The Gun Digest® Book Of Smith & Wesson

D1518864

Patrick Sweeney

©2004 Patrick Sweeney
Published by

kp books
An imprint of F+W Publications, Inc.

700 East State Street • Iola, WI 54990-0001
715-445-2214 • 888-457-2873

Our toll-free number to place an order or obtain
a free catalog is (800) 258-0929.

Library of Congress Catalog Number: 0-87349-792-9

ISBN: 2004093881

Designed by Paul Birling
Edited by Kevin Michalowski

Printed in United States of America

Introduction

I've been around S&W revolvers a long time. I shot them, off and on, when we went to the cabin up north when I was a kid. Later, my brother, Mike, bought a bunch of Model 57s in all three barrel lengths, and we shot them when on vacation or on "range trips." Then, in the late 1970s I began my path in firearms retail and gunsmithing at various gun shops in and around the Detroit area. When I started gunsmithing we had plenty of S&W revolvers to work on. Detroit had been issuing the M&P in .38 Special since the 1920s, and allowed officers to use personally owned revolvers for decades. Many police departments in the metropolitan area also issued the M&P, the Model 10, or other S&W revolvers, and some also allowed personally owned sidearms on duty.

The entire time I was working as a gunsmith, either as an apprentice or on my own, I'm pretty sure there was at least one S&W revolver in the shop for repair. Not because they were so fragile they needed work, but because they were ubiquitous. Every major city in the country was in the same situation; Colt had lost the police supply market to S&W back in the 1950s, and S&W revolvers were everywhere. I also had the advantage of Detroit allowing S&W pistols, so I saw the 39, 59 and later the second-generation pistols on a regular basis.

The only reason I knew how to disassemble a Mauser rifle before I knew how to disassemble an S&W revolver was that in Michigan (as in most places) the age at which you could own a rifle was lower than that of owning a handgun.

I've carried S&W revolvers and pistols for defense, and used them in almost every aspect of competition.

I've shot Steel, USPSA/IPSC matches, bowling pins, ICORE and IDPA with S&W revolvers and pistols. I shot indoor PPC leagues for years with S&W revolvers. I shot silhouette the first years it hit the ranges of Michigan with various M-29s and 57s. I've shot the Masters with an M-41. I've put a lot of ammo downrange using S&W handguns as the launching platforms.

And as I said, I've worked on them, repairing the results of neglect, abuse, bad luck and time. In the 25 years since I dove into the gun world, I have spent much of that time handling one S&W model or another on a daily basis. I've found them to be solid, reliable and accurate, with wonderful ergonomics and comfort.

In drawing up the idea for this book, my editors and I decided that we didn't need a simple listing of what guns S&W currently made. For that you can go to the current edition of the excellent *Standard Catalog of Smith & Wesson* by Jim Supica and Richard Nahas. No, we'd survey the current offerings of S&W with an eye to how they handle, feel, and shoot. What could you use them for? Is a particular handgun better suited to daily carry, competition or hunting? What kind of groups can you expect from one? And just how much does the .500 kick?

So if you want the details of every option available on a particular model, the current S&W catalog will give you that information. If you want to know production numbers for a particular model, to see if it is a desirable one to pick up for your collection, go to Supica and Nahas. But if you are looking forward to putting ammo downrange, and want to know what S&W will serve you best for a particular competition, or in daily carry, read on.

Table Of Contents

Acknowledgments

In any endeavor like this, you need assistance. In the case of a compendium of firearms, you need a) the guns, b) ammo to test them with, and c) someone to answers the questions that bedevil gun writers in the middle of the night.

Well, the guns part was easy. At least in the asking, for deciding which ones to include and which ones not to was not so easy. Unlike previous books, where asking sometimes got guns and sometimes got promises and no guns, S&W delivered. At times my delivery driver was at the door more often than the newspaper delivery person. Every gun I asked for, that S&W still made, eventually showed up at my door. As more than one member of my test fire crew said "Cooool!" At times it was not easy to keep track of what I was shooting, photographing, writing about or even handling. More than once I had to open the crane or peer at the side of the frame to remind myself which one it was.

Ammo is also a problem. Especially when the panoply of guns covers the spectrum of calibers. I had everything from .17 HMR to 500 SWM, and from 9mm to .45. Trying to reload enough ammo to test them all would have taken as long as the production of the book itself. Jeff Hoffman of Black Hills Ammunition sent me all I needed in the calibers he loaded. When my delivery driver wasn't bringing cartons of guns, he was off-loading cartons of ammo. (And don't think he doesn't know the difference!) Hornady sent me the biggest and smallest

calibers, their .17 and the first production lot of 500 they made. Peter Pi of Cor-bon sent me an embarrassingly large amount of .500 ammo even before S&W had the gun to me. I had plenty of time to stare at the ammo, wondering just what shooting it would be like.

And for the last, I had Herb Belin of S&W. He answered all my questions, tracked down the answers that he didn't know right off hand, and patiently explained to me the things that had changed at Smith & Wesson since I had last had long talks with the staff back in the late 1980s.

After all was said and done, I had learned a great deal. I had shot 10,000 rounds of various calibers, abused myself with recoil, been the envy of all I knew, and the source of information about these new and wondrous guns. I also had two gigabytes of disk space filled with digital photos, a pile of brass, and cartons of guns to ship back. There's the only drawback to the gun writer's world: we have to send the guns back. Despite rumors to the contrary (and some unscrupulous writers who took advantage) gun writers don't get to fill their safes with freebies. The manufacturers expect to get them back. S&W was kind enough to send me on the order of $15,000 worth of their exemplary products, and expected them back. So it was a sad day when I had to box up the last of them and ship them back. But the good news is that it's all here, ready for your perusal.

A Few Words About The Book

Your brand-new S&W has already been tested before you lay hands on it. Back when I was working in various retail shops, we would occasionally get a customer who wanted a "brand new, unfired Smith & Wesson" for their collection. We'd simply get them a new gun. Occasionally they'd complain that it had already been shot, and they wanted one unfired. It took some explaining that they were never going to get one that hadn't been absolutely unfired, because the factory test-fired every single gun ever made. I subsequently found there were some dealers who were cleaning up new S&W revolvers so the firing marks wouldn't show, and selling them as "unfired" collectors' pieces.

You must make sure your ammo works properly. This target load was too light for the S&W 4513TSW, as the gun was sprung for duty ammo.

Every firearm that leaves the S&W plant is test-fired before it heads out the door. There are employees assigned to test fire the guns, but everyone is encouraged to take a turn at it. As you'd expect, there are those who get competitive about such things. The record for the largest number of test-fire rounds in .44 Magnum was held for a long time by a petite woman who fired over 400 rounds through various Model 29s before quitting for the day. Test-firing is not the extended plinking session you'd think. There are a lot of guns and a lot of ammo to consume. The standard technique is to hold the handgun being tested in the right hand (for right-handed shooters) and insert the left index finger in the trigger guard. By quickly slapping your left hand back and forth you can launch rounds downrange a lot faster than if you fired in the normal fashion. (Somehow I don't see this happening with the .500.)

Pistols have a special magazine-loading machine. Magazines are stacked up in one feed tray, and random boxes of the appropriate caliber are dumped into the bin (without the cardboard or plastic/styrofoam, obviously) and the machine loads the magazines (I'd love to have that at my disposal!). Each pistol gets one to three magazines fired through it. The number varies depending on what the test-shooters see happening with a particular pistol, or with some models that need three just to make sure the random problem doesn't show up. Your pistol will get the magazines packed with it that were used to test-fire it, but they are all the same, so it doesn't matter. Revolvers get three rounds in alternating chambers fired through them. Every 300 or 400 hundred guns, S&W conducts what they call a "Level Check." Ten guns are selected at random from a production lot, and each of those 10 gets 300 rounds of ammo fired. S&W doesn't do any targeting of the groups, as targeting is a detail taken care of in the design, manufacturing and assembly process. (If a particular gun is "off" it is so rare that targeting the batch is a whole lot of time for usually no results.) Those 10 guns go into the "Used Gun" inventory. When the stack gets to be large enough, S&W sends out detailed lists to their distributors, who bid on the batch. So, if you've ever wondered where the guns you've seen in distributors fliers, the "ones and twos" stuff, now you know.

The recent change has been the inclusion of the little sealed envelope. Some states require a test-fire sample for their "database of fired case" projects. Never mind that it hasn't proven to work in a large-scale, nor that the mathematics and real-world tool wear experience doom it to failure. The database will be administered and built. The easiest way for S&W to handle it (and

Feeding frenzy at the test fire session. The volunteer crew lines up to test fire a bunch of S&W revolvers.

The Outers rest for test-firing handguns. With care you can do very good work from a simple rest.

their customers, too) is to simply provide a fired case with each gun. If they didn't each customer would have to turn over their gun to the state authorities for testing (can't have honest citizens just handing over a case and assuring the State Police it was fired in their guns, now can we?) and we all know who'd have to pay for that. So to save everyone the hassle, S&W provides the case. If you live in one of the places requiring it, don't lose it and be sure you know exactly where and when to turn it in. And if you get the chance, thank S&W for making it easier for you. And make sure you complain to your state authorities about the waste of time, money, effort and manpower. If you do not live in a state requiring the fired case, leave the envelope in plain sight in your gun safe, loading bench or bookshelf of gun books. Remind yourself every time you see it that you must vote in every election. (End of soapbox.)

Every time I have another project, I get a swarm of volunteers for the test-firing section. And it is a good thing, too. As much as I'd love to personally fire every single round dedicated to the testing of this or any project, I can't. First, the recoil would be too much. Oh, if I were testing nothing but 9mm, .40 or .45 pistols, I'd see that I shot as much as humanly possible. But this book

I was sparing in my use of the Ransom rest. I didn't have inserts for all guns, and I wasn't sure my setup would survive the .500.

called for more than that. The recoil from the 500 alone would have pounded me into the ground like a post. So I spread the wealth, and let my test-firers get in some fun.

And I always find useful information when I do. Since we aren't all the same, I find there are guns my volunteers like that I don't, and vice versa. And some are more or less resistant to recoil than I am, so I get different "takes" on what something feels like. One of my testers owns and shoots a Freedom Arms in .454 Casull. When he shot the .500, he commented: "That's not bad. The comp could work better. Got any more ammo?" (I must point out that none of them said anything remotely like that after firing the 329.)

The basic testing of all the guns was the same. Unlike the test-shooters at S&W, I'm looking to find out more than just "it shoots reliably" as part of the testing exercise. I need to know how they handle, how well they shoot, and if there are any idiosyncrasies I should know about. Once I'd handled them enough to make sure I knew where everything was and how it worked (you'd be surprised at how turned around you can get, handling different makes and models all day, every day) I'd take it along to the range with a supply of ammo. There I'd plink at the hill to get a feel for it and get a rough check on the sights. Then I'd shoot for groups, either standing or sitting at the bench, depending on what was avail-

able. I wanted to use the Ransom rest for everything, but found that there were models I could not get inserts for. It would not have been fair to compare some models with Ransom accuracy results with my standing or bench shooting results. So I used the Ransom rest sparingly, and for those firearms you'd expect the utmost of accuracy out of, to see what "the best" was. I'd also chronograph some of the ammo I was testing, as a check on its performance in the handgun du jour. At the group sessions we'd take turns shooting the various models on targets and the steel plates, to get a feel for how they worked and who liked what.

After that, the testing had to be tuned to the gun. If for example I was shooting the 945PC, I'd run a few IPSC drills and short stages. (With two magazines it isn't easy to do extended testing) Other models, you can't do that. While IDPA has a Back Up Gun division, USPSA/IPSC does not. Even if I'd had enough speedloaders, you will not find much joy running through a field course with a 442. And no one, I repeat no one, will willingly go through a 28-round field course a second time with a lightweight .44 Magnum. (most shooters would not finish.) Jim Cirillo retired from the New York Police Department some years ago after a long and distinguished career. His fame comes from his assignment to a team dedicated to stopping a string of armed robberies in the city, where the robbers quite often shot the store clerks

Jeff Chudwin testing the SW500. Lots of hunting power, way too much for defense except from large dangerous game.

You must test with what you plan to use. If all you ever shoot is competition, the full-metal-jacket may serve you well. If you plan to use one of the high-tech hollowpoints, you'd better make sure they feed in your gun before finding out the hard way.

even after getting the money from the till. The stakeout squads' job was to apprehend if possible, and stop if not. The predictable result was a series of shootouts. The bad guys didn't want to get caught. The good guys wanted to go home. The result, in sports parlance was Cirillo 17, Bad Guys 0. When Jim Cirillo talks about defensive shooting, it pays to listen. One of the ideas he has been working on for some time is the "Cirillo Index." Unlike aimed fire, you do not use the sights. But unlike "point" or "instinctive" shooting, you do aim. You simply aim with the whole gun. By interposing the pistol or revolver between you and the bad guy, and making sure you see just the back and not the sides or top, you are indexed on the bad guy to a reasonable distance. Reasonable as in gunfighting distances, not target competition. I tried the Cirillo Index with the handguns that were appropriate.

The carry guns got tested on the IPSC drills like the rest, then packed for a few days to see how they "rode." I also carried them at the gun club, to see how they were in the holsters I had. They were as expected. When you've got an all-steel full-size pistol in a tactical thigh rig, the exact model of it hardly matters. But concealed carry is a different matter. There, the models do matter, and lighter and more compact is easier to carry. Just harder to shoot.

Where I could (as in extra magazines to spare so I could finish a stage) I shot the S&W firearms that were appropriate in practice stages or matches. I did the accuracy testing off the bench with the aid of the Outers Pistol Rest. I could put it on one of our solid benches and rest the handgun I was testing in a repeatable manner. The steel construction kept it from changing shape as sandbags often do, and the fiber padding kept it from scratching the guns. And being relatively light, it wasn't a hassle hauling it down to the ranges from the parking lot. Another item from Uncle Mike's I found very useful was the patrol car Seat Organizer. Meant for police offi-

cers, to keep their gear organized, it works great for range trips, too. I found I could keep a notebook, pens and pencils, target stuff like a stapler, pasters and target overlays in it and keep it by the door. When I was packing for a range trip, I'd just pick it up, sling it over the headrest of the seat, and have what I needed ready to go. It also works great for those of us who do a lot of driving. With the organizer hung on the seat, you don't have a seat full of loose gear like maps, directions and snacks.

When the project got off the ground, I began searching for ammunition to shoot. As a full-time writer and trainer I have a lot on hand, but not enough to undertake a task such as this. I called Jeff Hoffman at Black Hills Ammunition to ask for some, and he asked how much I needed. Well, a case of .357 Magnum would get me through those particular guns. "No, how much for the whole book?" I said I'd have to call him back because I hadn't counted that far. When I called back with a figure, Jeff said "Great, fax me with calibers, bullet weights and specific caliber amounts, and I'll ship it as soon as we have it loaded." A week later my delivery driver staggered to the door with a bunch of cartons. A few days later he had more. By the third delivery I thought he was going to kill me. I added ammo from my own shelves to round out some of the calibers, and to offer a bit of variety. I also filled in on the calibers that Jeff doesn't load for. When I got the nod from S&W that there was a .500 Magnum set aside for me, I called Cor-bon. They developed it, and they'd be sure to have some. Despite working day and night trying to keep up with demand, they sent a supply of .500 ammo that kept my test-fire crew happy, and my hands sore.

When Hornady began loading the .500, they sent me a supply as well. That and the .17 HMR meant that I was shooting the most and least powerful handguns S&W made, with ammo from the same plant. And on the same day, too. That was a weird experience. One has so little recoil that if you hadn't heard it go off you couldn't be sure it went off. And the other recoils so hard you want to check your fillings after a few shot.

In all, the testing went through in excess of 30,000 rounds of ammunition. And for those of you who might be so snarky as to ask "With all that ammo, you ought to be a pretty good shot. Are you?" I can only say that when spread out over more than two dozen guns, in 15 calibers, the "practice" gets spread mighty thin. But boy was it fun.

In getting all the gear to the ranges each session, I found the usual method of multiple cardboard boxes just didn't cut it. Usually I'll have a gun bag or a shipping box with a couple of guns in it, and a cardboard box with a few hundred rounds of ammo. Drive to the club, park, haul the bag, haul the box, and set up. Not this set of sessions. Add a chronograph, camera and lenses, targets and pasters, lunch and then multiply the guns and ammo. It was not unusual to haul a dozen guns to the range, with 100 rounds of ammo for each. Or even more ammo in a common caliber with several sources. I found that Uncle Mike's makes a great case for the guns. Their wheeled gear bag is huge. I tested it by stuffing every handgun I could case and put into it, and the record is 37. (However, with that many guns in it, getting it into the back of a pickup truck may require a crane.) I found I could easily put a dozen guns, the camera bag, lunch and notebook in the bag without a problem. Then I could wheel it to the truck, and wheel it down to the range. That and a couple of sturdy cardboard boxes for the ammo and I could pack it all and carry it all and not kill myself just in the loading and unloading. If you need a good gun gear bag, or a huge luggage bag, then this is for you. It won't fit any overhead bin in any plane, but for checked baggage or for just hauling your gear on range sessions it is great.

The Drills

First is the "Bill Drill" named after Bill Wilson who developed it 20 or more years ago. In the IPSC setting the drill is simple. At 7 yards you face an IPSC target. You draw and fire six rounds as quickly as you can while still getting "A" zone hits. The old IPSC targets were a bit easier, with the A-zone a 10-inch circle. The new targets are a bit more difficult, with the A-zone being a 6- by 11-inch rectangle. The goal is to do a Bill Drill in two seconds or less with all A hits. If you drop a hit, you failed the drill. If you go overtime, you failed the drill. In the old days, if you could do a Bill Drill on demand you could walk on water.

As I did not have high-speed holsters for all of the handguns to be tested, I substituted the "Demi Bill Drill." Instead of from the holster, I took the draw time out (.8 seconds) and started from low ready. Thus, I had 1.2 sec-

onds by the shot clock to get six A-zone hits. Needless to say, I did not attempt it with the 500. And for the snubbies with only five shots, I dropped it to a second flat.

The Uncle Mike's large-wheeled duffle makes hauling a bundle of guns to the range for a test-fire session a snap. If the ground is too muddy, there are lots of straps.

Bill Drill times are very dependant on the gear you use and the class you're shooting in. To make it harder, some grandmasters have added to it, doing the "10-yard Bill Drill" or the "15-yard Bill Drill." If you are a grandmaster IPSC shooter, shooting an Open gun, a 15-yard drill is within reason. One approach for the really speed-inclined is to do an open-ended Bill Drill. Set the timer for 2.3 second Par time. It will beep to start, and beep to stop your shooting. (The .3 is for the average reaction time of most shooters.) Then see how many hits you can get in the time allotted. Remember, they must all be A hits, or you've failed the drill.

Next I did the Cirillo Index. I brought the gun up and indexed off the outline, to see if I could get fast hits close. I did the Cirillo Index test at 5 yards. Most guns I was able to shoot reliable pairs, where three quarters of the shots were A hits and the rest C hits.

The last IPSC drill was El Presidente. Again, the gear has changed things. The original drill was three targets, three meters apart, at 10 meters. (With the old 10-inch circular A-zone targets.) You started with your back to the targets. On the start, turn, draw, fire twice on each target, reload and fire twice on each again. The goal was 12 A hits in ten seconds. If you could do it on demand in 1978 when I started IPSC shooting, you were a demi-god. The current specifications are 10 yards, targets 1 yard apart, and the new rectangular A-zone target. An aspiring "C" class USPSA/IPSC shooter can shoot "par" scores with a Limited, Limited 10 or Production gun. (Par is the scoring equivalent of 60 points in 10

seconds.) The goal is to shoot "clean", all A hits, in the fastest possible time. A Grand Master with an Open gun can do "El Prez" in about four seconds, dropping a few points. My friend Rich Bitow shot El Presidente in the 2002 USPSA Factory Gun Nationals, 10 points down in 5.75 seconds with an S&W 25-2. Again, I did not try the El Presidente with the 500. And since I did not have a speed or carry holster for all of the guns, I again had to modify. I did Vice Presidente; starting facing the targets. And I stated in low ready. The difference would have taken maybe a second off the run times. The pistols were easy, I simply tucked the spare magazine in a magazine holder on my belt. The wheelguns were not so easy except for those using moon clips. Where I had suitable speedloaders I used them. Where I didn't I simply stuck with the earlier drills.

The common action target is the Pepper Popper. Some loads (.44 Magnum and larger) can dent or crater the steel, and you'll be in trouble if you do.

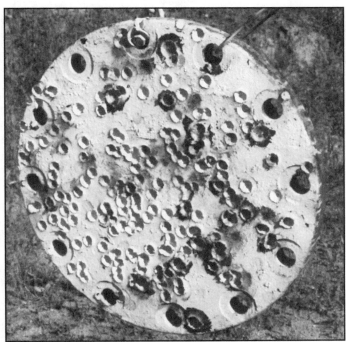

The result of cratered steel, now so dented as to be dangerous to shoot at close range (as in closer than 50 yards).

It takes a lot of ammo to test a bunch of guns. This is just one day's shipment from Black Hills. My delivery driver hates me, some days.

Gun Writer Specials

Writing this book was a lot of fun, but also plenty of work. Jeff Hoffman of Black Hills sent me all the ammo I needed in the calibers he loads. (Thanks again, Jeff!) I also shot a lot of my own reloads. And no one is impervious to recoil. Yes, it is possible to "build up" to recoil, get used to it. But too much, either in volume or ferocity, can actually set back your skills. And even cause injury. Fellow writer John Taffin (he writes about big bore revolvers for KP Books) once made quite a splash showing the x-rays of his shooting hand that was damaged by too much Magnum shooting. The bones were obviously displaced, even to the eye not medically trained.

The level of skill we writers bring to the table differs greatly. I know gun writers who can't shoot for beans. And some who could be world-class if they weren't always testing yet another different gun. Skill levels move up and

down depending on what the schedule is. When I was working on *Gunsmithing: Shotguns* I went eight months without firing a single shot from a handgun. As you can imagine it took a while to get back in the groove.

We don't get the secret handshake at the factories, sometimes they actually hide stuff from us. And they don't build special guns for us. No, there isn't some secret vault dedicated to "gun writer demo guns" or a specified gunsmith on staff, with 30 years of experience, who builds all the guns we see. Usually what happens is the contact person at the factory writes up an invoice and shoots it via e-mail to the shipping department. There, someone grabs the first one off the shelf that fits each stock number, packs it and ships it. I've gotten the wrong gun on occasion, as it is easy to transpose digits in a stock number. I've gotten shipments with more or less guns than the invoice said. And I've gotten guns out of the blue. Everyone involved, from gun writer to shipping clerk, are all human. And sometimes guns get through that shouldn't. But rare is the maker who doesn't make good on a product that is faulty. That said, no faulty guns came through from S&W. However, if they were sending "tuned" guns to this gun writer, you'd think they'd have done a better job. (Just tongue-in-cheek, here.) The most accurate gun I received was the economy 9mm, the 910. You'd think that all the Performance Center guns would have trounced it, right? That gun delighted in punching one-hole groups. If S&W was going to stack the deck and lure you into a life of poverty by purchasing their guns, you'd think they'd have done so to something other than the least-expensive 9mm they make.

No, they shipped what was on the regular shelf, and I benefited from the best 9mm made that day/week/month of 910 production. Not that any would be bad, but what you see is what you'll probably get. Except for the 910, where you may not see that in yours. And this one likely won't be anyone else's. I'll probably just take a breath, ask what the discount, if any, is for gun writers, and make a check out to S&W for the 910.

In all, a grand life. But not one in which to get rich, not with temptations like all these S&W's I've shot.

Patrick Sweeney
August 2004

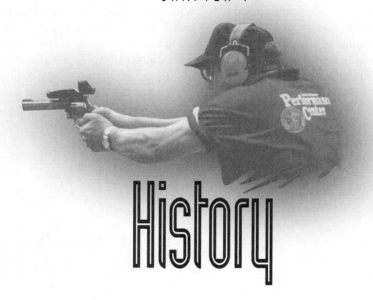

CHAPTER 1

History

Here in America we don't have the long history that other countries do. It isn't unusual to travel to Europe and clamber over sites that are 2,000 years old. To enter buildings constructed 1,000 years ago. To peer at books printed (or rather, transcribed) 500 or 600 years ago. No, we have to "settle" for things just a couple of centuries old. There are a select number of companies here in the United States that have been in continuous existence for over a century. And fewer that have been continuous manufacturers during that time. Just now passing their 150-year mark is Smith & Wesson.

Horace Smith and Daniel Baird Wesson met while working for another firearms manufacturer that would become Winchester. For those who don't know, the Winchester rifle we're all familiar with was first made as a handgun. The Volcanic Repeater. You can imagine the problems with a lever-action handgun, but at the time it sure seemed like a good idea. Mechanically it was. The problem was the state of the art of cartridge manufacturing wasn't up to the action of the handgun or the rifle it became. Despite making a number of handguns and rifles with lever-actions, Smith and Wesson left to form their own company. Oliver Winchester took the Volcanic firm, and with persistent infusions of capital, expanded it through the New Haven Arms, Henry Arms and into Winchester Repeating Arms Company. Horace and Daniel went a different way.

The big problem with a lever-action handgun was that you needed two hands to work it. If you had two hands free to work a firearm, a better choice would be a rifle. A handgun had to be a one-hand firearm. When the two were working out their ideas, the Colt revolver was still new, and swords were still viewed as entirely suitable martial arms. Then one of those great ideas came along, one that changed everything. As long as firearms were all muzzleloaders, you wanted the rear of your barrel

S&W has often led the evolution of ammunition. They brought out the .38 Special, the .357 Magnum, and interim advances like this old box of steel-jacketed ammo for perforating gangsters getaway cars in days gone by.

Continuing to lead the way, S&W with its Scandium alloy makes the world's lightest .44 Magnum, the Model 329 at just 25.4 ounces empty.

sealed. But when the Flobert cartridge was invented, another possibility emerged. The Flobert round was simple: if you took a percussion cap, and seated a small bullet in the front of it, you could fire the bullet with just the cap. Flobert made small handguns and rifle for "Parlor shooting." People would shoot in their parlor, or back yards, or gardens, for entertainment. (Imagine that today!) The Flobert firearms were not suited for hunting or defense, being too small, delicate and underpowered. The big advance came on April 3, 1855, when Rollin White was granted a patent for bored-through chambers in a revolver. If you then take a Flobert cartridge, and manufacture the case/cap with a rim so it doesn't fall through, you can fire the self-contained cartridge with the regular hammer of a revolver. No more loose powder, or delicate paper-wrapped powder and ball for loading.

D.B. Wesson learned of the patent almost immediately, and wrote to Rollin White. The two met and worked out a deal. The deal was decidedly to the advantage of Wesson and his partnership with Smith. They paid 25 cents per firearm to White for the exclusive use of the patent. White could not use the patent himself, and had to bear the cost of defending it against infringers. The idea was so useful that White spent large amounts of time, effort and money tracking down and suing infringers. The patent ran until 1872, so for the next 17 years the new firm of Smith & Wesson had a decided advantage over Colt.

The early S&W pistols were not powerful. The newly developed .22 Short was the round of choice. The problem was still making cartridges. In order to make a case soft enough to deform under the hammer and ignite the priming compound and thus the powder (at least the Short had powder besides the priming compound that Flobert cartridges used) the case has to be soft. Copper was the metal of choice. If the designer made the round too big, or had too much powder in it, the case would rupture, tying up the gun and possibly injuring the shooter. But for many, the .22 was plenty big enough. S&W made many of their Tip-Up .22 revolvers for use in the Civil War. Yes, it wasn't a .36 or .44, but the rounds were better sealed against moisture, could be counted on even in the rain, and any sidearm was better than none.

The manufacturing advances that come about as the result of any war had their effect during the Civil War, too. After the war the new central-fire cartridges became the new avenue of progress. Not the centerfire cases we think of, central-fire cartridges had the priming compound in the center of the case head but not in a separate primer. Think of a center-strike rimfire, and you'll have a good idea. Progress lead to the separate primer in a cupped-head case, and soon after that the Rollin White patent expired. The race was on! Colt went with the Single Action Army, a product-improved version of their cap-and-ball revolvers. S&W went with scaled up and

When Colt went to a hammerless model, they simply designed a shroud that could be bolted to a Detective Special or Agent. Unfortunately, your gunsmith had to drill and tap the frame to install it.

The shrouded Colt was still not hammerless, as the spur was exposed.

Just because S&W ruled the roost in olden days, doesn't mean they've given up against the newcomers.

The Chief's Special, and later in stainless, put the skids to Colt's production of the Detective Special. The Chief was more compact and tougher.

The Colt Police Positive tried to hang on against the .38 Hand Ejector, but always slipped.

improved top-break revolvers. Both had advantages and disadvantages. The SAA is marginally stronger, with its solid frame. But it is slower to extract the empties and reload. The S&W was a little less strong, since the action hinged in two to open. But the ejection was simultaneous, with all six empties or rounds being flung clear. And the open cylinder was faster to reload. So who won? They both did. S&W had the good luck to have their revolver seen by the Russian Military Attache, General Alexander Gorloff. In the course of the improvements the Russian Army wanted, the Number 3 top-break became a much better sidearm. It also made S&W a world-known firearms maker. In the middle of the 19th Century the Russian Army was large and well respected. To be selling sidearms to them, for issuance to their officers, was quite a coup. The military establishments of other countries also ordered S&W revolvers. The Russians alone ordered over 130,000 revolvers, with other armies ordering over 30,000. The S&W plant was so busy filling those orders and more, that they probably could not have delivered the revolvers our own Army needed. Thus cowboys then and now shoot primarily with Colt SAA, and not S&W Russian or Schofield revolvers.

Smith & Wesson had designed a double-action revolver a lot earlier than many think. Many tend to think of the DA revolver as a turn of the 19th century invention: not true. S&W offered DA revolvers (known then as "self-cocking") to the Russians early in the contract cycle for the single-action top-break Number 3. The early double-action revolvers were all top-breaks. A top-break revolver works by hinging open just like a double-barrel shotgun does. The barrel and cylinder tip up, and in the better ones the extractor raises the empty cases until they fall free, then snaps back into place. A top-break revolver is very fast to reload compared to a

Colt SAA. However, the top-break revolver frame is not as strong as that of the SAA with its single-piece frame. The goal of many was to marry the DA action to the single-piece frame.

Smith & Wesson did that with their Hand Ejector models, the I frame which came out in 1896, and the K frame which came out in 1899. The .32 Hand Ejector on the I frame is one many shooters will draw a blank on. That is because a half century later the design was changed from leaf springs to coil spring, the dimensions subtly altered, and christened the J frame. That's right, your Chiefs Special snubbie got its start in 1896. The K frame we all know, for it has been in continuous production ever since.

While the basics of many of the S&W models have been in continuous production for many years, that doesn't mean they are just old stuff in new guise. The .38 Hand Ejector your grandfather (or great-grandfather) could have bought in 1904 is a far cry from the K frame offerings of today. Scandium and Titanium aside, leaving out stainless steel, and ignoring the advances in adjustable sights, coil springs and optics you could mount, the model of today is a marvel by the earlier standards. First, the steel is far superior. We marvel over hand fitting of an earlier time, but if you want precise in a manufactured products, computer-controlled machining is far better. There were good guns made then, but there were lemons too. After all, the precision of measuring (as a part of the manufacturing process) is much better. As much as I love the old guns, if I'm looking for something to perform for me, to carry for defense, to use in a match, to go hunting with, I'll pick new.

In the first decade of the 20th century, S&W began the revolver run they've maintained ever since. With

Left to right, a .45 ACP, an Auto Rim, and two .455 rounds for the British .45 Hand Ejectors.

Compare the extractor rim of the .45 ACP on the left, with the headspacing rim of the Auto Rim on the right.

The .45 ACP and the .45 Auto Rim. The latter is a cartridge designed to fit the multitudes of Model 1917 revolvers that S&W made.

compact, medium and large-framed revolvers in calibers from .22 rimfire to the big .44 Special, they were set. With war clouds darkening the skies of Europe, the British army came to S&W asking for sidearms. They realized that British gun makers would not be able to produce everything else a war demanded, and sidearms, too. I wouldn't be surprised to find that a number of British officers and enlisted men also wrote to S&W asking for sidearms as well. It was quite common for officers to privately purchase sidearms for carry. (What can I say,

times were different. You could show up for a war with privately purchased everything: uniform, weapons, web gear, etc. Much less so now, especially the personal sidearm part.) And once the British were satisfied, the American Army then needed sidearms. Luckily S&W was able to provide both with what they needed, the British with .455, and the American with .45 ACP revolvers. Unlike the British, the American Army needed more. We were essentially starting from scratch, where the British had been fielding and equipping a larger army than ours for quite some time before the war started. While S&W provided the British with nearly 75,000 revolvers in .455, they did so in the space of a couple of years. When the American Army needed sidearms, they needed them faster than in a couple of years. (There wasn't enough 1911 production to arm all the troops that needed or required one, so the Army ordered .44 Hand Ejector models in .45 ACP.) The need was so pressing that in September 1917 the Army took over the operation of the plant and devoted it entirely to the production of M-1917 revolvers. At the peak rate of 14,500 revolvers per month, the plant ended up producing nearly 165,000 M-1917 sidearms for the war effort.

After the war things got nearly back to normal. While there were a lot of "surplus" handguns in circulation (mostly souvenirs brought back from the Great War) Prohibition soon created a demand for .38 Special revolvers for police work. Not everyone wanted a big .45. Developments in powders and metallurgy lead to the .357 Magnum in 1935, with the first guns called "Registered Magnums" made and sold as custom orders. Regular production Magnums also were made, but the Depression kept a lid on production.

WWII ended that. With the lessons learned from WWI, S&W and the War Department knew what was going to happen: production would have to be increased. Unlike WWI, the Army did not want M-1917 revolvers

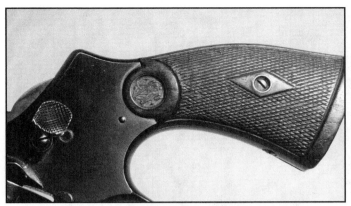

The original grips, ca. 1920s. Good until you start getting into recoil of more than .38 Special.

The British contracts all called for a lanyard loop. There are more than half a million S&W revolvers out there with a loop. And they are still useful.

The .357 Magnum K frame revolver was the standard police sidearm for several decades after WWII.

The Volume of Success

How successful has the Hand Ejector series been? Very. In the four decades from introduction to the U.S. entry in WWII, Smith & Wesson made 1 million K frame revolvers. To give you an idea of just how successful that is, compare them to Colt. Colt introduced the Single Action Army in 1873. It dropped production in 1941. In that time, the iconic cowboy gun totaled some 367,000 handguns made. With a 25-year head start, Colt made a third as many revolvers.

WWII saw the production of another million revolvers. (Not bad for a handgun considered "not a combat weapon" and made only for aircrews, plant guards and rear-echelon types.) Half that production went to British Commonwealth uses. With half a million revolvers made in .38 S&W, we don't see that many here simply because they were shipped off to the war and the Crown Colonies. And we didn't see many come back due to the irrational attitude that surplus arms were to be destroyed rather than sold off.

After WWII, the S&W .38 Special or .357 Mangum K frame revolver was the standard police sidearm. And many security companies also issued or authorized S&W revolvers. In the 105 years since its introduction, the S&W K frame is now closing in on (if it has not yet passed) the 7 million mark. Add in the trainloads of N frame .357, .44 and .41 Magnums, the .45 ACP and a smattering of other calibers, and you can have the S&W production totals over 10 million handguns. And we haven't even begun to count the J frame snubbies and the pistols. Is it any wonder that the name, logo and product of Smith & Wesson is so well known?

to augment 1911 production. But .38 Hand Ejectors, by then known as "Military & Police" models in .38 Special for the US and .38 S&W for the British Commonwealth armies, flooded off the S&W production lines. Once the serial numbers reached a million (starting from 1899) S&W started a new series, the "V for Victory" series with a V prefix. When a design change called for a new hammer-block safety, the design was implemented and the serial numbers altered to a "VS" prefix. After the war S&W focused on upgrading the revolver designs, and adding the pistol design, the M-39. They added the .357 Magnum K frame, to be the M-19 when models got model numbers and not names in the late 1950s. The late 1950s also brought the .44 Magnum. While it was introduced in 1955, it didn't really catch on in a big way until the early 1970s, with the Clint Eastwood movie "Dirty Harry." Once the memorable line "This is the world's most powerful handgun, and could blow your head clean off" was uttered on the screen, everyone had to have one. The demand was so great (and distracted many consumers from the other S&W advances like stainless steel) that dealers were charging premiums for any M-29, and putting customers on a waiting list.

The S&W explosion of models made for a rich collectors' field. What would be better than one of the few 4046 pistols made? One marked by the police department that once owned it.

Once accepted, the British guns were extensively marked. Markings add to a collector's interest.

The demand eventually leveled off, and things got back to more or less normal, but for a while there you could buy used M-29s, and the box of ammo originally purchased with same missing six fired rounds, for a decent price. Many who "had to have the Magnum" found they didn't enjoy shooting it.

In the 1980s, S&W leapt ahead of its competitors through a turn of events that had meant bad things for many other firearms manufacturers: they were sold to a conglomerate. The experience Colt had with a steady stream of conglomerate owners was that each treated Colt as a cash cow, siphoning money off for other divisions, and putting nothing back into R&D, design, capital improvements or plant. Tompkins PLC was just the opposite. They bought and installed computer-controlled machining stations, scrapping the many single-use mills and lathes. They invested in computer design software and training. And the company greatly expanded its product line. Before Tompkins PLC bought them, S&W would have, for example, the M-15. An adjustable-sighted .38 Special on the K frame, you'd find it in blue and stainless with three barrel lengths each. Now, S&W could shift manufacturing so quickly they could make it any way they wanted. (To swap a production line with a line of mills or lathes took a week or weeks. With CNC milling stations you can do it overnight.) The pistols burgeoned even more, rapidly going through two generations. It got so bad we were joking at the gun shop about the "S&W Gun of the Week Program." S&W even produced a wheeled guide to let you keep track of the models. We now are familiar with keeping track of models

The fiction of the Lend-Lease program was that we were simply loaning government surplus to the British, so they were marked as U.S. Property. Who were we fooling?

The collectors' field is wide open, for once you've collected all variants you can start in on the marked models.

The adaptability of the S&W design (and of revolvers in general) meant it was easy to make them in whatever caliber the customer wanted.

S&W revolvers have been police sidearms for a long time, as this 1920s-era .38 Special can attest.

Not all markings are cause for collector's delight. Some just tell you the model number and serial number. Of course, with those, you can write Roy Jinks and track down the production date of your S&W.

In the odd-caliber category, the .35 S&W takes the cake.

like the 4513, the 4006, and the 3926. Some of us even have the method memorized enough to tell what the pistols are without looking them up. But in the 1980s, it was overwhelming. And it also produced a whole bunch of handguns that are now the beginnings of a future S&W collection. If you did nothing but devote your collecting efforts to just second-generation pistols, you'd have a potential field of three dozen or so sight and length combinations. Add in the serial number transitions (the factory went to the three-letter/four-digit method right in the middle of the second generation in some models) and then add special models marked for police departments, experimentals, transitional models, and you could have 100 pistols and not have it all covered. The third generation models would be even larger. If you devoted yourself to just K frame revolvers made in the 20th century, in barrel lengths, sights, caliber and composition (carbon, stainless, aluminum) you'd have well over 100 guns to track down. Add in the production variants and police-marked guns and you could be at it for the rest of your life and never find them all. Aside from S&W and perhaps Roy Jinks, no one could have a sample of every model and variation S&W had made. Unless someone like Bill Gates with billions of dollars at his disposal tried it, there just wouldn't be enough time and money.

For serious collectors, one of the .35s can be topped only by one of the .32s.

The explosion settled down to the models that sold well, and special order models that distributors ask for. If you are a large enough customer, and what you want is technically feasible, S&W can make a run for a price. Just don't blink when the price is mentioned, or you won't get the run. (I've always had a hankering for a 10-shot .32 Magnum Airweight N frame revolver. I just can't swing the price of ordering a thousand of them.)

Since then S&W serial numbers have evolved even more, to the point where collectors obsess over them. (But then collectors obsess over everything.) The current serial number system is three letters and four digits. Where S&W had problems keeping serial numbers

straight, and having enough room (a seven-digit serial number of all numerals takes up space and is ripe for confusion) the "three and four" system provides an easy speaking and remembering method, and plenty of stock numbers. With three letters and four digits, you have 15.6 million potential serial numbers. When they run out, adding another letter on the end will give S&W another 405 million serial number at their disposal.

The current scene is one of abundance. With computer-controlled milling machines, CAD-CAM design, and exotic alloys like Scandium, S&W can make more models, variants and designs than even the collectors can keep track of. Hang on, it will be a fast ride for a long time.

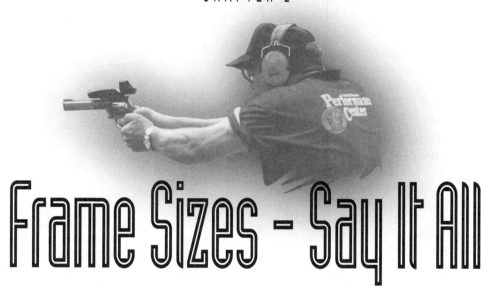

Frame Sizes - Say It All

It was never easy to simply say "big and small." Even when they only made top-break revolvers S&W made more than just two. The idea of having different frames sizes is common sense, really. After all, who wants to shoot a revolver the size and weight of a snubbie J frame that is chambered in .44 Magnum? (Yes, we all know some who would, but I'm talking the large group of us. Those who relish the idea of still being able to use a computer keyboard after a day at the range.) And the biggest frame, in the smallest caliber, is not much of a concealment gun, now is it? It also makes a difference to individual shooters. Some can't grasp a big revolver. My wife has trouble even with a K frame. So S&W was smart enough to offer guns in various frames, then and now.

Lets take them in ascending order, revolvers first.

J frame

The new J frame evolved from the old I frame, the original Hand Ejector. Named thus due to the ejector rod that you had to push to extract the empties, as opposed to the top breaks. In the top breaks, when you pivoted the front half of the assembly down it cammed the empties out. When you reached the end of the arc the ejector snapped back into place, ready for reloading. Those revolvers were called "automatic ejector" models. (Times change, mechanisms change, word usage changes.) The I

frame was designed around the .32, the Short and Long. In the early years of the 20th century the .32 was not sneered at as a "mousegun" or "wimpy pocket gun." When the Police Commissioner of New York City, Theodore Roosevelt (yes, the same one) determined that the police ought to be trained and armed, he selected the .32 long.

By the time WWII had ended no one was interested in a .32 handgun anymore. They wanted nothing smaller than the .38 Special. (Many wanted nothing bigger, making the choice pretty obvious) The new J frame was unveiled as a five-shot .38 Special snub-nose revolver at the 1950 annual convention of the International Association of the Chiefs of Police. The association was asked to name it, as in those days every model had a name. To no ones great surprise, they voted to call it the "Chiefs Special." Since then it has become the M-36, and is made in alloy frame, stainless steel, Scandium alloy and Titanium, and made with a standard hammer spur, shrouded spur and hammerless as well as hammerless with a grip safety.

The J frame is available in .32 H&R Magnum and .22 Long rifle, but for many when you say "J frame" or Chiefs special" the only response will be to hand you a box of .38 Special ammunition. Such was not always the case. In the 1950s the .38 S&W cartridge was still hanging on and somewhat popular. The J frame guns were made sometimes in .38 S&W. I had a customer with one when I was a full-time gunsmith. Our standard greeting was along the lines of "When are you going to give up that lightweight little mousegun and let me trade you for a real gun?" And the common reply would be "That Colt Lightweight Commander you've got would look very nice in my gun safe."

The J frame is the smallest revolver you can get that is chambered in a serious defensive cartridge (.32 Magnum or .38 Special) that you can depend on. There are others as small or smaller, but they usually are that small due to using a smaller cartridge.

The development of new alloys and heat-treating allowed S&W to chamber revolvers in frame sizes that would not have been thought of before. That, and the willingness to shoot same lead to the J Magnum frame. The J-M differs from the J only in that the cylinder, and the opening in the frame for it, are longer. The 640-1 Magnum came out in 1995, and it also required some extra machining in the cylinder stop to reinforce it against the recoil inertia of the .357 Magnum in such a small gun.

The J Magnum is now the only size made of the J frame (why make the smaller one and double the parts inventory?) and it comes, depending on the model, in carbon steel, stainless, aluminum alloy and Scandium.

The J frame is also the only frame to have three hammer types, the exposed, the shrouded and the hidden. The exposed hammer looks like any other S&W revolver except smaller. The shrouded hammer has the sides of the frame raised and machined to an arc that follows that of the hammer. Thus the hammer is protected from clothing (and vice versa) but the knurling of the spur can still be reached to cock the hammer for single-action shooting. The hidden hammer, or "hammerless" design completely encloses the hammer. It is double-action-only. While the standard hammer model J frames have been available with fixed sights or adjustable, the shrouded and hammerless have only ever been fixed-sight revolvers. Lest you think that the hammerless, double-action-only revolver is something new, or even semi-new in the latter half of the 20th century, guess again. When I first saw a shrouded-hammer J frame when working at The Gun Room in 1976, I thought it was a neat idea. Mike Karbon, who had an encyclopedic knowledge of guns, said, "No, the Safety Hammerless was first. Before the Spanish-American War." It turned out he was off by 11 whole years, the first Safety Hammerless models coming out in 1887. It was a top-break, and not a solid-frame, but it was a double-action-only concealed-carry revolver in a then-serious caliber.

The J frame started as a snubbie .38 Special. Back when all real guns were steel, it was the smallest and lightest you could get. We now have S&W snubbies that make the original J frame look like an anvil.

If you want a pro's backup gun, get yourself a K-frame 3-inch .38 or .357 Magnum with fixed sights.

K frame

The K got started in 1899, with the .38 Hand Ejector. The first models did not have a front locking bolt. That oversight was soon corrected, and if you have a vintage S&W that lacks a front locking bolt do not shoot it. It is far too valuable, and you may damage it if you use ammunition its old steel is not designed for. The K frame has been in continuous production except for six months of WWI, when the government assumed control of the plant to maximize the output of 1917 revolvers in .45 ACP. In WWII S&W continued to make K frames in .38 Special and .38 S&W for war use. The British and British colonial military units used it in .38 S&W, which they termed .38/200. The United States used them in .38 Special for aircrews, survival kits and plant guards.

In 1955, at the urging of the late Bill Jordan, S&W designed the K frame to take the .357 Magnum. Called the Combat Magnum, it became instantly popular. The improvements called for new steel, new heat treatments and precise fitting. As a result, S&W began the policy of no magnum parts for sale "across the counter." They didn't want their new .357 cylinders being installed in old .38 Hand Ejector frames, and being sued when the whole thing hurt someone. The policy became firmer when the .44 Magnum took off, as the factory didn't want back room "gunsmiths" installing Magnum cylinders and barrel into 1917 frames and hurting themselves or someone else.

The K frame was designed from the beginning to be a tough and reasonably compact .38 Special revolver.

In 1957 S&W embarked on the beginnings of the ultra lightweight journey. At the request of the U.S. Air Force, who was looking for every ounce of savings, they made a run of Model 12 revolvers. The initial Model 12 used an alloy frame AND an alloy cylinder. Subsequent testing showed that the alloy cylinders would not always stand up to use, and had an embarrassing tendency to break when fired. One of my other customers who could be counted on coming in once a year to have her sidearm cleaned, inspected and if need-be tuned, was a high-ranking Detroit Police officer. She had been issued the 12 when she started, and kept it the whole time she was on the force. Why not have the department's armorers look at it? "If I give it to them I won't get it back." As far as I know, she kept it to retirement. Out there somewhere is a DPD-marked alloy cylinder M-12, just waiting for a collector to get lucky.

In 1970 the K frame went stainless. At first the transition was a bit rocky, as the realities of hard use, lots of shooting, and the usual level of maintenance took their toll. But as each problem was uncovered (for a while there it was standard for gunsmiths faced with high-volume guns to do a bit of judicious welding to keep certain small parts assembled) S&W solved them. Today no one gives stainless a second thought except when faced with a nickeled gun. "Why nickel?" Because before stainless it was all you could do to slow down corrosion.

Right up to today, despite being chambered in .357 Magnum and smaller cartridges, the K frame has not been made in something larger. The cylinder just didn't have enough room for anything bigger. That had to wait.

The K frame was not ever made with a shrouded hammer or hammerless. If you wanted the spur gone you had to have a gunsmith cut it off and sculpt it to look good. K frames have been made with fixed and adjustable sights.

L frame

In the late 1970s S&W was running into a problem: K frame guns were wearing out and breaking faster than ever. The alloys were tougher, the heat treat was the best anyone knew at the time. But guns were showing up not just worn out but broken. What was going on? S&W was seeing the beginnings of the modern era of relevant training. In the old days, officers shot reloaded wadcutter ammo in their .38 Special revolvers, then loaded them with 158-grain lead roundnosed ammo for the street. And the volume of ammo used was small. A high-volume department might call for practice and qualification once a month. Most did it quarterly, semi-annually or only annually. The annual or semi-annual "Qual Course" firing might only be 50 or 60 rounds. The monthly courses would be less, only 20 or 30, but monthly was better than annually. In any case, an officer might shoot anywhere from 60 to 360 rounds of ammo a year. At 360 rounds of .38 Special standard pressure ammunition per year, you could go an entire career as a police officer and not wear out a gun. (360 rounds per year, twenty years, 7,200 rounds total.) And an officer who let it be known that he practiced more than what the department required might get a reputation as a "gunny" or someone looking to get into a shooting for status.

Then the "combat shooters" got involved. Actually, if there is any blame it belongs to the criminals who

The L frame came about to provide a home for high-volume .357 Magnum shooting. It is now a super-light seven-shot, and a real neat wheelgun.

insisted on resisting arrest. Police officers found that the old ways weren't so good any more. Especially bad were the old ways of practicing and qualifying with .38 ammo, then loading .357 Magnums on duty. The standard quickly became "If you carry Magnums, then practice and qualify with magnums." And there was a lot more practice going on. The combat shooters, or IPSC shooters, might (in the old days) greatly exceed those 7,200 career-total rounds in one year. I know of shooters back in the early 1980s who shot four and five times that much in a year's shooting. Of course they were mostly doing it in .45 ACP 1911s, but there were still revolver shooters shooting IPSC in the early days. They shot as much as the rest. And what we learned was that an M-19 could not stand up to a steady diet of full-power .357 Magnum ammo without regular overhauls.

And then it got worse. The standard bullet weight had been 158 grains in .38 and .357 Magnum. Then the shooting statistics began to pour in, and we found that the 125-grain jacketed hollow-point bullets did a better job of stopping than the 158s did. Departments that went with the 125/.357 equation soon found the guns died even sooner. Forcing cones eroded and cracked. Frames cracked between the barrel and crane. Cylinders went out of time and battered themselves to excessive endshake. The guns were not built for the load. Back when Bill Jordan talked S&W into it, the only ones who even came close to 5,000 rounds a year were Bull's-eye and PPC shooters. And they used .38 Special ammunition. When fed the steady diet of hot loads the guns weren't up to it, which anyone who stopped and thought about it for a moment would have known. And someone in the S&W design bureau came up with the perfect police revolver just in time for every police department in the United States to switch to pistols; the L frame.

We're all now familiar with computer morphing, where you blend one object into another on the screen. Well, imagine a morphed revolver. Take the barrel threads and their hole in the frame, and morph a K frame halfway to an N frame. Increase the diameter of the cylinder, and give it a larger shaft on the crane, to support it under recoil. Then, while you're at it, steal a line from Colt and make your new barrel look much like the Python outline. Gunsmiths for years had been showing off by fitting S&W K frame revolvers with Python barrels. The Python barrel was considered by many to be more accurate than the S&W, and you had to change the threads, but once done it was good looking. S&W now had their own in-house "Smolt." The changes did not include the frame at the grip straps, which remained K frame in size and shape. The K was far more comfortable to shooters than the grip size of the N frame, and the grip area was not the part breaking under heavy use. So the engineers left it alone. (Good for them.)

The extra weight of the barrel also helped dampen the felt recoil of the hot Magnum ammo. The thicker barrel allowed for a thicker forcing cone wall, and the heavier frame added steel to the topstrap and the web between the crane and barrel threads. First introduced in blue, the stainless version wasn't far behind. The 586 (blue) and 686 (stainless) were also available in a fixed-sight version for departments that didn't cotton to the "new-fangled" adjustable sights. In the expansion of the 1980s the 686 could be had in just about any barrel length, calibers up to .357 Magnum, blue and stainless (and even a few nickeled ones) but the writing was on the wall: the future was in pistols. The L frame offerings shrank to a few; the seven-shot version, a ported version, the basic gun. If you want a medium-frame revolver that can stand up to a steady diet of .357 Magnum ammo better than you can, the L frame is a far better choice than the K. If what you want is a lighter medium-frame revolver that can take occasional .357 magnum use but will mostly be used with .38 Specials, then you want the K frame.

The L frame also allowed for a larger cartridge in the cylinder. With the extra diameter it was possible to shoehorn a five-shot .44 Special cylinder into the L frame opening. It had been something I had been urging my contact at the S&W plant at the time to do ever since I first laid dial calipers on an L frame cylinder. What I had first been advocating was one of several options: a new caliber, the .41 Special. A cut-down .41 Magnum case along the lines of the .38/.357 and .44S/.44M, the .41 Special would have been a great round. And probably a financial flop. Hey, I was a gunsmith, not an industrialist. "If not a .41 Special, how about a .40 or 10mm?" Which is what S&W did from the Performance Center later, offering the Model 646, a five-shot .40 S&W using moon clips on the L frame.

L frames came out first with fixed sights, the model 581. They quickly acquired adjustable sights, but have not gotten the shrouded or hammerless treatment.

N frame

Work began on the .44 Hand Ejector in 1905. Offered to the public in 1908, it was the ultimate double-action revolver of its time. Not only was it available in the then-new .44 S&W Special, they were better-built than any revolver before, and for a long time after. The .44 Special was a powerful and accurate round designed just for the gun. The novel feature of the first models was the additional lock. The .32 and .38 Hand Ejectors locked the cylinder front and rear. The centerpin locked into a hole in the frame, and the front of the ejector rod was locked by a spring-loaded plunger under the barrel. The new .44 Hand Ejector had a third lock, a spring-loaded plunger inside the new oversized ejector rod shroud. The plunger locked into the front of the crane.

The first, the biggest for a while, and for a long time the hottest gun to have, was the N frame in .44 Magnum. Or in this case, .41 Magnum, which was in some ways better.

Known as the Triple Lock, the new S&W was everything you could want in a large double-action revolver.

While well-received, the Triple Lock was more expensive to make, and sales were not what the factory had hoped. The second model deleted the shroud and extra lock, and sales improved with the lower price. When the British realized that war was imminent in the summer of 1914, and that they could not make enough sidearms to arm their troops, they came to S&W. The first orders were so rushed that the British accepted the first batch as First Model revolvers in .455. While the revolver was fine, the extra lock and shroud were not. The British wanted more, but insisted that the extra lock and shroud be deleted. Since the British were willing to pay cash, S&W was all too happy to supply Second Model revolvers in .455, and the Triple Lock was not seen again. I've seen and handled two Triple Locks, one a pre-war in .44 Special and the other a custom order in .45 ACP. Both had been chromed by cretins working at auto plants who obviously tossed the disassembled parts into an empty chroming tray at the bumper line. The fishbelly white, partially flaking chrome did nothing to improve the looks. Both would have been premium collector's guns instead of shooting guns, had they not been chromed.

The U.S. had the same firearm shortage dilemma when we entered the war, and S&W simply switched production to the Model of 1917, a .44 Hand Ejector sec-ond model type chambered in .45 ACP and with the rear of the cylinder machined to accept half moon clips.

After the war S&W made a number of variations of the N frame in various calibers. In the 1920 and early 1930s the use of hotter-loaded .38 Special ammunition was all the rage. Known as .38/44 (a .38 cartridge in a .44 frame) we would now call them ".38 Special+P" rounds. The experimentation and interest lead directly to the .357 Magnum. Twenty years later S&W would up the ante with the .44 Magnum. As a pair of interesting backward steps, in the late 1970s S&W made two new models, one popular and one not. The popular one was the Model 25-5, coming out in 1978. By then the Model designations had been in use for some time, where the .357 N-frame was the M-27, and the .44 Mangum was the M-29, while the same revolver chambered in .45 ACP was the 25-2. It had been a popular and show-off task (although somewhat expensive) by some gunsmiths to take an M-29, a barrel for a 25-2 and a cylinder for a 27 and build a new gun. The late Skeeter Skelton was a vocal advocate of the job: The .44 barrel and cylinder would be removed (and sold for spares) the .357 cylinder would be lathe-reamed to .45 Colt, and the .45 ACP barrel re-fitted to the new revolver. A lot of work for a revolver that ended up being a ".44 Magnum Lite."

When the activity got to be too much, S&W stepped in and offered the 25-5 in .45 Colt. Quite popular with

Detroit cops and bowling pin shooters, it was strong enough to drop bad guys with factory ammo without the apparent need for high-tech hollowpoint bullets. As a bowling pin gun it could be loaded warmer than regular .45 Colt ammo was and broom pins off very well indeed.

The unpopular model was the M-520. It was a fixed sight .357 Magnum revolver made for the New York State Police in 1980. There were a few thousand made and never delivered. The NYSP switched to pistols and the 520s were shunted off to the civilian market.

If you have a Triple Lock, don't shoot it. It is too valuable to collectors as-is. If you have an "M-29" marked gun with a ".45 ACP" marked barrel that shoots .45 Colt ammo, you have a hand-built piece of history. And if you have a 520, you have the most durable .357 Magnum revolver ever made.

The N frame, as the .44 Hand Ejector, came out first with fixed sights. It has had adjustable sights for almost the entire time, first as special order guns when it was the Hand Ejector, then adjustable sights as standard when the N frame got model numbers. The only fixed-sight Magnum was the M-58, the .41 Magnum. The N never got treated to a shrouded or hammerless option.

N plus

The Performance Center does not take regular production guns and "tune them up" as some think. They machine the handguns they make from scratch, carving their custom models to precise dimensions. They make some eight-shot revolvers, the .357 Magnum and the .38 Super that are nominal N frames. But not quite. The cylinders are the same diameter as regular N frame cylinders, but the circumference upon which the chamber axes are aligned is farther out from the centerline than on regular N frames. The frame opening is the same as on regular N frames but the barrel is located higher on the frame front, to line up with the increased radial spacing of the chambers. You cannot fit the PC eight-shot cylinders and barrel on a regular N frame, nor fit regular N-frame parts to a PC frame. With a lathe, you could fabricate a new barrel to go on a PC frame, but you'd need more machine tool than most gunsmiths have to make a new PC cylinder. Were you to try and fit one to the other (frames and cylinders) you'd find the cylinder and barrel out of alignment by .040"! As a misalignment of as little as .005" calls for a frame to be re-worked or scrapped, you can see there is no way to reconcile the two.

The N-Plus frame can get you eight shots of .357 Magnum where there used to only be six.

The biggest and smallest S&W revolvers, the J and the X frame. If these aren't small or large enough, I don't know what to say.

X frame

The newest and so far the only handgun made for the 500SW cartridge is built on the X frame. Absolutely mammoth, the frame can easily handle the 500, better than many shooters can. As it is brand-new, with only two barrel lengths available, we'll have to see how it evolves. I'm wondering if when production catches up to the demand for .500 guns, we'll start seeing new variants. How about a seven-shot .44 Magnum? A nine- or 10-shot .357? Who knows? I've heard whispers from the factory, but nothing confirmed. If you really wanted to show off, the trick would be to figure out how many charge holes of .22 Long Rifle you could machine into an alloy cylinder to fit the X frame. That and a Scandium frame, and you'd have the lightest twenty-shot .22 Long Rifle handgun around.

Model designation follows the pattern of; Names, model numbers as two-digits and model numbers as three digits. The names are mostly of interest to collectors. The model numbers followed some internal logic in the 1950s, with the K frame in the teens, the N in the 20s and the J in the 30s. Then there were variations with the "dash" numbers, like the 25-2 that designated .45 ACP, or the 10-2, which meant a change in some internal or external parts, like a different sight dimension.

When stainless steel was introduced, the model numbers were bumped up to the "sixes" as in the 64, 65 and 66. Then when the changes started coming hard and fast, the revolvers got a three-digit model designation. The exact details are of interest mostly to collectors, but you must be aware of them because they do not always proceed in a rational manner. For instance, the 27 became the 627. The 25-2 became the 625-2. But the 10 did not become the 610. No, the 10 stayed the 64, and the 610 was the number given to the 10mm revolver.

When the three-digit revolvers started, the carbon steel guns were the "fives," as in the 586 and 581 series of L frame that came out with the 686. Then we got the "twos," threes," and "fours" the Airweight series in various frame sizes. It seems like S&W should come out with that wheel again.

Pistol frames

The earliest do not concern us, being the .35 (yes, a .35 caliber pistol) and the .32. We start with the 9mm, the M-39.

The single-stack first-generation guns have very comfortable grips and not much room for expansion. Should the urge to convert an M-39 to .40 ever come over you, lie down and apply cold compresses until it goes away. The 39 just wasn't built with that in mind. First generation guns are found only in 9mm, .38 Special and (ultra-rare) .38 AMT.

Late in the first generation S&W made the double-stack guns, the M-59. They too are 9mm-only guns and should not be viewed as anything but. Then it gets interesting.

Second generation

The second-generation guns introduced stainless steel, an extremely durable adjustable sight, and numerous small technical fixes. The second-generation guns still used two-panel grips that were held to the frame with screws. Second generation guns are found in 9mm and .45 ACP.

Third generation

The latest, the "3-Gen" guns feature one-piece wraparound grips. At first made of Delrin, they are now composed of Xenoy. The internals have been upgraded continually since the third-generation guns began appearing in 1989. You can find 3-G guns in 9mm, .40, 10mm and .45.

The first-generation pistols are the 39 and 59. The second-generation guns got the three-digit treatment where the first indicated the material and the last two the model. So a 639 was a stainless single-stack 9mm. The "5" was carbon steel and the "4" alloy. Then the third generation hit. The 39, 40 or 59 became the prefix, and designated capacity or caliber. The third and fourth digits became the combination capacity and trigger mechanism descriptors. You could make a chart, but the exceptions would clutter it so much it wouldn't be much use. You either have to remember them all, look them up, or make a wheel.

Design features of the S&W pistol.

From the beginning the trigger mechanism has proven to be very adaptable. It can be made in traditional double-action, single-action, decocking, DAO, and who knows what else. One interesting feature is the hammer pivot pin. It also acts as the slide stop cam shoulder, on the end of the arm that rests under the left side grip panel. The barrel is relatively cylindrical, compared to other designs. (mostly Browning or Browning-inspired.) The dual cam paths on the sides means the barrel can be CNC-lathe turned and finished on a CNC mill starting from a smaller-diameter steel billet. Smaller means less cost to procure, less time spent machining, and less wear and tear on the machine tools in the cutting.

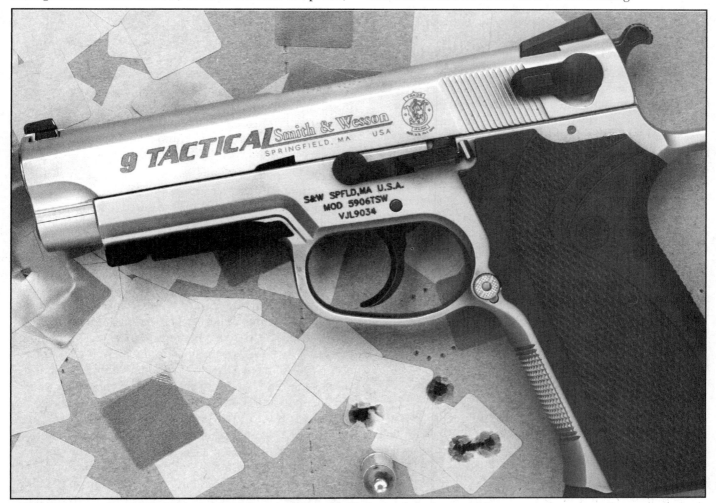

The third-generation S&W pistols are durable, accurate, and hold plenty of ammo.

Composition of S&W

The basic, beginning component was carbon steel. By including carbon in iron, we create steel. The amount of carbon and other minor metallic alloying agents, combined with the heat treatment, determines the strength and machineability of the steel. Early guns are softer simply due to less-exotic alloying agents and less knowledge of heat treatment possibilities. While "stainless" steel had been around for a long time it was expensive and too soft for firearms. When the problems were worked out, S&W introduced stainless models. Its use has expanded ever since; until now stainless is the standard and carbon steel the rarity. Steel is strong, can be easily machined, forged, cast or otherwise worked, and can be repaired should the need arise.

Aluminum is much lighter and softer than steel. What makes aluminum appear hard is anodizing. The hard-coat anodizing we are all familiar with is a surface treatment, not a through-hardening like heat-treatment is. Once you either wear through the anodizing, or break it, the softer substrate will quickly peen or propagate the crack. A cracked aluminum frame is gone, and must be replaced, where a steel frame could theoretically be welded and repaired. (Not that S&W will do that, nor will many gunsmiths. I'm just speaking theoretically here.)

Until the advent of CNC cutting machines, machining Titanium was expensive, difficult and slow. I recall seeing a sci-fi movie from 1950 where the engineer in charge comments "every ounce of weight costs us pounds of reactant mass. Try Titanium." Which was a real hoot because just working it wasn't possible until the 1960s. Even then it was ferociously expensive, something only the Department of Defense or aerospace industry could afford. Once the methods were refined and a sufficient supply was available it became possible to include Titanium in firearms. Titanium primarily comes in 3 common variants: 100% (CP/Commercially Pure) Titanium, 3/2.5 which is an alloy of 94% titanium, 3% Aluminum and 2.5% Vanadium, and 6/4 which is 90% Titanium, 6% Aluminum and 4% Vanadium. There are many alloys to be found, and sometimes minor changes or variations can have very useful properties.

Pure titanium was quickly found out to be pretty useless - very light, but so brittle as to be dangerous in most applications. (You do not want a brittle ICBM part for any application.) 6/4 alloy, invented in the 1950s was a very strong but not very ductile (rollable into tubes). 3/2.5 alloy was invented in the 1970s and is what you generally see in tubes, originally designed for military aircraft fuel lines. These alloys give amazing tensile strength for their feathery weight.

The cutbacks in defense spending in the 1990s opened up the availability of titanium in the commercial market, as producers and mills of titanium were all of a sudden without their biggest spenders. (And not to forget, their price-insensitive spenders.) Previously, you couldn't get specially-made titanium parts, but once the DoD demand slacked off, suddenly the titanium providers were willing to roll tubes or provide stock in many more shapes and forms than before.

Which is why you can find golf clubs, tennis rackets, firearms, etc. much more commonly, and relatively cheaper than even five years ago. And why do golf clubs lead the field? Golfers are not quite as price-insensitive as shooters, but much less so than the Department of Defense. And a golf club is a much less critical part to fabricate than a rocket part or firearm.

The big advantage Titanium has is its amazingly strong elasticity - much better than steel, and for much less weight.

Scandium is a rare metal that when alloyed with aluminum creates a very hard alloy. Unlike regular aluminum alloys, the Scandium alloys are hard through, and do not have soft cores. They do not upset on the surface as aluminum alloys do, and offer a great deal more strength than aluminum alloys did. One interesting change in design due to the light overall weight of the Scandium alloys is in the pivot pins of revolvers. The regular pins are steel, pressed into pockets in the side of the frame. In a Scandium alloy-framed handgun chambered in a magnum cartridge, the steel pins can break. The inertia of the recoil is just too much for them. So, when you see an AirLite revolver in a magnum chambering, the pins you see on the sides of the frame are Titanium.

The strength of metals can be measured many ways. One common one is to measure the "Tensile Strength" of a metal or alloy. By applying a measured load to the test sample, you see if it bends. As long as the bend returns to "zero" when the load is removed, the tensile strength has not been exceeded. (The exact details of the sample size, load, speed of application, speed of removal and measurement of "deflection" and return to "zero" are unimportant to this discussion, and require several semesters of study at a good Engineering college.) The various alloys of aluminum without Scandium have tensile strengths in the range of 40,000 to 50,000 pounds per square inch. (We'll just use "Kpsi" to make it easier.) Scandium alloy has a tensile strength in the 105-110 Kpsi range. The various alloys of steel, carbon and stainless used in firearms manufacture range from 120 to 140 Kpsi. (Special steel alloys can range up to 180 Kpsi, but they are too brittle for firearms use.) Thus the increasing use of Scandium in S&W products. For almost the weight of Aluminum you can have almost the strength of steel. Titanium has, depending on the alloy used, a tensile strength from 100K to 115K. Thus the use of Titanium in some applications.

MIM is not an invention of the devil. The way some shooters talk about it you'd think it was, but it isn't. MIM, from "metal injection molding," is a method of fabricating complicated parts that reduces costs while making better parts. The old way was to machine parts out of billets of steel or forged lumps. The "lost wax" or investment casting process requires a wax copy of a part, assembled on "trees" of parts with connecting wax rods, which is then encased in a ceramic slurry. When the slurry is built up, the coated tree is fired, hardening the ceramic and melting out the wax. The molten metal is then poured into the now-hollow ceramic mold. Once cooled the mold is broken, the parts separated from the tree, and then finish-machined. MIM involves an over-sized mould of the part. The powdered metal is mixed with a binding agent, and the mixture pumped into the mold. Once shaped, the part is heated. At a high enough heat (and a correct rate of rise and cool) the binding agent burns away and the powdered metal fuses into the part. With a known ratio of binder to metal, the exact shrinkage rate of the part when heated and cooled is known. Thus parts can be made that do not require fur-ther machining. Once cooled they are inspected, given a finish of some kind, and then used for assembly. The alloy of the metal determines the strength and properties of the part. As with any production process, learning on the production floor continues even after the research lab says things are finished and perfect. Some early MIM parts failed. (So what, some early parts of everything failed.) They do not fail now, and when they failed they failed early in use, so sufficient practice to make sure of a handgun's function would uncover them. So when you hear someone railing against the use of MIM parts, you know it is someone who only has part of the story. Without MIM and other production advances, we would not be buying handguns that actually cost less in real dollars than they did in the "good old days." As an example, my brother Mike bought his first M-57 revolver in the early 1970s for $289. At the then-current value of the dollar compared to today, that M-57 would cost $850 to $1,000. The current cost for a stainless 629 is around $600. Would the shooter who objects to MIM be willing to pay an extra $250 or more, for no MIM but also no stainless? I think not.

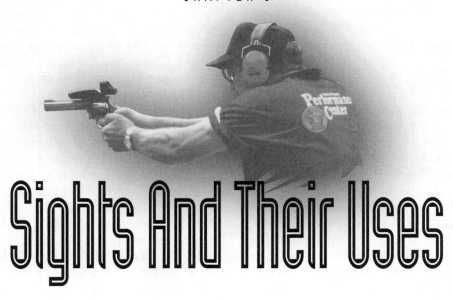

CHAPTER 3

Sights And Their Uses

One of the lesser controversies that rage in the gun magazines is aimed versus pointed shooting. Aiming is simple to describe, if sometimes hard to do. You line up the sights (of whatever kind) with the target and press the trigger. Pointing is less easy to describe. Point-shooting, instinctive shooting or reflexive shooting are different ways to describe the same apparent process. As it is usually explained, "You can point your finger quickly and accurately at anything. So you instinctively point the firearms at the target and fire."

Point shooting can be done in a range from the classic Western movie star shooting from the hip (usually on a blinding fast draw, to shoot the bad guy's gun or "just wing" him) up to a chest-high point, to pointing the handgun in the line of sight but not trying to look at the sights. The problem with point shooting is that we have no "instinctive" point, nor is our pointing all that accurate. We're all used to pointing at something and having our fingertip cover what we're pointing at. Usually very quickly. Except that it isn't all that accurate, nor quick. Our brain fudges any errors, since it knows what you're trying to point at. And instincts are far deeper in the brain than any skill at arms we might build. True instincts are those we are hard-wired with. Some even argue that the set of instinctive responses of the human brain are few, or even none. That we are a tabula rasa ("clean slate"). A true instinct is a duck migrating

1,000 miles, never having seen the route; not shooting a handgun quickly on a target. The latter is a reflex, a learned response. If you think pointing is accurate, try pointing out something to a friend. "No, there." "There?" "No, next to it, the little brown thing next to the blue thing." You could make a comedy routine of it, except that I'm sure it was old when Caesar was dressing for his last appointment.

Optics on your gun does not mean "slow on the range." Here Jerry Miculek is hosing through a stage at World Shoot XII in The Philippines.

For serious competitors in Open Division, a red dot scope is a requirement.

If pointing is so bad, then why did it get started, and why did it hang on for so long. Indeed, why is it that we're still arguing about it? In the beginning firearms had no sights. The whole idea of "accuracy" with a firearm was so ludicrous that putting sights on a firearm smacked of hubris. And military uses didn't require fine sights. Artillerymen were proud of being able to accurately fire, but they were usually firing at one stationary object while they were still. Hitting a particular corner or abutment of a fortress, five times out of ten, is hardly an achievement of marksmanship to crow about. (Doing so under return fire, that's a different matter.) Infantrymen were firing at opposing masses of infantry. If you were in the unlucky position of shooting at the enemy, you were shoulder to shoulder with your fellow soldiers, facing an equally packed mass of enemy soldiers about 50 yards away. You'd fire a volley, then close with bayonets. Accuracy just wasn't in the cards. Cavalry was as close or closer, but both riders were moving. Point and shoot was the order of the day, and statistics and personal luck would determine who got shot and who didn't.

The beginning of aiming came (as so many things did) in the American Civil War. Rifled muskets have enough individual accuracy that aiming became a profitable exercise in a military context. Because of that, the casualties in many engagements became horrific. As one example, the Michigan 24th Volunteers, of the "Iron Brigade" began the first day of Gettysburg with almost 500 men. They finished the day with less than 100. A good shot who was cool under fire could be certain of hitting a particular individual at 100 yards with a single shot. He could strike someone at random in a maneuvering unit out to 300 or beyond. In a statistical analysis of engagements of the Civil War, units that were chewed apart by rifle fire, the one that broke and charged first usually lost the engagement. The tipping point had been reached, where rifle fire trumped bayonets. It would be another half a century before the lesson was fully learned. Meanwhile, handguns, the weapon of the cavalry, were still pointed. The problem of two moving objects was not one that could be solved by careful aiming. It was not until WWI that cavalry became obsolete, so pointing hand-

Until just before WWII this would have been a radical, huge sight.

The thin blade on this pre-Depression M&P is as hard to use as it looks.

guns remained an accepted practice for that time. During the last half of the 19th century, the separation of target shooting from combat shooting grew. While target shooters proved you could shoot accurately by using the sights, many combat shooters and experienced gunfighters still pointed. The cause was a mix of things: sights, time and engagement distances, and experience.

The experience of many combat shooters (and the United States produced a large body of men, with a vast amount of experience) was that you didn't need to aim. They'd survived by pointing, so pointing obviously worked. The logical fallacy of that is that all those for whom pointing didn't work were not present to argue the point, and thus the argument had no rebuttal. But to a certain extent they were right. And the experience was buttressed by the time and engagement distances in which they worked. When shooting across a card table in a saloon in the Old West, pointing worked. Your opponent was a foot and a half wide, and 4 feet away. If you shoot first you'll probably score a hit. If you're in the trenches when the German assault wave swarmed over the lip of your trench, you had a nearly solid wall of gray wool-clad targets. Shoot fast, for if you don't there's a bayonet with your name on it. Target shooters fired at 25 and 50 yards (and Bull's-eye shooters still do) and for that you needed the sights. But in "real life" you shot the other guy at a distance a lot less than 25 yards. Sometimes 25 inches. And you had to do it first, or he'd shoot you. And the early sights were bad. No, let me re-phrase that: They sucked. So target shooters continued to use bad sights in broad daylight in a smooth range with liberal time limits, and punched small groups. While combat shooters concentrated on quickly hitting a target the size of a washtub at close distances.

And there it stayed for a long time. How long? Until the 1970s or 1980, depending on what segment of the shooting population you were in. The point where sights changed in each model is a subject that brings collectors to dizziness and delight. Indeed, to have consecutively serial numbered S&W revolvers, one with an old dimension or design, and the other with the new, would be the centerpiece of a serious collector's display. I'm not interested in exactly when the changes were made, just that the sights evolved. But before we discuss the change that came about in shooting, its causes and the inevitable resistance, let's look at the evolution of sights, as exemplified in S&W sights through the 20th century.

Sights In The Gaslight Era

I call it the gaslight era, but electric lights were no longer a novelty in the first decade of the 20th century. But sights hadn't changed much. The old top-break revolvers had front sights that were almost the thickness of a knife blade, less than .050 inches. And usually tapering towards the top. With a skinny little nub of a sight like that, it's no wonder point-shooting was preferred. The new Hand Ejector models were different. First, they were chambered in the new .38 S&W Special cartridge. It was powerful and accurate. So the sights were improved. Looking back from a century removed it is easy to make fun of them, but the sights were a vast improvement over previous sights. They just weren't enough. My oldest Hand Ejector dates from around 1912. It is chambered in .32-20, with a 5-inch barrel. The front sight is a willowy .057 inches wide at the top. The rear notch is hard to measure it is so small, but mikes out at .054 inches wide and .040 inches deep. Compounding the problem of

Yes, there is a notch in there, one you're supposed to use with the front sight. No wonder point shooting was considered a viable option!

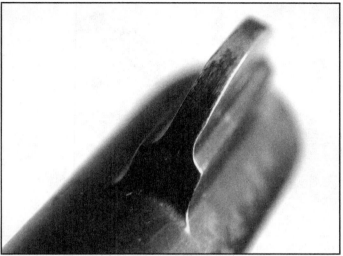
This sight may not seem like much, but it was a big step forward. Compared to the earlier M&P sights, it is huge.

aiming, the front sight is a semi circle, so the top edge is not clearly defined to the eye. And the rear notch is semi-circular. You are presented with the task of lining one rounded surface up with another rounded surface, and keeping them aligned while you fire. In the Ransom rest the .32-20 is nicely accurate. Trying to shoot it accurately without the rest is real work.

My next Hand Ejector is only 15 years older, but is a lifetime of development and progress ahead. For much of the 20th century the issue sidearm of the Detroit Police was a 5-inch blued S&W Military & Police in .38 Special. Once on the force and qualified, you could then carry a personally-owned sidearm. Better yet, you could carry anything you could qualify with on the state course. As one result, many officers put away their issued revolver and qualified and carried a larger-caliber sidearm. You could find .357s, .41 Magnums, .44 Specials, .44 Magnums and .45 ACP S&W revolvers in the holsters of Detroit cops. Many surrounding departments also issued 5-inch M&P revolvers. They were not all so willing to let their officers carry bigger guns. For many decades it was customary to allow a retiring Detroit officer to purchase his service revolver from the department. (We'll see if Detroit, having gone to .40 Glocks, and disallowed personal sidearms, continues the tradition of allowing retiring officers to purchase their issued sidearm.) My second Hand Ejector comes from a nearby department and was made in the late 1920s. The Grosse Pointe Park Police Department thought highly enough of it that they marked it, and did not let go of it until the 1980s. By the late 1920s S&W had changed sight dimensions. The front sight of my .38 is .081 inches wide at the top, with less taper than the earlier model. The rear sight notch (we're still in the fixed-sight era for "combat" guns) is

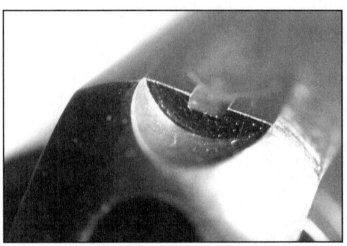
And we get a nice square notch to go with the wide blade, pre-WWII.

.094 inches wide. But better yet, the rear notch is milled as a square slot. It is still shallow, only .035 inches deep, but at least you can see vertical lines on either side of the front sight blade.

Jump forward another 15 years. S&W is working day and night to make sidearms for the World War II. While they are not making .45 revolvers as they did in WWI, there is a pressing need for .38-caliber sidearms for flight crews, wartime security personnel and rear echelon staff. The British colonial units all want .38 revolvers, but they want them in the older .38 S&W, no the newer .38 S&W Special. My third Hand Ejector is a pre-Victory model, before the serial number and lockwork change. Chambered in .38 S&W and shipped (based on the markings) to Australia, it isn't as pretty as the earlier ones. The finish is Parkerized instead of blued. The inspectors stamped it with all the markings required

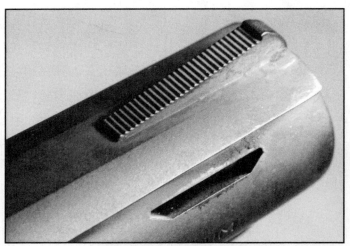
The evolutionary end of the line for fixed revolver sights. This thing is as wide as a 2x4 compared to earlier sights.

The S&W micrometer click adjustable rear. Hi-tech in the early 1950s.

by regulations. And the sights are the same as the M&P made in the 1920s. We'd have to wait until after the war for another change, and then we'd get two.

The first change was to fixed-sight revolvers. The sight blade was increased to .125 inches in width. The rear opened up to .137 inches, and the depth increased to .065 inches. My exemplar for this sight is a Model 65. During the 1950s S&W changed from naming their models to giving them model numbers. So the wonderful old Military & Police became the Model 10. The Combat Masterpiece became the Model 19, and so on. My Model 65 is a K-frame fixed-sight .357 Magnum revolver made in stainless steel. The Model 65 was introduced in 1974. Mine was made some time after that, but not too late. It had time to be purchased by and used in a police department, traded in and then swapped to the Second Chance combat shoot. At Second Chance it was used for a few years as an issued gun for the short-lived Subway Event. Then it ended up in the prize table, where I snagged it as loot. I rebuilt it and slicked it up, and carried it as a main and backup gun for many years. It went with me to a number of law enforcement firearms classes, and has been summarily dumped in sand, dirt and gravel in the course of training exercises. In all, it has done exactly what we require of a sidearm; be there and be dependable. And the whole time it has been an accurate shooter. The sights are large enough that you can see them well enough to aim. It will hit the 100-yard gong at our club six out of six if you do your part. I used it to fire the qualifying course at my local sheriff's department range. The indoor range then could not take .357 Magnum, so I had to use .38 Special ammo, but posted a 246 out of 250 with it. (Double-action weak-hand-only is where I dropped the points.) The evolution of fixed-sight revolvers stopped with these dimensions. There is no use in going wider than .125 inches for a front blade, and the only way to make them more visible is

to make the front and rears taller so you can have a deeper rear notch. During this time S&W took a slight step backwards. They introduced the Chiefs Special. The CS was a redesigned I frame made to hold the .38 Special, five shots and a short barrel and round butt. Meant for off duty and as a backup gun, it was viewed as a close-range concealment gun, so the sights got some of the old treatment. The front wasn't the old round blade, but it was made narrow, down to .070 inches. The rear notch was .080 inches and .040 inches deep. But when S&W went with the thicker front sights on their other models you could special order a heavy-barrel Model 36, and later in stainless, a Model 60.

The second change was to have adjustable sights on a sidearm. Early adjustable sights had been meant solely for target shooting. While they weren't fragile, they weren't meant for the rough and tumble of combat use. The early target sights (as early as the .38 Hand Ejector, available beginning in 1899) had tiny screws for adjustment. After WWII, with the redesign of many aspects of the action, the adjustable sights were overhauled. The new sights featured larger, more robust screws. And best of all, it was "micrometer click" adjustable. That is, you could feel and hear the clicks of each setting as you made an adjustment. If you overshot a change (common in setting sights) you could "click back" a click or two and be dead on. The new sights came in the new dimensions, with wide front blade and rear notches, and a relatively deep rear notch. My example is a Model 19-5, with the front blade .125 inches wide, the rear notch .127 inches wide and .075 inches deep. The S&W micrometer sights were just what target shooters wanted. And they were so popular that when S&W took the advice of the late Bill Jordan and came up with the K-frame .357, it came with adjustable sights. (The Combat Masterpiece, later the Model 19, it was for two decades the sidearm of choice for police officers who were the predecessors of

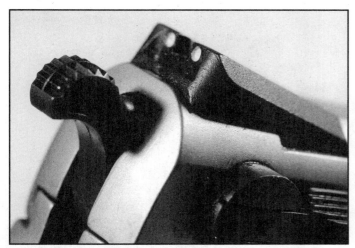

The Novak rear, with two of the three dots, was a definite improvement, but the three-dot sight is definitely 1980s. (People still love it.)

The front Novak, with the third dot.

today's "high-speed low-drag" operators.) The sight was so well thought of that when combat shooters using 1911 pistols wanted adjustable sights on their .45s they used the S&W micrometer sight. Consider how much work it entailed to weld up the old dovetail, file and polish the weld to contour it to the slide, then mill a longtitudinal slot and a cross step for the sight, drill and tap the screw hole and mill the locking step for the sight adjustment foot. You've got to love a sight to go to that much work.

Pistol sights didn't go through that much of an evolution. The first S&W pistol was the pocket pistol that was meant to compete with the Colt model M: the S&W 35. Not as in Model 35, but as in .35 caliber. The sights were smaller than the revolver sights of the time. After WWII, when S&W began the pistol project for the Department of Defense, sights were already recognized as something

you aimed with, and something that had to be properly dimensioned. The first S&W Model 39 pistols had good sights, and sights on pistols only got better. The culmination of pistol sights was the adjustable sight of the 1980s. So good were these sights I even mounted some on 1911 pistols for customers who liked them. A few years before it had been S&W micrometer sights on 1911s, then it became the adjustable pistol sights. Once Bo-mar came out with a specific model for low-mounting on 1911 slides, we gave up all the S&W hybrids. But for 10 years there, if you wanted adjustable (and low-mounted, combat-worthy) sights on a 1911, you got something from S&W.

The latest improvements to S&W sights are in making them more durable and (probably) making them easier to make. But they haven't changed much since.

But what did all this lead to?

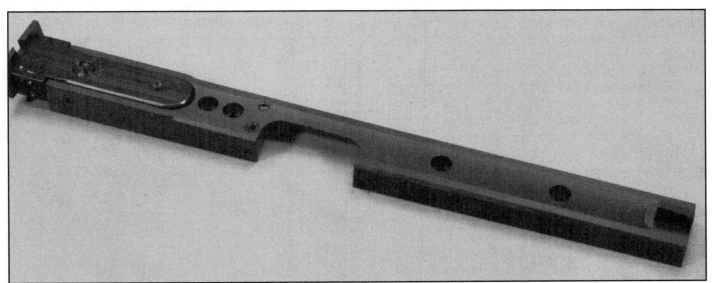

When PPC turned into an accuracy game and not practical handgunning, items such as this most-excellent Aristocrat rib started showing up on the firing line.

Combat Shooting Through The Ages

The first big change in combat shooting came about from the FBI. J. Edgar Hoover had just gotten legislation to arm his federal agents, and he wanted them to be the premier law enforcement agents. Many went with the then-new .357 Magnum. The Bureau designed a new training and qualification course. Like many other courses it required firing a substantial amount of ammunition (60 rounds) at all reasonable distances (5 to 50 yards) but it had some radical changes. The first was all shooting strings started with the sidearm holstered. Many police qualification courses (not that there were that many in the 1930s) had the officers start with their sidearms out and ready. To begin with a holstered handgun was new and radical then. It is obvious now. The second change was that all shooting was done double-action. No thumb-cocking the action to fire. Again, obvious to us, but back in the 1930s accurate double-action shooting was considered to be just a close-range expedient. The third change was that some strings of fire required more rounds than the revolver held, forcing agents to reload against the clock. Many qualification courses followed the basics of target competition, where all strings were five shots (or for police, six) with reloading done between strings. In a shootout you didn't get timeouts to reload, so the new FBI agents had to reload while the clock was ticking, and continue shooting to finish the string.

So far, so good. However, the FBI made two errors, one first then another later. The first error made at the time the course was designed, was to require one-handed shooting at close ranges. As we've discussed in the point-shooting section, the short time frames of real-life encounters "obviously" required one-handed shooting as the fastest shooting. And not just one-handed shooting, but one-handed point shooting. Agents were required to fire from a slightly crouched "chest point" with their weak hand clutched over their chest to act as a slight impediment to incoming fire. The second error was in not updating the course or the training that went with it in the subsequent decades of research, knowledge, practice and equipment improvement. The Police Practical Course as it was called also became engraved in stone as a competition, with changes few and fiercely fought.

In the 1970s, research by Jeff Cooper culminated in the formation of the International Practical Shooting Confederation. In the beginning it was not the "1911 exclusive zone" that it later became. Many shooters used other firearms, and as a lot of them were police, they used double action revolvers. And they found out that if you measured the actual times, and let shooters do things the way they wanted, you came up with surprising results: Two hands won. Sights won. Standing up won. Everyone who shot one handed, crouched, or pointed, or used

The gold bead, first from McGivern, then Jerry Miculek, and now SDM.

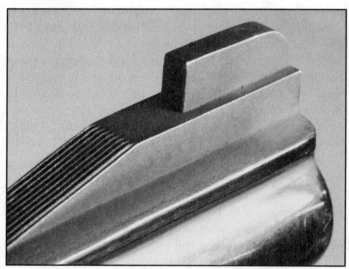

The flat target blade was great for competition but hard on holsters, especially concealment holsters.

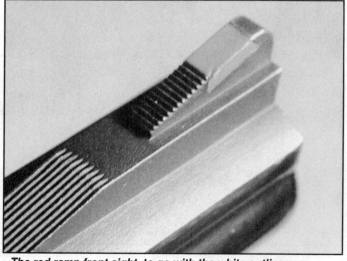

The red ramp front sight, to go with the white outline rear.

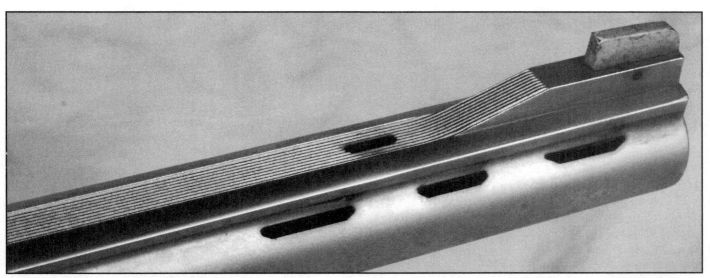

In an earlier day, we just painted the sights. This paint job has lasted almost 20 years, 14 Second Chance shoots and a veritable slew of pin, steel and IPSC matches.

some combination of those three, lost. The knowledge had to be teased out of open competition over the course of more than a decade, but by 1976 it was clear: the old ways didn't work as well as the new. They didn't even work as well as we had thought.

And part of the evolution was possible by the new sights that had been evolving through the decades of traditional target competition. Without the large, bold sights the Bull's-eye shooters had developed, the fast shooting of IPSC would not have been possible. PPC as a competition was in a crisis. New developments in holsters made the draw much faster. New techniques in gunsmithing made guns smoother in action and the easier trigger pulls resulted in higher scores. But the real change came with speedloaders. The original times for the PPC had been laid down in the 1930s, when officers or agents loaded their revolvers from belt loops or loose ammo in their pockets. As an example, the 7-yard line time of 25 seconds for six shots, reload and six shots is fast when loading from belt loops. If you're reloading six from the belt or pocket, you'd better crank off your first six quickly, because you're going to be spending 10 seconds or more of that time reloading. A speedloader holds six rounds, and you can reload in a few seconds. A clumsy reload might take up six or eight seconds. With a fast holster and speedloaders, anyone could shoot a perfect score on the old PPC target with its dinner-plate size "5" ring. Rather than cut the times, PPC shrank the rings. The 5-point ring became a 10 ring, and went from a dinner plate to a playing card in size. The center "X" ring shrank to almost a business card-sized oval. PPC became a sedate target shooting affair, rather than a training for real-life busniess. Meanwhile, IPSC was still shooting at dinner plate-sized (or larger) X rings, and letting the

shooters shoot as fast as they could to win. But the FBI was not paying attention. The training methods and accepted standards of the early 1980s were pretty much the same as they had been in the late 1930s. Agents still shot double-action, from a crouch, one-handed at close range, with one arm clutched over their chests. The problem they had was that they no longer could recruit exclusively from the "adult male population with jackets larger than 42 inches" pool. They had to accept women, and women training to be agents were flunking the firearms course at disproportionate rates. In the court of law, if the FBI standards could have been shown to be relevant to real-world performance and the duties of an agent, then the standards would have held. They were not. The training standards had things like tests for trigger pulling. An agent in training had to be able to pull the trigger of a revolver a certain number of times within a stated time period, or fail. (28 times in 30 seconds. Sitting here at the computer I just did it in seven seconds. But I'm not a 5'2" female recruit who has never held a revolver prior to entering the FBI academy.) The test had no real-world relevance. Also, agents in training were required to use the issued K frame revolvers on the training and qualification course at the academy. With a small hand, the K was too large. However, if they were tested on the qualification course with J frame revolvers (allowed after graduation) they could shoot passing scores on the course. I think you can see where this was headed. Basically, what the court asked was if the agents in training could perform all the mental, investigative, procedural and court testimony tasks of an agent, but the firearms training was so archaic that they would be flunked, then why was the firearms training not up to modern standards? The FBI had no good answer, and so they were required to update

If you are hunting, the only "rules" you have to worry about are those of fair chase and your state hunting regulations. Get a scope if it helps and is allowed.

If you mount a scope, you're in Open Division, if they even allow it. Before you have Scott Mulkerin of SDM mount one, make sure the match rules allow it.

An SDM Fabricating fiber optic sight. It fits the spring and plunger front on some S&W revolvers.

Another SDM sight, this one with a gold bead and made for drilled and pinned front sights.

the firearms training procedures and standards.

I don't want it to sound like I'm beating up on the FBI. The episode is so informative, and the lesson so valuable, that it bears repeating. The lesson is that sights work, and we should use them. But there is another lesson: We should not get so caught up in what we do, and how we do it, and so proud of how well we do it, that we fail to look for better ways of doing it.

Sights Today

Now we have large, clear, easy-to-use sights. So why do, as my wife once put it while watching shooter after shooter on the Back Range at Second Chance, "Some shooters think 'aim' is a four-letter word?"

Heck if I know.

You can get a plethora of sight options on your S&W. The basic black goes with everything. A black ramped sight with a black rear (adjustable or fixed) will work well for many applications. However, many shoot-

ers like something different, and so we have other sights. The most common you'll see is the factory combination "RR/WO" otherwise known as red ramp with white outline. The ramped front sight has a dovetail milled in it, and the dovetail is filled with a plastic insert or epoxy casting. Usually red. The rear blade (only on adjustable sights) has a white paint outline around the notch. Ideally, the red ramp (which looks like a red square to the shooter) fits neatly into the white "U" of the rear sight. In low light the colors fade but are still visible. If you like the idea, but are not enamored of the color red (some shooters don't see it well) you can replace the front sight blade with a plastic sight in one of an assortment of eye-searing colors. If your revolver does not have a pinned front sight you can have the barrel machined to take one. Mag na Port makes the sights, and can machine your barrel to take them. The bright colors were quite popular at Second Chance, as the backdrop behind the pins changed from year to year. One year it might be black, the next camouflage, and the one after a dark blue. If you showed up with "black on black" sights on your

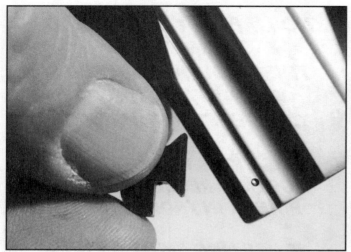

The spring and plunger sight, coming out.

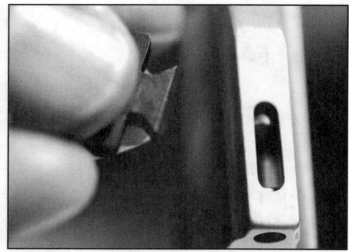

The sight out, ready to be replaced with another.

handgun, and the backdrop was black, you could lose your sights between pins.

One oldie but goodie that keeps coming back is the McGivern Gold Bead. The gold bead is installed on the rear face of a post sight, and when you are sighting it rides in the notch of the rear sight. You can be fast, accurate, or both with the gold bead.

The modern replacement of the gold bead is the fiber optic sight, like the HiViz that comes on some S&W models, or the replacement SDM blades you can get for your revolvers. The fiber optic rod has a unique property: it reflects light on the inside surfaces of the tube, not allowing it to escape through the sides. Thus, light collected by the tube is allowed to (primarily, not entirely) shine out the ends of the tube. The tube, as a dot in the front sight, shows in the light. And the level of brightness is directly related to the ambient light, appearing to adjust to the light level. In bright light you have a bright dot. In subdued light you have a dim dot, not so bright it overpowers your vision. The only disadvantage to the fiber optic sight is fragility.

Pistols come as either plain black or three-dot sights.

And you can also get night sights, where the three dots are replaced by small vials of Tritium. The radiation from the tritium causes a small amount of phosphorescent material in the rear of the vial to glow, creating dots that you can see at night. Some like them, some don't. Some find them useful.

Sight construction

Front sights come one of three ways: integral, pinned, or spring and latch. The integral sights are formed with, and machined out of, the barrel forging or blank. Or in the case of an Airlite gun, machined out of the shroud itself. If an integral sight is damaged you must either machine the barrel to take a pinned or spring and latch sight, weld up the sight, or replace the barrel. A pinned sight is held on by a cross pin. The sight extends down into the barrel rib, and the cross pin goes through the rib and sight blade. A damaged pinned sight can easily be replaced. The spring and latch uses a spring-loaded plunger and a cross pin to clamp the pyramid-shaped foot of the sight in place. A spring and latch sight can easily be replaced when damaged, and even replaced with a different looking sight. As long as the two sights (original and replacement) are exactly the same height when install, the zero will not be changed.

A Final Word

So that about covers sights, except for the most important directive of all. Use them. Without sights you can't really know where your shots are going. Shoot enough ammo that acquiring the proper sight picture becomes second nature. Smith and Wesson handguns can be exceptionally accurate tools in the right hands. To see these guns achieve their full potential, use all the benefits they have to offer.

CHAPTER 4

Disassembly and Maintenance

Revolver Maintenance

For many, "maintenance" involves simply wiping the outside of their wheelgun with a silicone cloth, poking a brush and patches down the bore and the charge holes in the cylinder, and putting the gun away until next time.

That can lead to problems. A friend of mine once fired some blanks and gave his beautiful nickel M-19 the usual cursory cleaning. Too bad they were black powder blanks, and the pitting was a mess even through the nickel finish. If you are out in the rain, fall in the water, drop your revolver in the sand, dirt, mud or surf, you'd better do a better job or suffer the consequences. First we'll go over the tools, the disassembly, then the cleaning and lubrication.

Tools

You'll need a proper set of screwdrivers. The screw slots on the grips and sideplate will not be the same. You want a properly fitting screwdriver for each. You do not want to use the standard screwdrivers found in most home toolboxes. They are not proportioned for use in firearms, and will mar the screw slots. You'll need a modified screwdriver when you get to the interior parts, a bore and chamber brush, patches, bore cleaner and lubricant. A padded surface on which to work also helps. The modified screwdriver is for removing the rebound block. You need a screwdriver with a shank the same size as the hole bored in the rebound block. The blade has to be ground or filed narrow enough to fit inside the rebound block spring. Or, you could just buy a special tool from Brownells for removing and replacing the rebound block. If you decide you must remove the cylinder stop you'll need a screwdriver the size appropriate for work on eyeglasses and a narrow-nosed needle-nose pliers.

Disassembly

Make sure it isn't loaded. I do this in every book and magazine article, and every writer I now of does it too. Why? I don't know about them, but I used to work at a gun shop. We lost count of the number of times a prospective customer would assure us "Oh, it isn't loaded" just before opening the action and throwing one or more rounds of ammo out onto the counter, floor or our feet. Make sure it isn't loaded.

Remove the grips. On factory or other two-piece grips you'll see a screw on the side. Unscrew it and pull the grips off. If they are tight, resist the temptation to pry at them with the screwdriver. (In fact, resist the urge any time it occurs to you to use a screwdriver as a pry bar. It is always a bad idea, for the screwdriver, the firearm and you.) One-piece grips will have a screw in the base. Unscrew it and pull the grips down off of the frame.

Use a screwdriver that fits properly. If you don't, you'll chew up the screw slots.

The front screw on the sideplate allows the cylinder and crane to be removed. The other two keep the sideplate on.

On the right side of the frame you'll see a screw under the cylinder, slightly forward of the trigger. Use a properly fitting screwdriver and unscrew it. On older models the screw will be a single piece. Later models will have a hollow screw with a spring-loaded plunger inside. Set the screw someplace you will not loose it and not get it mixed up with the other sideplate screws. Now open the cylinder and place the revolver on its right side on your disassembly mat. You can remove the cylinder and crane one of two ways. One is to hold the cylinder while you pull the crane out the front. Then lift the cylinder and set it aside. The other is to line up one of the cylinder flutes with the crane pivot boss and slide crane and cylinder off the frame together. Then you can pull the cylinder off the crane and set it aside. Obviously if your cylinder is unfluted you'll have to take the first route.

Action disassembly, assembly and lubrication

To remove the sideplate, turn the frame over. Look at the sideplate. If it is the earliest model you'll see four screws, one of which you've already removed. Later models will have only three. (The "five-screw" model S&W you might have heard about used a screw in the front of the frame to push the cylinder stop spring. More on that later.) Remove the screws and keep them in order. They are fitted to their particular hole, and swapping them does not help things on reassembly. With the screws out, hold the frame loose in your left hand (but not so loose it will fall free) and tap the frame at the grip straps with the handle of your screwdriver or some other wood handle. You want the inertia of the sideplate to pop it free when you tap the grip frame straps. If you tap too lightly it won't come free. If you whack too vigorously

the sideplate will come free, spin through the air and fall to the floor. According to the dictates of Murphy's Law ("Anything that can go wrong, will.") the sideplate will be bent, nicked or otherwise damaged as a result of hitting the floor.

In the tapping you might also dislodge the hammer safety. When you lift the sideplate free, look for a small strip of steel with a loop at the bottom. That's the hammer safety. Take a moment to look at it. It rides with the loop over the small stud on the trigger rebound/return bar. The safety slides up the angled track you see in the sideplate. When you release the trigger after firing, the safety slides up the track and comes to rest between the hammer and the frame. (On later models, it blocks the hammer from the frame-mounted firing pin.) To continue disassembly, pull out the safety and set it aside.

If at this point you want to watch the action in motion, you'll have to do two things: pull the cylinder release back, and keep the parts in the frame. The cylinder release latch has an interior bar that interlocks with the action. When the cylinder is open or out, the latch moves forward and blocks the action from moving. Why? To prevent someone from opening the cylinder and loading the cylinder, then cocking the action and then closing the cylinder with the hammer cocked. Or cocking the hammer and then opening and closing the action to load or unload it. To defeat the interlock to watch the (partially disassembled and definitely unloaded) action work, you have to hold back the latch. As the action cycles it will try to lever itself up out of the frame and launch parts across the room. You'll have to push the parts back down with your thumb from time to time.

Once you've watched the parts in action (note the timing of the double-action sear, on the hammer, and

Tap the frame straps with a hammer handle to loosen the sideplate

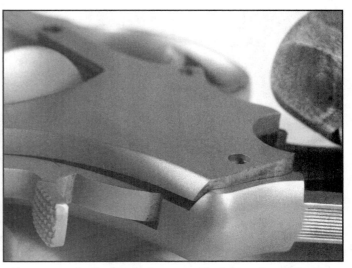

Done properly, the sideplate pops up but doesn't go flying.

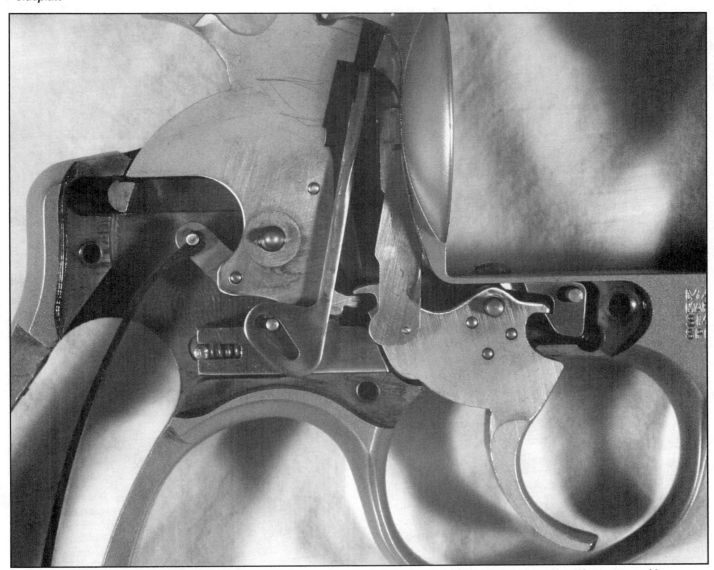

You can see the parts in their proper relations. Either memorize this photo, or remember this page number. You may need it.

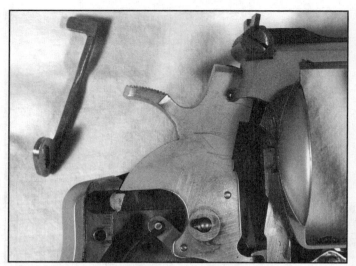

Take out the internal safety...

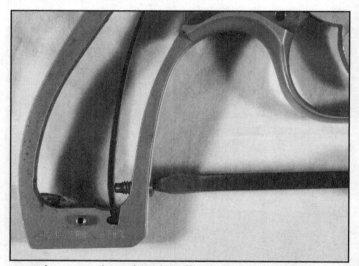

...and unscrew the mainspring. (The factory has a neat way of taking it out without unscrewing the strain screw. Do it wrong and the spring is bent, or flying across the room. Take it the easy way and undo the screw.)

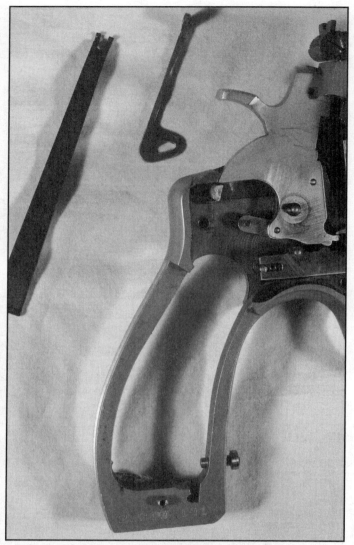

Place the spring where you can find it.

Use a special tool to lift the rebound block from its seat.

the cylinder stop bolt as the front of the trigger cams and releases it) you can continue with disassembly. First, the mainspring. On the frontstrap is a large screw. It tensions the mainspring. (Coil-spring models like the J frame obviously don't have a strain screw. You remove the spring by cocking the action and putting a paper-clip or other wire through the hole in the guide strut. Then relax the spring and remove the spring and strut.) Loosen the screw. Once you get enough free play you can unhook the spring from the hammer hooks. Pull the trigger back, grasp the hammer and lift it straight up off of its pivot stud. Ease the trigger forward. Now take your modified screwdriver and remove the rebound block. Fit the tip of the tool in the block hole, next to the retaining stud. Lift the block, but do not let the block or spring

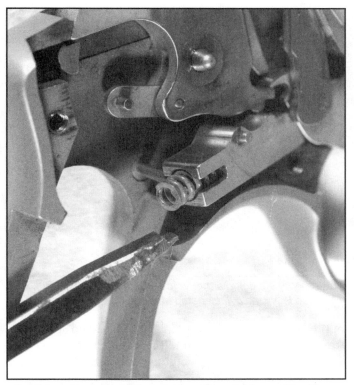

Don't lose the spring, it is unique and cannot be replaced by anything lying about your house.

fly free. In many models you'll find a small rod inside the rebound block spring. It is the trigger overtravel stop. Rather than have a stop on the frame or trigger, where it can be bound by debris, some clever engineer or gunsmith at S&W designed the in-the-block stop. It is also a very easy way to adjust overtravel. While assembling a revolver if the gunsmith or assembler determines that there is too much overtravel, he can pull out the rod, measure it, and substitute it with one marginally (and measurably) longer.

With the rebound spring and block clear of the retaining stud, lift them out and set them aside. Remove the hammer by pivoting it partway back to clear the firing pin from the frame, and lifting it straight up off of its pivot stud. To remove the trigger, lever the hand back only until it clears the frame side, then lift the trigger and hand straight up off of its pivot stud. You are now done. You can clean the gunk, dust, grit or whatever out, lube and reassemble. Just in case you feel the need (or have a really nasty cleaning job from say, falling into sandy surf and need to clean everything) here is how you remove the cylinder stop: Use the tiny screwdriver to pivot the bolt down so the top of it clears the frame. Grasp the bolt with the needle-nose pliers. Now use the tiny screwdriver to compress the spring in the front

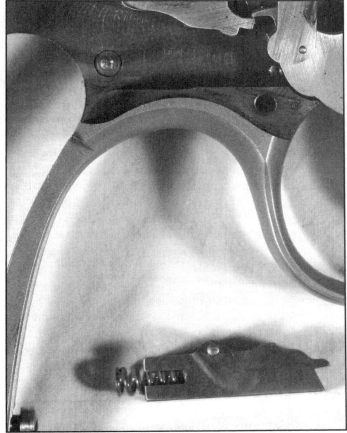

Set the rebound block and spring aside.

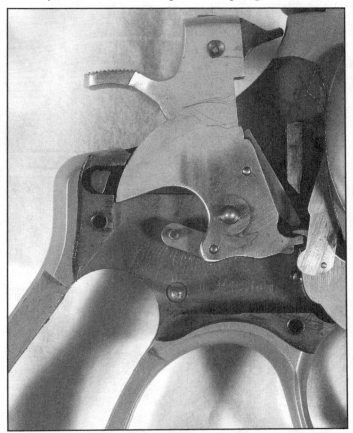

Pull the cylinder latch back and pivot the hammer partway back, to clear the frame edges.

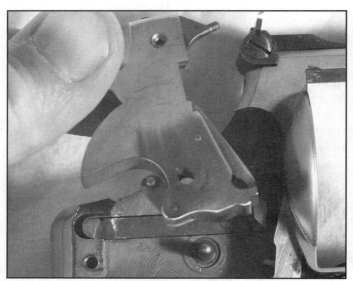

Then lift the hammer straight up...

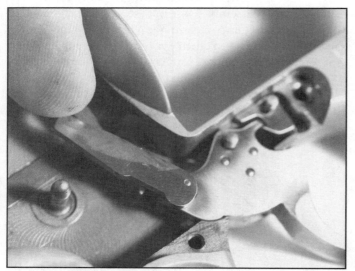

...pivot the hand out of the frame...

...and lift the trigger and hand up at the same time, as a unit.

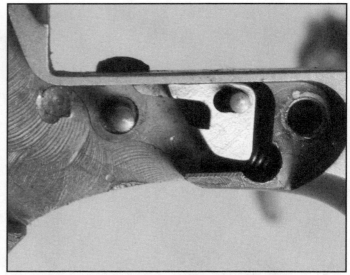

Unless you are doing a trigger job, or adjusting the timing, you can leave the cylinder stop in place.

of the bolt. Once compressed, lift the bolt and spring straight up off the pivot stud. If you simply grasp the bolt and wrestle it straight up you'll probably kink the spring, thus the complicated job of compressing it as much as you can beforehand.

Scrub all the parts clean. When you go to lubricate the parts, put a drop of liquid lubricant on each surface that has metal-to-metal contact: the pivot studs, the hand and DA sear, the single-action notch, the cylinder stop bolt, the springs, etc. If you've hosed the interior with an aerosol cleaner then you'll want to get some lube into the slot in which the cylinder release latch rides. To reassemble, grab the cylinder stop bolt with the pliers, and keeping the spring in place, press it down on the pivot stud until the spring hits the frame. Then use the tiny screwdriver to compress the spring (don't kink it if you can help it) enough to clear the milled opening. Press the bolt and spring down until the spring goes into the drilled hole. Check to make sure the bolt smoothly pivots on the stud. Take the trigger with the hand and press it down on its stud, pivoting the hand back enough to clear the frame opening. Once down, check its function. Now press the trigger halfway back, and slide the hammer down with the firing pin clearing the frame and the single-action and double-action sears on either side of the trigger sear. Once it is down all the way you can pivot the hammer and trigger to the rested position. Now place the spring and stop in the rebound slide and press the front of the slide against the rear of the trigger, locating the trigger link in the machined seat on the front of the rebound slide. Using your modified screwdriver or the Brownells tool, compress the rebound spring until you can press the whole assembly down in place in front of the retaining stud. Check the action again to make sure it is functioning as it was before. If it does not, you have something out of place and need to back up and start over.

Once the parts are back in place, hook the mainspring over the hammer stirrup, and then slide the angled seat of it into the notch in the frame. Tighten the strain screw. Now place the safety bar on the rebound block actuating stud, with the safety bar "flag" pointing into the frame. Push it up until it rests between the hammer and frame. Hook the top lip of the sideplate into the frame and press it down into place with your fingers. Once it is lined up and partly in place you can tap it with your screwdriver handle or plastic mallet to seat it. Return the rear sideplate screws to their appropriate holes and tighten them. You want to leave the front one out until you have replaced the cylinder and crane.

Lubrication Of The Action

You can use a light liquid lubricant to keep things moving smoothly. However, if you are going to be doing a lot of shooting and want the action as smooth as possible you might want more. Competition shooters who plan on shooting a few thousand rounds each week or two do not want to be pulling the action apart every few days to scrub and oil. For the maximum smoothness and for a durable lubrication job, go with Brian Enos' Slide Glide. Apply some to the rebound block, the trigger tip where it contacts the cylinder stop, the hand pivot and the DA sear. Also, apply a small dab of it at the base of each pivot stud, for hammer, trigger and cylinder stop.

It will last a lot longer than liquid lubricant will. It will also act to seal from environmental debris the surfaces that were greased. Powder residue, dust, dirt, lint, and other stuff will get trapped at the first surface encountered, and be less likely to work into the working surfaces.

If you're worried about temperature, you can use a light enough grease (Brian makes it in three grades) to not freeze in the winter, or heavy enough to not melt and run out in the summer.

If you go with a grease that's too-heavy in cold weather with your action "tuned" with lighter springs, you may find the trigger return a bit sluggish. The answer is to not use the light return spring. It was just slowing down your shooting anyway.

Bore cleaning

Your bore gets dirty from the powder residue. The friction of the bullet's passage leaves behind traces of the jacket material or the lead of lead bullets. Lubricant on the lead bullets helps, but does not eliminate leading. The forcing cone gets blasted by the blow-by of the hot powder gasses when the base of the bullet completes the jump from cylinder to barrel. Because the residue is deposited by high temperatures and high-pressure gases it can be particularly resistant to cleaning.

Getting the bore clean is a simple operation. You run a brush (bronze, not stainless) down the bore to clean the gunk out. You then apply patches with bore solvent, let them sit, and swab clean. Repeat until the drying patches come out clean. If you use lead solvent and the

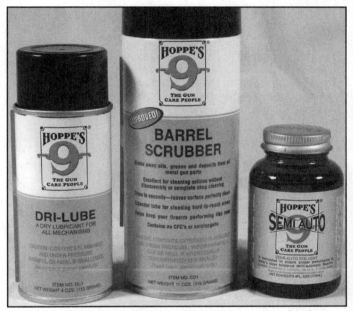
You need solvents to clean, and lubricants once you're done.

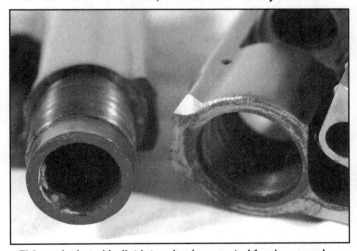
Firing a jacketed bullet into a lead-encrusted forcing cone has been known to crack it. Don't blame S&W; take it like a man and get a new barrel.

The barrel is tough on the threads and inside the frame, and can take a lot of abuse. But the forcing cone is hanging out there on its own.

The cylinder face can be cleaned, if it is steel. Don't try to restore a Titanium cylinder to "like-new" looks, as you might cause excessive wear.

patches come out black, there is lead still in there. If you use copper solvent and the patches come out green, there is still copper in there. (Be careful that the copper you're "seeing" in the bore isn't off of the brush you use to scrub the bore.)

In shooting pistols it is customary (and pretty use-less) to shoot a few jacketed rounds to "clean out" the lead left behind by lead bullets. In pistols it doesn't help but it doesn't hurt either. I have, however, heard from more than one revolver shooter who cracked the forcing cone of their revolver doing exactly this. So, I am com-pelled to tell you not to do it. I haven't done it, nor am I aware of any controlled experiments to see if it could be duplicated. However those who have done it are quite clear and vocal about how they came to do such an ex-pensive thing, and that they will never do it again.

To clean the bore (and forcing cone) of a heavily leaded revolver, you need one of several tools. You can use J-B bore paste, or a Lewis Lead Remover. (Both from Brownells) The J-B is simple: find a worn bore brush well under size and wrap it with a large cleaning patch. You want a snug fit in the bore, but not one that requires a mallet to get it down the bore. Then wipe a good dol-lop of J-B on the patch. Scrub the patch back and forth a couple of dozen times. It will come out so disgustingly black you won't want to touch it. Wipe the bore with two consecutive clean patches and rebuild your J-B patch with a fresh patch and dollop and repeat. Repeat until your second cleaning patch comes out clean. The J-B is

not easy to apply to the forcing cone. For the bore and forcing cone cleaning, the Lewis Lead Remover is great. You use the bronze screen and an appropriate size bore plug to scrub the lead out of the bore. You'll have to do a short copper-removing cleaning to get the residual copper off, but that is easy. For the forcing cone, push the Lewis rod through the bore. Then fit the cone plug and a bronze screen onto the rod. Pull the rod forward until the bronze screen is in contact with the forcing cone, and then rotate. Rotate until the forcing cone is clean.

Cylinder maintenance

The main thing about working on your cylinder is to keep the crane and the chambers clean, and the crane lubricated. Once the cylinder is off the frame you can simply pull the crane forward off the cylinder. Scrub the chambers with a bronze brush. If you are in the habit of shooting short brass in long chambers, you'll need a chamber cleaning reamer. The use of .38 Special am-munition in a .357 Magnum revolver, .44 Special in a .44 Magnum, or .45 Scofield or Russian in a .45 Colt will result in powder residue and bullet shavings building up in the front of the chamber. No problem if all you ever shoot is the short stuff. However, if you then proceed to chamber the magnum ammo, the front of those cases will be in the region gunked up by the short cases. When you fire, you may find you can't easily (or at all) extract the empties. To prevent the problem, use the chamber clean-ing reamer to cut the gunk out.

The face of the cylinder can become crusted with residue if you have an inefficient load or one where the lead bullets are not properly lubricated. To clean the cylinder face, use the bronze screen of the Lewis Lead Remover. Do not go brushing vigorously with a handled brush, as you may round the edges of the chamber throats, leading to a loss of accuracy. If the cylinder face is merely scorched black, you can clean the front of it with a dab of Simichrome and a cleaning patch. Apply the Simichrome to a patch and rub the surface with the patch, using your fingers for pressure. Stainless and nickeled cylinders can be made as clean as new this way. Blued guns benefit, but you'll be hard-pressed to see the difference. And it won't make any difference in performance, so don't worry about wearing away the face of the cylinder.

Wipe the crane clean, and lube the crane before putting it back in the cylinder. While you have the crane off, the ejector rod is vulnerable to being bent. Take care not to knock it out of alignment. You can also check to make sure the ejector rod is tightly screwed together. The rod is a two-piece assembly, and can come loose. Just try turning it with your fingertips. If it is loose it will turn. If it is not it won't. To tighten it you really should have the special wrench (again from Brownells). I've seen many ejector rods with plier or vise marks on them from shooters attempting to tighten the ejector rod without the tool. It doesn't cost that much, and saves having to explain how your S&W got marred. Tighten it finger tight. Do not try to torque it on tightly, and do not use a thread-locking compound of any kind. If the next time you find it loose, tighten with a bit more force. The threads are small, and you do not want to strip them by over-tightening the rod. The repair is expensive.

Place the lubed crane back in the cylinder, and slide the assembly back in the frame, using the cylinder flutes to clear the crane boss. Or, hold the cylinder in place next to the frame and slide the crane into both the cylinder and frame at once. Then replace and tighten the front sideplate screw. Check function, and you're done.

General cleaning notes

The best thing to use on a blued revolver to scrub gunk and the very slight pitting that happens when out in the elements is 0000 steel wool and light oil. Spread enough oil on the surface to float the debris so it doesn't scratch, and scrub. You can wear the finish with this combo, so be careful. But with a light touch you can clean without harming the blue, or at least not harming the blue any more than the rust already has. Wipe the slurry off with one cloth, and use another to lightly lubricate the surface for storage.

Stainless revolvers are much less likely to show any pitting, but when they do you aren't going to simply scrub the pitting off. For a stainless alloy to have been attacked severely enough to show even a little pitting means it was really neglected. Scrub off what you can, but the pitting will still show, unlike the blued gun. Both blued and stainless benefit from a slight film of oil to keep them protected.

Nickel guns are different. You won't see any pitting until or unless the nickel is flaking off or bubbled. And then the only solution is to get it re-nickeled. To clean a nickel gun you need the aforementioned Simichrome, which is a metal polish well thought of by those with chromed motorcycles. You can find it and a similar product, Flitz, at automobile stores as well. Use a cleaning patch with a dab of polishing goo on it, and rub the surface. Periodically wipe the surface with a clean cloth to wipe the oxidized slurry or goo off. Once you've cleaned the gun you have two choices: store for protection or store for show. At the first gun shop I worked at we always polished up used guns with Simichrome, then left them dry in the display case. Dry, they shone like a new penny, and anyone with the slightest weakness for a nickel gun (stainless was brand new at the time, and not as well liked, at least not in the looks department) was tempted. We made many sales just because the guns looked so good. But even nickel guns benefit from a slight film of oil on storage. It slows down the oxygen in the air, keeping it from dulling the finish as quickly as it otherwise would. But for show, the oil dulls the mirror look of a properly nickeled gun (and S&W factory nickel jobs are the definition of proper) and makes it less attractive.

Titanium and Scandium parts require a different approach than that of steel. First, while they are both strong, abrasion resistance is not high on their list of attributes. To clean the powder and lead residue off of your Titanium cylinders, use solvent and a patch or plastic bristle brush. (I don't even use a bronze brush.) Avoid like the plague stainless brushes. Do not use abrasives like Flitz or Simichrome. Do not use a ScotchBrite pad or 0000 steel wool. You probably won't be able to get all the discolorations off. If you try, you could damage the finish. Ditto with Scandium alloy parts. Yes, they are a lot harder than the older aluminum alloys, but they are still aluminum. Don't go scrubbing with steel wool or any of the other abrasives. As time goes by I'm sure we'll see clever solvent makers coming up with formulas to clean Titanium and Scandium alloys. Until then resist the temptation to apply elbow grease.

Grips are best left alone, unless the wood is so dry that you simply must apply some linseed oil to keep them from cracking. However, wood grips that are finished with a lacquer, varnish or polyurethane will not benefit form linseed oil and must be spot-treated if possible or stripped and refinished if not.

Cylinder slinging

We've all seen it in a movie, TV show or at the range. Someone opens a revolver by pressing the cylinder release latch, and then snaps his wrist to the side, slinging the cylinder open. Or closes the cylinder by snapping his wrist. This is very hard on the gun. The opening cylinder's inertia must be stopped by the crane, and can twist it out of alignment. On closing, the centerpin stops by hammering against the far side of the axis hole drilled in the frame. You can peen the hole to an oval, or put a kink in the centerpin. Don't do this! There are competitive shooters who did some variation of this when the situation called for it, but they did so knowing that they risked harming the gun, and risked harming it right there and then and possibly causing their score to suffer as a result. They were willing to take the risk. I'd rather you didn't.

Having told you not to do it, I have to tell you of one (extremely rare) occasion where it is OK: In the event you find yourself in a shootout, AND you must reload, AND you find one hand or arm isn't working, you can snap the gun open and closed. Just know that if you do it, there is a chance the gun will be harder to operate (bent cranes or kinked centerpins can cause binding) and the gun might require the services of a good gunsmith afterwards. Considering that you may need the services of both a good doctor and a good attorney afterwards, I wouldn't worry about damaging the gun.

Pistol maintenance

The S&W pistol design is incredibly durable. Back when S&W had a shooting team (in the early, "inflationary" period of IPSC many manufacturers had sponsored Teams) they developed a cartridge to run in their guns called the .356 TSW. The .356 TSW was a cartridge equivalent in power to the .38 Super, but the same overall length as a 9mm Parabellum. If you wish to gain the same velocity out of a shorter cartridge that you can get from a longer cartridge, you have two choices: use a slower powder, or increase the operating pressure. As the 9mm case had no extra room for a slower powder, they upped the pressures. The standard load for a .38 Super or a 9mm is on the order of 34,000 psi. (The longer Super can gain more velocity as it is slightly larger and thus able to either hold more powder or use a slower powder.) To make the .356 TSW with its 9mm length run at the same velocity as the .38 Super, the pressures were pushed up in the middle to high 40,000 psi region. (The round was never accepted by SAAMI, the standards board for the firearms industry, so there was never a well-defined ceiling.)

The .356 TSW ran at 125 percent of the regular pressures of the 9mm the S&W pistols were originally built for, and stood up to years of hard, steady practice by

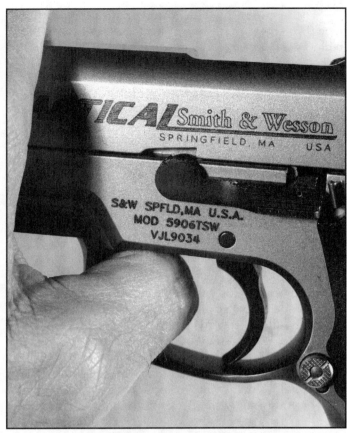

Line the slide stop notch up with the slide stop pivot shoulder, and press the slide stop out of the frame.

Grand Master level competition shooters. So I wouldn't be worried about wearing out a 5906, 3906, a 3913 Ladysmith or any other S&W pistol simply by shooting it.

But you can neglect a pistol to death. Regular cleaning avoids that.

To clean the S&W pistol you need all the usual cleaning supplies, brush, rod, patches, solvent and lubricant. You'll also need a drift pin and hammer to remove the grips. Older guns will have the grips held on by screws, with the separate mainspring housing held on by the crosspin. For those you'll need the drift punch, hammer and a screwdriver.

Make sure the pistol is unloaded. (We've been through this before. I'm not picking on you, just do it.) Remove the magazine. Then press the slide partway back, until the slide hold-open notch lines up with the circular shoulder on the slide stop lever. Press the slide stop lever from the other side of the frame, pressing it free and then lifting clear of the frame. Ease the slide forward. On the SA/DA guns, as the slide runs over the decock lever in the frame it will drop the hammer. Don't be alarmed. Slide the upper assembly off the frame and set the frame aside.

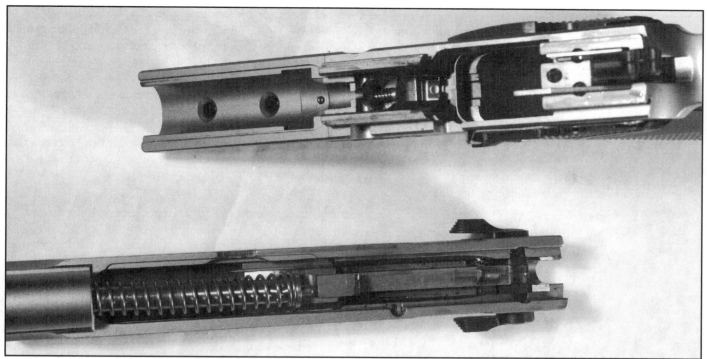

With the slide stop off, remove the slide and barrel as a unit.

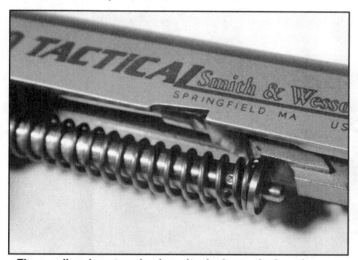

The recoil spring stays in place, hooked onto the barrel.

Pivot the spring down off the barrel.

Slide and barrel

The recoil spring is held in place by the guide rod. The rod fits into a notch machined on the underside of the barrel. Press the rod towards the muzzle, and then pivot it away from the barrel. It is under a fair amount of spring pressure and can be launched across the room (or into you) with some force if you let it fly. Once free, pull it out and set it aside. Unlike the Model 1911, the S&W has no barrel bushing except for special models and very early Model 39 pistols. Remove the barrel by pressing on the chamber though the ejection port until the hood and chamber end of the barrel comes free of the slide. Then pull the barrel back out of the slide.

Notice that the S&W barrel does not use a link or kidney-shaped oval like Browning-designed guns do. The barrel has a pair of cam paths milled onto the side of the barrel foot. When the action opens the cam paths strike a shoulder in the frame which cams the barrel down out of engagement with the slide. The barrel is stopped once unlocked, and the slide continues its merry journey. On closing, the slide contacts the hood and pushes the barrel ahead of it. The fronts of the cam slots contact a different shoulder to pivot the rear of the barrel up and lock it to the slide. The last travel over-rides the shoulders, locking the barrel up to the slide. While it is relatively simple to fit a 1911 barrel, fitting an S&W barrel requires proper tools, training and knowledge of how the mechanism works. If you need a new barrel and a replacement does not simply drop in, you'll need to turn it over to a qualified gunsmith.

At this point cleaning is easy. Scrub the bore clean with brushes or solvent-soaked patches. Depending on if you use lead or jacketed bullets you'll select the appropriate solvent. An error in selecting lead bullets or a load

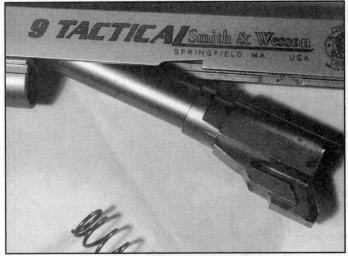

With the spring out, pull the barrel down and out.

for them may result in an episode with J-B bore paste or Lewis Lead Remover. Be sure to scrub the chamber clean and leave it dry. The recoil spring and guide rod simply require a wiping down. The slide can be scrubbed with a brush and lubricated. Or, if it has been exposed to a harsh environment you can clean it with an aerosol cleaner and then lube it. Disassembling the safety mechanism, extractor and firing pin is not a user-serviceable item. If you are having problems with your safety that cannot be corrected by cleaning the sand, dirt, lint or other gunk out, you need to take it to a qualified gunsmith.

To reassemble, insert the muzzle end of the barrel into the slide and press forward and up until the barrel locks into the slide. Then press the recoil spring and guide rod forward until you can catch the shoulder of the rod in the notch milled in the underside of the barrel.

Frame maintenance

There isn't much to do with the frame. You can do a thorough cleaning by hosing it with aerosol cleaner and wiping the frame rails and cam shoulders clean. If you need more (that falling into the mud or surf thing again) you can remove the grips. Or on older pistols, the grips and mainspring housing. On the old guns it works just

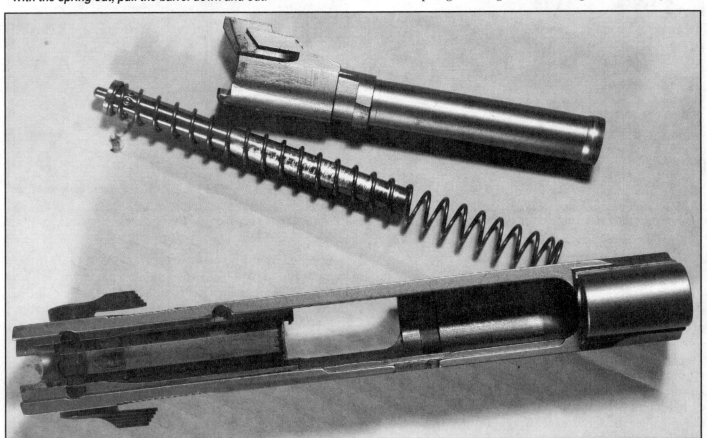

With the slide apart, you can scrub away.

The trigger levers will get grungy if you don't wipe them clean now and then.

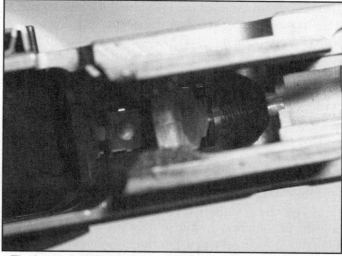

The frame ahead of the magazine gets a lot of powder residue; spray and scrub it clean.

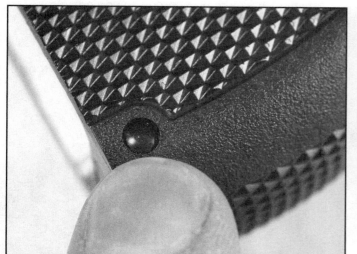

The grips are held on by a cross pin down at the magazine opening.

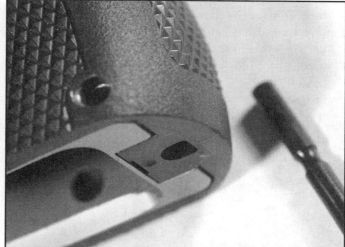

Drive the pin out to remove the grips.

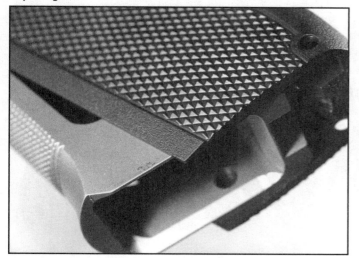

With the pin out, pivot the grips free. You may have to spread them a bit to clear the grip straps of the frame.

like the 1911: drive the crosspin out, pull the mainspring housing clear and be sure not to lose the spring and cup. On new guns, drive the crosspin out. Then pivot the grips (which are molded one-piece plastic) away from the bottom of the frame. The grips have little molded tabs inside that keep them tight to the frame cutouts, and you may have to slightly flex the side panels to get these tabs clear of the frame. Once free, retain the spring and cup. As with the safety, you do not want to be taking it down past this. There are a bunch of small springs and parts, and each variation on the SA/DA trigger mechanism has a slightly different set of parts. How bad can it be? Consider that at one time S&W had to print and distribute a circular slide rule to indicate what models had what features and just what the model number was. The trigger mechanisms can be: traditional SA/DA, where the safety drops the hammer and stays down. SA/DA spring, where the safety drops the hammer but springs back up to the "Fire" position. SA/SA where the safety cams down but doesn't drop the hammer. DAO, where there is no safety and the trigger works like that on a revolver: don't press the trigger if you don't want it to fire. And finally, SA/DA Decock, where the safety is a lever on the right side of the frame that drops the hammer and springs back up, like a SIG-Sauer. All these require slightly different trigger parts. Unless you know exactly how the one on your bench works, you shouldn't go messing with it.

Hose the parts with your aerosol cleaner, lube the moving ones, and reassemble.

To get the grips back on old style, use the mainspring housing to compress the cup and spring over the hammer strut. Slide it into place in the frame and press the crosspin through. Then screw the grips back on. On new guns, flex the grips enough to clear the frame and press it up to the top of its cutout in the frame. Pivot it close to the bottom of the frame. Then place the spring and cap over the strut. Compress the cap until you can push it into the recess in the grips that keep it in place, and then press the grips fully forward on the frame. Drive the crosspin through.

Reassembly

Make sure your hammer is down. If it isn't, reassembly will be more difficult. To lower the hammer, insert an empty magazine and keep a thumb on the hammer. Pull the trigger and ease the hammer forward.

Take the assembled slide and start it on the rails from the front. When you get to the back of the magazine well, press down the levers you see. The left one is the ejector, the others are disconnector and hammer drop (if your model has the hammer-drop safety). Once you've cleared them, run the slide back far enough to line up the slide stop notch with the slide stop hole. Press the slide stop through until it bottoms against the frame. Check for proper function. You're done.

Cleaning

You must have the proper tools to properly clean your S&W handguns, or any handgun, for that matter. While you can keep a sidearm going in bad conditions with patches cut from worn clothing, and found tools like screwdrivers and old toothbrushes, the proper tools make the job a lot easier and thorough.

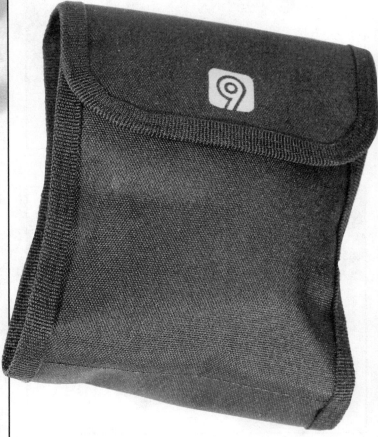

The spring and spring cap, riding on the hammer strut as they are supposed to.

A compact cleaning kit can be a Godsend if you're out hunting, or at a match, and need to do some quick cleaning.

You should have a cleaning kit: Everything you need in one box, bag, carton or case. That way you won't go to clean, and find you've left the (insert necessary part here) at home when you went on your hunting trip or to the big match. One way to have a cleaning kit is to get one ready to go. The Hoppe's Universal Field cleaning kit has all the basics, rod, oil solvent and patches. If you add a bore brush or two of the right size in tubes, and a cleaning brush, you're set. The case is compact enough to toss into your daypack when you go out hunting. (What, you don't wear a daypack when you hunt? Are you crazy? Where do you carry lunch, the GPS, your matches and space blanket?)

If you like, you can also throw in a Bore Snake as well. The Bore Snake is one of those "why didn't I think of it?" ideas. It is a bore-sized rope with a section of brass bristle brush as the beginning. Open the action, drop the weighted end down the bore from the chamber, then pull the whole thing through the bore and you are done. The "rope" has 160 times the surface area of a patch. (I've never measured it, but it seems reasonable.) The worst bores might benefit from a scrubbing with a brush before "snaking" but most will not need extra scrubbing. Just

the snake. I found out how useful it can be at the World Shoot in South Africa in 2002. I was shooting with the South African Modified Team, and after lunch each day it was "Time to snake those bores!" At first I thought I was going to see some weird South African ritual. No, they were simply taking care of the needed maintenance required at their range. You see, the super-fine dust in that region coated everything with a layer of talcum-like dust in a matter of hours. Oh how I wish I'd had something like it at Second Chance. There, we'd go through hundreds of rounds a day for a week or more. Cleaning was a nightly process that could take hours. With the Bore Snake I'd have had a lot more time for sitting around the campfires talking about guns.

One thing you don't want to do is use a stainless steel bristle brush on your bore. I've talked to more than one custom barrel maker who says they can immediately tell when a handgun bore has been subjected to a stainless brush. The scratches are that plain to see. Once I had my hands on a bore scope, I could see them too.

You need to get the lead out, and the jacket fouling if you're shooting jacketed bullets. Use a cleaning solvent formulated for your problem, a brass bristle brush, and

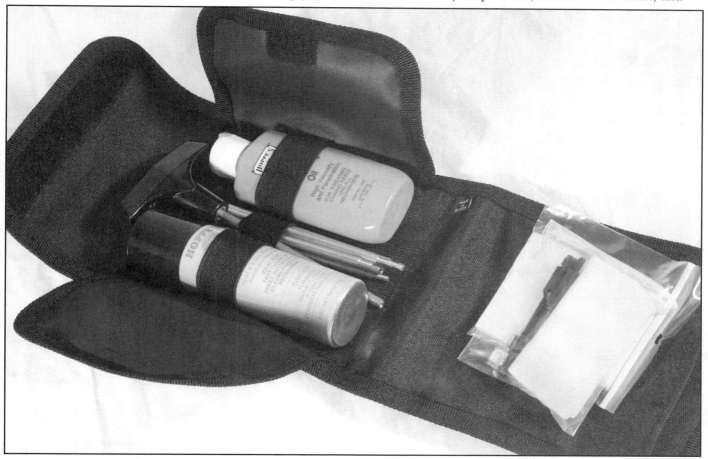

Inside the Outers field kit you have what you need for regular maintenance. Add a caliber-specific bore brush and a screwdriver that fits your handgun, and you're good to go.

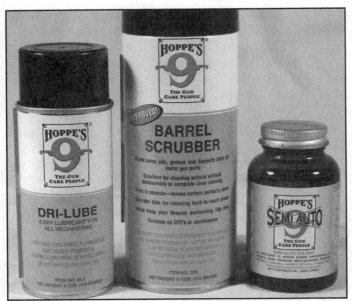

You need solvents to clean, and lubricants once you're done.

The BoreSnake scrubs the bore quickly, easily and thoroughly, but they are caliber-specific, so get one for each caliber you have.

The BoreSnake even has a section of embedded bronze bristles.

follow up with clean patches. If you're cleaning lead then the patches will be black or gray until the bore is clean. If you're cleaning out copper, then the patches will be blue or green until the bore is clean.

Wipe the powder residue from any place it collects. On revolvers that would be the breechface, crane, cylinder and forcing cone. On pistols you'll find powder residue on the breech and underside of the slide, around the barrel, and on the frame around the feeding ramp area of the barrel.

Lube heavily enough to reduce friction but lightly enough to not attract grit. What you need varies according to where you are. In coastal Alaska you'll need more to slow down corrosion. In Iraq you'll need less to avoid collecting wads of oiled dust bunnies and sand castles. Use the cleaning brush to brush away packed lint, dirt, and whatever else builds up. If you have proper ventilation you can use aerosol cleaners and lubricants. The Xenoy grips of third-generation S&W pistols are impervious to all known solvents, including New Jersey tap water. If you have a super-aggressive carburetor cleaner you might experiment on a corner just to see what happens, but if it is formulated for firearms, it is safe on your S&W.

Oil lightly, reassemble, and either store or load for carry.

CHAPTER 5

The 332:
A pocket gun with a fine round

The little 332 is a marvel of compactness, if not of power. Chambered in .32 H&R Magnum, it is not intended to be a pocket rocket like larger-calibered handguns. The .32 H&R Magnum was introduced in 1984 with the intention of it being a small game hunt-ing cartridge and a ".38 Special Lite" defensive round. It serves well in both, but has not gotten the success that it deserves. Many prefer to go with a rimfire, the .22 Long Rifle or .22 Magnum, for small game hunting. In small-bore silhouette the .32-20 has elbowed the .32 Magnum

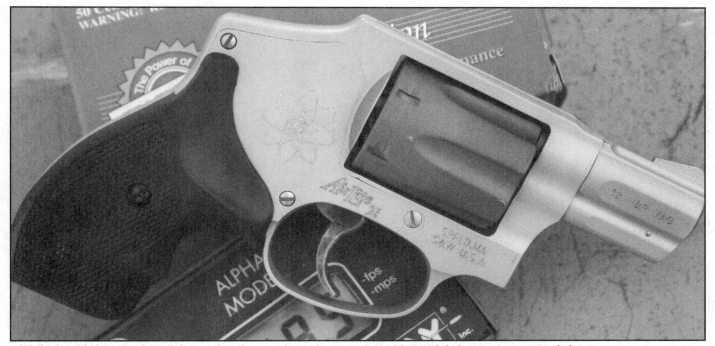

While the .32 Magnum doesn't have a lot of power, it can be enough, and it certainly is easy to carry and shoot.

aside. Used in Thompson Center single-shot pistols, the .32-20 with its longer case allows more powder and thus more velocity. However, the .32 Magnum has not given up the ghost.

The exterior

The 332 is an AirLite hammerless J frame revolver with a Titanium cylinder. As such it is so light you might not notice it. On the left side the stubby barrel is marked "Smith & Wesson" while the frame has the S&W logo, the cylinder latch and the action lock. On the right side is the caliber designation on the barrel, ".32 H&R Mag"

(the barrel isn't long enough for "Magnum") and the S&W atomic logo, "AirLite Ti" and the two-line S&W address. The hammerless frame isn't really hammerless, it just encloses a hidden hammer, leaving the 332 a double-action-only revolver. The short barrel causes a reduction in muzzle velocity, but the six-shot cylinder gives you one more shot than the same size .38 Special, the 442 has. The grips are round-butt rubber, of the style known as a "boot grip," made to be easy to carry and conceal, while still being reasonably useful for shooting. I find many to be just a bit small, but the compactness is a small price to pay for making the gun so small and easy to carry.

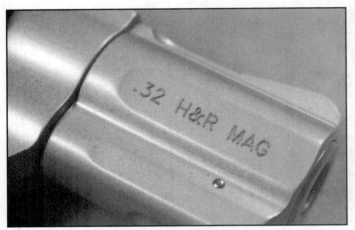

You might not say "I carry a .32" very loudly in mixed company, but S&W has clearly marked the 332.

The Airlite 332 uses the new S&W barrel tube in a sighted shroud style of assembly. It doesn't hurt accuracy.

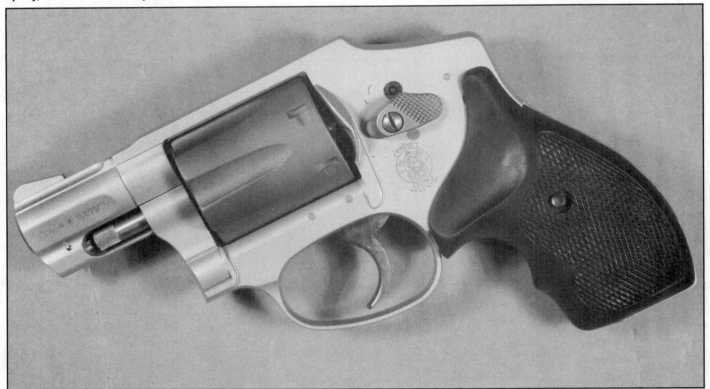

The compact 332 is easy to pack, with its boot-grip-style grips.

Carry and shooting

Despite my admonishments that "pocket guns" should be carried in a holster, if you are going to ignore my advice and just drop something in your pocket the 332 would be one to select. The compact size, the light weight, the lack of sharp edges and controls that could be wiped, levered or pushed off, make it very carry-friendly. As a main gun for someone with recoil issues, or who wants the lightest possible gun, the 332 would be great.

As a backup for someone who already has a bigger main gun to depend on, the 332 would be great. And it is a perfect handgun for the "Back Up Person" that my friend Mas Ayoob has defined.

We think of back-up guns as the second or third gun we go to when a defensive situation has gone really bad. But not all back-ups are equipment. Sometimes they are people. A couple of examples to demonstrate: Say you're going to make the night deposit for the company you

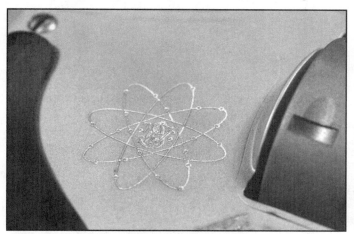

AirLite, Scandium and Titanium make the 332 ultra-light and easy to pack.

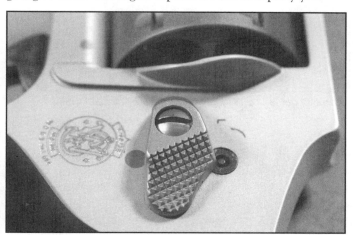

The cylinder release and action lock.

The 332 holds six shots of .32 Magnum.

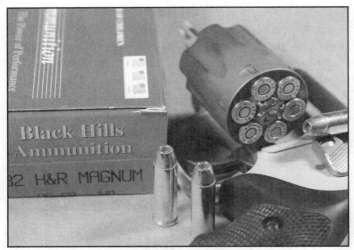
You can get all the .32 ammo you need from Black Hills.

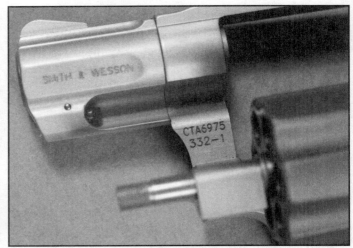
The ejector rod is not full-length of the case, so be sure and eject vigorously.

own or work for. The shift manager rides along. When you get to the bank, and go to make the deposit, a car pulls out, full of obvious miscreants. You are carrying, but the shift manager isn't because he isn't licensed. Even though he's an experienced shot, and knows what to do, he doesn't have a license, so he can't carry. The two of you can take cover, and you can hand him the backup 332 while you depend on your main gun. It would be best if you checked with an attorney, but in many locales such an emergency use would be OK. If you're in a predicament where you are legally in the right using lethal force, then handing a spare gun to someone you know you can trust would also be covered. A similar situation might occur with a deputy making a call in a remote location. He (or she) arrives to find the caller waiting (who else can point out the exact problem?) but unarmed. If the Deputy knows the person, and can trust his or her judgment, then handing them the 332 gives him or her another set of eyes to watch for trouble, eyes that can do more than just point and shout "Over there!"

And when you're handing a backup gun to a backup person, you don't want to be handing them a lightweight magnum. One shot from the 340 (for example) and your assistant is not going to be hitting anything with subsequent shots. The .32 may not be a powerhouse, but the low recoil will encourage aiming and hitting.

And that was easy to do with this 332. The group pictured was only average for what the 332 could do. I found it easy to shoot tight clusters of holes with it, despite the double-action-only trigger. The 100-yard gong was easy when I paid attention to the sights. The short sight radius made follow-through vitally important, and I lost more than one shot twitching the sights left as the last of the double action trigger pull went sideways instead of straight back.

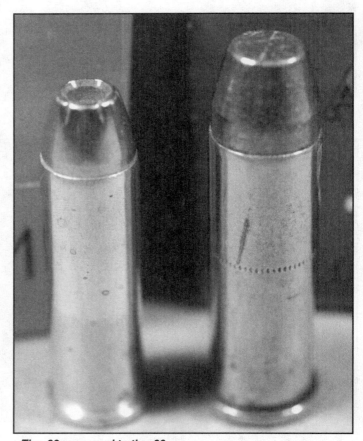
The .32 compared to the .38.

With the light recoil Bill Drills were a snap. It was not much more work than shooting a .22 rimfire, and I could easily keep the front sight in the A zone of an IPSC target while cranking off six shots in just over a second. The Cirillo Index was a bit tougher, as the short barrel made it hard to keep the index, but out to 5 yards

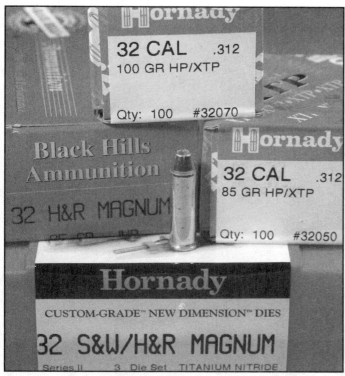

If you want even less-costly practice ammo, you can reload the .32.

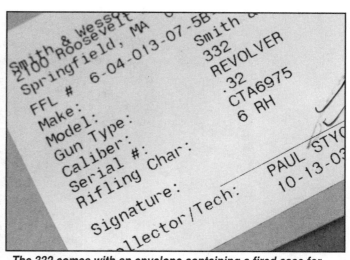

The 332 comes with an envelope containing a fired case for those who need it for their paperwork.

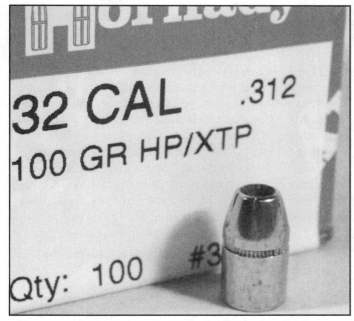

If you need performance, the Hornady XTP is tops. You can go "heavy" at 100 grains, or lighter if you wish.

For mild, paper-punching accuracy, load a wadcutter. Berry's plated are great for indoor shooting where you may not be allowed the use of lead bullets.

I could keep all shots in the A zone. Lacking a speed-loader for it, I couldn't try the El Presidente, but I have no doubts about being able to pull it off.

The .32 H&R Magnum ammo comes in two flavors, a jacketed hollowpoint for defensive use, and Cowboy loads for even lighter practice. With no power factor in Cowboy Action Shooting, some competitors have found that a .32 is better than a .38 or .44. While the traditional cowboy .32 is the .32-20, it is not without its faults. It can be picky to reload with its bottleneck shape and sometimes thin neck walls. The .32 Magnum is much more forgiving, and so is being seen more and

The 332 is also an accurate little blaster, as this double-action (what else?) group demonstrates.

more at Cowboy Action Shooting matches. And since the CAS requirements are for lead bullets, no jackets, and velocities under 1000 fps, you will have low-recoil practice ammo. If that isn't soft enough for you, you can use .32 S&W and .32 S&W Long ammunition as practice ammo, too. It may not be common, and it may not be cheap, but often it is quite inexpensive. If you go to gun shows you can sometimes find tattered old boxes of the two for not much cost, as no one wants them. As practice ammo it works fine. Just be sure to scrub your chambers after firing, as the shorter cases (both are shorter in over all length than the .32 Magnum) will leave lead and powder residues on the chamber walls after firing. When you use the longer Magnum cases you can potentially find the cases bound in place, expanded from firing and trapped by the residues left behind by the shorter cases.

The short barrel does hurt velocity, with the Black Hills jacketed hollowpoints registering only 848 feet per second. With an 85-grain bullet, that gives a power factor of only 72, where 125 is considered Minor for many competitions. However, defense is not competition, and anything is better than nothing. The decision for many people is not between the 332 and something larger, but between the 332 and something smaller. As light in power as the .32 H&R Magnum seems to be, it is way ahead of something chambered in .22 Long rifle, which may post a power factor of only 35 or so.

If the lightweight .38s pound you too much, the 332 is just the ticket.

CHAPTER 6

The 342Ti:
Taking lightweight to the extreme

For those who did not find the regular Airweight snubbies feathery enough, S&W came out with the Ti series. Replacing the steel cylinder with one made of Titanium shaved another 4 ounces off the gun, but it also brought problems. It is peculiar, and particular, but it can be a problem depending on your usage: If you shoot hot loads with lead bullets, you can find the bullets jumping the crimp, moving forward and perhaps tying up the gun. Especially if you are accustomed to using reloads of indifferent quality, you may

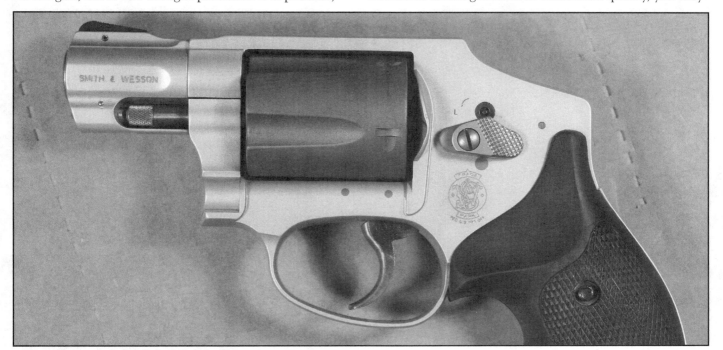

The compact and ultra-light 342, left side.

encounter this problem. That said, I never did. I depended on Black Hills ammo, with some extra tests with my own reloads and some other factory ammo. None jumped the crimp. However, the problem has been reported and commented on, and so it must exist for some shooters. Test your ammo before depending on it.

The 342Ti is the lightest possible five-shot .38 Special revolver, and I for one do not want to fire one that is lighter. At least not with ammo suited for defensive work. However, as a carry gun the 342Ti is a joy. The weight is so light you could stuff it in a pocket and not notice it. At 10.8 ounces, I have older PDAs that weigh

more than the 342Ti. The enclosed hammer is not going to catch on anything, and it certainly won't be a point of ingress for all the usual stuff that collects in pockets.

The finish is clear-coat bright aluminum alloy with a rough matte finish, and the cylinder is left in Titanium gray with a matte finish. The frame contour of the 342 differs from the 442 on one point; the rear corner of the butt. There, S&W machined the backstrap and installed a lanyard loop. You can use a small clip, or tie some cord to the loop, and then attach a lanyard so you won't lose the revolver in hard use. If you are using the 342Ti as a backup and sleeping bag gun, a lanyard can be very

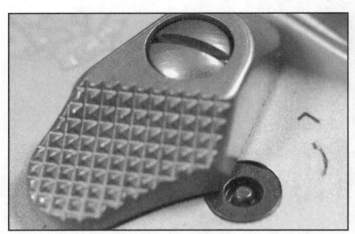
The cylinder release latch and action lock are nicely sculpted.

The barrel tube clamps the sight and ejector shroud in place.

The barrel is short, for compactness, so the ejector rod isn't as long as the shell case.

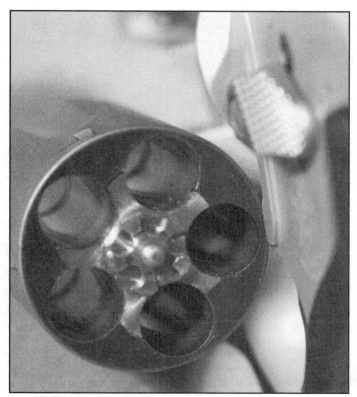
The Titanium cylinder holds five rounds.

useful. With it clipped to your wrist you know you won't lose track of it while sleeping. And the DAO trigger means you needn't worry about inadvertently brushing the trigger in your sleep. If you are a real "belt and suspenders" type you could put a layer of paper tape over the trigger guard, enough to keep the trigger from being brushed by clothing or objects, but not so much you can't tear through it on the trigger stroke. That way you can sleep secure, knowing you have every safety advantage and yet still have a convenient sidearm handy the moment you need it.

The S&W atomic logo and AirLite logo.

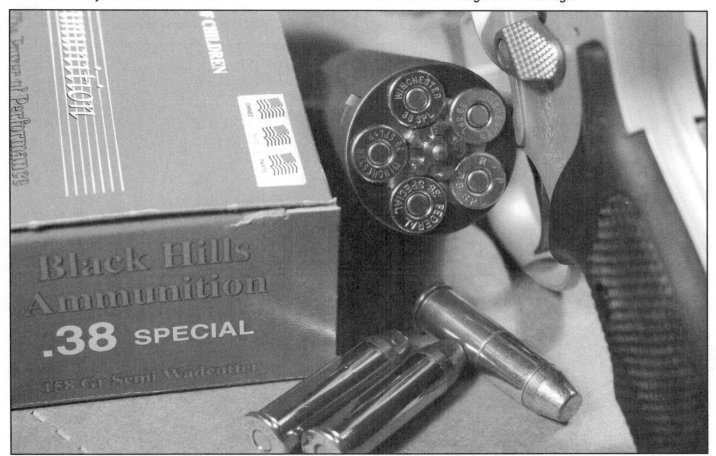
Black Hills reloads get the job done.

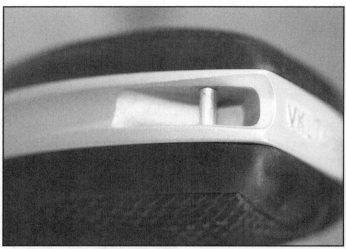

The lanyard ring/bar on the 342 lets you keep it close on those dark and stormy nights.

Every surface is sculpted to reduce weight.

Shooting and carrying the 342

As light as the 442 was, the 342 is lighter still. And easier to carry as a result. But also tougher to shoot. Where the 442 offered sharp recoil only with the hottest defensive ammo, the recoil of the 342Ti became noticeable with stout regular ammo. The .38 Special+P loads that could be fired in the 442 with some work became noticeably objectionable in the 342Ti. There were those who did not find the 342Ti such a problem with +P ammo, but I noticed they did not come back for seconds.

To carry the 342Ti, I would spend more time than I would with the 442 getting accustomed to the recoil, and keep practice with the +P ammo to a minimum. Not for the gun's sake, but for mine.

The drills were somewhat abbreviated. The Bill Drill with only five shots and no draw becomes a sub-second

Reloads are not always the most powerful load, but for practice, you don't always want full power.

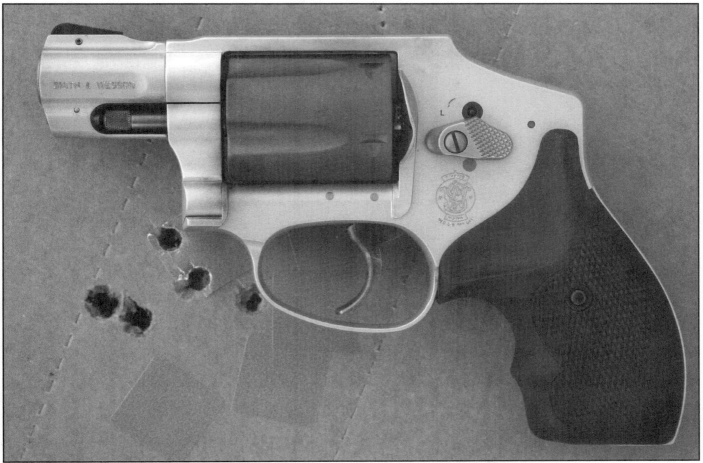

Five shots double-action into just over 2 inches at 15 yards, standing. I'll take it.

attempt at getting five A hits. With the 342Ti and practice ammo, wadcutters and soft-shooting roundnose, it is doable. With the +P defensive ammo, keeping the sights on the A zone while you deal with recoil and work the trigger becomes a real challenge. I was able to do it several times, but the sharp recoil soon took its toll. When I realized that my times were getting worse, I stopped.

The compact size and short barrel makes the Cirillo Index more work, too. But as with the Bill Drill, practice will improve your score. With only five shots in the gun and no J-frame speedloaders on hand, I didn't even try the El Presidente.

The 100-yard gong was safe from most of the test shooters. The hard recoil, the short sight radius and the double-action-only trigger made it tough to score on the plate. I managed five for five on one occasion, but the snappy recoil soon had me missing again. The short barrel takes its toll on velocity, too. You will not be getting the full .38 Special or .38 Special+P velocity from the just under 2-inch barrel of the 342Ti that you'd get from a 3- or 4- inch barrel.

As a backup, or ultra-light concealed carry gun the 342Ti is superb. But to be able to make efficient use of it you must practice, practice, practice.

CHAPTER 7

The Model 442:
Compact, powerful and hard-working

The S&W Model 442 Centennial Airweight and its brother the 342Ti are the culmination of the compact, lightweight personal defense revolver that S&W has been making in one form or another almost since the company began making firearms. The Model 442 sports an aluminum-alloy frame with a steel five-shot cylinder. It is built on the J Magnum frame. The 442 was introduced in 1993 on the standard frame size, but later the frame was enlarged to the J Magnum. (Probably to keep the number of parts needed for all models as small as possible. After all, why have both J and J Magnum frames in inventory?)

The 442 is a compact .38 snubbie, and even though it isn't the lightest, it is plenty light and compact.

The idea of a compact but powerful handgun that could be carried concealed has always been attractive. In earlier eras when clothing was much heavier, guns that were carried "concealed" were generally much larger than today. The introduction of the Chiefs Special, later called the Model 36, gave concealed carry a new impetus. As compact as the first J frames were, the hammer spur was always a problem. Unlike the K and N (and later L) frames, bobbing the hammer on the J was not always so easy. The hammer looked odd (and to many users and owners, what looks good is as important as what works well) but also lightening the hammer could cause ignition problems.

Not so much from the mere fact of it being lighter, but the problem of the lighter hammer having to plow through lint and pocket debris that had collected on the gun. Many shooters preferred a shrouded or concealed-hammer model. And, hammer spurs tore clothing.

Within a few years after the Chiefs Special, S&W had both. The Model 40 and 42 came first. They were "hammerless" models, where the hammer was completely enclosed in the frame. They also sported a grip safety on the backstrap, which kept them from being fired unless the grip safety was depressed. Later, the Model 49 came out. The hammer spur was shrouded but exposed, and there

The sideplate, with S&W logo and Airweight markings.

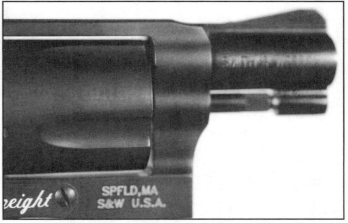

The short barrel, exposed ejector rod and ramp sight are all classic S&W snubbie hallmarks.

Five shots, and then you'll need more.

was no grip safety. I can imagine the reasons for both. Many shooters, then and now, can't shoot a J frame accurately DAO. The Models 40 and 42 gave you no other choice. I can well imagine the experience locally, of an officer at the Detroit Police Department trying to shoot a qualifying score from the 25-yard line, double-action-

The barrel is all steel, not a tube in a shroud. But with the accuracy of the latter, how much longer?

only on a 2-inch barreled .38. The shrouded but exposed hammer of the 49 could be thumb-cocked. And since a revolver is double-action-only, what's the need for a grip safety? Fewer parts meant less cost and complexity.

Fast forward 40 years, from 1952 (the Centennial coming out) to 1993, the 442. We now know a few more things: that you can shoot a revolver double-action accurately. That 25-yard qualification strings are not really as useful as they used to be, and many departments have deleted them. And pocket lint still exists even with lighter clothing.

The 442 is a great little pocket gun. (And need I remind you that we call them "pocket guns" but we still carry them in holsters?) At an ounce less than a pound, the 442 is the lightest steel-cylindered revolver in a serious caliber you can get your hands on. I liked the one they sent me so much that I really hated to send it back.

All matte black except for the markings, the 442 is a business-like little revolver. Up front it has a nominal 2-inch barrel with a ramp front sight. The rear sight is a notch milled into the rear corner of the frame. The

A compact gun under a sweater goes unnoticed.

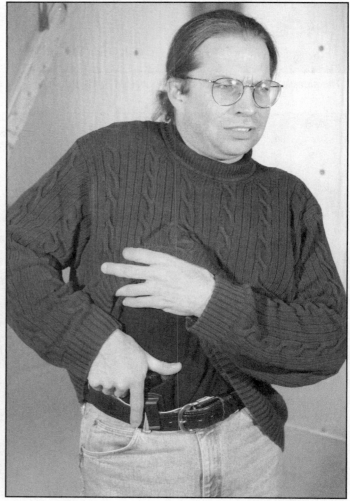

Lift the sweater...

frame fully encloses the hammer, and the contour of the rear corner continues down into the grip straps. There is no delineation between "frame" and "grip" on the rear contour, letting you place your hand as high as comfort and dexterity allows. The grips are rubber, of the "boot grip" design, very comfortable and yet still compact and concealable. If you plan to carry it under a coat, jacket or shirt, you should as with all rubber grips check to see how well the fabric slides. If it grabs the grips, you could move and inadvertently disclose the 442.

The alloy frame uses steel pivot pins for the lock work. You won't see the ends of the pins flush with the frame, as the finish hides them, unlike some Scandium-framed revolvers we've seen.

The barrel is marked "38 S&W SPL+P" on the left side. You can shoot +P ammo, but your hand probably won't like it much. The weight of the 442, as with all lightweight wheelguns, produces a sharp recoil sensation with hot ammo. But you should practice with what you carry. If you practice with light ammo to start with, the recoil becomes manageable as you become accustomed

to it. On the left side of the frame, you'll see the S&W logo, the cylinder latch, the built-in trigger lock, and the head of an internal pin. If current S&W manufacturing practice holds, this pin is titanium where the rest of the internals are steel. It is the only pin that shows bright through the finish. The trigger lock blocks the mechanism for storage when the supplied special key is used to turn the lock counter-clockwise.

On the right side of the frame is the large S&W logo, "Airweight" in script, and the new two-line S&W marking. Old S&W guns had the four-line marking, but the new two-line version makes everyone happy and takes less time and cost to laser cut. (If you think the accountants don't calculate the cost of every marking, operation, design change or detail, you're seriously mistaken.) Underneath the barrel, the ejector rod locks into the standard front locking bolt on all non-shrouded S&W revolvers.

The hidden hammer means the 442 is a DAO revolver. If you are going to carry it you must put in sufficient range time to shoot it accurately DAO.

...produce the "equalizer"...

...and get the muzzle on target as soon as possible.

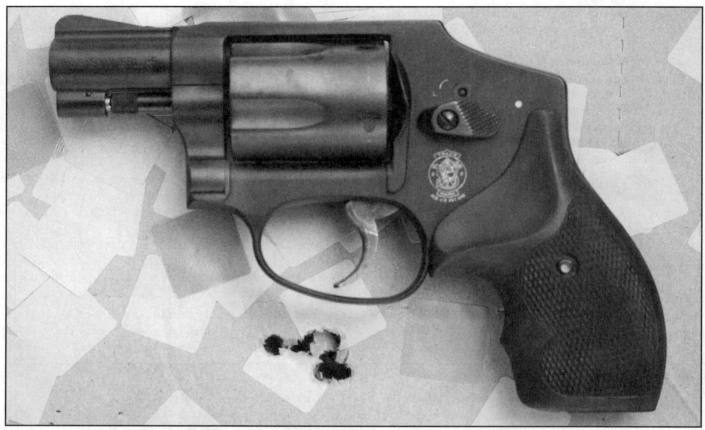

The 442 shot very well. As a double-action-only revolver, it takes some work, but the work is amply rewarded.

Shooting and carrying the 442

To carry the 442 is to almost forget you have it. It is so light that if it had a flatter profile it would be forgotten in your wardrobe until you went to run things through the wash. Only the bulk of the cylinder kept reminding me that I had a revolver on. Obviously the enclosed frame kept the mechanism free of dust, lint, pocket debris and all the other stuff that gets into your carry gun when you pack all day long. On the draw, the grip came easily to the hand provided I had cleared clothing on the draw. With a sidearm this small you must make sure you don't have billowy clothes on. If you have too large a shirt (you needn't go with an old disco-tight shirt) you might end up grabbing cloth along with the gun.

In shooting, the impression depended on the ammo. The soft-shooting Black Hills wadcutter ammo was a joy to shoot, if a hassle to reload. After a few fumbles I let my mind drift back to my PPC days of speedloading wadcutters, and let the speedloader float to the gun. Without forcing it, I was much faster. Still, round-nose and hollowpoint ammo loads much faster than wadcutters do. The stouter loads produced a sharper recoil, but not so much that I couldn't handle it. At the usual conversational ranges of most altercations, and on close-in

IPSC stages it shot accurately. (Using a five-shot revolver on a 27-round field course ends up being a lot of work.) As you can well imagine, trying my hand at the 100-yard gong was an adventure. The short sight radius required an extraordinary amount of concentration to keep lined up as I crept through the trigger pull. As with the short barrel and reduced velocities that resulted, I had to hold about 6 inches over the top of the plate. But hit the plate I did, and often enough that I didn't feel like I was wasting ammo.

For fast, close work the 442 pointed well for me. While I'm not an advocate of point shooting, I was able to get good fast hits using the "Cirillo Index" on targets out to 5 yards or so.

If you don't need the last ounce of weight pared off of an already lightweight carry gun, the 442 just might be the gun instead of its brother the 342Ti. While the Ti model pares 4 ounces off the already feathery 15 of the 442, for some the weight difference is not enough to give up a steel cylinder. For me, the 442 just felt so good I may have send S&W a check for that gun when the book is complete. You can't have too many good guns, and this one is too good to let get away.

CHAPTER 8

The .22 AirLite:
Perfect for just in case

merica is different than many places in the world. In a lot of places you can't get lost, for the walk of an hour will certainly get you to someone who can tell you where you are and how to get where you're going. In other places, getting lost means you are there until you get lucky and find some-

one. Which could take days, weeks months or never. (Of course, with GPS units and cell phones rapidly becoming ubiquitous, that all changes.)

And in many places you sure don't want to be out walking, lost or not, packing a firearm. To do so will get you thrown into a jail where it is a long walk to daylight.

The .22 AirLite is a compact little Kit Gun, inexpensive to feed and soft in recoil.

Only here could you be lost, need to walk out, and be able to arm yourself for the walk. Or pack a handgun "just in case" while hunting with a rifle or shotgun. Thus the Kit Gun. The idea of a Kit Gun was to have the smallest, lightest and most compact firearm that could be used for survival hunting and signaling. The old I frame, and later the J frame were perfect for the job. Chambered in .22 Long Rifle they could be stashed in our gear along with a box of ammunition, and the weight not noticed. But if light is good, lighter is better. Thus the Airweight Kit Guns. And now the AirLite.

The AirLite .22 is an eight-shot .22 Long rifle built on the Airweight J frame. With adjustable sights it serves well as a companion gun in a hunting trip. If you're out on a several week hunting trip, you can only pack in so much stuff. And even hungry hunters get tired of re-constituted dried foods. But shooting a convenient (and where legal) rabbit, squirrel or other dinner target with your hunting gun is not always wise. The 7mm Magnum you're packing along for moose won't leave much left that is edible on the rabbit you're eyeing. But the .22 of the AirLite will.

The grand tour

The frame is a standard lightweight spurred hammer J frame, with a few exceptions. The firing pin is contained within the frame, and the flat face of the hammer strikes the firing pin, driving it into the cartridge rim. On the left side are the standard small S&W logo, cylinder release latch and trigger lock. "Smith & Wesson" is laser-etched on the left side of the barrel. On the right is the name "AirLite" on the sideplate, with .22 Long Rifle on the barrel. The sights are a "V" rear notch and a HiViz fiber-optic rail up front. The fiver optic collects light along its length, but only allows the light to escape at the ends. As a result, the front sight literally glows. It doesn't do so at night, but in the daytime the bead glows from light, and the brighter the light the brighter the bead glows.

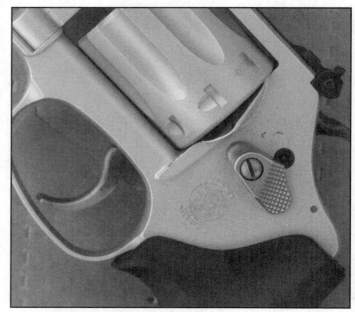

The sideplate carries the AirLite logo.

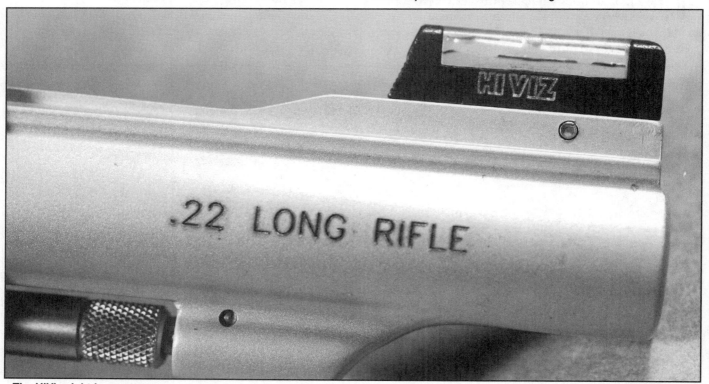

The HiViz sight is easy to see.

The rear sight is a standard assembly attached to the top of the frame, while the front sight is a blade with the fiber optic built in that is pinned to the barrel. If you desire another color, or the sight becomes damaged, you can drive the pin out and replace the blade.

The alloy cylinder holds eight rounds of .22 Long Rifle. The action is standard S&W single- and double-action. If you need a precise shot (say for that rabbit) you can cock the hammer and fire. For plinking you can shoot single- or double-action.

The accuracy is superb, with eight shots under an inch standing at 15 yards as my best group. I found it reliable in ignition with every brand I had along, and the differing points of impact between the brands were minor.

The barrel of the AirLite is the new sleeve-and-shroud method S&W has developed, and if the accuracy of this revolver is indicative of what others using this method can deliver, then lets have more of them.

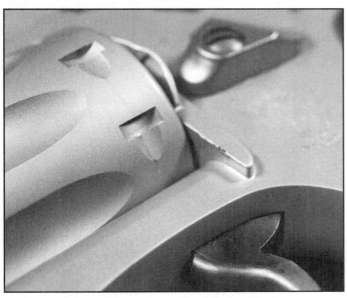

The cylinder retention stud is a simple bar on the frame.

The rear sight is a "V"-notch express sight.

Eight shots of .22 Long Rifle and a box of 50 hardly weighs anything. Stuffed in a daypack, you'd never notice the weight.

Shooting and carry

Shooting the .22 AirLite is a blast. The whole thing is so light you hardly know you're holding a handgun. The recoil of .22 Long Rifle is so miniscule that even the light gun doesn't kick that much. Accuracy-wise it is quite accurate, but I am not a fan of the fiber optic notch sighting system. Were I the owner of this neat little blaster I'd swap the front sight for a standard blade and either change the rear blade or machine it to a standard notch. Despite not liking the HiViz sight (I must be an old fart) I was able to shoot it quite well. Off the bench at 15 yards I was able to post clusters just over an inch in size. The 100-yard gong was not in any danger of damage from the little rimfire, but paying attention to the sights produced a small "tink" with satisfying regularity.

As a carry gun you have to realize that the AirLite is meant as a packing gun on a hiking, camping or hunting trip. It isn't my first (nor second, third or fourth) choice

The crane and centerpin, proportioned for a .38 Special revolver, are stout enough for a lifetime of .22 shooting.

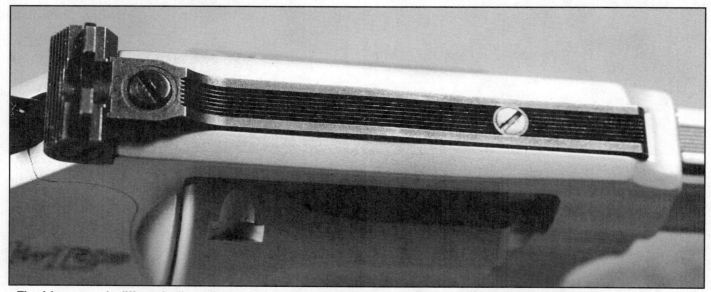

The J-frame rear is differently dimensioned than the K-, L- or N-frame sights. It goes all the way to the front of the frame.

as a defensive firearm. For use as a kit gun, it would be great. You could pack it and a box of ammo and never notice the weight. Kept in camp for getting dinner it would be unobtrusive and ready at a moments notice. However, if you did select it for defensive use it would work well. As long as you kept in mind the limitations of the .22 Long Rifle, which is no great powerhouse, it could do the job. After all, many people have no desire to get shot, even from a rimfire. Many encounters are "settled" simply from the sight of a handgun. And a determined defender who can hit what they aim at can make even someone who isn't readily impressed by small guns stop their nefarious activity. The big advantage the .22 AirLite would have there would be the cheap cost of practice ammo, the low recoil, and the excellent accuracy.

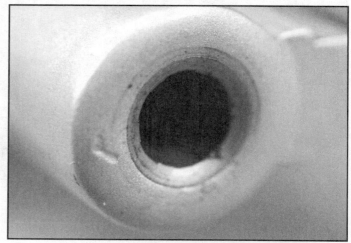

The barrel is a sleeve in the sight and ejector rod shroud.

Eight shots at 15 yards standing. Not bad, and plenty good enough to keep you fed in the backcountry if need be.

Doing Bill Drills with a rimfire snubby is a strange experience. There isn't enough recoil to shove you around, so the only movement you see in the sights is what you put there. But the sight radius is so short that any movement means you've just shot a "C" instead of an "A." With a little practice I was able to shoot eight-shot (a cylinderful) Bill Drills under par time. I could keep all shots in the A zone in the Cirillo Index. I didn't try the El Presidente, as I had no speedloaders.

The only thing I can see S&W doing to change it would be to chamber it in one of the .17 rimfires, the Hornady Magnum Rimfire or the Hornady Mach 2. But then it would be the ".17 AirLite."

CHAPTER 9

The 17H:
The newest in a long line of small revolvers

K frame revolvers in a rimfire chambering have a long history at Smith & Wesson. Indeed, the first S&W revolvers were in .22 Short. Starting in 1931 S&W began offering the K-22. The idea was that Bull's-eye shooters who were using revolvers in the rest of the match would want a matched revolver in .22 Long Rifle for the rimfire portion of the match. As the K frame guns evolved, so did the K-22, into the K-22 Masterpiece, the K-22 Combat Masterpiece, and the Model 18. The refinements did not change the essence of the K-22; a six-shot double-action revolver chambered in .22 Long Rifle that delivered superb accuracy and almost no recoil while operating exactly like its bigger brothers.

Then Hornady came up with the .17 Hornady Magnum Rimfire. Built on a .22 Magnum case, the .17 HMR delivers velocity like the .22 can't. And even less recoil.

The 17H is a K frame stainless double-action revolver chambered for six rounds of .17 Hornady rimfire. The 17H is pure modern K frame all the way. It has the mod-

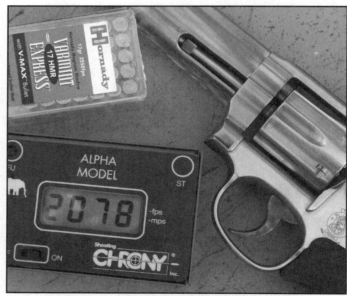

The .17HMR delivers plenty of velocity from the 8-inch barrel.

The .17 came from Hornady, and the barrel markings proclaim it.

Despite the velocity, the bullets do not harm good steel targets. But check before you go using it on the club's rimfire silhouette targets.

Six shots of Hornady Rimfire Magnum per cylinder.

ern adjustable sight, which can be removed to expose the scope-mounting holes. In the old days we used to have to drill and tap an S&W frame in the rear sight channel to mount a scope. Modern S&W revolvers come already drilled and tapped, making shooters' lives easier and taking one more job out of the hands of gunsmiths. One change that further dampens the already miniscule recoil, and improves the looks, is that the barrel is the full-lugged design. Like the old Python barrel, and similar to the design S&W instituted with the 586 series of revolvers, the 17H has an underlug that extends to the muzzle.

The chambers (or charge holes, if you prefer the older terminology) differ from those of other models or chamberings. In the centerfire models, and other rimfire chamberings, the recess reamed for the cartridge rim is

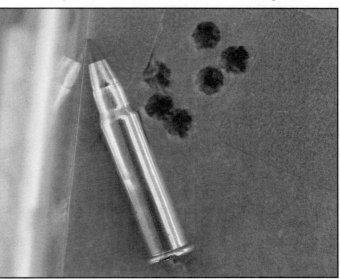

The size of the holes throws off our perspective. The group is under an inch, center to center at 20 yards from a rest.

The hard part of the .17 wasn't hitting the 100-yard gong; it was hearing the hits.

a squared step. On the 17H, the rim recess is reamed as a cone on the extractor and a stepped square on the cylinder. The only reason I can see for the change is that the angled surface of the ejector acts to tip the cases out, away from the center of the cylinder, to aid ejection.

Handling and firing the 17H

First, the accuracy. The accuracy with irons was superb, and I'm sure you could do even better with a good scope attached. On the club's 100-yard range I was able to easily select a bit of scrap paper or wood on the hill at will, and make it jump by plinking at it. The level

of accuracy was so good it was scary. The 100-yard gong was no problem to hit; however telling that I'd hit it was a problem. At that distance the little 17-grain bullet made so little noise when it hit that I couldn't tell half the time. Considering my performance plinking, the idea that I'd missed a 10-inch gong was silly. But half the time I couldn't hear any sound from the hit. On the bench at 25 yards I managed to place cluster after cluster of six shots well under an inch. As well as I was doing, I apparently had had too much coffee in the morning, as I was not able to shoot the tight, six-shot cluster of all shots

The .17HMR started from a .22 Magnum rimfire case.

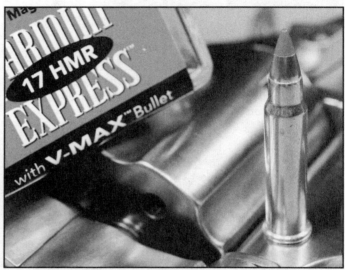

"Varmint Express" indeed. Expressing them right out of the neighborhood.

With groups like this, you can't go blaming the gun. And you could shoot even better if you mounted a scope on it.

A closeup of the curiously beveled extractor star.

touching that we all love to post for others to see. But groups three quarters of an inch or less are nothing to be ashamed of.

Considering the intended use, small game, was there any point in trying the standard IPDC drills? I did one Bill Drill. At 7 yards, with the inconsequential recoil of the .17 and the long sight radius of the 8-inch barrel, I shot six shots in a grand total of .92 seconds. First try. Then I went plinking.

The chrono results were at first as puzzling as the gong test. I couldn't get the .17 caliber bullets to register on the skyscreens. With a little fussing and moving the screen rail around I was able to get the tiny bullets' shadows to register on the screens, and was it fun! The 8-inch barrel of this 17H delivered the 17-grain bullets at an average of 2086 fps. You would be hard-pressed to get a .22 Long Rifle bullet within 500 fps of that, and even the .22 Rimfire Magnum would not be much higher than 1700 fps. However, the high velocity is gained by using a very small and light bullet. For varmints at close range it is plenty good enough, but we're still talking about a load with a 35 Power Factor, where a 9mm has to post 125 to be scored at Minor in competition.

The velocity had me a bit worried: would it damage our club's steel plates? We use falling steel plates for many of our matches, and non-falling for some matches and a lot of practice. We are very protective of them, as damaging them can create a safety hazard for members. Anything that craters or punches holes in the steel is prohibited. (We don't worry about rifles on the 100-yard range. The splashback cannot come back that far, so we simply assign the steel on the 100-yard range sacrificial status, and replace it when it becomes too worn to use.) Would the high velocity of the .17HMR cause a problem? We have previously banned full-power .44 Magnum or larger handguns, and the .30 Carbine is a known steel-damaging round. What of the .17? There was only one way to find out. I selected a structural member of one of the steel plates for a test-firing. (If the .17 damaged it, I was fully prepared to load the steel in my truck and take it directly to the club's welder for repair.) One shot on the angle iron leg produced no damage. So, I risked six shots directly onto one of the target plates. No damage. All they did was scuff the paint, and left an impression less than that of the target loads we usually strike plates with. The fragile bullet, meant for varmint shooting, probably had a lot to do with the lack of damage to the steel. That, and the light weight of the bullet.

As a varmint gun and a small game hunting gun the 17H is great. And the 17 Hornady Magnum Rimfire certainly delivers everything it promises: high velocity and no recoil. For a dedicated small game or varmint hunter who is determined to use a handgun, you need only put a scope on yours to get 100-yard performance. The question of "Does it harm steel?" was more than one of not damaging my club's steel and then having to pay for repairs. The light recoil and superb accuracy will no-doubt have many shooters thinking about using it for rimfire silhouette. So long as the targets are made of a good grade of steel, and the organizing body of your matches approves it, I'm sure you'll do well.

The .17 Hornady Magnum Rimfire has caught on so well a year after its introduction that Hornady is running the production line 24 hours a day, seven days a week trying to keep up. Well done, Hornady and S&W.

CHAPTER 10

The Stainless K-22:
100 years of work to achieve perfection

The new K-22 is the culmination of the century of effort that S&W put into refining the K frame and making .22 Long Rifle handguns shoot. The frame is the K frame made of stainless steel, but with the 21st century manufacturing precision that comes with CNC machinery. The K frame is large enough to be useful in holding a .38 Special cartridge, without being so large as to preclude its use by most people. Many find the larger N frame to be too much to hold. When you then take the .38-sized K frame and chamber it in .22

The typical game: a squirrel. With an accurate .22, it's just a matter of holding and squeezing.

Long Rifle, the result is a bank vault that holds accurate ammo. The 6-inch full-lugged barrel it came with no doubt aided the accuracy of the sample gun. The recoil of a .22 LR in this gun was inconsequential, even with the "full power" ammo (The .22 long rifle is dangerous, and can injure or even kill, make no mistake. But it is not the V-8 engine of the firearms universe.)

The newest version of the venerable K-22 is all stainless with a full-lugged barrel. It holds six rounds of .22LR. The one shipped to me had a 6-inch barrel, and

the balance was decidedly muzzle-heavy. The sights were a plain black post and a plain black blade, just the way I like sights to be. The rear sight covers the drilled and tapped holes for a scope mount, which for many small game hunters is an essential addition.

The K-22 is an S&W, with all the modern features you've come to expect. The cylinder latch on the left side of the frame (with the action lock just above it) opens easily, and the heavy cylinder has plenty of wall thickness to hold the .22. The action is double- or single-

The S&W K-22 has always had a reputation for accuracy. The current stainless version of it continues that tradition.

The old cylinder retention stop was a stud staked into the frame. The new is machined.

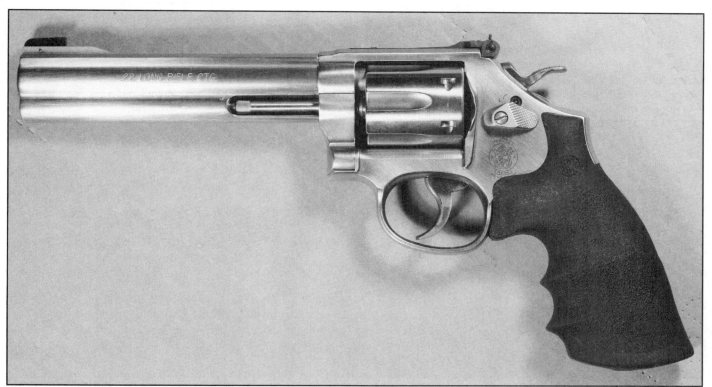

With a 6-inch barrel, the K-22 is nicely balanced, but not unwieldy.

action. In double-action the K-22 is perfect for teaching someone to shoot DA; the springs are light enough to pull, but the heavy cylinder times up with authority. For someone who is trying to learn DA shooting, the only drawback to an afternoon and a brick of .22 ammo is the potential for a sore trigger finger.

In single-action the pull is clean and light, 3 pounds and with no creep. For offhand shooting at the 100-yard gong the 22 provided plenty of entertainment. Members of my crew of volunteers are more likely to go after the exotic guns and ammo when I show up, but left to themselves they'd be happy to burn large amounts of cheap .22 ammo.

Many pistols show decided preferences for one ammo over another, in accuracy or sometimes even function. I've had pistols that were tack-drivers when you fed them what they like, then scattered shots when you fed them

what they didn't. And some even refused to work with the "wrong" ammo. Not so the K-22. It worked with everything. And it all was good enough to go six for six on the 100-yard gong at one time or another. It proved so accurate that plinking at dirt clods or broken target sticks on the 100-yard hill actually became boring. "Line up the sights. Press the trigger. 'Pop' there goes the stick." As you can imagine, the lack of recoil made a Bill Drill simply a "dry fire session with holes in the cardboard." The sights moved more from my trigger finger working the trigger than they did for the recoil of the .22. The long barrel made the Cirillo Index a snap. Lacking speedloaders I did not try any El Presidentes, but assuming I can reload the K-22 reasonably quickly, beating a Par time and score would be a snap.

The only thing I'd change would be the barrel length. If it was for hunting I'd go with an 8-inch barrel, and for

The cylinder latch is nicely sculpted, even better looking than the old ones.

The click-adjustable S&W micrometer sight works very well.

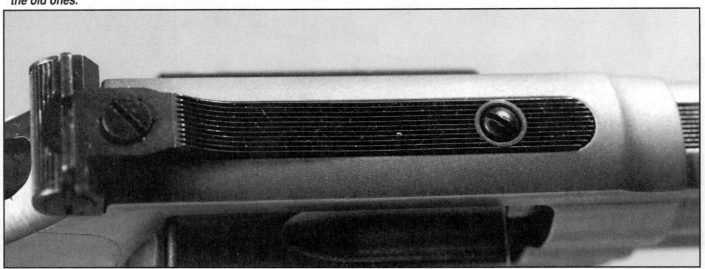

If you want to scope the K-22, remove the rear sight and you'll find scope mount holes underneath.

Six shots. You could have more, but six is often plenty.

The recesses for the rims are cut as square shelves, something the centerfire revolvers lost years ago.

The underlug goes the full length of the barrel.

The front sight is pinned in place, and you can change it for something else if you like.

training someone on the basics of marksmanship I'd prefer a 4-inch tube. And if the small game hunting was to be with a scope, then the 4 would work as well as the 8.

Of all the handguns in the test, this one got the most ammo through it. Where some got a few hundred (or less, as with the SW500 or the 329) and some got more, I shot the K-22 a bunch. And so did my test-fire crew. How much? So much that I actually cleaned the gun before I shipped it back to the factory. I didn't want the crew

there thinking I was renting it out on weekends or something. Once I'd cleaned it up, I almost decided to keep it. A couple thousand rounds of .22 ammo is nothing in the life of a good handgun, and this one is a good one.

The 340PD:
A lightweight powerhouse

The 340PD is an expert's gun. While it is just another 442 when you feed it .38 Special ammunition, its character changes when you go with Magnum ammo.

The 340PD is a Magnum J frame, hammerless and made of Scandium alloy. At 12 ounces empty it is among the lightest handguns offered by S&W in a serious caliber. And the .357 Magnum is definitely a serious caliber.

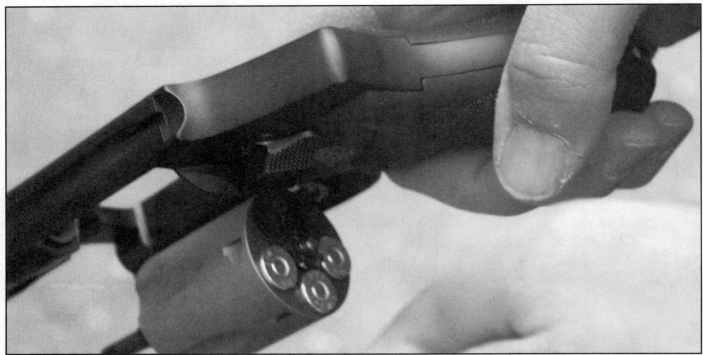

The 340 is an expert's gun: light, compact and five-shot.

The combination of the two makes for a real handful, and one you should take time to work up to. On the left side the barrel is marked "Smith & Wesson" while the frame has the small S&W logo, the cylinder latch and the action lock. On the right, the frame has the S&W atomic logo, "AirLitePD" under the cylinder and the two-line S&W address. On the barrel shroud it is marked ".357 S&W Mag" and "No less than 120 gr bullet." The barrel is the new rifled tube in a shroud design, and very accurate. Why the marking admonishing heavy bullets? Recoil inertia. The recoil of the 340 with hot loads is very sharp. The neck tension and crimp of factory am-

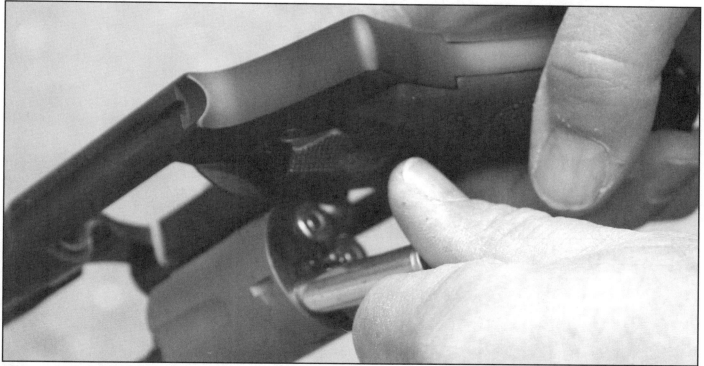

You can load one at a time...

...until you get to five. Or you can use a speedloader.

Hang on!

The usual result of shooting .357 Magnum ammo in the 340PD.

The 340 ready to go.

Here, fired with "only" .38 Special+P ammo, it still comes up hard.

Despite the harsh recoil, the 340 can be accurate. Here is a double-action group at 15 yards off the rest, with .357 Magnum Black Hills 125-grain JHP ammo.

munition can only hold against so much recoil, and then bullets start to pull. Why the limit on lower weights and not heavier? Ammunition has the bullet protruding from the case. When you lighten the bullet you remove lead and copper from inside, where it adds friction to resist bullet pull. Below 120 grains the bullet is so short there isn't enough surface of bullet to case to resist inertia. Bullets start moving forward under recoil. As for reloaded ammunition, you will have to experiment. You may well find that even some heavy bullets move under recoil, especially if your loading dies do not create enough neck tension. (All the more reason to depend on factory ammo for defensive use, and not reloads.)

The cylinder is titanium, and holds five rounds. The sights are fixed, with a notch in the rear and a red ramp on front. The front sight is pinned in place, so if you wanted to change the sight to some other style or height you

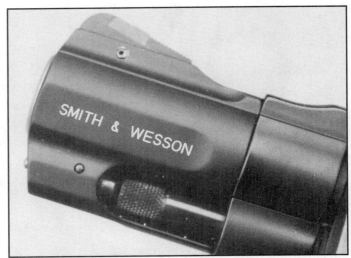

The short barrel leaves the ejector rod less than case length, so eject briskly to make sure the empties get out.

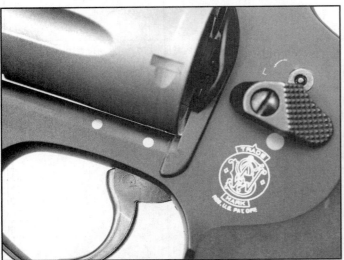

Notice the white pins flush with the frame. They are titanium, to stand up to the recoil.

And the admonition against light bullets lets you know you're in for some recoil!

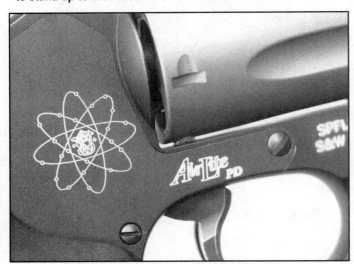

The atomic logo lets you know it is a Scandium frame; the AirLite lets you know it is a Titanium cylinder.

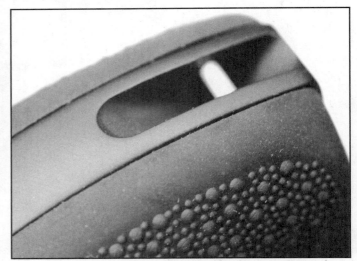

The lanyard loop lets you secure the pistol to your person in a stressful environment.

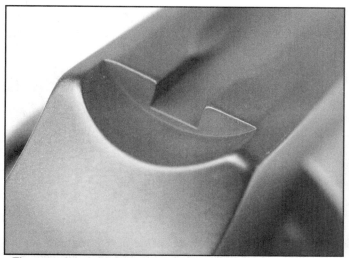

The rear sight is just a notch in the frame.

The front sight is the classic S&W red ramp.

It may only be five shots, but you can't get five more powerful shots into something this small.

could. The hammerless frame makes the 340 a double-action-only revolver. At the bottom of the frame, which has rubber boot grips, there is a lanyard loop. The lanyard allows you to secure the pistol to your person in case you need it someplace where you may have to suddenly grab for security, and don't want to lose the 340. A boat, for example. Or to keep it in your sleeping bag and not lose it down by your feet while you sleep. With its lack of external controls, and double-action-only trigger, sleeping with the 340 is a lot safer than many other options. And if you are in an environment dangerous enough to require loaded firearms immediately upon awakening, sleeping with a handgun suddenly seems a lot less hazardous than it might whilst snug in your own bed at home.

The best-performing load for defense is also the hardest to shoot well, the 125-grain .357 JHP. Practice up to this load; don't start with it.

Carry and shooting

Carrying the 340PD was like carrying any other Airweight snubbie. Once parked in a simple Uncle Mike's belt holster, or snugged in the belly-band holster, it rode without a problem. As the frame is hammerless, it could not work in an ankle holster, as the strap is designed to work with a hammer. The grips are comfortable, and work to keep it concealable.

Shooting is the "work" part, not carrying it. With .38 special ammunition it is a handful to shoot. With the light weight the "snap" of the recoil from regular .38 ammo is noticeable. With .38 Special+P ammunition it starts to be more than new shooters like to shoot, or can handle well. You could easily work a new shooter into a flinch, with the 340 and .38+P ammo. As for the Mangum ammo, do not go lightly there. It is work. Even an experienced shooter can easily work into a flinch shooting the 340 with magnum ammo. I did most of the magnum shooting with the 340 using 125-grain jacketed hollowpoints. My hand was sore after emptying a few cylinders. While it was objectionable with 125s, it was downright obnoxious with 158-grain full-power Magnum ammo. So bad, in fact, that while I tried a few Bill Drills with the 125s (Five shots, one second, all A

hits. Never happened.) I didn't even try it with the 158s. There just wasn't any point to it. I wasn't making my hits or time with the 125s, and the 158s kicked even worse. Why beat myself up? Ditto the Cirillo index. I ended up shooting the 125s far slower in the magnum loads than I did with the same gun and .38 Special +P ammunition. My advice for those who want to pack the 340PD as a defensive gun is this: spend most of your time practicing with .38 Special or .38 Special +P ammunition, and end with some .357 Magnum. Practice as often as you can without developing a flinch or persistent soreness in your shooting hand. Once you have built up recoil resistance, then and only then carry it with .357 Magnum ammunition. And if you fall off your practice routine for any time (like more than a week or two) go back to the .38s until you can build back up to the magnums. Otherwise, you will simply build a flinch. It will be difficult to overcome later, and will negatively impact your ability to use the 340 in a defensive situation.

The 340 is one of those guns that I'm glad I had a chance to shoot, but I'm also glad I've got other options for defensive carry.

CHAPTER 12

The Model 640: A carry gun you enjoy shooting

T he light guns get all the "oohs" and "ahhs" but the 640 is the tool of the pro. An all-stainless J magnum frame, the .357 Magnum 640 is what you want to be shooting, if you have to shoot a snubbie. I found the light guns work but are not all that pleasant to shoot, but even with magnum loads the 640 was enjoyable.

The J frame Model 640 holds five rounds of .357 Magnum. It can also use .38 Special and .38 Colt ammunition. You could practice with increasingly more power-

If you want to shoot it, leave the big grips on. For carry, find small grips to ease concealment.

ful .38 ammunition, then go to .38 Special+P loads, and finally graduate to the magnums. And be a much better shot for the work. One thing that makes the 640 easier to shoot are the grips. Large for a carry gun, they are soft rubber and have subdued finger grooves. I usually don't find finger grooves are in the right place for my hand, but the swells and grooves of these grips didn't annoy my hands like many others do. For the most compact carry option possible, you could replace the bigger grips it came with, with something smaller like the boot grips that come on the 442. If you do so, realize that you'll be trading off some shooting comfort for that conceability.

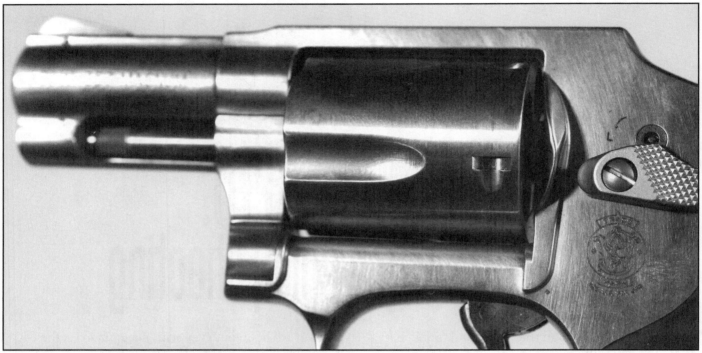

The all-stainless 640 is one tough gun, and worth the weight.

The five-shot J frame brings enough ammo to get started, but you'll surely want to be carrying spare ammo in a speedloader or speed strip.

Not bad, for double-action over sandbags at 15 yards, with full-power .357 Magnum ammo.

The hammerless frame completely encloses the hammer, so there is nothing to catch on clothing during concealed carry. And no slots to allow lint, dust and "who knows what" to get into the action. Like all S&W revolvers it has the action lock on the left side of the frame above the cylinder release.

In carry it is a bit heavy. But as a J frame it isn't so heavy you can't carry it, and the weight does come in handy when you touch off a magnum round. In shooting, I did five-shot drills, and Bill Drills with any .38 load were easy. They were a bit more work with the magnums, but once I got my timing and a feel for the trigger I could shoot passing times on the Bill Drill. The Cirillo Index was a bit harder, as the short barrel and stout recoil would drive me out of the A zone if I wasn't paying exact attention to what I was doing.

The 640 makes a fine concealed carry gun for someone who felt five shots (and reloads) were enough. For those who like to start with more, the 640 in an upside-down shoulder rig, as a backup gun, would be an exemplary choice.

When it came time to ship the guns back I was really torn between all the guns. Which could I afford to pay for and keep? I had to decide if I was going to hang on to any, and the 640 was on the short list. I haven't sent it back yet. In the famous words of Jack Benny, "I'm thinking!"

CHAPTER 13

The 686:
A step up from the K frame

The 686 frame was created because the K frame was not up to the increasing amount of .357 Magnum ammunition police departments were using. The original intent when the Combat Magnum (later the Model 19) was designed was that police would practice mostly with .38 Special ammunition, some Magnum, and carry Mangum ammo on duty. In the mid-1950s that was common practice and seemed like a good idea. By the early 1970s it didn't seem like such a good idea any more. What departments found was that police officers

The 686 can be had with the Power Port barrel, a factory-machined compensator. It works, but be aware that some shooting competitions won't allow its use.

who had practiced and qualified with .38 Special ammunition often could not hit what they were shooting at when they were using .357 Magnums on the street. The noise, recoil and sometimes even the point of aim were different. The administrators who were paying attention changed their procedures; officers who carried magnums on the street would practice and qualify with magnums.

The all-stainless 686 is built to take .357 Magnum ammo as a steady diet. The re-designed cylinder release latch is less likely to bite your thumb on recoil.

Then another change happened, and the wheels fell off the whole firearms cart. The old .357 Magnum load had been a 158-grain lead bullet at 1,500 fps. It was plenty hot, too hot even for regular use in N frame guns, so by the 1970s it had been downloaded. In the early 1970s factory .357 Magnum was usually a 158-grain bullet going 1,250 to 1,300 fps out of a 4-inch barrel. It wasn't so bad on the guns. But the invention of reliably expanding hollowpoints for handgun cartridges caused a shift to jacketed bullets. And expansion was better in the lighter bullets. In short order the "gold standard" for reliable stopping power (in as much as any handgun can be said to have "reliable stopping power") was a .357 Magnum with 125-grain jacketed hollowpoints. Out of a 6-inch barrel that bullet would be going at or over 1,400 fps. The jet of gas on the forcing cone was hot, abrasive and sharp on impact. Forcing cones eroded and cracked. Top straps got flame-cut. Guns went out of time in a relatively short period of shooting. S&W had to do something.

What they did was make the cylinder, frame and barrel at the forcing cone closer to the dimensions of the N frame. They left the grip straps the same as the K frame. And the parts in between were proportioned to match up and work properly. To aid in recoil, the barrel was changed to a full-lugged design for extra weight out front. And not coincidentally, similar to that of the Colt Python.

The Power Port barrel comes as a six-shot gun. You can have a seven-shot 686, but you can't have it with a ported barrel unless you port it yourself.

The result was the finest police sidearm that could be had, just in time for police departments to stampede to the auto-loading pistol as the issue sidearm. But not before the L frame was firmly established and proven.

The 686 provided for the test was the 6-inch Power Port, a model where the barrel at the muzzle is machined with an integral compensator. The sight is directly behind the port, safe from expansion gases. As an aside, I spent a trip at Second Chance shooting a 1911 where the expansion chamber of the compensator had been bridged with a strap to hold the front sight. The original owner had expressly asked for that design, not wanting to give up the inch of sight radius. The gunsmith (a master at the craft) had machined the sight rail as a dovetail from front to back, fitted the sight rail (with integral sight) and then silver-soldered it in place. It was beautiful. My main gun had decided to break a week before Second Chance, so I borrowed this gun. After shooting over 1,000 rounds of hot pin loads through it, and right in the middle of a run on a three-man team event, I started hitting 3 feet low. The bridge had busted loosed of it silver-soldered dovetail on the front, and was bent upwards. I had to borrow yet another gun to finish (and repair the gun when I got home.)

All this is to try to dissuade you from the idea that you can have both the full sight radius and the compensator, by bridging the port with a sight rail.

The comp on the 686 works, by the way, and quite well, too. To jump ahead for a moment, with full-power magnum ammo it was by far the most fun to shoot of any gun I had to test.

On the left the barrel is marked "Smith & Wesson" and back on the frame is the small S&W logo, the cylinder release and the action lock. The 686, as all new model S&W revolvers have, has the cylinder retention shoulder machined as an integral part of the frame. The right side has the four-line S&W address/trademark rollmark, and ".357 S&W Magnum" on the barrel. The frame is drilled and tapped under the rear sight for a scope mount. The hammer spur is serrated, but the trigger is narrow and smooth on its face. The sights are post front and black blade rear, but you can have red ramp and white outline sights as an option.

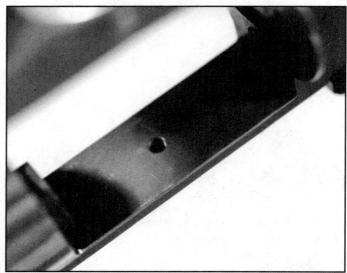

For those who want scopes, the 686 comes drilled and tapped for a scope mount. Remove the rear sight and the scope base holes will be revealed.

The 686 was one tack-driving gun. This is only an average group, fired with full-power Black Hills 125-grain jacketed hollowpoint .357 Magnum.

The 686 I received was a six-shot model. You can also have seven-shot models, but without the porting. You'd think it would be easy enough to offer it as an option, but there apparently just isn't enough demand for both options. But if you were to luck onto a Power Port barrel, and had a seven-shot 686 to work on it would be easy enough to swap barrels.

Carry and shooting

Carrying this particular 686 is a simple thing: since it is either a competition or hunting gun, you pack it in the appropriate holster. This one is not a concealed carry gun, although in the 4-inch or shorter barrel it could well be. With the right holster the weight is no big deal.

In shooting, this 686 really stood out. The port worked well to dampen felt recoil, even with the hottest bowling pin loads. One of my favorite loads, a 180-grain Oregon Trails lead truncated cone, over 7.9 grains of Accurate Arms #5, was quite fun to shoot. And as always broomed pins off quickly. With the Black Hills ammo it was almost sedate, especially with the 125-grain load which offers lower bullet mass and lots of gas volume to work the comp. For accuracy, I was easily able to punch a demo group that was just over an inch center to center at 25 yards off the rest. As for the 100-yard gong, it was toast. Even off hand it was easy to go six for six. And any test crew shooter who sat down to shoot could guarantee six hits from six shots. As a long-range plinker this 686 made hitting target stick debris on the 100-yard hill fun. At least once or twice per six rounds we could make the stick jump, which is the desire of every plinker. With .38 Special ammunition it was so light in recoil it would be no problem for a new shooter to learn the skills for shooting. As long as your new shooter has hands big enough, and strength enough to hold it up, the 686 would be an exemplary learner's gun.

Bill Drills were boringly easy. The smooth double-action and the compensator kept the sights in the A zone with ease, and even the hottest factory ammo was no problem. I tried a few runs with bowling pin loads, and that isn't so easy. But definitely do-able. Lacking a speedloader for the L frame (I spent all my time shooting PPC using K frame revolvers, so I have a coffee can full of K frame speedloaders,) El Presidente was not possible. I ran a few patched-together El Prez runs, doing each half against the clock, and then adding the runs plus an average reload time, and to no great surprise found par scores on the El Prez were easy to do.

If you don't already have a 686 in your gun safe, and you prize your reputation as a serious shooter, collector, competitor or expert, you simply must get one. I've had a dozen or so L frame guns pass through my hands through the years, and I have not yet seen one that would spoil their reputation. My friend John Simon carried a 581 (blued, fixed-sight L frame) as his duty gun for many years until the department switched to 9mm autoloaders, and he never failed to qualify with it. He even used it in IPSC matches, winning revolver class until he, by his actions, made it mandatory for me to show up with a wheelgun to give him some competition.

CHAPTER 14

The Model 386P:
The P stands for Perfect

The 386P is perhaps the perfect defensive revolver for concealed carry. Light in weight, it is accurate and reliable.

Built on a Scandium L frame, the seven-shot 386P is dark, with its blue frame and gray Titanium cylinder. The front sight is a "red ramp," with a red plastic insert

The 386P is a large but lightweight concealed-carry gun. You'll need a good holster more for its bulk than its weight. When you need defense, you'll be glad you had the 386P with you.

to catch the eye. The front sight is pinned to the barrel shroud. The rear sight is adjustable. The barrel is the new S&W "tube in a shroud" design the Airlites have. The hammer spur is serrated but the trigger is smooth. The action pivot pins are flush with the frame but white, showing off against the dark frame, demonstrating their Titanium content. The barrel and frame have the standard S&W markings, "Smith & Wesson" on the barrel, and the logo on the left side of the frame. On the right the barrel is marked .357 Magnum, and the frame has the atomic S&W logo, AirlitePD and the two-line S&W rollmark. The frame has a steel insert above the forcing cone. The hot gases from magnum loads create a jet coming out of the gap between the cylinder and barrel. On steel-

The atomic logo lets you know it's Scandium, and light. The AirLite name is the clue to the Titanium cylinder, if the color didn't give it away.

Note the titanium pivot pins, flush with the frame and brighter than the aluminum alloy.

The seven-shot cylinder will require a special speedloader, rather than a regular L-frame .357 one.

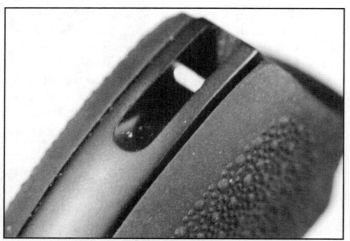

The lanyard pin lets you secure the gun to you in the wilderness, while sleeping, or someplace where you dare not drop it.

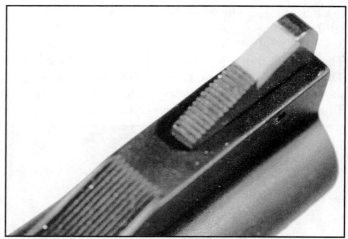

The red ramp front sight is not going to hang up on the draw. It is pinned in place, so if you need to, or want to, change it, you can.

The steel insert takes the blast of flame from the hot .357 Magnum loadings you'd use in defense.

A plain black rear blade, the way I like them. If you do not like the blade, it is easy enough to change.

framed guns the jet flame-cuts the topstrap, but soon stops as the cut gets a few thousandths farther from the gap, and the surface builds up a coarse, powder and lead residue. On the Scandium frames the cutting would be worse and go deeper. Thus the steel insert to take the flame.

The action is the single-action/double-action trigger mechanism that S&W is famous for, with a very nice crisp single-action and smooth if heavy double-action. The grips are larger than the smaller snubbies, making it easier to get a good grip on the gun. You'll need it. The rear corner of the frame is machined for a lanyard, with a cross pin through the grooved backstrap.

The Titanium cylinder holds seven rounds of .38 Colt, .38 S&W Special or .357 Magnum. It comes in the standard blue plastic S&W box with all the usual accessories.

Carry and shooting

As for carrying it, the 386P is light, compact and holds a bunch of rounds. For a small increase in size over a five-shot revolver (when you add in a holster) the seven shots of .357 Magnum of the 386P are a lot. Packed as a backup in a shoulder rig you'd never notice it.

In accuracy the 386P was amazing for a lightweight snubbie. The 100-yard gong was easy to hit. The flat trajectory of the .357 Magnum made holdover easy: hold

You wouldn't think a lightweight carry gun could shoot like a Bullseye or PPC gun, but this 386 does. A real sleeper for competition, too.

the top edge of the plate and you couldn't miss. Tumbling dirt clods and busted off chunks of target frames on the 100-yard backstop was easy. (The rifle shooters are always missing the target and hitting the frames, leaving shattered bits of the target holder sticks on the backstop.)

While the 500, used at the same range session, was the star of the party, everyone went back to the 386P several times. It was stout enough in recoil to be fun without beating you up. It did sting the hand with the

hottest loads, but with anything even mild by .357 standards it was a blast to shoot.

If you like revolvers and want something big to carry without getting to the N frame bulk, the 386P is an easy-to-carry blaster that deserves your consideration. Would I want to shoot a bowling pin match with it? Not a chance. But I'd gladly shoot an ICORE match with it, and have a real fun day doing so. And as a main gun for carry, it is superb.

CHAPTER 15

The Model 627-5:
The .357 Magnum, plus two

The 627-5 is probably my favorite wheelgun in this book. Built by the Performance Center on a modified N frame, it is just what it says, an eight-shot .357 Magnum. As mentioned earlier, the Performance Center does not just take frames from production and "clean them up" as I've heard some shooters claim.

They machine from scratch (or from forgings) their guns using their own specifications. They do just shoehorn an eight-shot cylinder into an otherwise standard N frame, but there's more to it than that. The distance from the centerline of the cylinder to the centerline of the chamber/bore on a standard N frame is .536." That is, from

The eight-shot .357 is a slick-looking wheelgun.

the center of the ejector rod (the axle) to the axis of the firing pin/primer/case/chamber/barrel/bore is .536" and every cartridge made in a standard N frame has to conform to that dimension. If you make your cartridge smaller, you'll have thicker chamber walls. You can only get so large before you run out of chamber walls, which is why there is nothing larger than a .45 Colt in an N frame. And why the .45 Colt should be limited in chamber pressure. If you want to add more rounds, you also have only so much circumference to work with. So if you want to add rounds, as in .38/.357, you can't just consider the wall thickness from axle to chamber and chamber to outside wall. To fit more rounds on the circumference isn't possible past seven .38/.357 Magnum at the standard axle-to-axis spacing, which is why the Baumann conversions of the 1980s and 1990s were only seven shots. To add another round, S&W increased not the cylinder diameter, but the distance from axle to axis. The 627-5 has an axle-to-axis dimension of .576" which may not seem like much. But it precludes putting the new

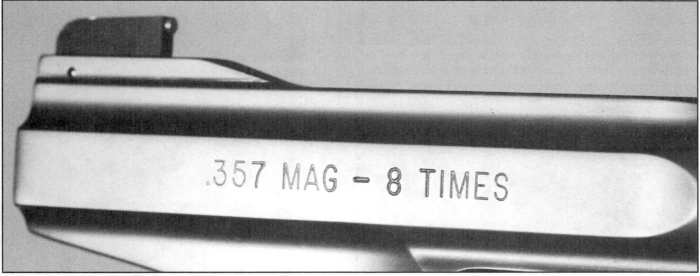

Just in case no one noticed what you had, the barrel is clearly marked.

Here you see the eight-shot cylinder swung out.

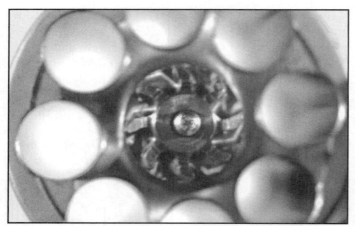
The ratchet requires some very particular and precise machining, and as for timing it, you'd better know what you're doing.

The 627-5 comes with a gold bead front sight.

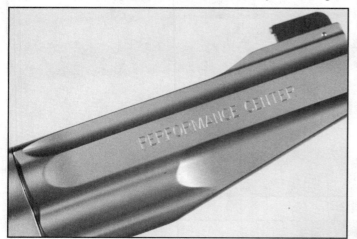
The barrel sculpting carries over to the offside of the ejector rod shroud.

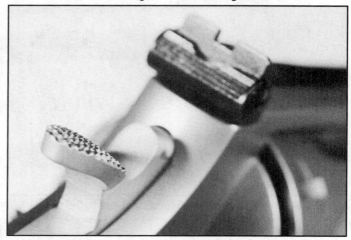
To go with the gold bead front is a plain black rear blade.

The left side of the frame gets the Performance Center logo.

cylinder in old frames, and as a result, you couldn't just install an eight-shot cylinder in your 27 or 672, should you somehow lay hands on one. What the small added amount does is greatly increase the circumference of the cartridge axis. The math is simple: Pi times R equals circumference. The N frame has a .536" reach, giving a circumference of 1.683". The 627-5 has a reach of .576", giving a circumference of 1.809" adding 0.126" to the circumference. That's enough to add an eighth round.

The extra circumference comes at the expense of wall thickness to the cylinder exterior. However, that wall was already plenty thick. Where the eight-shot cylinder becomes possible, it also makes it incompatible with the regular frame: the axle-to-axis distance. Since the axis of each cartridge is farther from the axle, the location of the barrel must be, too. Since the chambers sit .040" higher, the barrel must be that much higher in order to line up with the chambers. Were you to install that eight-shot cylinder on your standard N frame (the cylinder would fit in the frame opening) the chambers and barrel would be mis-aligned by .040"! No amount of forcing cone funneling will allow that to work. You would end up injuring yourself or others. Don't Do It!

The 627-5 has a 5-inch sculptured barrel. Think of it as a cylindrical barrel slabbed down, and a rib machined on the top. The underlug is tapered back to the shroud, and the rear of the barrel is sculpted to blend with the front of the frame. The ejector rod is enclosed but not locked on the front as almost all other S&W revolvers are. Like the many PPC revolvers built with new, bull barrels, the crane is kept closed via a ball plunger and a recess in the frame.

The sights are a McGivern/Miculek gold bead on a patridge post front, and a plain black notch rear. The rear sight is the standard new-model N frame rear, where the front is rounded and set into a round-ended slot on top of the frame. The new sight is much more robust than the old design, but does not fit old frames, so you can't just install the new if you wished.

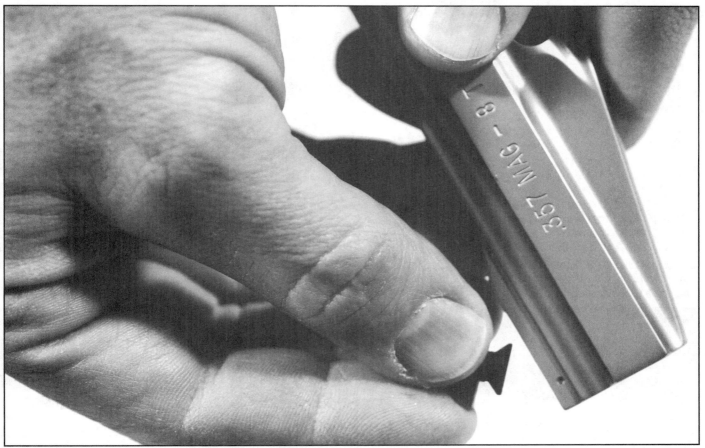

The revolver uses a spring and plunger to hold the front sight in, so you can change it by hand whenever you want to.

Once you've pulled and levered, just lift the blade out.

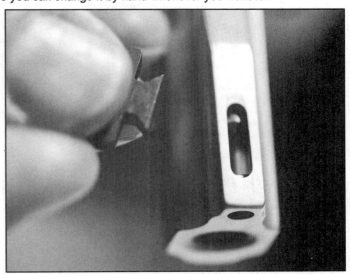

The spring and plunger stay in the barrel so you can't lose them.

The eight-shot shoots as good as it looks. Eight shots of Black Hills .38 Special wadcutter at 25 yards. You can win a lot of matches with accuracy like that.

Just over an inch, center to center.

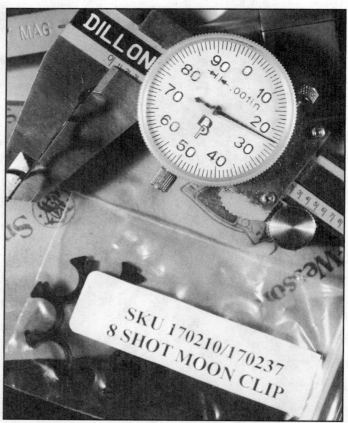

The eight-shot is set up to use moon clips. You can use it without them, but you give up a lot of advantage in a match.

And just to cap it off, the eight-shot comes in a snazzy hard case from the Performance Center.

The left side of the barrel is marked ".357 Magnum – 8 Times" on the barrel, with the Performance Center logo on the frame underneath the cylinder latch and the action lock. The right side has "Performance Center" on the barrel and the S&W logo and patent line markings on the frame.

The round-butt 627-5 comes with finger-grooved wood grips. They would be the first, and probably only, thing I'd change. I have yet to find finger-groove grips that fit my peculiar hands. I have large but not over-sized hands with skinny fingers. (Yes, "surgeons hands") Every finger-groove grip I've ever held so far has had the grooves in the wrong places. I'd probably change them for the Hogue/Miculek one-piece grips, or an N-frame Pachmayr round-butt rubber grips, depending on the match I was using it in. The 627-5 comes in a lockable Performance Center case, padded and with all the usual accouterments: cable lock, owner's manual, registration card, and an envelope containing a fired case. Now I love to shoot, and I'd probably like the test-fire duty at the factory, but the Performance Center 627-5 has to have

been miserable duty: you have to load the moon clips, test fire the gun, then unload the moon clips and save one case to put in the envelope.

The cylinder of the 627-5 is fluted, and the rear machined to accept the full moon clips. The hammer is flat-faced, with the firing pin spring-loaded and inside the frame. The moon clips are not slotted like the 10mm clips in the 610 are. With eight shots in the cylinder there isn't room to slot the clips between rounds. The clips themselves are quite thin, only .023" thick spring steel sheet stock. In comparison, my Baumann-converted M Model 28, with seven shots of .38/.357 Magnum uses clips .025" thick, while the 610 and 25-2 use clips of .036" thick spring steel. Why the difference? The 610 and 25-2/625 uses the extractor groove of the pistol cartridge rim to hold the case. The 627 and all those meant to use a revolver round require the undercut of the rim to hold on. What you might not know is that the rims on cases are lathe-cut. In the manufacture of brass, the extruded cups, when they get that far, are fed into automatic lathes that spin the cases and turn the

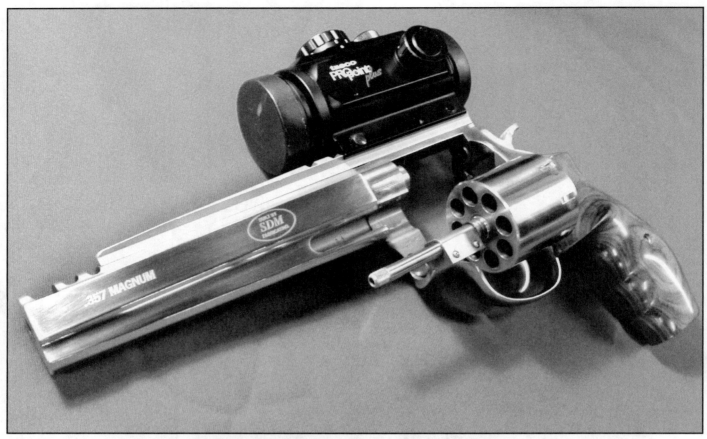

And if stock isn't enough, this custom 627 from SDM Fabrication is just the ticket to tear up the circuit in ICORE Open class.

rim to dimension. To make the forward face of the rim perfectly square, the cutter goes into the case a small amount. Remington cuts larger access slots than others. The slot is not just "taller" that is, longer from front of rim to rear of recess lathe-turned, but also the diameters differ. A "deeper" slot turned farther into the case body affects moon clip function. In the .38/.357, I can only use Remington brass in my Baumann revolver. The 610 and the various 25-2 and 625s I have do not care about cases. The extractor rims of pistol cartridges have a large enough area that the small differences between them does not matter. But in revolver rounds converted to full moon clips, it does matter. If you load your full moon clips with all Remington brass in the 627-5, you may find the rounds are too "floppy" and getting reloaded quickly can be difficult. You should segregate your brass so that you are using only one brand of brass in your 627-5, and split your supply between .38 Specials for light loads and .357 Magnum brass for heavy loads. I found Winchester and Federal brass to be tighter than Remington in the 627-5. (In my Baumann M-28, I cannot use Winchester or Federal. They won't fit in the moon clips.)

Shooting and carry

The 627-5 shot just like you'd expect an N frame .357 to shoot. The large stainless frame absorbed recoil quite well. When fed .38 Special ammo it was so sedate that shooting was a pleasure. Even with full-power .357 Magnum ammo it didn't hurt to shoot, and it was possible to get an afternoons worth of practice out of it without pain. As for accuracy, it was great. The gong was in mortal peril on every shot. My best group was a 25-yard off-the-bench group of just over an inch, with Black Hills target wadcutter ammo. While they would be hard to reload quickly even in moon clips, the wadcutters (as they usually do) shot so well they were the standard to measure against. Even non-wadcutter ammo shot very well, although trying to shoot tight groups from the bench with full power .357 Mangum ammo isn't fun.

As for holsters, the 627-5 is meant to be a competition gun, so holsters are not a problem. Anything that fits an N frame will take the 627-5. Any open-topped Kydex or synthetic, or competition holster that does not enclose the frame up to the rear sight will work fine and super-fast. Uncle Mike's nylon holsters that come up that far are a bit of a squeeze, but the holster has enough give to let the gun fit. The squeeze is for the flat-topped gold bead sight. It will tear up a lot of holsters in quick order, which is why competition shooters use open-topped or low-cut front holsters. If you have a custom-fit N frame leather holster for your other N frame guns, your 627-5 might not fit because of the sight. I tried several of my holsters, and some would, and some wouldn't. But I did not have enough on hand to get any idea of a pattern. The best thing to do would be to contact the holster maker of the brand you are considering and ask them if their holster will take the 627-5. As most shooters will be using it in competition, I don't see a problem. The various Kydex holsters, and my Safariland competition holster doesn't cover the frame, and the dimension doesn't matter.

Competition

For those where a revolver can be used, save two, the 627-5 would shine. Those two are PPC and IDPA. PPC only shoots six-shot strings, so the extra shots wouldn't help. In fact, they'd be a hindrance, for you'd have to load a moon clip with only six rounds and be sure you indexed them properly to fire six shots. And IDPA only allows six-shot revolvers. USPSA/IPSC allows extra-shot revolvers, but you can only fire six shots between each reload. So, load a full moon clip (to make it easy and not worry about indexing) and shoot six and eject. Or, shoot your 627-5 in Limited 10 Division. Yes, you're giving up a couple of shots to those pistol shooters with 10-shot guns, but you aren't giving them up to all pistol shooters. There will still be shooters in Limited 10 shooting 1911 pistols with seven- or eight-shot magazines. With them, you are on parity or one shot behind. It would be very good practice (and satisfying indeed) to shoot a wheelgun and beat some pistol shooters.

One arena where the 627-5 can shine is in bowling pins. The Five-Pin event is one where the .357 Magnum has plenty of power to broom pins off. And in the Five-Pin Event there is traditionally a capacity limit: eight rounds. The as-made 627-5 will meet any Stock gun rules, so you are set. With an out-of-the-box 627-5 you have as many rounds as anyone on the line, you have enough power (with handloads or Remington 180 JHP hunting loads) and another advantage: the New York Reload. You're probably wondering why I recommend the Remington 180-grain factory load, since the moon clips are floppy with Remington ammo. Because it is customary in 5-Pin to allow the New York Reload, which is to draw or snatch another loaded gun off the rail when

the first one runs dry. The second gun does not usually have to be a revolver although it is smart to be using one. Richard Davis began the rule at Second Chance for a simple reason: were he carrying a revolver for defense, he'd carry a back-up instead of spare ammo, just as many NYPD officers did. (And Chicago officers too, but it never got called a "Chicago Reload.") So if you have the 627-5 and another N frame, you're stylin' for bowling pins. Start with the 627-5 and keep your spare in a holster or on the rail, table, whatever in front of you. Take a cardboard box with an old blanket in it to the line. On the start signal, start shooting with the 627-5. If you need more than eight shots, drop the 627-5 into the box, snatch the spare and keep going. When you step to the next table, fish the 627-5 out, drag the box, reload both and get ready. More than one shooter at the old Second Chance matches shot well and won loot shooting a pair of six-shot revolvers this way. Starting with eight gives you even more of an advantage.

If you wanted to shoot in Pin Gun instead of Stock, the lack of porting might be a hindrance. However, the difference between the 627-5 and other N frame is mostly the frame. A good gunsmith could thread a bull barrel to fit it, and fix sights to the barrel. You could have a longer sight radius, ports and comps, and extra weight right up to the weight limit if you wanted, by changing barrels. (There is the little matter of the crane lockup, but as I said "a good gunsmith" can solve your problems. But you'll have to find someone who knows his stuff, like Scott Mulkerin of SDM Fabricating.)

The real reason for the 627-5, its raison d'etre, is ICORE. The International Confederation of Revolver Enthusiasts is a revolver-only endeavor. All others need not apply. All shooting strings are revolver-neutral, that is you can fire them with a six-shot revolver at no handicap. However, you can shoot faster if you can make up mistakes without reloading, and that is where the 627-5 comes in. Loaded with .38 Special ammo (there is no Major/Minor scoring) you have very little recoil, and any floppiness of the moon clips is minimized. With practice and good trigger control you can post some smoking times in ICORE with the 627-5. Of course all "advantages" depend on skill, and other people with the same gear can beat you if you don't practice. The gun itself is not going to vault you to the top of the standings. And the 627-5 is a Stock or Limited gun, so all the Open shooters will be attempting to crowd past you with their compensated and red-dot equipped revolvers.

CHAPTER 16

The 610:
The revolver for a pistol round

I f you've got a large-frame revolver tough enough to stand up to just about any cartridge, you're going to have a group of shooters asking for their favorite cartridge. In the late 1980s, the buzz was for a 10mm revolver. The 10mm was still hot in some circles. Bowling pin shooters were hot for it. The 10mm cartridge was (and still is) strong enough to sweep pins off of the tables with ease. The brass was tough as old boot leather. And in a double-action revolver it would be just the ticket. So S&W made a run of revolvers beginning in 1990. By the time they were in regular production, the bloom had gone off the 10mm rose. The .40 S&W

The left side of the 610. If you want a gun for both IPSC and IDPA, this is probably it.

The 610 has an unfluted cylinder.

was the hot new round. And many bowling pin shooters found they could forego the cost of a new gun and simply load hot ammo in their existing guns. The 610, which never even made into the catalog, was dropped after being made for two years.

What brought it back was a need for a light-recoiling gun, one that could be reloaded with full-moon clips. IDPA brought it back. Some IPSC (International Practical Shooting Confederation) shooters who had been active early in the formation of IPSC, formed the International Defensive Pistol Association. The IDPA founders had not been happy with the way IPSC evolved. Specifically, the equipment race and the development of Raceguns, with their high-capacity magazines, compensators and red-dot optics. That, and the use of high-speed competition holsters, prompted the creation of IDPA. Feeling that the IPSC had gotten too far from its martial roots, they left and formed the new group.

The new competition had four categories. The one of interest here is Stock Service Revolver. No competition-derived equipment or modifications were allowed. What was allowed were full moon clips when they came

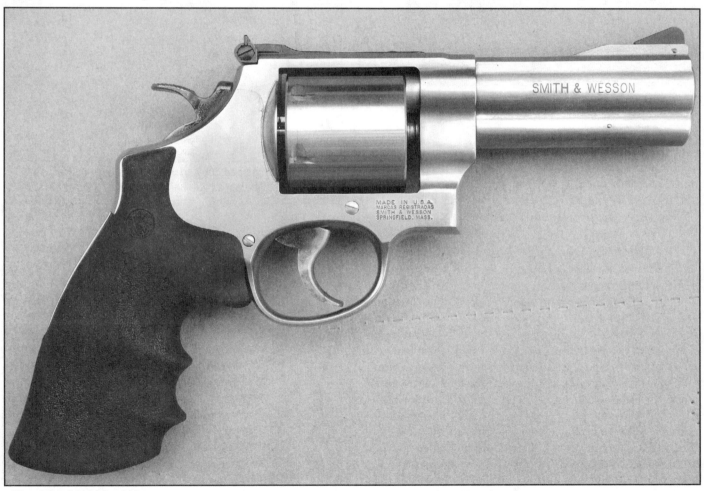
The right side of the 610.

The 610 comes with a ramped, plain black front sight.

The plain ramped sight is easy to change, since it is spring-loaded.

You can clearly see the spring tunnel for the front sight.

The model is stamped, the serial number is laser-etched, and there is no ball detent as you find on some of its bigger brothers.

that way from the factory, which lead to an inadvertent equipment race. (These things happen.) You could order up a super-custom revolver from the Performance Center and use it as a "Stock" service revolver. But you couldn't have your local gunsmith modify your existing K or L frame S&W to take "moonclips."

To keep shooters using .38 special revolvers in the sport, the threshold Power Factor for SSR was set at 125. That is, the bullet weight in grains times the velocity in feet per second, divided by 1000. So a 125-grain bullet going 1,000 fps is right on the threshold. (You have to be at or above the threshold to post a score. Under it, your score is zero.) The decision created a slight problem. A .38 Special revolver had the right power, weight, balance and accuracy. But reloading it was slow even with speed-loaders. (The scoring in IDPA is time. Your time to finish the stage, plus any penalties you garnered. Faster was better.) A 25-2 or 625-2 was a lot faster to reload, but the .45 ACP recoil cost time. It could be loaded down, but not easily and the resulting load was almost always dirty in burning. The solution? Find an old (at that time out of production) 610, and load its moon clips with .40

The chamber throats measure a nice, consistent .401″.

The cylinder retention stud is shaped to keep the cylinder in place with or without moon clips.

Smooth, medium-width trigger.

The rear sight is a white outline version.

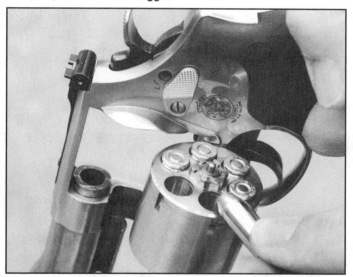

You can load and fire without moon clips. (Not recommended, however.)

The 610 study

S&W ammo instead of 10mm. The 40 could be loaded very soft without running dirty, it reloaded almost as fast as the 25-2 and 625-2 did, and accuracy was plenty good enough. The other "advantage" of the 610 (mostly illusory) was that the shorter 40 brass was faster and more likely to completely eject from the gun. I've been shooting a 25-2 for many years in IPSC and bowling pin shooting and I've never had the empties "short-stroke" on ejection. Indeed, I've had full moon clips bounce off my person on ejection, I've gotten them out of the gun so vigorously. However, some shooters feel the need for any advantage, real or imagined. So they shoot 40s in their 10mm wheelgun.

It didn't take long for S&W to hear the demand, and they brought the 610 back after a six-year hiatus.

The 610 is built on the N frame, and from its model designation it would seem obvious that it is a stainless revolver. The sights are the new models, with the front sight held in place via a spring-loaded plunger. If you want to change the sight, push the sight rearward against the (stiff) spring and then lift it out. Installing the new is as simple, press the base of the new back against the spring until you can fit it under the retaining pin. The rear comes as a white-outline blade. If you wanted to hunt with the 10mm you could remove the rear sight and bolt a scope base in the drilled and tapped base holes hidden under the rear sight assembly.

On the 1990 to 1992 production guns the firing pin was fixed to the hammer, as all earlier N frame guns had been made. The 1998 and later guns have a float-

The big 610 ready to go.

In full recoil, 10mm ammo comes back pretty hard.

If you don't use moon clips, extraction becomes something of a problem.

ing firing pin in the frame and a flat-faced hammer. And to meet the needs of IDPA shooters, the 4-inch barrel became standard. (The IDPA rules used to allow 5-inch guns, but it was changed to 4 inches because the shorter length was "more concealable.")

On the left side the barrel is marked "10MM" and the frame has the small S&W logo, cylinder release latch and trigger lock.

On the right side the barrel has "Smith & Wesson" and the frame has the standard four-line "made in USA" rollmark. The grips are rubber/synthetics from Hogue with the S&W logo molded into them, and the frame of the 610 is the round-butt design. Some years ago S&W decided that while round-butt frames could have square butt grips installed and work just fine, the reverse was not true. To cut down on the number of frames they'd need to make and inventory, they decided to make just round-butt frames. They didn't stick with that, but the current-production 610 got the round-butt treatment, probably because it was intended for IDPA unlike the earlier 610 which was intended for IPSC and bowling pins.

The cylinder is unfluted, and the cylinder retention stud is machined as an integral part of the frame.

The cylinder is long enough to hold 10mm ammo in the moon clips. The clips themselves bear some study. When the Model 1917 was introduced, the "half-moon" clip was the norm. Each held three rounds, and reloading (or even loading) the .45 ACP round was made possible. Fast forward to the early 1980s. Bowling pin shooting is really starting to catch on. IPSC has not yet driven (via high round-count stages and super-fast shooting times) revolvers from the field. Those in the know want something faster to reload their S&W 25-2 revolvers. Back in the 1970s someone got the bright idea of welding a pair of half moons together to create a full moon clip. The loss rate was high, but luckily half moon clips seemed to exist in the billions. (Wartime production for two wars demands billion-unit production lots) When word got out, it wasn't long before we started seeing real moon clips, not weld jobs, courtesy of Steve Crawford at Ranch Products. Circa 1975, the setup was complete, just waiting for the right matches. But the original style, half or

The 610 shoots nicely even with full-power 10mm ammo. Here is a six-shot group with Black Hills 155-grain JHP at 20 yards from a rest.

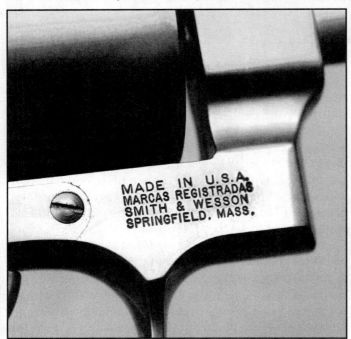

The S&W four-line address.

After a day of shooting full-power 10mm ammo all it needs is a little scrubbing.

full, clips had one problem: variances in case dimension sometimes made it tough or impossible to seat or unseat the brass.

The 610 moon clips solve that problem by using a slot between each cartridge opening. Each leg of the clip that holds a cartridge can flex to accept a case. Of course, dropping a loaded moon clip can result in lost rounds, but dropping ammo is not a good way to improve your score.

Shooting and carry of the 610

As you can imagine, shooting the 610 with 10mm ammo is not unlike shooting any other magnum. That's what the 10mm is. The original specifications called for a 200-grain bullet going 1,200 fps, the old Norma load. And it did that, at least out of a 5-inch 1911 barrel. At a power factor of 240, no one is going to be using any of the old stuff in an IDPA match. Even current ammo is hot by IDPA standards, with power factors at or slightly above 200. Recoil is sharp and stout, and you would not expect it to be any less. For someone who is fond of the 10mm the 610 would make a very good backwoods or bear gun. By reloading it to the gills (the old Norma load is no more, nor does anyone load up to it any more) you can boost a 200-grain bullet to nearly 1,200 fps out of the 4-inch barrel. You could even load hard-cast 220-grain bullets to 1,100 fps, for even more penetration. If you feel a handgun is sufficient for four-legged defense in the backwoods, then the 610 loaded with a hot load such as this will probably suffice.

In IDPA SSR competition, you want to use 40 S&W ammo in your moon clips. For a 180-grain bullet in a .40 S&W case to exceed the IDPA threshold, you only need push it to 700 fps. The 180/700 combination in such a big gun creates so little recoil that anyone who can get their hands around the grip can shoot it without fear of recoil. And should you want to shoot the 610 in USPSA/IPSC competition in Revolver Division, the threshold for Major is only 165. So you need only get your 180-grain bullet over 916 fps and you're there. In my squad of revolver shooters at the 2003 USPSA Factory Gun Nationals, a third were shooting the 610 they usually use in IDPA competition. You can produce those ballistics out of either .40 S&W or 10mm cases, as it is easily within the reach of loads for either.

The chambers are cut for 10mm cases, and in a pinch you can use 10mm ammo without the moon clips. The rounds will seat on their mouths (provided you have not crimped them too tightly) and will stay put for the firing pin to strike the primer. However, ejection will be troublesome, as the ejector star has nothing to grab on to. If you need six shots in a pinch, then you can go ahead. But be aware that getting the empties out will be work. Depending on the pressure of the load, it can be anywhere from simply turning the gun over and shaking the empties out, (light loads that burn clean) to poking a stick, pencil, pen or other object in the front of the cylinder and pressing the cases out. (Hot loads will take more force.) As I cannot endorse putting your hand out in front of the cylinder, I have to tell you to either never lose the moon clips, or consider using the 610 without them as an extreme emergency measure only.

At either load, the 610 would last so long that you would not wear it out shooting it.

As for drills, the Bill Drill was a snap. I could easily drop six shots into the A zone with the 610 and IPSC loads. It was even easier with IDPA loads in .40 S&W cases. The El Presidente was a bit tougher, as it has always been with a revolver. The reload is critical on this drill. The actual shooting is easy, and should only take about six seconds at most. So that leaves four or less seconds for the reload. In the Cirillo Index the 610 passed, as the big cylinder give plenty to index off of.

CHAPTER 17

.41 Magnum:
Better than you think

The .41 Magnum is the best cartridge that never had a chance, and thus is worth some time and space. Introduced in 1964, the .41 Magnum was to be the "handgun for everyman." The idea was to offer the ammunition in two flavors: a 210-grain lead flatpoint at 950 feet per second, and a 210-grain jacketed hollowpoint at 1,280 feet per second. And S&W would make revolvers for it, the gloss blue adjustable-sight

The Model 58 was only ever offered in a 4-inch length, for police duty carry.

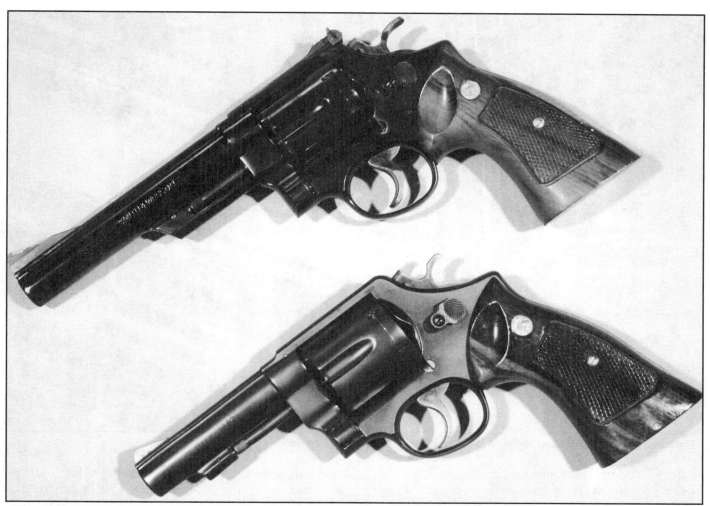

The .41 Magnum came in two models: the adjustable-sight Model 57 and the fixed-sight Model 58.

The Model 57 came in 4, 6 and 8 inches; the new M-657 comes in 7.5 inches.

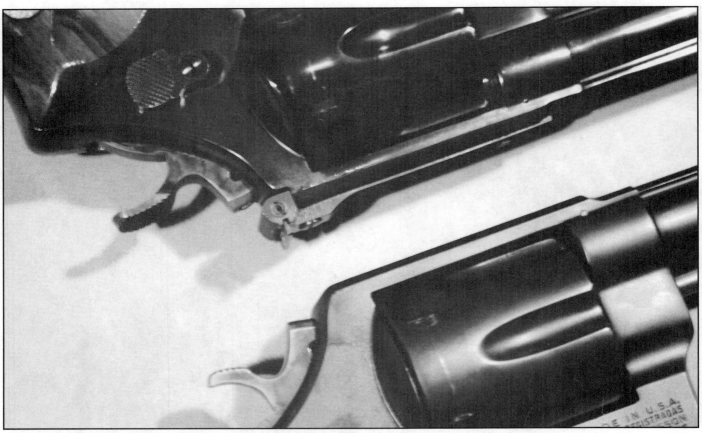

The frames of the .41s differed slightly to accommodate the sights used by each.

Model 57, and the matte finished, fixed-sight Model 58. The end result was pretty much as you'd expect. No one wanted the fixed-sight gun except for a few police departments and big-bore carry revolver fanatics. And everyone got the ammunition confused. The Detroit Police Department allowed officers to carry whatever they could qualify with until the whole department mandated Glock 40 pistols. Every spring with the start of the annual qualification cycle we'd get officers showing up looking for ammo to shoot. The smart ones made sure they'd gotten the lead load, for the jacketed wasn't allowed. (Can't have hollowpoints, you know.) Even if they could hide the jacketed ammo from the range officer, trying to qualify with 210s going 1,280 was not easy.

There are a number of things that could have made a difference. By 1964 the revolver world was already divided between the .357 Magnum camp and the .44 Magnum camp. The .41 was too big, It would only fit in the N frame, so the .357 camp wasn't interested. They had the perfect gun in the Model 19, the K frame .357. And the shooters who could get their hands around the N frame already had the .44, so why use a "lesser" caliber? Had Remington and S&W come out with a .40 or .41 just before the .44 Magnum, things might have been different. The .40/.41 could have gotten a foothold, and

been competing directly with the .44, instead of coming along nine years later once the .44 was well-established.

If S&W had made the guns, and Remington the ammo, as .41 Magnum and .41 Special the Magnum would have been the 210-grain JHP at 1,280 fps load, and the Special the 210-grain lead at 950. It would have saved confusion between the loads, and placed the .41 fully in the pattern shooters were accustomed to with the .38/.357 and the .44S/.44M. I don't know that the .41 Special could have been fit into the K frame, but it would have been a perfect fit when the later L frame was introduced. A five-shot .41 Special L frame carry gun would have sold well in the Detroit area if offered as an option in 1980 when the L frame came out. The WonderNine Wars had only gotten started, and there were many revolver holdouts.

One curious boost to the sales of .41 Magnum guns came in 1971 with the movie "Dirty Harry." The now-famous scene "This is the most powerful handgun in the world…." caused shooters to line up at gun stores to get their hands on a .44 Mangum. S&W couldn't keep up. Some stores formed waiting lists, or took deposits. Others charged full retail, or even retail-plus for their Model 29s. Yet there were still .41 Magnums to be found. My brother Mike and his high school football buddy had to

The standard bullet weight in the .41 is 210 grains. You can load it mild or wild.

have Magnums. Larry held out for a real .44, paid (as I recall) $450 for his, and waited months. Mike found a dealer upstate who had a .41 in the counter at the standard price of $289. By the time Larry had his .44, Mike had three .41's (4-, 6- and 8-inch barrels) and practice shooting them. Many other shooters went the .41 route as a substitute, and found they had a good gun, not just a "substitute magnum."

The accuracy is superb. Mike and I used to amuse ourselves on summer vacations by plinking at empty coffee cans with his .41 Magnums. At 100 yards. Offhand. Dad told us to knock it off whenever a club member came to the range to sight in a deer rifle. He didn't want us shooting better at 100 yards with a handgun than some hunters did with their rifles at 50 yards sighting in.

The brass is tough, standing up to many magnum loadings, and relatively easy to find. Back then you could scour gun shops and not find much or any .44 Special. But there was always .41 Magnum ammo on hand. The bullets were quickly in the catalogs of all reloading component makers, and all casters offered at least one bullet weight or style for .41 Magnum. You used the same primers and powders that you'd use for a .44 Magnum, and loading data was everywhere. Back before silhouette shooting became more specialized, and we used off-the shelf guns and ammo, the .41 had a small advantage: the trajectory was flatter. If you zeroed a .44 load of a 240-grain bullet at 1,250 fps at fifty yards, it would drop 5.8 inches, while the .41 (210 grains at 1,350) would drop 5.1 inches. No big deal. But at 200 yards, where the Rams stood, the drop for the .44 was 41 inches, the .41 dropped only 37. Today shooters don't worry about such small differences, but back then it could make the difference between winning and not winning.

The currently S&W offers only one gun in the .41 Magnum: the 657, a stainless 7-1/2-inch full-lugged barrel N frame with adjustable sights. But you can find many Model 57 blued revolvers in 4-, 6- and 8-inch barrel lengths, and some 4-inch Model 58s and 4-, 6- and 8-inch 657s of earlier production. What you have is a powerful, accurate heavy-duty revolver that lives up to the S&W reputation. Don't let anyone convince you otherwise.

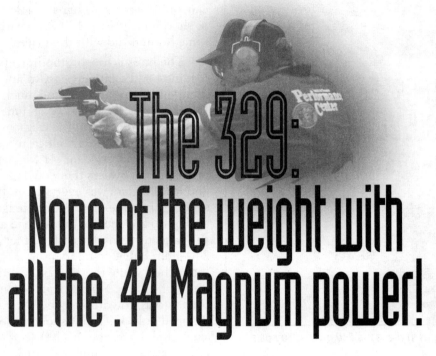

CHAPTER 18

The 329:
None of the weight with all the .44 Magnum power!

he 329 arrived in the last batch of firearms shipped to me by Smith & Wesson. I had thought the 500 was hard-kicking, and the 340PD and other Airweight guns had been hard on me. The 329, chambered for the .44 Magnum, is tops of the list of "easy to carry but hard to shoot" guns we all want. Everyone who ever carried a concealed weapon has at one time or another wished they were packing something lighter in weight. But not necessarily something less effective. In the old days we'd swap a government

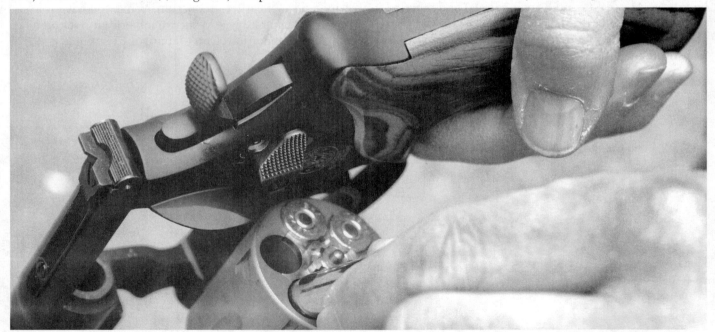

The 329 looks and works like any other N-frame .44 since S&W dropped the Triple Lock Model of the .44 Hand Ejector; it is just a lot lighter.

model for a Lightweight Commander, and enjoy a bit of reduction in size and weight without losing power. Or we'd swap a Model 19 snubbie for a Model 12, and get a weight reduction at the loss of .357 Magnum power.

But not until Scandium and Titanium could we lose weight without losing power. And the result is something we don't always want to shoot. At 27 ounces empty, neither I nor any of my test-fire crew was under any illusions as to how hard it would kick.

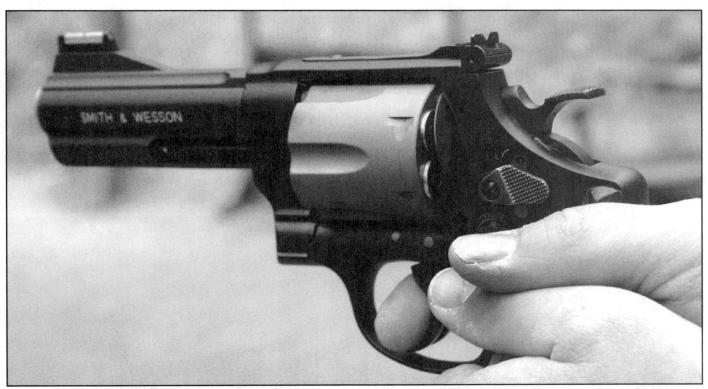

The 329 is a compact, lightweight, powerful sidearm for when you need it. If only it didn't kill on one end and cripple on the other!

I'll admit this is not a good group. It is, however, a double-action group with full-power .44 Magnum ammunition.

The 329 is an N frame made of Scandium alloy. The Airlite PD sitting on my desk as I type this is blued, with a Titanium cylinder. As is visible from the front, the barrel is the new Airlite "tube in a shroud" that offers light weight and increased accuracy. While at first glance it appears like the old S&W barrel contour, it is more sculpted and has 16 flats, flutes and lines on it besides the ribbed sight line on the top. The front sight is a HiViz fiber optic, this one in orange. Pinned in place, the sight can be replaced if you damage it, desire a different color, or want a different sight. To match the dot on the sight, the rear blade is a "V" notch instead of the rectangular one. The rear sight is adjustable. Underneath the rear sight the frame is drilled and tapped for a scope mount. Why you'd want to double or more than double the weight of the revolver by mounting a scope on it, I don't know. (Damp-

en the harsh recoil?) But S&W gives you the option. The barrel is marked ".44 Magnum" on the right, and "Smith & Wesson" on the left. Back on the frame, the right side has the S&W logo with the atomic symbol, and "Airlite PD" just under the cylinder on the front of the sideplate. Forward of that is the new two-line S&W marking. The left side the frame has the S&W logo, the cylinder catch and the action lock. You can see the action pivot pins in the side of the frame, left in their titanium color. (Maybe the finish that goes on the Scandium aluminum alloy doesn't "take" on Titanium. Maybe nothing takes on Titanium.) The hammer and trigger are the wide style. While the hammer is serrated, the trigger is left smooth. I much prefer smooth triggers for fast double-action work, as they are less likely to abrade your trigger finger. (The purpose of this gun is fast double action. Make no mistake.)

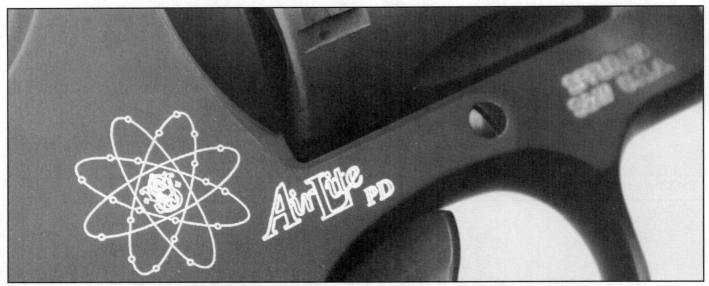

The right side of the frame, with the atomic logo and AirLite on the sideplate, and the two-line address forward of that.

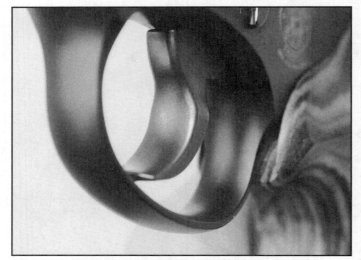

The trigger is smooth and medium-wide, the best combination.

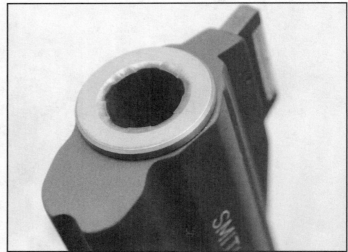

The new barrel is a tube screwed down through a shroud for the sight. It's an S&W design.

The Titanium cylinder has a stainless steel extractor. The axle hole for the centerpin is bushed with a steel bushing, to support the rod against the recoil forces of the .44 Magnum. The firing pin bushing is also steel, set in the Scandium alloy frame. The firing pin is spring-loaded and captured in the frame, activated by the flat front of the hammer. In front of the cylinder, above the forcing cone, the frame has a steel liner pressed into place. The hot .44 magnum gases would otherwise flame-cut the Scandium alloy. To prevent that, the steel liner takes the jet of gas. Considering the recoil of this gun, I imagine you'd give up before it would. The ejector rod is locked in by the standard S&W plunger in the barrel shroud. The grips are good-looking finger grooved wood, fitted to the round butt of the 329 grip straps.

The cylinder holds six rounds of .44 Russian, .44 Special or .44 Magnum.

The 329 comes in the standard S&W blue box, with a Hogue rubber grip to replace the wood one if you wish, cable lock, owner's manual and fired case. George Grasso collected the case in mine on April 19, 2004. If George also fired it and a rack of other 329s to collect the sample cases, my hat is off to him. I have even more admiration for him if he figured out a way to get others to do the shooting so he could simply put cases into envelopes.

Purpose

The purpose of the 329 is simple: to provide the greatest amount of power in the lightest possible package for emergency use. You can use less power if you want to. But for those who need the most, the 329 delivers. If you are looking for a bear gun while flyfishing in Alaska, you may not want, or cannot pack, the weight

The steel insert protects the frame from the flame-cutting from the cylinder gap.

The six-shot Titanium cylinder looks like any other until you pick it up.

The HiViz fiber optic sight. If you don't like it, you can replace it with another.

The rear sight is a "V" as an express sight, not a notch like the patridge design.

of a full-sized .44 Magnum or larger gun. Even a 4-inch Model 629 may be too much weight, depending on how you get to your flyfishing river. Something even bigger, say in .480 Ruger, .475 Linebaugh, or the 500, may just be more weight than you can pack or want to have. The person who wants a big defensive revolver but not the weight can load it with relatively mild .44 special ammo and have the lightest gun holding that kind of power. By some measures the old .44 Special lead round nose ammo might not be much, but consider this: the .45 ACP is considered a real manstopper. It launches a 230-grain bullet at just about 800 feet per second. The .44 Special hikes a 246-grain round nosed bullet out in the low 700s. Just how much difference can there be? A Cor-bon load of a 200-grain jacketed hollowpoint turns the .44 Special into a modern fight stopper.

Carry and shooting.

Carry is simple: Can you say "hardly noticed it?" With a holster that is reasonably comfortable and keeps the gun tight to the body, the 329 rides like it isn't there. Shooting is another matter. My test crew is composed of experienced shooters. A few are relatively new, but even they've put a bunch of ammo downrange. The average shooting experience of my crew is probably in excess of 20 years of high-volume shooting. Some are experienced competition shooters who put tens of thousands of rounds of ammo downrange annually. When I had the Model 500 to the range they lined up to shoot it. At the same session they were less happy about shooting the 386P with its light weight and seven shots of .357 Magnum. The 340PD, the J frame Airweight .357 gave some of them pause. The 329 was not the popular gun. Oh, they handled it, hefted it, dry-fired it and talked about it. But none volunteered to shoot a second cylinder of full-power .44 Magnum ammo. Most did not finish their first

cylinder of 240-grain Black Hills .44 Magnum ammo. And no one shot it with the 300-grain ammo.

The typical reaction to shooting a few rounds of the full-power ammo was for the shooter to open the cylinder and holding the open gun shake their shooting hand. They'd then hand it to the next shooter and go on to something less stout in recoil. Several shot multiple cylinders of .44 Special ammo, which with Cowboy ammo is kind of nice. With standard .44 Special ammo it is somewhat stout. But even they moved on to the other guns as soon as they could. Several of my test shooters shot the 500, commented "That's not so bad" and asked if I had any more ammo along to shot. None did so with the 329.

My first session was typical: I was shooting a bunch of the guns with Rob Gaffney, a longtime club member and multiple test crew volunteer. Rob has shot a lot, and back during testing the Gun Digest Book of the 1911 he took such a shine to the Springfield .45 Super that he had to have it. Rob shoots big bores, and is not afraid of recoil. After three rounds of 240-grain full power ammo he opened the cylinder and handed me the 329. I found I could fire two rounds and had to quit. Later I had rested, taken a bunch of aspirin, and wore some gloves, and I could fire a full cylinder. It still was not fun, not like many of the guns I've tested for this book.

After shooting a cylinder of the standard .44 magnum ammo, I tried one round of 300-grain ammo. It brought tears to my eyes. Black Hills could ship me all the free 300-grain ammo they want. S&W could give me this gun for free. I'm still not going to shoot a second round of the 300s through it. If anyone shoots this gun, and comments truthfully that "It isn't so bad" they are not only a tougher man than I am, they are likely a tougher man than anyone you know or will ever meet. In talking with Mag-na-Port I found that not only can they easily port this or any other Airweight gun through the shroud

The left side of the barrel reads "Smith & Wesson."

On the right side, the promise of pain to come:".44 Magnum."

The original Model 29 weighs in at 43 ounces, and it still hurts with some loads.

and barrel tube, they are seeing many S&W Airlite guns showing up. After shooting this one, I can understand why. With a set of ports, or better yet dual sets of ports, you can take enough of the edge off the recoil that shooting it doesn't become an exercise in masochism.

That said, would I own one of these guns if I had the need? You bet. As ferocious as the recoil is, it is worlds better than bear teeth on your anatomy. With its super-light weight you can pack this gun and a couple of speed-loaders of ammo and never notice the weight. And with ports, it might actually be fun to shoot. As this gun is a loaner from the factory I can't go and get it ported just to find out, but my experience with Mag-na-Porting has been such that I'd send the gun off right away were it mine.

Considering the harsh recoil, any shooter who simply completed an El Presidente would be an exemplary competitor. If he were to do it with 240 factory ammo in par, he would never have to buy a drink again. Such toughness would be the stuff of legend. I did not shoot drills. Well, not with factory ammo. I shot a few El Presidente's with the .44 Special Cowboy ammo Black Hills sent, and with the mild ammo shooting par was not a problem.

Loading for performance

Were I in the situation of packing the 329 for back-country wear and bear defense, I would not use factory ammo. The standard 240-grain ammo is loaded to deliver as much velocity as possible. You do not need the velocity for penetration. In an extreme emergency such as a bear about to chomp on you, you want excessive penetration. Expansion will not save you. Indeed, it may well be that nothing is going to save you, but if anything will it will be penetration. For that, you need bullet design, a hard-cast flat-point or truncated cone bullet to be exact. I'd load an Oregon Trails 240 TC or a Cast Performance 255-grain wide flat-point and only boot it to 900 to 1,000 fps. Yes, it would be less than it could be. But I could fire all six as aimed shots quickly when I needed to. Were I to load a more robust load, say a 300-grain bullet to 1,000 or 1,100 fps, I'd get off one shot. While I was recovering the bear would be on me and I might get the second off.

Bullet penetration is not the intuitive thing you'd expect. What experimenters have found is that as you add velocity you gain penetration, but only until the increased velocity begins to cause bullet deformation in tissue. Then penetration slows or even decreases. A hard or very hard, cast bullet at a moderate velocity will often penetrate to a greater depth than a jacketed softpoint, especially if the softpoint has been pushed hard enough to expand. The increased frontal area of the softpoint acts to slow the bullet. Does the moderate-velocity hard bullet do less tissue damage? Yes, but. Extensive damage that does not reach to vital organs is not useful when you are attempting to stay in one piece. Penetration that punches holes through organs, and breaks bones is far better.

I'd rather have a bunch more bullets on target, even if they didn't penetrate to the theoretical maximum, than one that does. Even at that, the 255 at 900 to 1,000 fps is going to penetrate to an amazing degree. The bullet is designed so as to penetrate, and the velocity is not so great as to cause bullet deformation or upset, both detrimental to penetration. And I can stand to shoot it; especially if the gun is Mag-na-Ported. It would serve for bear country. (In as much as any handgun "serves" in bear country. Sometimes you just need a rifle.)

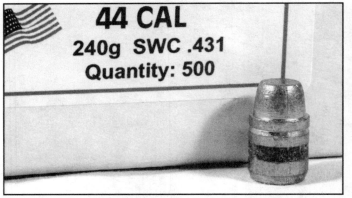

Or, if you are a traditionalist, you can get penetration with a 240-grain bullet from Oregon Trail at 950 to 1,000 fps.

For penetration without crippling recoil, try a Cast Performance 255-grain bullet at 950 to 1,000 fps.

My postal scales says this 329 weighs a mere 25.4 ounces empty. Oh, this is going to hurt...

CHAPTER 19

The 629-6:
It's designed for hunting

The "dash six" is a hunting gun. While the basic 629 can be had in a compact (relatively speaking) size for concealed carry, hiking or compact duty, the hunting gun is full-sized for bagging your deer, elk or bear. The Performance Center turns this one out ready for hunting.

The 629-6 is built on the N frame, in stainless. The barrel is a special contour, 8 inches long with an integral muzzle brake. Personally I'd prefer a brake that was less sleek and contoured, and one that was a bit more bulky and worked more. But I'm definitely a "works over looks" kind of shooter. The barrel has a rib on top, and the underlug is sculpted from the ejector rod housing to the muzzle. On top is the scope mounting base cover with

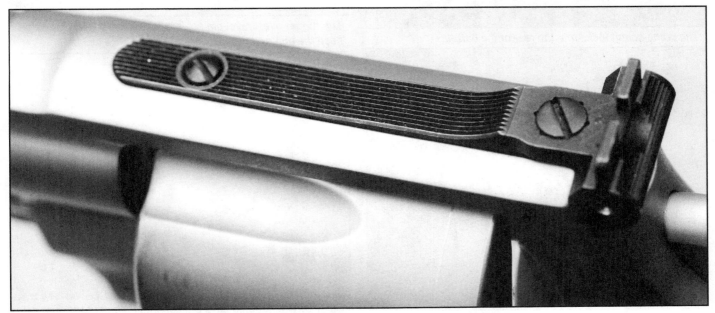

The new model rear sight for S&W covers the scope base holes drilled and tapped in the frame.

Part of the "looks" treatment of the PC 629 is the open-port ejector rod housing.

its cap screws. The front sight and rear are taller than usual, both to clear the scope base cover and to allow the hunter more sight for long-range shooting. While the rear is a tall S&W blade, the front is a dovetail design with red paint on it. From the look of it I'd say S&W is simply buying the sights from Millett rather than fabricate sights themselves. (Nothing wrong with that, Millett makes good sights, and many firearms manufacturers buy small parts rather than tool up to make them.) The frame is normal N frame, with the usual markings, action lock and cylinder latch. It has the Performance Center log on the left, and the S&W logo on the right side of the frame. The barrel is marked ".44 Magnum" on the left and "Performance Center" on the right side.

The tuning for hunting is obvious, even beyond the cosmetics of the barrel shape and sights. The crane has a spring-loaded ball set into its front face, and the rear of the ejector rod housing has a large notch in it that corresponds to the ball. While not the mechanical marvel of the

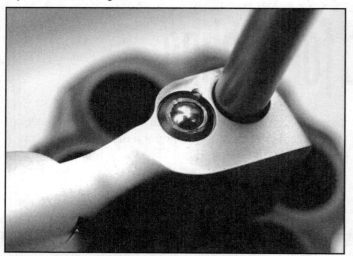
The crane detent locks into the rear of the barrel.

The trigger over-travel pin set into the rear of the trigger helps keep the gun on target.

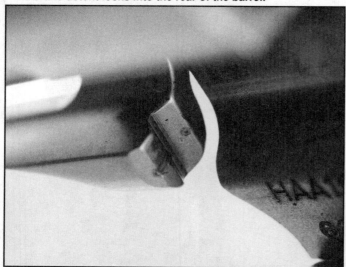
The detent notch in the barrel shroud makes for a firm lock-up.

Older S&W magnums have big square hammer spurs. The new style is egg-shaped.

old Triple Lock, the detent ball does offer extra locking strength to the 629-6 under the recoil of heavy hunting loads. The trigger also gives the intent away. On the rear of the trigger is an overtravel pin. For the finest accuracy you do not want the trigger moving once it has released the hammer. The overtravel pin limits the amount the trigger can move once it has released the hammer.

The hammer spur is egg-shaped and checkered, and offers plenty of purchase for cocking the hammer for single-action shooting. One curious thing I found was that even though the barrel is machined to take a scope mount, the frame is still drilled and tapped, also for a scope mount. You can use either (but not both) to mount a scope.

Unlike the other Performance Center guns, the 629-6 did not come in a hard case. It came in a soft case with the Performance Center logo embroidered on it. Inside were the usual items, the cable, lock, fired case, owner's manual, and a spare grip. The fired case was collected by George Grasso, and from the number of guns that

arrived with packets with his name, he's a busy guy. The wooden grips that came on it could be swapped for the Hogue rubber grips included. While I found the wood grips plenty comfortable, the rubber ones could come in quite handy were you to be working up a stout hunting load. Should you be looking to load bullets of around 300 grains as hunting loads, you'd definitely want to be shooting the gun with the Hogue grips in place. Also in the case was a brochure for the Performance Center, and nestled in the midst of the paperwork, the scope mount. The mount simply replaces the cover, and nestles over the oval shoulder machined on the top of the barrel, out of the rib. With a tight fit between the shoulder and corresponding recess in the scope mount, the mount isn't going to move under recoil. The mount is machined to accept Weaver-type rings. Simply remove the cover, bolt on the base, and then secure your scope in your choice of rings, using two or three of the cross-slots with your two or three rings. (You might not be able to find a scope that all three will fit.)

The rear sight is taller than standard.

The model is stamped, the serial number laser-etched.

The 629 before firing.

Carrying and shooting

The 629-6 is a hunting gun, so thinking in terms of a concealed carry or duty holster is silly. You want a sturdy belt or chest holster that provides protection while not making the draw too slow. As for shooting, it was fun. Unlike the smaller calibers, the .44 Magnum, when a round hits the gong, makes quite a noticeable sound. Where the .22 is barely perceptible, and the .38 or .357 make a little "snap", the .44 Magnum slaps the gong. There is no question, if you hit it you know it. The recoil was not too bad compared to some standard 629 and 29 revolvers we had along. Whether the reduced recoil was due to the comp, the extra weight, or some of both, I don't know. As I mentioned, I would prefer something more efficient (the Power Port on the 686 comes to mind) rather than the little slots the 629 came with. The

The 629 in recoil is stout, but there are bigger guns.

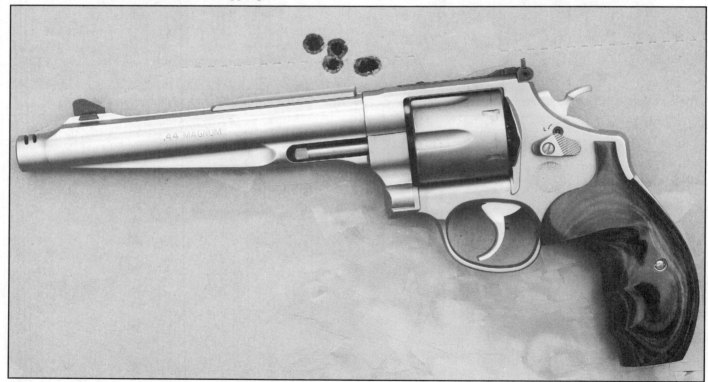

Not a bad 25-yard group in the rest, with 240-grain Hornady XTP hunting ammo (1,350 fps).

small transverse slot design is one IPSC shooters tried, and abandoned in about 1986. But the trick would be to make something more efficient that was as good looking as this unit is.

As for accuracy, the 629-6 as it in spades. After hammering the gong I sat down to shoot some groups for the camera. (Yes, I should have done it in the reverse order. What can I say? I was having fun.) I promptly

The Performance Center made it, and they are happy to put their name on it.

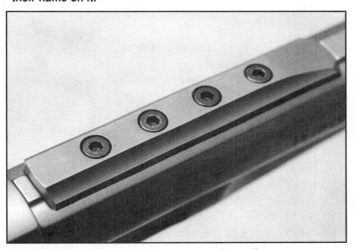
The barrel-mount scope-base cover works well.

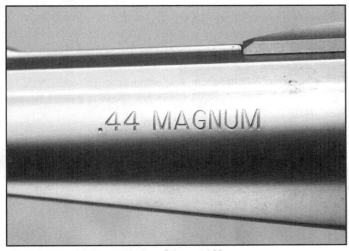
In case you had any doubts, it is a .44 Magnum

shot an inch and a half group at 25 yards with iron sights and Black Hills 240-grain jacketed hollow-point ammo. Objective attained.

The question becomes what do you feed the beast? Considering the accuracy it delivers, you feed it bullets appropriate to the game you are hunting. Were I going out for Michigan whitetail I'd feed it the most accurate factory 240-grain ammo, as demonstrated from the Ransom rest. Any factory 240 is going to penetrate fully, and most likely exit the far side, of any deer in Michigan. Using factory ammo makes the job simple rather than trying to develop the best handload for the job. Deer are simple. Elk, on the other hand, would call for work. First, I'd try Hornady 240 XTP factory ammo. If that load delivered the kind of accuracy I'd desire, less than 3 inches at 50 yards, then I'd go with it. If not, then I'd try loading Hornady 240 XTP bullets myself. If I couldn't get them to group (that would be a rare occasion!) then I'd default to deep-penetrators: Oregon Trail 240 semi-wad-cutters, 300-grain flat points, or Cast Performance bullets, their 255 Wide Flat Nose bullet. Whichever one of

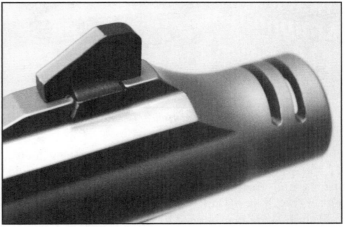
While we might prefer a more-efficient comp, this one gets the job done.

The Performance Center logo on the frame identifies this model.

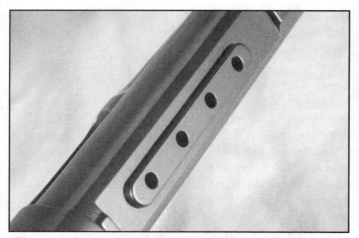
The scope-base cover off, revealing the shoulder inset.

For deep penetration, a hard-cast bullet like the Cast Performance works well.

If you want weight, you can get it, either jacketed or hard-cast lead.

To resist recoil, the machined lug fits in the scope base.

those bullets shot the smallest group at hunting velocity (1,350 fps for the 240 and 255, 1,150 for the 300) would get the nod. As for bear, there would be an easier choice: either the Oregon Trail 300, or the Cast Performance 300 grain Wide Flat Nose. The one of those that shot the best would be the bullet I'd go with.

Where expansion on a whitetail can be desirable, on the bigger (and in the case of the bear, more dangerous) game you need penetration. More is better and too much is not enough. If you can have your bullets exit the far side of a big critter like an elk or bear, with velocity to spare, you're making progress. Handguns do not have anything like the power that even regular rifles like the .30-06 deliver, and you must make clean wound channels with two holes. Having both an entrance and an exit wound allows for more blood out and air in.

The question some might have is, "Is the 629-6 up to the task of shooting 300-grain bullets?" You will not be able to get the kind of velocity you can generate from a Ruger Super Blackhawk, Redhawk or Super Redhawk. They are larger guns. I'm not sure what would give out first, the gun or the shooter, but it wouldn't be pretty trying to generate 1,300 fps from a 300-grain bullet in a 629. You'd probably quit before you threw the 629 out of time, and neither you nor the gun would like it. After all, in the 629 you're talking about a revolver that weighs 47 ounces, to the Ruger's 54. Those 7 ounces may not seem like much, but when you're getting up to the 400 power factor (a stout pin load is 200!) every ounce matters. Take it easy on yourself and your 629-6, and leave chasing the last few fps to the guys who like recoil. A hard-cast 300-grain bullet at 1,150 fps is going to penetrate very well. Then it is up to you to place that bullet correctly on your quarry.

CHAPTER 20

The 25-2:
The royal family of .45 ACP wheelguns

The 25-2 is the penultimate .45 ACP revolver, the refinement of the Model 1917 that got started during the War to End All Wars. After S&W made the military production, they didn't need to make many for quite some time. The nearly 165,000 revolvers were surplus to the U.S. Army. Along with the several million Model 1917 Enfield rifles produced, they were unceremoniously stuffed into storage. The plant made special order guns, some large orders of model peculiarities, and a relatively large Brazilian contract of 25,000 M-1917 revolvers just before WWII. Except for some individual special-order revolvers that might have been made with adjustable sights, the vast majority of the .45 ACP revolvers were fixed-sight guns.

After WWII handgun competition picked up where it had left off. Not to disparage the efforts of early gunsmiths, but early Bull's-eye pistols weren't all that good. A top-quality revolver from S&W was not only more reliable and accurate, and would have a vastly better trigger, but would cost less than a 1911 pistol and the gunsmithing needed to make it even close to competitive. Bull's-eye shooters shot the 1911 because it was required in the Service Pistol portion of the matches, but not all shot that. Many used it only there, and a matched set of revolvers for everything else. Just as the K-22 was introduced to match the K-38, the target shooters of the time wanted a .45 target revolver. Which they got, in

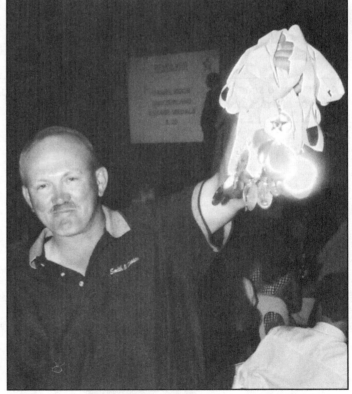

If you want to win in revolver competition, you'll eventually have to lock horns with Jerry Miculek. Here he shows his haul of stages win medals at World Shoot XIII in South Africa.

The regular .45 ACP rim and the .45 Auto Rim case, designed to eliminate the need for moon clips.

The Model of 1955 guns have large spurs for fast thumb-cocking.

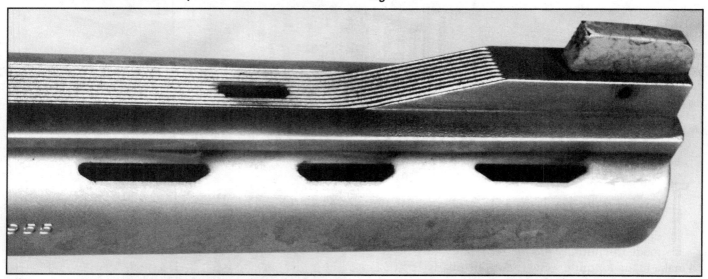

If you want to shoot fast on pins, ports to control recoil help. Of course, you'll be in Open when shooting this gun, but you still won't be at a disadvantage.

Also, the 1955 has a large, serrated trigger.

the form of the Target Model of 1950. It had a skinny barrel, adjustable sights, and a square front sight blade. No ramps for Bull's-eye shooting, what they wanted were clean-edged posts. What made it great was only half-done. After all, if a skinny barrel was good, a fat barrel was better. In a few years, we had the Target Model of 1955. The barrel was full diameter from frame to muzzle. Within a few years it would have its name changed and then its raison d'etre yanked away. In the model number reorganization of the late 1950s it became the Model-25-2. The "dash two" meant it was a .45 ACP revolver, to distinguish it from the occasional special-order gun built in .45 Colt, the "dash five."

It was blue steel, highly polished, built when things were built well (and well before CNC machinery) and never got the respect it deserved. At the same time it came out, S&W unveiled the .44 Magnum. Those who wanted power needn't worry about trying to pump a .45 ACP up with hot handloads. The .44 Magnum did that

All action shooting with revolvers is now done double-action. No more thumb-cocking.

right off the shelf. And Bull's-eye shooters soon abandoned it. In the very early 1960s gunsmiths had finally figured out how to have it all, accuracy, reliability, a good trigger, and do it on the same gun for a reasonable price. Jim Clark, Sr. who had been for the 1950s the man to beat in Bull's-eye shooting, offered a conversion at his gun shop: send in your Colt 1911 in .38 Super, and he would send it back converted to feed and fire .38 Special wadcutter loads. Just like that, things changed. Where it had always been a struggle to fight back the .22 LR pistol competitors with a revolver, the wheelgunners had been doing fine in Any Centerfire and .45 divisions. Now, a shooter could shoot a High Standard in .22, a Clark conversion in .38 and a Clark-built .45. All felt the same, all worked the same, and none needed cocking to fire each shot.

During the whole time, the factory made special-order guns in .45 Colt, called the 25-5. They were the Model of 1955 with the cylinder and chamber machined so that they accepted .45 Colt (without moon clips) instead of .45 ACP. To find a pre-production special order 25-5 would be every S&W Collectors dream. The 25-5 was made a catalog item in 1978. I was working in a gun shop bordering Detroit then, and the excitement of the DPD officers over the introduction of that model was electric. Yes, they could use the 25-2 in .45 ACP, but due to the peculiarities of departmental regulations, they had to load with 230-grain hardball. With the 25-5 in .45 Colt they could use the factory 255-grain lead bullet, a much better "stopper" by their estimation. (They were

The 625 V-comp is great for IPSC, IDPA or ICORE.

there, I was not, they had shot people with both rounds and they preferred the Colt to the ACP in that application.) Hi-tech hollowpoints were years in the future, and prohibited by DPD policy anyway.

Every change went against it, and the 25-2 fell on hard times. PPC didn't want it, Bull's-eye no longer needed it, and anyone who wanted power went right up to .44 Magnum. And beginning in 1964, .41 Magnum, too. Then the wonder-nine pistol wars began, with everyone trying to come up with a better 9mm double-action pistol. And the Dirty Harry movies made a .44

The loaded moon clip.

When you eject, the ejector star lifts the moon clip and not the rounds. Thus you can be a lot more aggressive in chamfering the charge holes of a moon-clipped gun than other revolvers.

The whole assembly, clip and ammo, goes into the cylinder.

Magnum a red-hot "must-have" handgun item. What kept it going were places like Detroit or Chicago. Where the police carried them, and residents depended on them. Then a new handgun match involving bowling pins began. It was called Second Chance. And while that's not how the match got it's name, that's certainly what it gave to the 25-2. The idea was simple, then and now: blow five bowling pins off a table as quickly as possible. Do it faster than anyone else, and you win. Scoring was simple: the time from the start signal to the last pin hitting the ground. And when things were kept to five pins (unlike the 12-, 15-, 20- or 30-round stages in IPSC) revolvers kept up. Many records were set, and

much loot earned, by shooters wielding wheelguns. Since you needed enough power to take the pins off cleanly, you needed a big gun. But if you used too much power, recoil would slow you down. It turns out that the .45 ACP loaded a bit hot was the perfect ticket. (Although many other calibers could do the job.) And the 25-2 with hot loads worked great.

What really got pin shooters scouring gun shops was a new optional event, the 8-Pin event. Unlike the 5-Pin, where if you ran out of ammo before finishing a table revolver shooters could perform a "New York Reload" (Drop the empty gun, draw a loaded spare and keep shooting, pistol shooters need not apply. If you were shooting a 1911 you had to reload.) The 8-Pin required a reload. No one was fast enough with a speedloader to keep up with someone using one of the new "full moon clips." To win the event, you simply had to have a 25-2 and the relatively new "full moon" clips that were introduced in 1975 by Ranch Products. We stalked gun shows, called gun shops, scoured classified ads all in the quest to have a 25-2. Me, I built one. I found a Model 1955 barrel at a gun show for $20. I located a surplus Model 28 at Jack First Gun Shop for $100. I bought a cylinder from S&W, and I learned to build an N frame.

And then S&W dropped it. The beautiful old 25-2 just didn't have enough customers, especially not with stainless everywhere. But that didn't mean the idea of a .45 ACP revolver was dead. It simply got replaced in stainless. What brought it back was IPSC. I ran into Tom Campbell at the S&W Dealers seminar in Ohio, the summer of 1988. There he showed me the new gun, the 625-2 "Model of 1988." Offered in 5 inches, the length

The 1955 Target and a 4-inch 1989.

Where allowed, I prefer the 25-2 for its longer sight radius. I can't shoot this gun in IDPA, as the 6.5-inch barrel is "too long" to conceal.

The 1988 and 1989 625-2s are often the choice for USPSA/IPSC revolver competition.

the revolver cognocenti had been lusting over and special-ordering from S&W since the 1920s. Skeeter Skelton and Bill Jordan wanted it. Elmer Keith tried it. Everyone who handled one felt the 5-inch length was the length to have. And now S&W had it as a regular item.

Want to know why the 4-inch came out right away? I take part of the credit/blame, whatever you want to call it. In talking with Tom, (he and I had at that point "gone way back," meeting early in the evolution of IPSC) I mentioned that "5 was great but it isn't stock." Tom had just been telling me that it was perfect for bowling pins. I told Tom that I had been talking with Richard Davis at Second Chance, and that for the match the 4-inch guns would not be considered Stock in the 8-pin event. They had to be 4 inches to be Stock. I think Tom didn't hear the "8-Pin" part of the conversation, and promptly told the factory that if they wanted to have a Stock gun for Bowling pins it had to have a 4-inch barrel. We saw the 4-incher appear right away.

The 625-2 is a stainless N frame of almost identical appearance with all the stainless N frames that have appeared since. It has shown up mostly in full-lugged barrel trim, as even hard-core shooters appreciate the recoil-dampening weight on a heavy barrel. It has been seen with unfluted and fluted cylinders, there have been Mountain Gun versions, snubbies and special commemoratives done. Included in that have been the 625-5, the .45 Colt version.

For your consideration, we present three guns in the evolution of the N frame .45 revolver:

25-2

Blued steel with a 6-1/2-inch barrel (late production went with even 4-, 6- and 8- inch barrels, from the 4-1/4-, 6-1/2- and 8-3/8-inch lengths) the 25-2 was standard in the 6-incher. If you wanted a 4-inch barrel you either custom-ordered it or had a gunsmith shorten one. In 8 inches you only had one choice, factory order, and wait. In 25 years of working on guns, working in guns shops and cruising gun shows, I recall seeing only one 25-2 with an 8-inch barrel. And regret not getting it when I had the chance. The earliest guns are mid to late 1950s so the lockwork is always the newest version. They came standard with large, target hammers and triggers. Very popular with IPSC and bowling pin shooters, so you'll often see them with replacement hammers and triggers, or the originals altered. A smaller hammer spur and a narrowed and smoothed trigger are the most common changes.

For anyone more than average size, the 6-inch "hangs" better in aiming than the 4-inch. But the gun is so large that for duty carry, the 4-inch was most popular. The cylinder is machined to accept moon clips. The originals are the half-moons, holding three rounds. Later came the full moons, holding all six, with a brief time where you could buy "third moons" that held just two rounds each. I don't remember seeing them anytime recently, I can't remember who made them, and I have no idea why you'd want to take the step back.

The blued one is a box-stock gun just as the factory made it. The chrome gun is my "pseudo 25-2" which is a Model 28 that I rebuilt with the 1955 barrel and cylinder

The well-equipped revolver shooter goes to the line with a holstered S&W and a belt dripping with moon-clipped ammo.

to 25-2 specs. The blued gun is my current IPSC gun. It has been through the hands of four different shooters in my club, and as far as I know has been to Second Chance three times. It has been to the USPSA Nationals twice. The hard-chromed gun is a Second Chance Pin gun for 5-Pin or 8-Pin. It has been to Second Chance 10 times, and has won me many times its cost in loot from the prize tables of both matches.

625-2

The basic stainless N frame, with (in the case of the revolver in question) a 4-inch barrel. The "standard" has been 4 or 5 inches, depending on in which production lot your gun was made. The most recent production guns have the action lock, requiring a key to lock and unlock for storage. The cylinder is fluted, and cut for full moon clips (of course) and in the case of this gun, a gold bead front sight. How I came to own it back in the early 1990s is one of those stories from a match that even the "losers" like to tell. I had shot at Second Chance and done well enough to get on the prize table. At Second Chance the prize distribution was simple: the winner walked up and took what he wanted from the appropriate bin. As there were some 20 bins, you had to be careful. You also had to be fast, for the "30 second rule" applied. If you stood there for 30 seconds and hadn't picked, the guy behind was then allowed to reach past you and grab what he wanted. My friend Rich Bitow had earned the slot ahead of me to the prize table (I no longer recall what category it was) and he walked up and rooted around. He grabbed something and walked off. I walked up, and there was

In action shooting with revolvers, the reload is everything. To learn, watch the top shooters. Jerry Miculek is THE top shooter, and his loading bears study.

this 625-2 peeking out from under something. I grabbed it before the next shooter had a chance, and got it logged off the books to me.

The next morning, I was having breakfast in town before making the drive home, and Rich sat down behind me. "Say Rich," I said "why'd you pick whatever you took, instead of the 625?" He looked at me with his eyes goggling. "Because I couldn't find the damned thing, is why." He thought he knew how many guns were in the prize table for that category, and was pretty sure there was still a gun left, but there was so much loot in the table he couldn't locate it. But he made his choice and never complained. (One of the reasons many like to shoot is the lack of whiners in competitive shooting. And what some find most fun about it is when they can make fun of the occasional whiner who shows up. Rich isn't a whiner.)

The 625-2 is a 4-inch version, with round butt and gold bead sight. In using it for IPSC shooting I became dis-satisfied with its accuracy. I clamped it in the Ransom rest and found it only casually accurate. I then tested it chamber by chamber, and found that several of them shot one-hole clusters. But all of them had a different point of impact, so the distribution was to make it average. I sent it back, and S&W replaced the cylinder. When I told Herb Belin about this, he remarked that "the early 1990s was before we were boring our cylinders on CNC machines. We bore them all on CNC machines now, and our indexing and uniformity are much better. About as perfect as you can get."

The 4-inch version is not my favorite IPSC gun, but as an IDPA gun it is just about perfect. Loaded with Berry 185-grain hollowbase jacketed round nose bullets (that have an exterior shape the same as 230s) over Tite-group, they are remarkably soft in recoil, nicely accurate, and reload like a dream.

625 V-Comp

This is a performance Center gun built for IPSC, pins and ICORE. The barrel is a slab-sided but ovaled heavy barrel with a threaded muzzle. You can put the provided compensator on it, or have a gunsmith machine one for you to your specifications. Or, if you want to shoot Stock you replace the comp with a thread protector. The cylinder is unfluted for extra weight. From a special production run in 1999, this is a compact and accurate revolver for those who want it all in a short (relatively speaking) barrel. Without needing a gunsmith you can take off the rear sight and install a red-dot sight, put on the comp, and have an Open gun. Or go back to iron sights and no comp for Stock. Load it light for IDPA or ICORE, or load it heavy for pins.

The 625 V-Comp with its lugged barrel and thread protector.

The right side.

The 6525V is a 4-inch gun, to meet IDPA rules.

The unfluted cylinder of the V.

The thread protector can be removed and replaced with a compensator for matches that allow it.

Accessories

A 25-2 of any vintage needs moon clips. The original still works, but half moons are not as fast for competition, so few use them any more. There is one other option. Back in the 1920s, Peters cartridge made the ".45 Auto Rim" cartridge. It is a .45 ACP with a rim that fills the gap of the moon clips. You can use these instead, but you will have to load your own brass as there is no more ammo being made. But with the popularity of .45 ACP, that is what everyone uses, and moon clips.

When I built mine, I began acquiring clips whenever I came across them. Guns in trade, if there were spare clips I snagged them. When I saw clips at gun shows, I bought them. I now have a small coffee can full of moon clips, a lifetime supply. But clips have to be loaded. The old way was to press each round into the clip one at a time. The new way is to get the "Re-mooner" from California Competition works. I met Bill Palazzolo at Second Chance almost from my first day there. He first designed, made and marketed a pair of pliers to remove fired cases from moon clips, the De-mooner. The same tool can be sued to install them, but not as easily. With the Re-mooner you drop in six rounds, the clip and press the legs closed. The De-mooner is as easy; drop the empty moon clip onto the top post, then squeeze the handles and lever

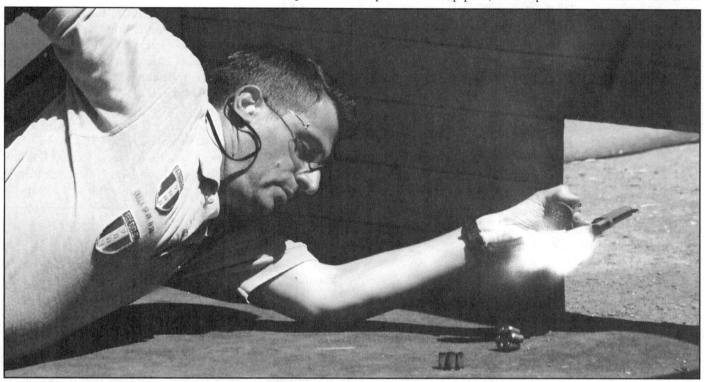

Reloading prone isn't fun any time, but with a revolver, it takes some extra planning and flexibility.

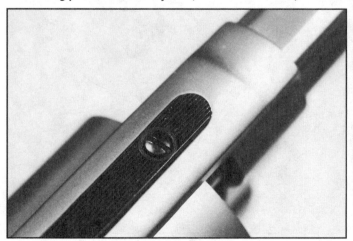

The 625V has the standard S&W adjustable rear sight. You can remove it and install a scope if you wish.

The CCW "Shoot the Moon" carrier in the standard carry mode (as in IDPA).

The CCW "Shoot the Moon" as most IPSC shooters use it. Much faster, but hard to conceal.

two empties free. Turn the moon clip a third of a turn, press and remove two more, and again for the last two.

The way to carry your clips in competition is with a "Shoot the Moon" ammo carrier. The spring clip and internal locator keep the clips in place and lined up for use. It isn't uncommon to see a competitor in an IPSC match with a belt full of Shoot the Moon carriers, each with a loaded moon clip on it. To get through a big field

course might take 28 rounds, and you can't always be sure you'll need them in multiples of six. A field course might require four, four, six, four, six, etc. You can't do a standing reload, so every time you move to another shooting position, you're reloading. For those 24 rounds just counted, you'd need five moon clips with 30 rounds, plus spares. (Every miss adds time and a reload.) It isn't unusual for a competitor to come to the line with seven or eight moon clips on his belt, with another in hand to load when told to do so.

Strength of the 25-2

While the .45 guns are built on the same frame as the .44 Magnums, you can't assume that they can take as much pressure as the .44s. First, you have a larger case head with which to generate thrust on recoil. And, the larger rounds leave less wall thickness to deal with pressure. The limits of the .45, in the .45ACP+P load, are as much as you'd want to put into an N frame .45. Which is nothing to sneeze at. At the top end, a 25-2 with a 6-inch barrel or 625-2 with a 5-inch barrel loaded with .45ACP+P ammo should be able to launch a 230 JHP at just over 1,000 fps. While that is a large difference from the .44 Magnum specs of a 240-grain bullet at 1200 fps,

One advantage revolver shooters have over pistols is that a holster can be fast and secure. The Safariland holster is shaped to clamp on the cylinder and not come loose inadvertently.

Here Jerry is shooting a 1988 with the 5-inch barrel.

it is still plenty good enough for many things. And all competitions and defense can be handled by that or less. At least defense from people, not bears. If you're looking for a bear gun, my first suggestion would be something besides an N frame. If you've settled on the N frame, then a .44 Mangum or a 10mm would be much better choices than a .45 ACP or .45 Colt.

I once had a customer ask that I ream his 625-2 out to .45 Winchester Magnum. He wanted the full moon clips and the power of the Win Mag. I declined, as I thought the power was too much for the gun. As far as I know it is still in one piece, but I'd still turn down the job.

Loading the 625

What you feed it depends on what you intend to do with it. The loading books are full of data that will allow you to do well in IPSC or bowling pins. For IPSC the Major threshold is 165,000, so you need merely get a 230-grain full-metal-jacketed bullet up to 717 feet per second and you're there. There are pages and pages of data for just that load. For Bowling pins you need a 195 PF, where you must then get that same 230 (or a jacketed hollowpoint) up to 850 fps. Again, there are pages of data for that, mostly in the .45ACP+P load section.

What you will be hard-pressed to find are loads to shoot ICORE or IDPA with. The threshold for ICORE is 120, for IDPA 125, both "powderpuff" loads in a .45 ACP. You're trying to get an accurate and clean-burning load, of a 230-grain bullet at 545 fps? It isn't going to happen. The problem is, both competitions require quick reloading, and if you go to anything except the jacketed round nose bullet you compromise reloading. One approach would be to go with a bullet like the 200-grain jacketed round nose from West Coast Bullets. There, a 135 PF load only requires 675 fps, low but within reason. Better yet, Berrys makes a 185-grain round nose with a difference. It is a hollow-based plated bullet, with the same profile as the 230. (Don't get it mixed up with a real 230, or your loads or scores will suffer) A 185 needs only go 729 fps to produce a 135 PF load. Now we're talking. If you load the Berry 185 hollow-base over five grains of Hodgdon Titegroup, you'll be in the ballpark. I've found sometimes large variations in velocity between .45 ACP revolvers when the loads get very light, so you'll have to use a chronograph and adjust for your gun. But with the Berrys or the West Coast bullets, you'll be able to shoot light loads in our 25-2 or 625-2 and keep up with the .38s in ICORE and IDPA.

CHAPTER 21

The Biggest Magnum:
S&W designed a whole new frame for the mighty .500

The evolution of hand cannons has been with us ever since someone got the bright idea of making a firearm that could be fired with one hand. For those who think what we've got now is big, in the days of smoothbore muskets it wasn't uncommon for "horse pistols" to be as large a .70 caliber.

The modern evolution of hand cannons waited on two things: the .44 Hand Ejector and a cowboy by the name of Elmer Keith. The original Triple Lock models were not as strong as later models (and far too valuable now to do any experimenting with), but the later ones were plenty strong for what he had in mind. He also had the advantage of new powder developments, something that has always driven experimenters in the field of hand cannons. His work began in the 1920s with the .44 Special and progressed to the .357 Magnum, then the .44 Magnum in 1955, and things were pretty linear. He would take a standard round, boost its power in its parent frame, and see what happens. Then things got complicated. The .41 Magnum was, to some, a step back, a less-powerful cartridge. After the .41 Magnum came the .44 Auto Mag, a step sideways into an unreliable autoloader. Later we got the Desert Eagle in .44 Magnum, which some wags then described as the "world's only crew-served handgun." They thought it big, and if only they knew. Dick Casull was experimenting with a suped-up .45 Colt. His early experiments involved such arcane

My brother got a big magnum before I did, a .41. Now I've got the bigger one. He doesn't seem to be jealous. To give you an idea of scale, Mike wears a size 48 jacket.

It may be big, loud, hard-kicking and expensive, but boy does it shoot! I almost didn't sit down to test it, the recoil seemed so fierce. Now I'm glad I did.

tactics as triplex loads, where he'd carefully layer three different types of powders, then more or less lock them in place in the case with the bullet compressing the column of powder. The problem he had was that any gun chambered for the .45 Colt was far too weak to hold his R&D efforts. The solution was two-fold, a new case, longer than the parent case (where have we heard that before?) and a new gun to hold it, the Freedom Arms. Built more like a bank vault than a handgun, the Freedom Arms revolvers were so durable and accurate that they actually caused a rift in the ranks of silhouette shooters.

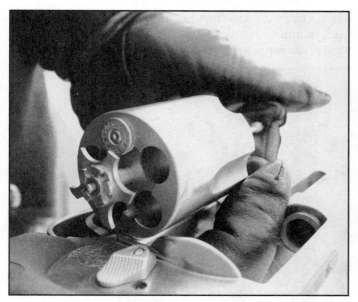

The massive cylinder holds only five rounds of .500 S&W Magnum ammo — plenty for herds of buffalo and triceratops.

This is the kind of recoil you can expect with factory Cor-bon 440-grain loads: muzzle straight up

The biggest and smallest centerfire revolvers S&W sent me: the .500 and the 442. Both are five-shots, but there is a world of difference between them.

Silhouette shooting calls for large amounts of power (relatively speaking, from a handgun) to knock over steel targets out to 200 meters. In the late 1970s you didn't have a lot of choices of handguns with which to shoot silhouette. You could use a Ruger Blackhawk, or you could use an S&W M-29. The experimenters used M-57's in .41 Magnum. The problems were many: the Ruger had a hammer fall like a ball peen hammer. And the trigger pull was not always that great. A lot could happen in the time it took the hammer to come crashing down onto the firing pin. The S&W's were accurate, the triggers superb, but a steady diet of factory 240-grain ammo would soon have them on the gunsmiths bench,

getting re-timed and re-tuned. And the ammunition of the period was not always up to the task. At 200 meters you had to hit an area of about two square feet (not two feet square) to knock over a ram. I spent many an afternoon lying in the sand at the 200-meter line trying to figure out just what my hold for drop and wind would be on the rams. Not every gun could keep all its shots inside the "sweet spot" of the rams at 200 meters even from a machine rest.

The Freedom Arms revolvers were just about handbuilt. They were machined with precision, not production, in mind, and they shot. The .454 Casull round they were chambered for had more than enough power to

The compensator the .500 comes with in the 8-inch version.

The muzzle end: a hole big enough to stick a fingertip into.

The five-shot cylinder, showing plenty of cylinder wall thickness. Say, a seven- or eight-shot .44 anyone?

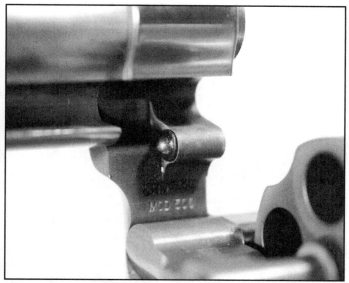

The cylinder detent that locks up against the crane is tough enough for this gun.

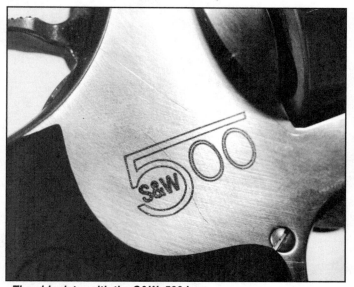

The sideplate, with the S&W .500 logo.

The top rear of the frame is taller, to contain the cylinder, with a hammer to match.

tip over a ram at 200 meters if you could make the shot. They shot so accurately that the organizers of sanctioned silhouette matches decreed a "cost ceiling." No gun that retailed for more than a certain amount could be used as a Production Gun. And the ceiling was always under what the Freedom Arms sold for.

The .454 Casull ushered in a new age for handgun hunting. With plenty of power to deliver, hunters could consider larger game. Or, hunters who would not have otherwise thought of hunting decided to get into it, since there were now powerful handguns capable of the task. And as usual, there were some who thought the .454 Casull was just a wee bit wimpy. Now, we're talking of a cartridge that delivers a 240-grain bullet at 1,800

fps, or a 300-grain bullet at 1,600 fps. But the real power merchants didn't think velocity was the be-all and end-all of handgun hunting performance. They wanted weight and frontal area, and velocity was something a step behind that.

While the .454 Casull was happening, and its successors were being developed, there were a bunch of other cartridges vying for the title of "The World's Most Powerful Handgun." The .445 Super Magnum came out, but it had two strikes against it in the power department: it was a stretched .44 Magnum, and thus limited to bullets made for the .44 Magnum, and it could be had only in Dan Wesson revolvers and Thompson/Center single-shot pistols. The designers wanted a round that

He's 6-foot, 8-inches, 280 pounds, and the muzzle still comes up past 45 degrees. And this is the medium load!

would get more velocity out of a .44 Magnum, to flatten the trajectory to the 200-meter rams, and deliver more energy to those rams. There was the .50 Action Express, for the Desert Eagle. The .50 A.E. has a rim the same diameter as the .44 Magnum, so the Desert Eagle can use the same bolt for the .50 A.E. as for the .44 Magnum. But while it delivered power it was not what the hunting mavens wanted. (And to be fair, there was also the matter of social status: those who hunted large or dangerous game with a handgun wanted to be seen using high-zoot custom revolvers, and not production pistols.)

The experiments involved taking rifle brass, .348 Winchester, .45-70 or .50 Basic, and cutting it to handgun lengths. Then, the experimenters would take Ruger frames (Superblackhawk, Redhawk, SuperRedhawk) and install new barrels. The new guns would get custom cylinders. The experimentation settled on .45-70 cases, with barrels in .475" bore diameter, with cylinders chambered for five rounds of .475 Linebaugh. There was a new Sheriff in town, and he delivered a .475-inch diameter bullet of 400 grains at 1,300 fps. This was enough for almost anyone. It was certainly enough for anything that walked the earth. In fact, it was more than some needed, and many a .475 Linebaugh custom gun was shot with loads that didn't come close to the red line. Ruger,

The cylinder latch, S&W logo, and the unavoidable action lock. Even the .500 gets one.

ever ready to jump into the fray, came out with the .480 Ruger. The case for the .480 Ruger is shorter than the .475 Linebaugh, so you could consider it to be the ".475 Linebaugh Special" except that the pressure ceiling is no different. The .480 Ruger does have one advantage, and that is that it fits into Ruger production guns.

And there it stood for a couple of years. Then S&W talked to Cor-Bon about a new cartridge. In particular, Herb Belin, the Handgun Production Manager at S&W called up Peter Pi at Cor-Bon and asked if he could come up with a cartridge to put S&W back into the lead. The "Most powerful Handgun in the World" title that S&W had enjoyed since the Dirty Harry movie of 1971 hadn't been true for a number of years. But public perception didn't catch up with ballistic reality until Ruger unveiled the .480 Ruger in 2001. After all, if a custom maker made something more powerful than the .44 Magnum (as with the .454 or .475) they were just custom guns, right? But to have a direct competitor like Ruger one-up S&W, well, that couldn't stand. So Herb talked to Peter, and Peter the next day had a prototype revolver case that could do the job. He sent it to Herb, who said "Yes" and set the design engineers to work. First, they had to make a cylinder to hold the round. In the old days that would involve a whole lot of slide rule or desktop calculator work, then machining a prototype out of steel. In this modern CAD/CAM world, they plugged the strength of the steels into the computer, tossed in the working pressure of the cartridge, added a safety margin, and let the computer ruminate for a fraction of a second. When the dimensions came out, they fed those into a CNC machining station and produced a cylinder. Which went the way of all things mechanical when the test program is titled: "Test to Destruction."

With a cartridge and a cylinder known to take the load, they then went back to the CAD/CAM computer and designed a frame and internal parts to go with it. With the parts designed, they began making the SW500, and S&W was once again manufacturer of "the Worlds Most powerful Handgun."

Walk around and kick the tires

And a long walk it is. First, the barrel. The barrel is a tube inside the shroud, screwed into the frame and then tensioned from the front. The design makes it possible to deliver startling accuracy from the .500, while keeping barrel production costs down. The barrel is tensioned, that is, using the barrel as the bolt to hold the shroud on stretches the barrel. The tension of being stretched acts to stiffen it, making it work as if it were thicker and more stable than its thickness might lead you to believe. On the front is a compensator, and while some of the test shooters liked it, most expressed a desire for a more effective one. It might well be that custom gunsmiths could make a name for themselves producing a muzzle brake to replace the factory one, that works better and doesn't look like a goiter.

The frame is massive. With a 2.3-inch cylinder to contain, it would have to be. The rear sight covers the scope mount holes, where you can bolt on a scope base, and attach rings and a scope for more accurate shooting. The cylinder holds five rounds, so the locking slots in the cylinder fall between the chambers. Unlike six-shot revolvers, the .500 doesn't have the locking slot acting as a weak point against the chamber pressure. The cylinder locks into the frame on the centerpin in the rear, and via a ball detent in the frame, acting on the crane. By putting the ball behind the crane, recoil works to lock the ball tighter into its recess in the crane. (And boy, there's plenty of recoil to lock that puppy in there!) The hammer is serrated, the trigger smooth, the sights white outline and plain black front post. The grips appear odd. They are proportioned for the shooter, not in proportion scaled up as the rest of the frame is. As a result they seem

The Barnes 275-grain hollowpoint is the "lightweight" load, but it still kicks.

The 440-grain Cast Performance bullet is one big slug, and it delivers all it promises.

a bit small when you first look a them. That's because your eye has not yet gotten accustomed to the large size of the gun itself. Once you get hold of it, and realize that you're holding the normal-sized part of it, you realize just how big the gun is.

On the right the frame is marked with the "SW500" logo, while the left of the barrel is marked "500 S&W Magnum." The grips are soft rubber or synthetic, and welcomed. The trigger pull is very nice, not at all what you'd expect from such a beast of a handgun. The good trigger pull is a benefit of the CAD/CAM design, where the frictional and camming forces of each part can be calculated, and the trigger pull designed to be good. The trigger is certainly an aid to good shooting, even if the recoil isn't. And since the reason for being of the 500 is power, let's get right to it; how does it shoot?

The test crew experience

My volunteers were all on hand when it came time to shoot the 500. Cor-Bon had kindly sent me a supply of ammo (and Hornady would later, as soon as they had finished the first production lot) so I had plenty of all three loads: the 275-grain jacketed hollow point, the 400-cast and the 440-cast. The 275-grain bullet which comes from Barnes Bullet, isn't really a copper jacketed bullet as all who see it suspect. It is entirely copper, and the test crew's response to shooting it is "That's not so bad." At over 1,600 fps, it isn't. While those numbers would be murder in an N frame, the big 74-ounce X frame gun handles it with aplomb. The 275-grain bullet would the be choice for deer hunting, but you'd have to have a big deer to justify it. You'll need a big corn-fed Midwest

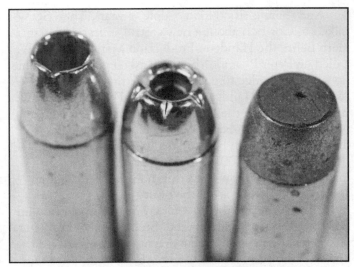

Here you see the Barnes, Hornady and Cast Performance bullets.

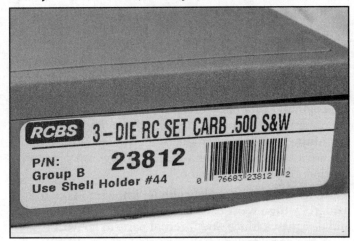

You are definitely going to want to reload ammo for the .500, to reduce both recoil and cost.

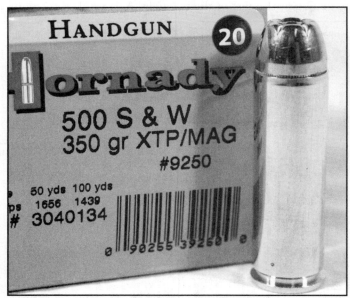

Hornady is no slouch when it comes to good ammo, and their .500 is a hot load.

The 400-grain JSP is for those who want performance but must use a jacketed bullet.

If you use the .500 on your club's steel targets, the welder will have to repair them, and you'll be charged with the repair. At least at our club, you will. Ask before you shoot!

the 275-grain ammo, only one fired more than a cylinder of the 440 load. Later, another test shooter blasted off a cylinder of the 440, and asked, "Got any more?" but he owns a Freedom Arms in .454 Casull, and is used to recoil that will loosen his dental fillings. The 440-grain Cast Performance load will without a doubt penetrate to great depths. If they could make the bullet just a bit harder, it would probably shoot through a diesel engine. It will certainly perforate anything that walked the North American continent since the mastadons died out.

Had I not held out some ammo for accuracy and chronograph testing, they'd have cleaned me out of the 275-grain load. And I noticed that while they shot five-shot cylinders, they often turned in four empties. I lost some of my supply of brass for future reloading endeavors to their brass sample library. Later, the Hornady XTP loads arrived. When I first saw the box I was not at all enthused about shooting it. The label clearly states it is a 375-grain XTP bullet at 1,900 fps. The 400s at 1,600 were bad enough. What were these like? Not bad, on a par with the 400-grain loads, as they were "only" in the low 1,600 range. I later asked why, and my Hornady source tells me that out of the test barrel it delivers 1,900 fps, so that's what they put on the box.

One thing we all looked for was the "recoil double." The legend goes, the recoil of the .500 drives the gun back so fast in your hand that your finger comes off the trigger, it resets, and the muscular tension of your finger pulls the trigger again. Well, if it happened to someone else it never happened to us.

As for accuracy, we beat our gong half to death with the .500. When I sat down to shoot a group I was not at all looking forward to it. Who wants to shoot something this powerful from the bench? With lots of padding, aspirin, rest breaks and concentration I was able to shoot groups. The best was an inch and a half at 25 yards, center to center. I was as amazed as anyone, and really nervous on the fifth shot that I'd yet again trash a good-looking group with a flyer due to my own trigger mashing.

The latest word from the factory is that there is a new model, with a 4-inch barrel (the initial model has an 8-inch barrel) with a more effective compensator on it. After shooting the big one, the smaller one has to be even more of a wild ride. If someone shoots the "snubbie" .500 and tells you "that wasn't so bad" you are either in the presence of a liar, or someone far tougher than me or any on my test-fire crew.

If you have to have the biggest, you must have the .500. If you need something big to go after large or dangerous game, the .500 should top your list.

buck, not one of those dainty little Texas deer. Going up in size, the 400-grain bullet, is a jacketed soft point slug from Hawk Bullets. The 400-grain bullet at (again) over 1,600 fps puts it ahead of the standard "thumper," the .45-70, for woods hunting. You have plenty of penetration for anything you might wish to hunt.

Last is the heavy hitter, the thumper par excellence, the "winna an still champeennnn!" the 440-grain Cast Performance bullet. A hard-cast bullet at over 1,600 fps, the 440-grain load gave all but the most experienced at heavy recoil pause. The reaction was typically that the shooter would shoot, and the recoil would whip the muzzle vertical. They'd then haul it down, pause, look down at the gun as if it had tried to hurt them, and then turn back to the crowd. Someone would ask, "Are you done?" and the reply was invariably "No, I'm going to finish the cylinder." While they lined up to polish off all

CHAPTER 22

The long and short on barrels

S&W revolver barrels could not be simpler in their design: they are screwed into the front of the frame. What complicates things are the details. The barrel must protrude a certain amount out of the rear of the frame, to come close to but not contact the cylinder. It must be lined up correctly so the front sight is a correct indication of the point of impact of the bullet. And the barrel cannot be turned too far one way or the other or the locking bolt underneath will not properly lock the ejector rod tip.

Further complicating things, the thread sizes for any given frame have not changed since the frame was introduced. The common thread sizes are the root cause of the "no magnum parts" policy. After all, no one in their right mind would install .44 Magnum parts into a wartime production Model 1917 dating from the Fall of 1918, would they? You bet they would. So, while it is possible to rebuild an S&W revolver and even change the caliber, you should exercise some common sense when planning to do so. As a general rule, don't plan to go up in power when rebuilding. So, don't go and try to fit a barrel and cylinder from an Model 19 into a 1920s era .38 Hand Ejector or Military & Police. But if you want to take a modern .38 Special and install a barrel and cylinder from a .32 H&R Magnum into it, you'll probably be fine. "De-tuning" a .44 Magnum by fitting .45 Colt parts to it

would be no problem, just so long as you are not under the illusion that you now have a ".45 Magnum" and try to juice it up.

All pistol barrels, even those with a "supported" chamber, have a thin brass wall between the chamber and the outside. The barrel can't completely enclose the case, so you do not want to exceed the standard pressure in your pistol, or risk blowing out the case.

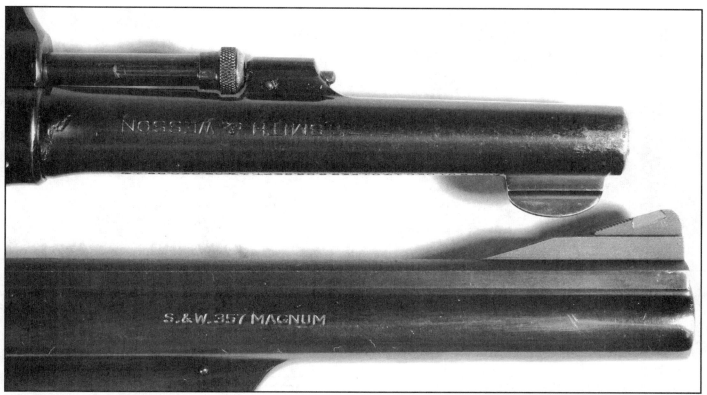
Old "pencil" barrel and a new "ribbed" barrel.

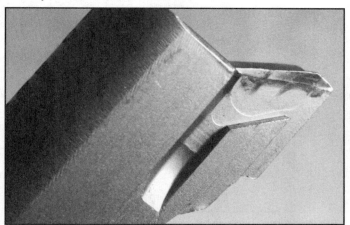
S&W pistol barrels use side cams, and not a link, to unlock and lock the barrel.

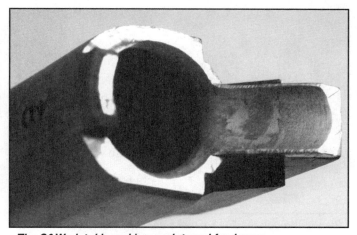
The S&W pistol barrel has an integral feed ramp.

One small problem that extreme accuracy mavens discovered (and the factory probably knew about a century ago) is that tightening a barrel into the frame crushes the shoulder into the frame. It also constricts the threads at that point. While many of us are quite happy with the accuracy of S&W revolvers (and the level is quite high) those who want more object to the constriction. They have gone so far as to develop the process known as "fire lapping." In regular lapping you cast a lead slug into the bore, and then coat the slug with an abrasive compound. Working the slug back and forth polishes the bore and evens the internal dimensions. However,

to do it correctly requires precise tooling. Instead, the fire-lapping process uses lead bullets with the abrasive compound in place of a lubricant. Each bullet fired polishes the bore. The process has its own peculiar details, do please don't go smearing valve grinding compound on your bullets and fire them. You'll ruin the bore. If you want more accuracy (and sometimes you don't get it, so be ready for a lack of results) get a proper fire-lapping kit for your caliber and follow the instructions.

S&W barrels were traditionally made by forging where the heated steel for the barrel is pounded by a drop forge. Once cooled the forgings were deep-drilled,

You can see that the barrel, with its ramp, does not require any frame ramp as part of the feeding process.

Barrels through the 20th century were simply screwed in.

The long thread secures the barrel well, but the shoulder can squeeze the bore if tightened too much, harming accuracy.

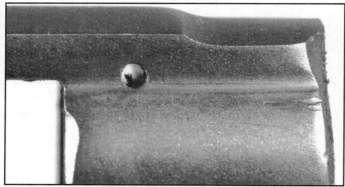

Note the pin to lock the barrel in place, used through most of the 20th century.

Older guns required extra machining to clear the head of the ejector rod underneath the barrel.

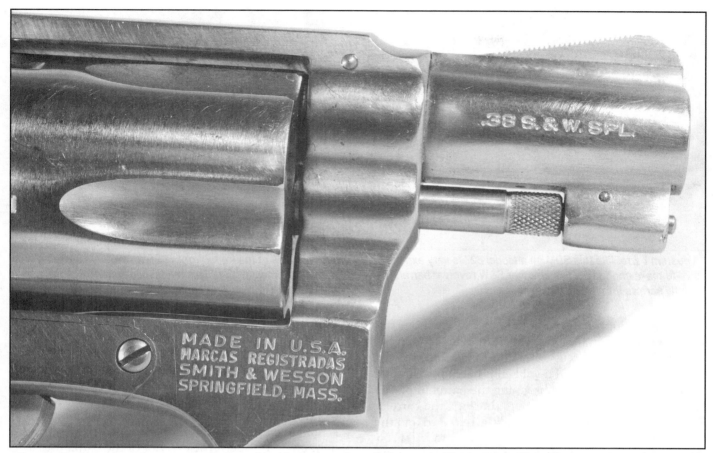

Even a short barrel can be accurate. Note on this J frame how the cylinder nearly fills the frame. Thus the extended magnum frames on new J-frame pistols.

the exterior profiled, the bore reamed, polished and broached, then finish machined for installation by the fitters. There are still barrels made this way, and they work just fine. The broaching machine dates from the 1930s, and Herb Belin tells me that it will certainly be working in the 2030's and beyond. A forged barrel is traditional and tough. But not always needed. S&W barrels are also made from extrusions, where a billet of steel is heated until it is plastic, then forced through a die to create a cylindrical tube that later becomes a barrel. The last method of barrel making is to machine the barrel from a piece of bar stock. Known in the custom automotive field as "billet" parts, you can have a barrel made from bar stock with less heat and noise, fuss and muss than forging or extrusion. You simply feed the appropriate-size bar stock into an automated mill and lathe, with the correct cutters at hand and the cutting paths programmed. Once you've paid for the investment in (very expensive) machines, your parts drop off the machines 24 hours a day minus maintenance time.

Once machined, the barrel has to be rifled. The traditional method is broach cutting, where a hooked cutter is pulled down the spiral path of the rifling to cut a groove. In the days before industrialization, gunsmiths made barrels by cutting the grooves one at a time, taking 10 or 20 passes per groove. The "modern" method is the multi-cutter broach. Looking like a steel Christmas tree, the broach has a row of spiraled cutters for each groove. Each hook is slightly larger than one ahead of it. One pass and the whole bore is rifled. The newest method of rifling bores is electrical discharge machining. In standard EDM, you bring an electrode in close proximity to the part to be "cut." You then pump a huge electrical charge into the electrode. The current jumps the gap (just like a spark plug) and the arc erodes the part to be cut. Since the arc can only jump a certain, and small distance, the electrode faithfully cuts an impression of itself. All the rest are details: feed rate, arc distance, electrode wear, lubricant, etc. To rifle a bore, you fabricate an electrode that goes down the bore, with the tops of the electrode where you want the grooves of the rifling to be. As you pull the electrode through the bore it cuts the grooves of the rifling. Traditionalists complain that it isn't "real rifling" and that there must be something wrong with it. There can't be too much wrong with it, as the .500 uses the EDM process for its barrels, and they are remarkably accurate. Herb says they may even be the most accurate barrels they make.

A custom barrel like this SDM on a Model 627 is very expensive to make and fit. But like all other S&W revolver barrels, it simply screws into the frame.

Here is a view of the frame front of S&W revolvers showing the barrel/frame junction. This model has a pinned barrel, and note the rear-sight locking screw.

When fitting a new barrel to an S&W, you have to keep a few things in mind. Older guns, at least when barrels are the topic of discussion, fall into two categories: pinned and not-pinned. The old guns had a pin through the frame above the barrel, trapping the barrel in place. You must remove the pin before unscrewing the barrel. A new barrel, once fitted must then be removed and the groove filed to clear the pin for it to be reinstalled. (You can simply decide not to replace the pin, but the gun will look unfinished.) The pin was to keep barrels in place. The older barrels are thinner than the new ones, with less of a shoulder to bear against the frame. Depending solely on the thread crush and shoulder friction seemed not enough I guess. Newer guns do not have the pin. Their wider shoulder provides enough tension to keep the barrel in place.

If you are going to replace the barrel on your revolver you simply must have the correct frame wrench and inserts. In older gunsmithing books you'll see the advice to "clamp the barrel in a padded vise and put a hammer handle through the frame opening" which is a good way to twist a frame. Use the padded vise, but get a frame wrench (Brownells has several) and the insert for your frame. You'll find the added leverage makes the job easier. And the cost of the wrench and insert is less than the replacement cost of a new frame.

Recent developments

The increase in interest for the lightest possible handgun led S&W to Aluminum and later Aluminum/Scandium alloy frames. And Titanium. And into a problem. Especially with magnum chamberings, getting the barrel tight to the frame to withstand the vibration was not easy. The solution (and also shaving a little more weight off) was to turn the exterior of the barrel into a shroud. The actual barrel is a sleeve inside the shroud. The barrel keeps the shroud on in the simplest possible manner: it traps it. Time for a little mental exercise: Imagine the barrel as a bolt with a hole bored down its length. Rifle the hole. Now slide the bolt into a shroud, and tighten the bolt into the front of a frame. Viola. The barrel locks the shroud in place. The act of trapping the shroud tensions the barrel lengthwise, and avoids the bore constriction at the shoulder that older revolvers could suffer from.

It is entirely possible that all S&W revolvers in the near future will have their barrels attached this way. On the lightweight guns, where it is obvious that the bore material is different than the shroud material, there won't be a problem. But on the all-steel guns it may come to pass that some new gunsmith who doesn't know which is which may try to remove a new barrel the old way, or an old barrel the new way. It will be interesting to see what happens.

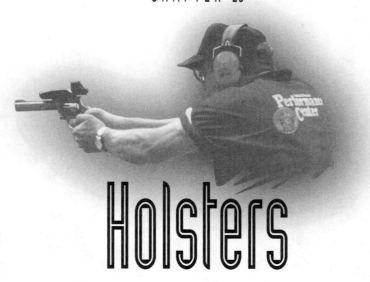

CHAPTER 23

Holsters

The days of carrying a handgun in your pocket are over. Oh, we've all done it. Well, those of us who've got old stories, old habits or stories of poverty as college students have done it. Pockets are very good for carrying many things, but handguns are not tops on the list. When I have done it, I did so for practical and short-term reasons. Usually I'd be packing a spare or backup at the gun shop, when we'd just gotten a visit from a group of suspicious-appearing "customers." And I'm sure every gun shop in the country has had at least one staff member do so as recently as yesterday. I've seen jewelry store clerks, pawn shop staff, and pharmacists with guns in their back pockets. And despite all that, and our successful experience at it, I'm going to go on record and say you should not carry a loaded handgun except in a holster. I might even be so bold as to say that carrying it in a pocket or tucked in your belt or waistband is negligence. The waistband-carry is called "Mexican" carry, by some. It is even more hazardous than are pockets. A friend of mine, a chief of police in another state, was trying to decide if he would continue to allow his officers to carry their off-duty guns in the waistband or in a pocket. One day while a group of his officers were talking in the department's Ready Room one of the off-duty officers simply had his pistol slipped in the waistband of his sweatpants. While talking, it slipped and was going to fall. In grabbing it to keep it from falling, his finger went

inside the trigger guard, and the pistol discharged into the newly carpeted floor. No injury except to pride. The next memo out of the word processor was from my friend the chief dictating that all firearms, on- or off-duty, were to be carried in a suitable holster. The officer? A letter in his file mandated remedial firearms training, and a rotating set of nicknames from fellow officers for the next year or so. He was lucky, he knew it, my friend knew it, and everyone in the Ready Room knew it.

It could have been worse. Who in this day and age wants to be standing in court when the judge hears a loud "thunk" and asks "What was that?" Do you really want to be explaining it to your supervisor or chief? Or, in grabbing for the falling handgun, cause it to discharge and have a limp for life? To be medically retired from an injury due to one's own negligence, carelessness or haste? Or worse yet, to die or cause the death of someone else from the negligent discharge of a handgun carried in a pocket, waistband or belt without a holster? Get a holster. Get a secure one. And learn to use it.

Despite the descriptor we give some handguns as "pocket pistols" you do not want to be carrying a firearm in your pocket. Smith & Wesson makes safe handguns, but if you work to negate the safety features you can expect only loud noises. You may not be so lucky as to only shred a square inch of newly installed carpeting.

While pockets are common, carrying a loaded handgun in them should not be. We've all done it.

Ideally, we can get a grip, and draw...

...to present the perpetrators with a severe problem. But if anything goes wrong, you could be in trouble.

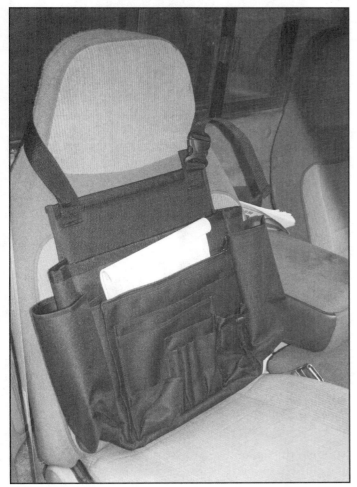

And you should never leave a loaded gun in your vehicle. This Uncle Mike's carrier is perfect for report forms, log books, pens, pencil and a thermos, but is not the place you should be stashing a loaded defensive sidearm.

When selecting a holster you have to consider a number of variables: comfort, security, speed and concealment. Where will you wear it? How is it secured; belt, waistband, web gear or vest? Does the manufacturer make a holster for the handgun you will be using? And in competition, do the rules allow it? A shoulder holster is a sound choice for concealed carry in the winter. But no match will allow its use. IDPA has an approved holster list. If a particular holster isn't on the list, you can't use it for score. Make sure before you show up with the wrong gear.

Holsters are made to fit a number of uses, which describe in many cases the kind of holster they are. The main categories are concealment, duty, open carry, hunting, competition, and service and tactical. And with all, regardless of if you are carrying for defense or competition, you have to have spare ammo. Lets take them in order, with some examples I have found useful.

Concealment

With so many states going to shall-issue concealed carry laws recently (42 states at last count had either "shall-issue" or reasonably obtainable carry laws) there are many shooters now carrying. One thing that all have in common is that "concealed" means concealed. The inadvertent showing of your concealed handgun can be something as simple as a verbal warning "Joe, get a better holster. That cheap one you've got is showing your gun again." to revocation of the license, fines and jail time. The until-recently vague in many jurisdictions "brandishing" law is a big problem some places. Back when only the police, those politically connected and criminals carried handguns, it was simply assumed

Concealed means concealed. No one should see it, nor have a hint of it, until you produce your sidearm when you need it.

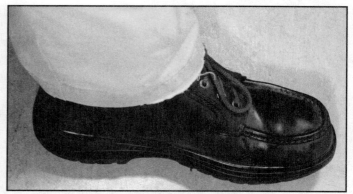

Properly done, no one should see an ankle holster.

To draw, lift your trouser leg to clear the cuff.

Bend over or kneel, and grasp the grips and press through the thumb break.

that if someone saw your gun it was because you wanted them to see it as a means of threatening them. (I say "until-recently vague" because with many people now carrying the courts are quickly defining exactly what is brandishing.) In some jurisdictions, the police were in the habit of showing a holstered handgun when in plainclothes as a step up the ladder of force escalation. (Not that it was called such in those simpler days.) Now, many departmental Use of Force policies forbid such a display. And with many people carrying, there are many more opportunities for someone to inadvertently see a "concealed" handgun. With lots of people carrying, that assumption that an observed handgun is one that has been brandished is not always valid, but you may still find yourself in trouble because of it. (Many laws are written that when simply observed, a handgun has been "brandished, while in other locales you must actually use the observation as a threat. Check with your attorney.) And, it is tactically unsound for people to see that you are "packing" for it alerts them to take aggressive actions.

After all, the firearm you are carrying is in itself a valuable piece of property worth stealing, if only the bad guy can figure out how.

Concealed carry involves three locations: ankle, waist and "shoulder holster." Called thus because the gun rides under your shoulder, not on it.

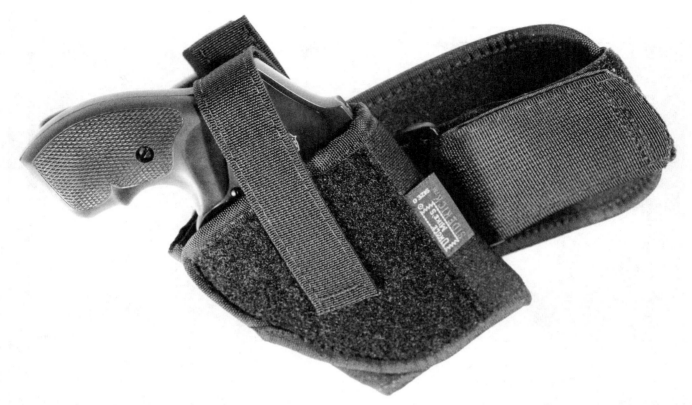

The ankle rig, with unloaded snubbie inserted. Now fit the holster to your ankle (with unloaded gun). Once the holster is fitted, then draw, load and re-holster.

The ankle rig is the one we are familiar with if we've seen older police movies. As a location to store a firearm it has several shortcomings: It is uncomfortable, easy to spot, slow to draw and prone to loss. In order to keep the gun in place you generally have to pull the straps pretty tight. You cannot wear anything except baggy-ankle pants or your gun is both impossible to draw and easy to see. Straight-leg chinos or boot-cut jeans are giveaways to an ankle rig. Spotting an ankle rig is not that hard: look for someone who hides his feet when he sits down. Who has a really, really bulky pair of socks on. Who never puts his feet up. The draw is slow simply because you have to bend over, kneel or lift your leg to draw. As for losing a gun, if you haven't tried to run down a suspect while wearing an ankle rig, and had the gun go flying you don't know the words "incident report/firearm loss." Every step you take tests the limits of the retaining straps on the holster.

All that said, I've had good luck with an Uncle Mike's holster, the 8820 ankle Holster. Made of ballistic nylon it comes in one color, black. The nylon is a good choice for those in hot weather, because you can run it through the wash once it has gotten funky from sweating on it. The main body is padded and has a holster stitched right to it. The holster has a thumb-break strap that goes over the hammer. You must use a revolver with a hammer spur in order for this holster (or almost any ankle

rig) to be secure. If you try to lock a hammerless model in, the strap has nothing to hold on to, and you'll eventually part company with your handgun. An extra strap goes above your calf muscle, and secures to the ankle rig. You have two straps to keep it in place, keep it from falling down and keep it in place on your leg. A word about location: The traditional location is on the inside of the leg opposite your strong hand. That is, right-handed shooters should wear it on the inside of the left leg, grip to the rear. It will be accessible there to either hand. One trick my friend Mas Ayoob pointed out to those wishing to pack in the holster and keep it a secret is to wear a larger pair of socks to cover the holster. A black sock with a bulge could be a wrapped ankle from a sports injury. But a holster is… well, a holster. The 8820 is comfortable for daily carry, washable, and you can get it for a number of handguns. I just wear a J frame in mine, as I'm old school and look on backup guns as something chosen from the revolver rack, and not pistols.

To put it on and make it comfortable, first insert the unloaded revolver in the holster and adjust the thumb-break strap. Then remove the revolver and wrap the holster around your ankle and tighten the main strap. Then insert the handgun you'll be wearing (unloaded) and check the fit. It may be that "tight enough" lacking the gun is too tight once you have the extra tension of the revolver in there.

Just because you can carry someplace doesn't mean you can carry everyplace. Check before you travel, or you may be in trouble.

Shall Issue

Not so many years ago, getting a concealed carry permit was not easily done. In many locales it was simply impossible despite the wording of the law. You had to in many jurisdictions prove need of a firearm. And as soon as the need went away, so did the permit. In Detroit, getting a permit in the old days was easy if you were a big political contributor, the owner of a party store or a retired police officer. Everyone else could spend months or years trying, and fail. Or having succeeded, get issued a "CCW" with so many restrictions it was practically useless. In New York, fuggedaboudit. Your chances of acquiring a home permit (keep it at home, don't carry it) were slim, and a carry permit was the provenance of the few, the wealthy, the politically hyper-connected. And don't bother getting something from Upstate, as no one (and I mean No One) had a valid permit to carry in the City unless it was issued by the City. In California, you could get a county permit that was good in the state, but only if you had a residence in the issuing county. Chicago had banned handguns, so a carry permit was simply a fantasy.

Then things began to change. Thanks to grass-roots work the laws were changed, updated or enacted to read "shall issue." The difference is simply this: in a "may issue" state, the legal body administering the permits looks at your needs or training or both, and may or may not issue you a permit depending on if they determine your need is sufficient. The big Catch-22 was simple: you proved need by depositing large sums of cash at the bank, or transporting compact valuables such as gems. Once armed, you could not use the firearm except in defense of yourself, not the valuables. So danger to your person was not enough to get a permit, but the only condition under which you could use it. I know, it makes little sense, but that's how it was.

In a "shall issue" state, you simply have to meet the threshold requirements. Usually, a citizen or resident alien, no criminal record, take a class and prove ability. Once you have met the requirements, the issuing agency must either prove why you are disqualified, or issue you the permit. They "shall issue" the permit unless they have clear proof otherwise.

The changes have happened in many states, but there are still holdouts. New York City is still a bad place to try to own a firearm. You cannot even carry there as an off-duty police officer unless you are an NYC officer. (Federal agents have special dispensations, but even they have restrictions.) The whole State of California is the same way. I was told point-blank by officers from both places not to carry even with a badge, for it would do no good. Chicago is, well, Chicago. But the rest of Illinois is "safe" for off-duty visiting police officers. Not so Wisconsin, which is hard to figure.

The thing you have to be aware of is this: just because you can carry where you are doesn't mean you can carry where you're going. Learn the law, read up on your vacation spot, and if at all possible make some law enforcement contacts. They can advise you on what is common practice even if it isn't black-letter law, on the place where you're going.

Once you have the holster body and revolver positioned, strap the upper strap around your leg over the calf muscle. Then run the connector strap down and Velcro them together. Pull the trouser cuff down over the holster and take a few steps around the room. Adjust if needed. If you find yourself out of the house and need to adjust, find a restroom and get into a stall. Don't simply find a convenient corner that is "unobserved" and adjust. You never know who is going to step around the corner and find you with your pants up.

The 8820 works for any J frame with a hammer spur, so one of the Airlites with a hammer spur would be perfect. You could, if your wardrobe would hide it, add a K frame snubbie with a hammer spur to the mix, although you'd have to select the correct holster from the Uncle Mike's catalog. One application for the ankle rig that many have discovered is for drivers. If you're seated and belted in, getting to a belt holster can be nearly impossible. A shoulder rig will do, but an ankle rig works well also. The only drawback comes for those of us with big feet. In some vehicles, if you have big feet there may not be enough room in the footwell, and under the steering wheel, to get to the gun. You definitely want to practice with an unloaded handgun in your garage with the door closed before you go depending on an ankle rig.

Waistband

You can hide anything at your waist if you have a cover garment (jacket, sweater, Hawaiian shirt) to put over it. Most who carry use a sports jacket or suit jacket, but in the summertime the Hawaiian shirt option is quite popular in some social groups. The trick is finding something that is both concealable and comfortable. Some are quite happy with an "inside-the-waistband" holster, while others find that anything but an on-the-belt is agony to wear. The difference is in where the holster rides. Does it go inside the belt, between you and the belt? Then it is an in-the-pant design. An on-the-belt model puts the holster and gun outside the belt. (Although you can wear many outside holsters between belt and waistband by running your belt through the loops the "wrong" way.) Two special cases of outside holsters are the "paddle" holster where you have a stiff backer on the holster that slides down between belt and waistband or belt and waistband and you, and the "pancake" which has loops front and back, rather on the backside of the holster.

One outside I have is the Galco COP. It is a pancake design made of leather, and uses loops on either side of the holster body to secure to the belt. The front has two loops so you can wear it either straight up and down, or tilted forward, the "FBI Cant." The thumb break strap

The Galco COP is a very comfortable thumb-break pancake holster.

keeps the gun secure. The model I have is for the Glock and Sigma. The strap keeps it secure, and there is also a tension adjustment at the rear, tightening the holster on the trigger guard. You can adjust the tension to the point that even doing a handstand the Sigma will stay in place with the thumb break strap unsnapped. To put on and adjust the COP, take the empty holster and loop your belt through the loops. Tighten your belt and insert the unloaded handgun. Check fit, comfort and your ability

to draw. Look in the mirror to see if it is truly hidden by your jacket. If everything checks out, load up and go. (don't forget to put your CCW in your wallet!)

Wilson Combat makes a lot of gear that will be useful to the owners of the SW1911. One is the "Tactical"

The strap goes over the back of the slide on the SW9.

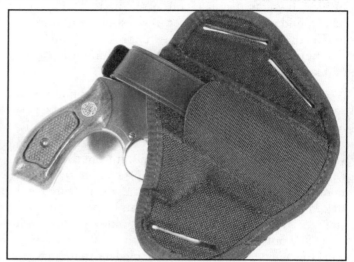
Uncle Mike's makes a synthetic pancake holster. The two forward slots give you two choices for the angle the holster rides on your belt.

On the draw, lift the sweater or windbreaker...

...grasp the handgun (the 5906TSW in an Uncle Mike's Kydex rig)...

...thrust up and forward...

...getting both hands on the gun...

...and get the sights to your line of sight.

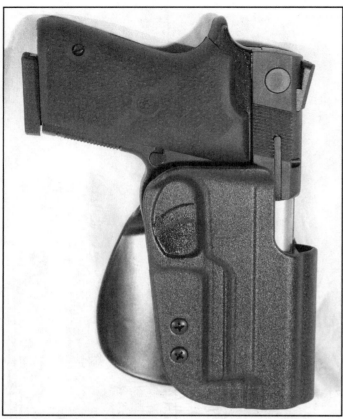

Uncle Mike's Kydex paddle holster with the S&W 4040PD in it. A compact and comfortable carry combo.

TA1 holster. IDPA approved, it holds an SW1911 high and tight. A little high for me, but my wardrobe problems are not yours. For many shooters it is quite comfortable. I have to quit wearing it after about eight hours. The Tactical is a compression-formed open-topped holster with a tension retainer at the trigger guard. It has a back panel and loops to hold it to your belt. The wear is very slightly tilted forward, not enough to require breaking your wrist as in the FBI cant, but not straight up and down. Suede-lined and offered in leather and sharkskin, the holster is stiff and secure but fast.

The synthetic world gained a new application when holstermakers figured out how to use Kydex in making holsters. Kydex is a sheet-made synthetic that can be cut and formed to create holsters. You can create two sheets and screw or rivet them together, or you can wrap one sheet completely around a firearm. Uncle Mike's makes the wraparound type, and bolts a belt adapter to the back. The tension comes from two sources: the wrap of the Kydex, and the compression of two screws down behind the dustcover, which both squeezes the Kydex wrap and bulges two rubber washers to provide friction. Kydex holsters are legendary for their durability, as they shrug off most abuse with aplomb. The worst you can do is scuff or gouge a Kydex holster You can't get a knife through it. A holster like the Uncle Mike's Kydex 5319 can be concealed with the right jacket, as the gun will

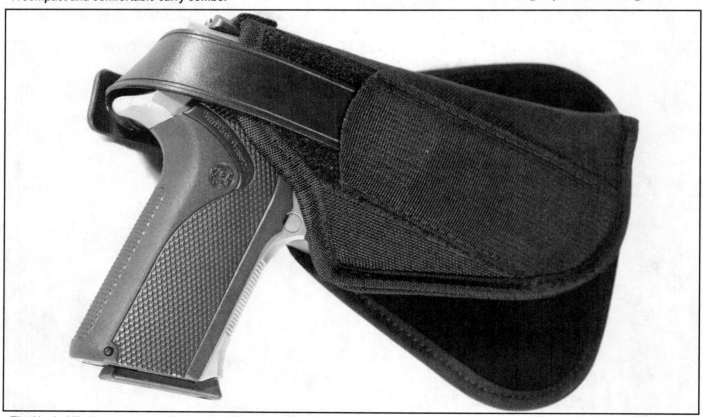

The Uncle Mike's cordura paddle, with a "grippy" paddle back to keep it secure.

stand out from your belt some. But it won't fall out, and you'll find the draw plenty fast.

A paddle holster I like is the Uncle Mike's 7815. Unlike a lot of designs that use hooks or knobs to provide friction on your belt (and thus keep the holster in place) the 7815 uses a very "grippy" synthetic on the paddle itself. The synthetic resists sliding across the fabric of your clothes. You can use a paddle holster without a belt, provided your waistband fits tightly enough and is of a heavy enough fabric to hold the weight. If the fabric is too light you'll find your handgun flopping around, exposing it to view or falling off. Even if it doesn't fall off, a loose holster tires you out from the beating you take from your own gear. To adjust or put on a paddle, you have to loosen your belt or your waistband. Loosen, insert empty holster, tighten. Check fit, install unloaded handgun. If you need to adjust, unholster, loosen, adjust, tighten and check again. It may take some doing, but you can find a comfortable location.

The Uncle Mike's Kydex paddle holsters use a retainer, but a very secure one. The paddle is secured to the back of the holster body (Uncle Mikes makes the holster bodies so they will fit on any one of the several securing/attachment systems they make) with a pair of screws. The paddle has an "S" shaped tab bolted to it near the bottom that will grab your clothes if you attempt to pull it out. I'm not sure it will stay put against a determined gun grab, but it certainly isn't going to come out inadvertently. As with all paddle holsters, it puts the

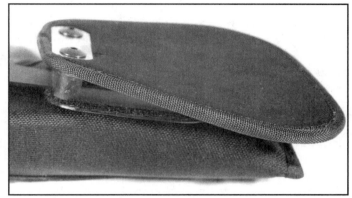

The grippy back does not use hooks or loops.

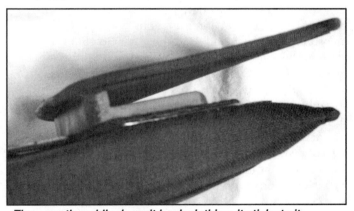

The smooth paddle doesn't hook clothing, it sticks to it.

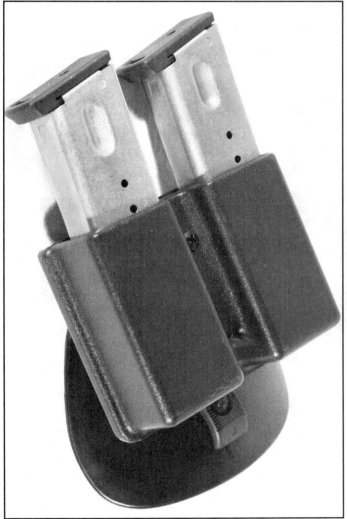

Note the hook, under the magazine boxes, that catches on your clothing to keep the mag pouch on your belt.

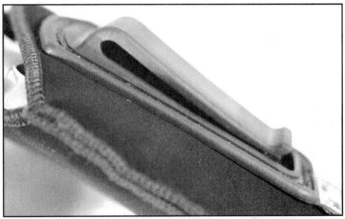

The back of the simple open-topped Uncle Mike's belt holster. Slide the holster in your pants and hook the clip on your belt. Yes, it's that simple.

handgun in a higher ride than I often find comfortable. Depending on the style handgun I'm wearing, I can find some paddle holsters OK, and some push the gun so high that I feel the sights in my floating ribs. You may also find the same thing, and the only way to know is to try. You will probably (as all long-time gun wearers have) end up with a box full of old holsters, holsters that don't fit, holsters that aren't comfortable, holsters that fit guns you no longer own.

One location some like and some hate (put me down in the hate column) is the small of the back. The idea is to put the gun behind you where it is less likely to be seen and detected. For me, it simply translates into agony in short order. The only way you can tell if an s.o.b. works for you is to try one. It will only take a couple of minutes to tell if it isn't.

A deep-concealment holster that works better for me than the s.o.b. is the belly band holster. Think of a money belt with a handgun in it, and you'll be close. You wear it above the belt and not below as most money belts are worn. The body of the holster (Uncle Mike's #8746) must be selected according to your waist first. Most holsters are solely selected for the gun they hold, but the belly band must fit you first, and all the way around. A word of caution here: don't use your "vanity" waistline measurement. We've all seen the guy who claims his waist is the same size as it was in high school, because he's wearing the same size jeans, right? Except he isn't fooling anyone, what with his belly drooping over his struggling belt. No, measure your waist above the midsection, where the holster will go, and get the correct one to start with. Don't use your belt length as the measure, actually wrap a tape measure around yourself and order a band from that measurement. The band goes around you with the Velcro strap under the secure loop and attached to the band body Velcro stripe. Once you have it comfortably located (an undershirt helps for comfort) then attach the correct holster body to the belly strap. The holster location depends on how you expect to use the holster. If you plan on a two-handed draw (left hand lifts shirt, right hand draws) then putting the holster over on the left side of your body works fine. If you contemplate a one-handed draw (right hand fished under shirt, lifts to holster, draws) then over on the right side is the place for it to be. In any case you are not going to be setting any quick-draw records. The holster exists to let you carry in the worst summer heat: you're wearing a Hawaiian shirt, shorts and deck shoes. Where else can you carry a gun, for goodness sake? I find wearing the band just over where my belt runs is quite comfortable. In addition to the Velcro strip that holds the holsters, the band is sewn so that there are pockets in the mesh of the band where you can put other items. One I'd be sure to add would be

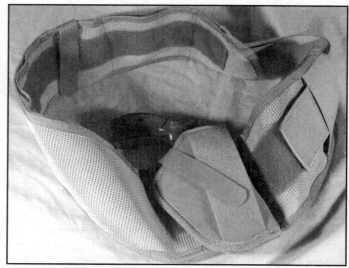

The belly-band holster.

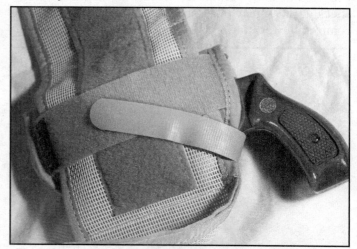

The holster attachment to the belly-band holster. Once assembled, you put it on and then don your Hawaiian shirt.

a carrier for your CCW, which you must have with you when you are armed.

Sometimes the simplest is the best. A simple, open-topped, clip in the belt, inside the waistband synthetic holster gets the job done as well as the expensive stuff does. This is especially true for someone who will be carrying concealed in a highly controlled environment, like working behind the counter in a store. With a counter between you and the customers (and the "customers") you won't have to worry about a wrestle and gun grab attempt. You aren't going to be chasing anyone. And you may only be carrying while on premises, so easy-on/easy-off makes a difference. The basic Uncle Mike's clip-on holster works. I know, because we sold a lot of them at the gun shop. For a lot of people it was an entry-level holster, the one they got because they needed a holster and didn't want to spend any more than they needed to in order to get started. But many found it was all they needed.

To adjust the strap, insert an unloaded handgun in the holster body.

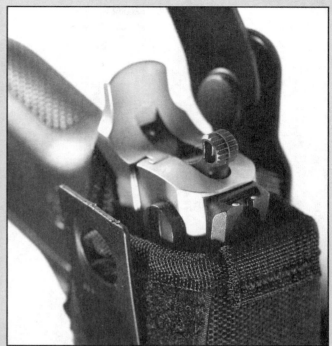

Secure the snap.

Adjusting the Velcro universe

In the old days we'd struggle to get tightly fitted leather straps to go over the guns for which they were designed to fit. If a leather strap was too short you were stuck. If it was too long you had a loose fit, and the gun finish would wear from rubbing and movement. With synthetics everywhere, we now have the "one-size-fits-all" Velcro-secured strap. Except no one seems able to fit them. The easy way is to use a flat plastic paddle (which many makers pack with every holster) to slide the straps. The method is as follows:

Take the holster and the unloaded firearm. Slide the handgun in the holster and the paddle or paddles between the Velcro strap and the holster body. If the strap does not have an exterior securing layer, just peel it up. Now snap the two halves of the strap together, the thumb-break portion and the snap portion. Slide the thumb-break portion down into the channel with the paddle between the strap Velcro and the holster Velcro. (or secure it to the holster body) Adjust it so the thumb-break points straight up. Now slide the paddle out and press the Velcro parts together. Push the other leg over the back of the handgun, and down the channel, with the paddle riding between the two Velcro surfaces. Once tight, slide the paddle out and press the Velcro together. If the

Bend it over and insert into the velcro tunnel with the paddle between strap and Velcro attachment panel.

The paddle must go between the two sections of Velcro.

thumb-break flap is metal-backed, bend the metal just above the snap to create a "V". If it is plastic, you may have to readjust the strap so the flap is pointing towards your body. You want a "V" in the snap for your thumb to ride in as a wedge.

As a refinement, orient the straps as much as possible so the force of the gun trying to come out when secured acts in a straight line on the strap. You do not want the strap at an angle to the forces trying to open it. If you have it at an angle, it will eventually peel away and leave you unsecured.

If your holster was not shipped with a paddle, and you don't have one from another holster, you can use a popsicle stick, tongue depressor, or unsharpened training knife (called a "drone") as a paddle. Under no circumstances should you use a knife with a live blade. You will be pushing and struggling, and sometimes using vile language. One slip with a plastic paddle does no harm. One slip with a sharp knife and the fit of your thumb-break straps may be the least of your concern. At least until the stitches come out.

Pull out the paddle and press the Velcro to lock it.

The shoulder holster gets a lot more use than you'd think from what you see at practice ranges and competitions. Most competitions don't allow them, and many ranges that cater to the general public don't allow holster work of any kind, so how would you know? Work the counter at a gun shop in a high-percentage carry location. My first exposure to a shoulder rig that worked was at the old Gun Room run by Mike Karbon. I was working the counter when an obvious police officer in plain clothes asked if we had speedloaders for the S&W M-29. I said sure. He asked if he could try them to make sure they fit. (The HKS speedloaders were new at the time, and speedloaders in general had a poor reputation before then.) He reaches inside his leather bomber jacket, produces an eight inch blued M-29 and flips open the cylinder and unloads before anyone can say a word. My, oh my! You see, he was all of 5-feet, 8-inches tall. Since then I've had a fondness for shoulder rigs. My favorite is an old one, an upside down rig with elastic holding the trigger guard inside the holster body. The two other methods of holding a handgun are the horizontal and the vertical. The horizontal works when you have enough body depth (and a short enough handgun) to keep it from "printing" through your shirt or jacket. The vertical can be very comfortable, but you are again limited in overall length.

The shoulder rig is very popular in cold climates. Many police officers carry a backup gun in a shoulder holster. Under a winter jacket it is easy to access, comfortable, and not trapped by the seat belt and seat cushion of a patrol car.

Hunting

The basic open carry holster can work quite well for hunting. The main things to be aware of are the hunting regulations and how they apply to concerning concealed carry. Draping a coat over your gun to protect it from the rain or snow will be fine, right up until the DNR officer wants to see your CCW. You know, the one you don't have. For those who do, and want to have a concealed carry that is open and secure, the Safepacker is great. Made by The Wilderness, it looks like a map case or gear pouch. The Velcro on the back can be strapped to a pack, belt, bandolier or cargo bag. It also has a strap on top for clutch carry like a purse, or wrist carry where you stuff your hand through the strap and let the pouch dangle. The strap unbuckles to expose a partial tear-away pouch that holds a handgun and spare magazine or speedloader. The one designed for a Government model not only holds the SW1911, but also all the full size 39, 40 and 59 series, the SW9 and SW99, and with a little coaxing, the ultra lightweight 329. While it isn't a speed holster it is a lot faster than a gun stuffed in a pouch on your backpack, or hidden under a couple of layers of clothing.

For open but protected carry you need an Uncle Mike's flapped holster. The shoulder or chest rigs will carry even the biggest handguns protected from the weather but also obviously openly carried as a hunting rig, and not concealed to cause you hassles.

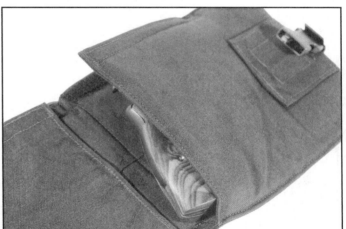

Undo the snap and you have a hint of things to come.

The SafePacker closed. What's in it? Only the shadow knows.

Mr. Bear or Mr. Mugger is in for a big surprise.

Competition

There are three kinds of competition holsters; speed, speed with concealment, and "don't let it drop on the floor" standards. For ICORE, USPSA/IPSC, Steel Challenge, Handgunner Shootoff and Bianchi Cup you want speed. For IDPA you want speed with concealment. And for PPC, just don't let it fall. Speed rigs will work for PPC, so if you're going to switch back and forth between the two types of shooting then get a speed rig and stay safe. For IDPA you will have to select something from the IDPA Approved Holster List.

The speed holster I've had the most luck with comes from Safariland. The Model 002 is an open-topped holster with a muzzle flap to keep the muzzle from tipping out if you have to walk or run with it. I simply took the flap off, as I found that the retention by means of the tension of the holster on the cylinder was more than enough to keep it in place. The holster is a laminated and heat-molded structure with a soft inner layer that should keep the finish from wearing when you practice your draw and dry fire. The outside is a tough basketweave surface that is waterproof and easy to clean. In between them is a tough, flexible synthetic that provides the tension to secure the revolver. The 002 takes advantage of the supposed drawback of revolvers: the cylinder. The big round thing in the middle provides a perfect

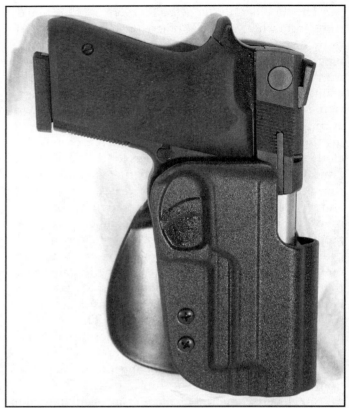

A Kydex holster, when for the intended gun, will retain the sidearm even when you are greatly exerted.

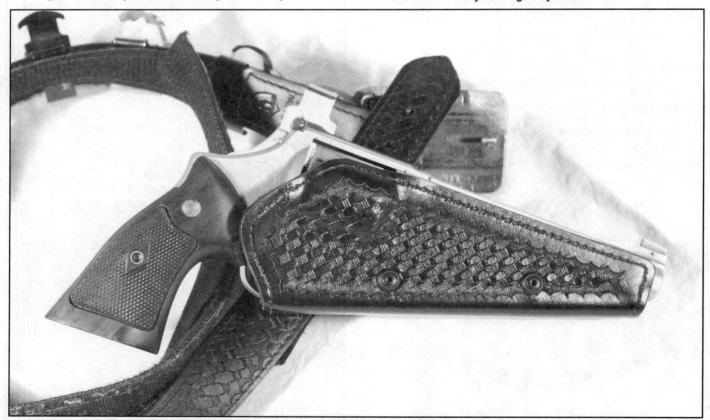

Competition holsters, like this Safariland, only have to be secure enough to keep you from being DQ'd for dropping your gun.

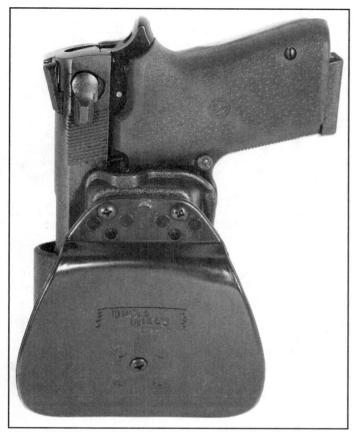

Some holsters are meant to be "high-ride" holsters. I find some of them ride too high on me.

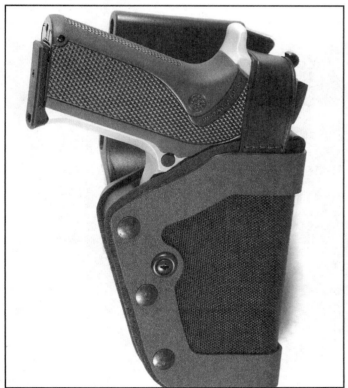

The Uncle Mike's Triple Retention duty holster, shown here for a 59/40, works very well.

securing place for the holster to grab. Where pistols, being flat, need something hanging on to the trigger guard, or a muzzle plug, or both, to be able to hold on, the 002 simply clamps around the cylinder. Your draw is what you want it to be. You can grab the grips and shove the gun forward, although that will not be the fastest draw. The best draw is to grasp the grips and "pop" the gun up out of the holster, towards your line of sight, and pivot to the target as it comes up. Once the gun and the cylinder have moved 2 inches or so, the friction of the holster to hold the cylinder is gone. I wear mine just forward of the hip line on my right side. I have long arms and a high waist, so the less I have to move my hand back to draw, the better I like it. High-ride hip holsters often leave me drawing by yanking the gun up into my armpit, a very slow and uncomfortable process.

Duty

When in uniform, a police officer has a unique problem that the rest of us don't: his gun is open to view by bad people who are accustomed to doing bad things. They may try to take it away from him. Carrying concealed, no one knows you have a gun, and so can't plan to grab it from you. (One of the very good reasons to keep a concealed gun concealed.) When hunting, you are unlikely to find yourself walking through groups of people, some of whom might be recent parolees, or real, live gangstas. But the police officer would be. His holster must be reasonably secure against unwanted attention. Weapon retention is not just a holster, it is also training and practice. But the right holster helps. There are several levels of retention. The simplest is friction fit, not a good thing for a duty holster. Competition holsters and concealed carry holsters can depend on friction alone. Duty holsters cannot. It isn't prudent. The first step up in security is a thumb-break strap. The Uncle Mikes PRO-2

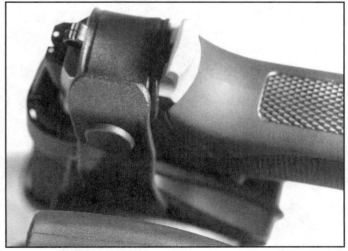

Note the thumb-break strap.

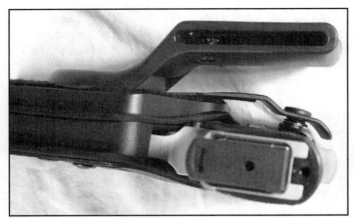

The jacket slot offset keeps the gun and jacket apart for a clean draw.

The back of all Uncle Mike's duty holsters give you angle adjustments so you can make it sit correctly for you.

uses friction and a thumb break to hold the handgun in place. If the snap comes undone, the friction will keep it in place, but not resist a grab attempt. For many officers, it is enough. I prefer more. The Uncle Mikes PRO-3 uses a thumb break strap, friction, and a trigger guard lock to hold the gun in. If someone tries to grab the gun, and doesn't know which direction it takes to rock the gun to disengage the third lock, they won't get it. However, you must practice the particular draw from your holster. You must practice it enough to be reflexive in its use. I train police officers in Illinois, and have heard more than one instance where a police officer was issued a new "secure"

holster but not given sufficient training to use it. (Would a chief or sheriff hand someone the keys to a patrol car not knowing if he or she had a drivers license? The keys to the traffic copter? So why issue a holster with no training? I don't get it.) One officer found himself in a lethal force situation, and could not get his handgun out. He'd practiced for 18 years with a plain thumb-break holster, and the new secure holster resisted his efforts. It also resisted the effort of the offenders, so he suffered only a severe beating and not the execution with his own sidearm they intended. Had he gotten the correct training (and enough of it) he could have avoided the beating as well.

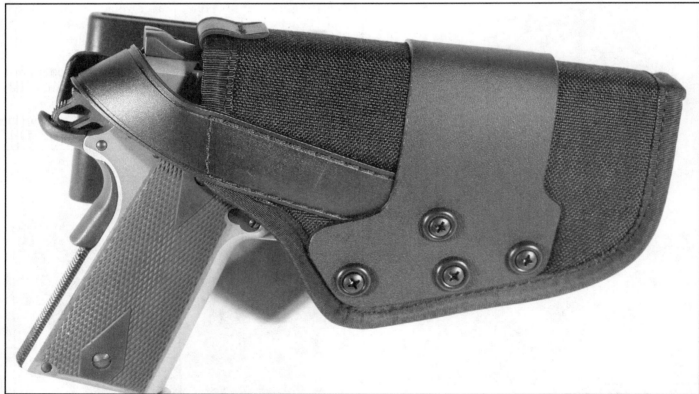

The dual retention from Uncle Mike's keeps the gun in place.

Service/Tactical

The categories used to be separate, but the changes in both police and military uses have changed and converged) so much that they are much the same. The typical tactical holster now is one of two choices: a thigh holster or a vest holster.

The trigger guard retention plate inside the Blackhawk CQR. This holster works so well I have to pry it back from the hands of the DEA Agent I had loaned it to.

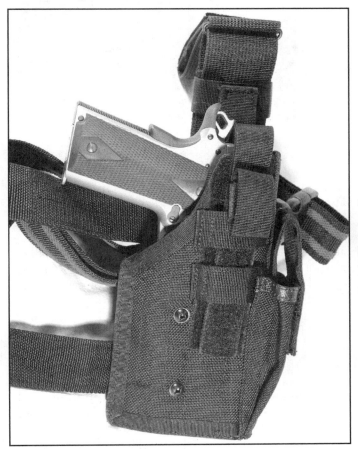

The Blackhawk CQR, side view.

I have several thigh holsters that I have found to be very useful. The first is the latest, a Blackhawk CQR. The problem with a lot of tactical thigh holsters is that they are made of fabric. Synthetic fabric to be sure, very durable and washable, but still fabric. I found on a recent class that the holster I had been using then would not keep the thumb safety of the 1911 I was wearing "On." On two occasions I drew to find the safety already off. Not a comforting feeling. The Blackhawk CQR (which is available for a number of handguns, but only the SW1911 from the S&W line) has a rigid tensioned interior that holds the handgun by clamping on the trigger guard. Most other tactical rigs simply use the thumb break strap (which the CQR has) to keep the handgun in. But the CQR also holds with the inner holster. At a class right after it arrived I found the CQR fast, secure and the safety never came off. (Safeties come off from moving in the holster, rubbing the lever off. Since the handgun can't move inside the CQR, it can't rub.) One thing I have found with Blackhawk holsters (and other makers, too) is that they make the drop straps for average guys. Shooters like me who are long-legged and high-waisted, can often end up with the "tactical jock strap"

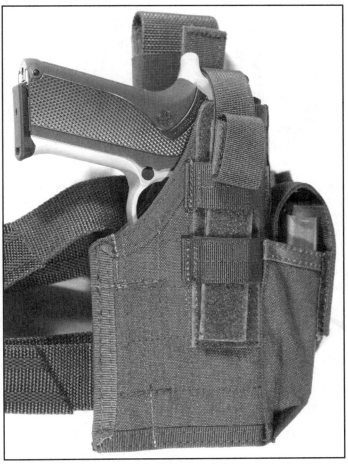

The London Bridge Trading Company lightmount tactical holster keeps a pistol and a light.

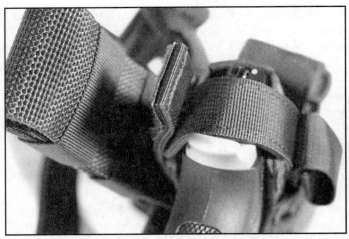

The LBTR tactical holster thumb-break strap is all about retention.

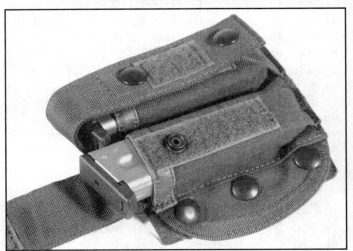

The Blackhawk SpecOps pouch, with three snaps to make it fast on or off.

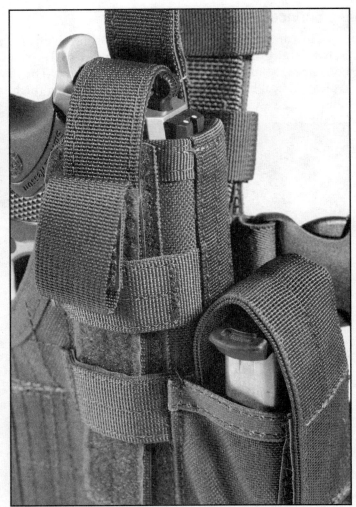

The spare magazine pouch, and fast-secure Velcro retention strap, coiled on the side help keep things in place.

effect of a holster trying to ride too high. If you have this problem, be sure and get the drop-leg extender to go with your holster.

Another holster maker I am fond of in the tactical arena is made by London Bridge Trading Company. They sent me a holster for handguns with tactical lights attached. For those using the 5906TSW or the 4006TSW with the light attached, the LBTC light rig can be just the thing.

Blade Tech makes a tactical thigh rig of Kydex, with friction and thumb-break retention. As with all Kydex holsters is isn't flexible, so if you happen to roll over on that side you will find the handgun and holster a stout lump under your leg. However, laden with all the gear SWAT team members wear, the extra lump of the Blade Tech holster is not going to be unique.

Any tactical holster needs magazine pouches. While they all have a spare magazine pouch on the holster itself, if you need the handgun you probably need more

than the one spare. One convenient mag pouch is the Blackhawk Special Operations pouch. It holds two magazines with a flap that has both Velcro and snaps. The snaps are positioned to hold either standard-length magazines or extended length magazines. If you're carrying a 5906 or a 4006, you can have the standard magazines on. Something that uses extended magazines (like 20-shot magazines for the 5906) won't be left out, as the second snap fits right in place for the longer magazines. You can even use single-stack 1911 magazines that hold 10 rounds. And if your magazines are an odd length, and don't fall right to the snaps, the Velcro still holds the pouches shut. The outside of the flaps have small Velcro panels so you can secure them open if you want to have an open-topped pouch for speed. The SpecOps pouch uses three snaps on its securing flap to attach to your belt or a cargo or webbing strap. There is a Velcro panel on the back to hold it in place. Unlike many other pouches that require partial undressing to add them to your gear, the SpecOps can be attached or removed just by unsnap-

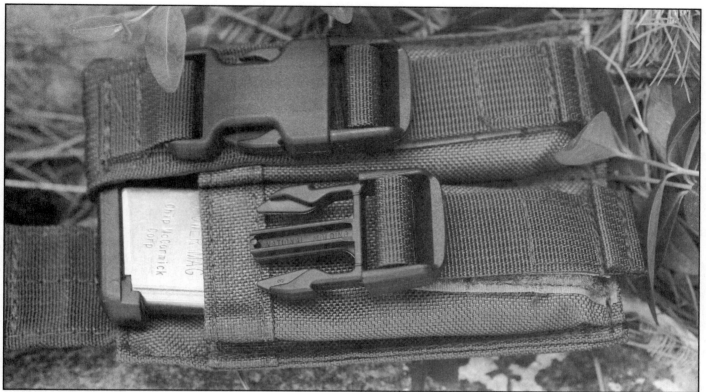

The SOE Gear dual-mag pouch is tough enough to get dropped, stepped on or kicked and not show the wear.

The dual-mag version of Uncle Mike's Kydex magazine pouches.

ping it and prying the Velcro away from wherever it is. You can add the pouch in a few seconds when gearing up, or take it off and toss it to someone who needs it more than you do at the moment.

Another pouch that is hell for tough comes from SOE Gear in southern California. While it does not have the easy-on/easy-off flap of the Blackhawk, it is secure, adaptable and tough. At a class last year I had to put it down to do some armorer's maintenance, and forgot to pick it up when done. (A perfect demonstration of why you attach everything you need or plan to use to your person.) A few hours later we discovered it when one of the students kicked it across the range while walking to the targets. It had obviously been stepped on several times, and kicked, and it was none the worse for the experience. Nor were the magazines inside. John Willis of Special Operations Equipment knows how to make tough gear. He must, many of his customers come from the ranks of Marine Recon units. If they have a problem with his gear they are certain to complain.

Any holster you select should be one you have tested for the ability to draw. Can you get your hand on the gun in a full firing grip (except for your trigger finger) before the gun ever leaves the holster? If you have to pluck the handgun out with your fingertips, then get a good grip, that is not a good holster. And despite the open-trigger design being very popular for cowboy shooting, I would

Uncle Mike's also makes a belt slide attachment for those who do not want a paddle, pancake or clip-on.

loader pouches is that they can often be mistaken in this digital age for cell phone or pager pouches, or PDA carriers. While the holster is clearly a holster, the smaller pouches for the rest of your gear are simply glossed over when seen, mistaken for something else.

Competition is different, both in that no one is alarmed when they see you (at least not on the range) and speed matters more than comfort or security. For competition I go with open-topped mag pouches. Uncle Mikes makes Kydex carriers, both belt and paddle. You can get them in singles or as pairs, for any sized magazine you might be using. Fobus also makes synthetics that are very useful and quite fast. Serious competition shooters will go with the fastest, regardless of how expensive they are. Unless you are going to be slugging it out with Dave Sevigny for the Production Division title at the next USPSA Nationals, you do not need to spend $20, $30 or $40 per magazine carrier. (Then again, Dave doesn't, either.)

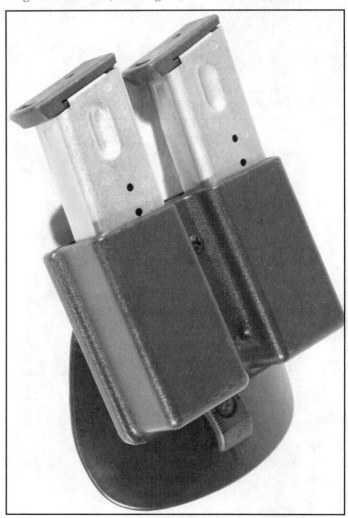

You should take spare magazines with you if you leave the house armed. After all, if you're unlucky enough to need a loaded gun, who says you'll be lucky enough to solve your problem with only the ammo in the gun?

pass on any holster that doesn't cover the triggerguard when the handgun is holstered. You have enough to worry about when drawing in a stressful situation than adding to your worries with a trigger open to your trigger finger. Many traditional (and currently-made) holsters have open trigger guards. I'd advise passing on them. It is easy enough in this day and age to get a holster that covers the trigger. Get one.

Spare ammo

You simply cannot walk out of the house without spare ammunition. Yes, statistically you will probably not need the extra ammo. But if you were going by the odds, you wouldn't have a gun on, now would you? At the very least you need a spare speed loader for a revolver or a spare magazine for your pistol. To carry them you need a pouch of some kind. The simplest pouch for a speedloader is the Velcro-flapped belt pouch from Uncle Mike's. You can pay a lot more, but what you'll get are dressier looks and not greater function. Magazines require belt pouches. The good thing about magazine and speed-

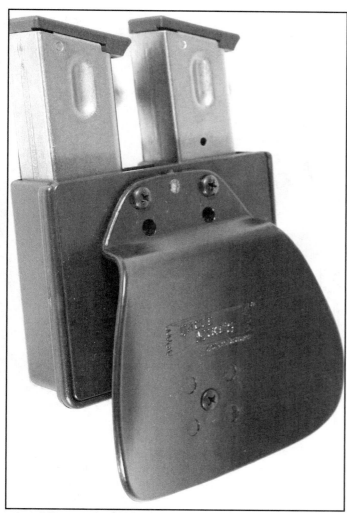

A paddle mag pouch is easy-on and easy-off for those who need to "unload" their belt repeatedly during the day.

Revolver competition, where you'll be using moon clips, adds another problem. You have to grasp the moon clip itself to pull if from your belt and put it in the revolver. Unlike speedloaders there is no knob or handle. The best solution is the "Shoot the Moon" carrier from California Competition Works. It is a sheet steel clip with a plastic center that keeps the moon clip securely on your belt. However, competition shooters can always find a way to improve things. Most shooters lock just two of the rounds in the carrier, leaving the rest of the moon clip sticking out from the carrier. The moon clip is secure (at least by competition standards) and quickly accessible.

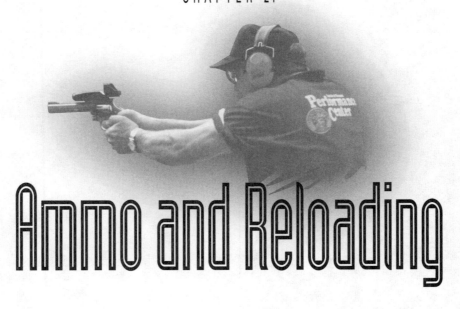

CHAPTER 24

Ammo and Reloading

Smith & Wesson handguns have been chambered in almost every handgun caliber offered in the 20th century. There are a few exceptions, you won't find an S&W pistol in .41 Action Express. Or the 9mm rimmed. But all the common ones will be there. Just so you have a reference, I've listed the calibers, and for those who plan to reload their own ammo, a few tips and dimensions that I've found useful through the years.

Reloading for S&W

In many respects, reloading for the whole line of S&W handguns is almost as simple as falling off a log. There is a whole raft of issues that you needn't worry too much about. Things that groups like Glock shooters and those fond of Single Action Army revolvers have to contend with simply don't exist in the S&W universe. And the fussing that 1911 owners go on about tuning extrac-

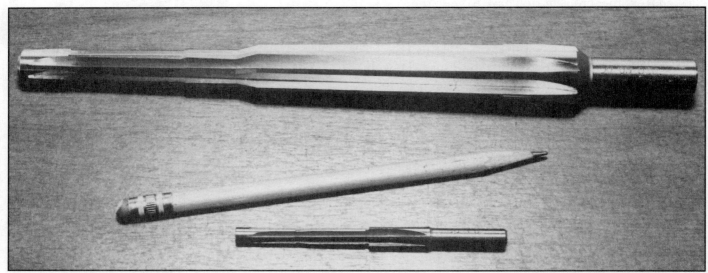

While S&W handguns have been chambered in many cartridges through the century, there are limits. You can't have an S&W in just anything.

tors and getting loads just right are also puzzles to S&W owners. First, the things you needn't worry about.

Lead Bullets

Lead may be a heavy metal, and hazardous in some regards, but it is not the problem for S&W shooters that it is for Glock shooters. Glocks are extremely unfriendly to lead bullets. They were designed for jacketed ammo, and that is what they want. Feed them lead bullets and you can suffer accuracy problems, and may even crack a frame or barrel as a result of lead buildup. S&Ws don't do that. Their rifling is cut and of the Enfield design, not the polygonal of Glocks. And as lead was the customary bullet material for decades of revolvers shooting, S&W has a lot of experience with lead bullets. You would be well-served by loading hard-cast lead bullets in pistols, and lead of the correct hardness for the revolvers, depending on the application. The hardness that is appropriate for a wadcutter bullet at target velocities is not appropriate for a .44 Magnum hunting load. (You want the wadcutter dead soft and at a low velocity, while the hunting load should be as hard as possible and will usually be at the highest velocity.) Lead may be viewed by the State of California as a Plutonium substitute, but it isn't a reloading problem for S&W owners.

S&W handguns don't care about lead or jacketed, just so long as the bullet is the correct diameter for the caliber and application.

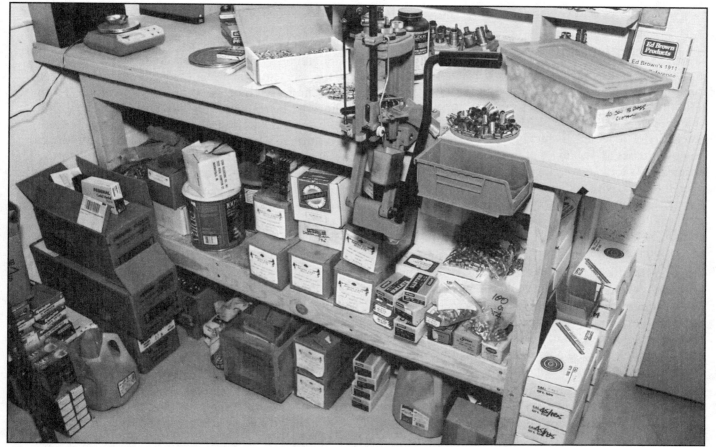

You don't need an elaborate reloading setup to turn out large amounts of good ammo.

Chamber & throat dimensions

SAA owners are famous for measuring the chambers, bore, throat and forcing cones of their revolvers, and figuring out the best compromise of bullet diameter and softness for best accuracy. It isn't uncommon for the nominal .452" bulleted .45 Colt to have a throat of .459", and for a .44 Special with its nominal .430" bullet to have throats of .425" to .427." Such mis-matches in bore, throat and bullet diameter are infamous for causing accuracy loss and leading problems. You will not likely find those problems in S&Ws. If you have a .44 Magnum, you can count on the bore being .430" to .431" and the throats likewise. You may find some Model 25-5 revolvers with throats a bit over the .452-.453" they should be, but with the SAAMI specs maxed out at .459" it is understandable if your 25-5 throats come in at .454". For the most part you can count on the dimensions being what they are supposed to be. No wild swings in diameters, or mis-matched bore and throats. My friend Dave Manson even makes a special fixture and reamer for gunsmiths who need to adjust throat size. For those revolvers with undersized throats, he can provide the tool to ream them to the correct (and uniform) dimensions. As much as Dave would like to sell all of them he makes, you're probably buying a paperweight if you get one "just in case" for your S&W revolvers.

Extractor tension

S&W pistol extractors pivot, not flex, and the feed ramps are one-piece. The magazines of the S&W pistols hold the rounds high and in a straighter line with the chamber than does the 1911. (Except, of course, for the SW1911.) The feeding is slick, fast and even, without the bumps, hitches and changes of direction that the 1911 is heir to. As long as you have a cartridge of the correct overall length, with sufficient neck tension to prevent setback and enough crimp to keep the case mouth from catching, your ammo will feed. They are so forgiving that ammo you can feed an S&W might choke other pistols. You could get into bad habits if you weren't careful.

And the things to worry about? Make sure your belling stem is the correct diameter. Use tungsten carbide or titanium nitride sizing dies. Don't be cheap, pass on the steel dies. And buy good bullets. There is probably a reason the "cheapest cast bullets in town" are that cheap. Get them the correct diameter for your caliber, and the correct hardness for your application.

When it comes to crimping, the important thing to remember is this: The crimp does not hold the bullet under recoil, the neck tension does. Crimping in pistols is done to ease feeding, so the sharp corner left at the case mouth by firing and sizing is ironed out of the way.

Black Hills doesn't just reload, they also load new. And with few exceptions, you won't need to trim handgun brass.

A hard roll crimp on revolver rounds can help accuracy and uniformity by providing resistance to the initial burn of the primer and powder. But neck tension is what keeps the bullet in place. If you do not have enough neck tension your loads will suffer. Make sure your belling stem (the powder drop activator on many progressive presses) is the correct diameter for your bullets.

One subject that comes up with amazing regularity is trimming brass. Rifle reloaders do it on a frequent, sometimes even every loading, basis. Rifle brass is a special case. Rifles operate above (in some instances far above) handgun pressures. Rifle cases are bottlenecked, with a large capacity and a small bullet. Rifle cases flow on firing, and stretch on sizing and neck expanding. Handgun cases, being cylindrical, shorten when fired, and rarely extend back to full length when sized. The only two times to trim brass to a uniform length are the most exacting target loads and full-throttle hunting loads. The target loads need to be uniform for greatest accuracy. By making the cases the same length you create uniform neck tension, bullet release and crimp. For hunting, you want them the same for uniform burning of the large amounts of slow-burning powder you're using. And when you operate at the maximum pressure for a cartridge you do not want a stray, overly-long case coming along. It will be crimped harder than the rest, and cause an increase in pressures. Even a tough 629 or SW500 can be undone if you spike an already maximum operating pressure.

The overall length of the loaded round is subject to change with different bullets. The length depends on the bullet construction and shape. A flat-point bullet will load shorter than a pointed round nose, all things being equal. The manufacturers locate the crimping groove where they think it best (or customary) for the caliber in question. A bullet with a deep hollowpoint will load longer than the same weight as a soft-point. Usually. You

Did my testers and I shoot all this? All this and more! (Thanks again to Jeff Hoffman at Black Hills Ammunition!)

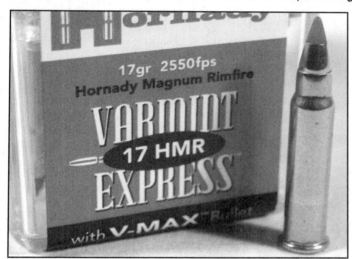

The .17 Hornady Magnum rimfire is one hot little number.

Derived from the .22 WRM, the .17 has its priming compound inside the rim, which must be crushed to fire.

see, the bullet manufacturers try to keep the bullets with the same weight proportioned so that they all have their bases at the same level in a loaded case. That way all bullets of a given weight and caliber have the same size combustion chamber. Keeping the combustion chamber the same simplifies generating loading data. If they did not, there could be large changes in the loading data for two different bullets of the same weight from the same maker, and we all know someone out there would get the data mixed up.

If you are going to be serious about competitive shooting, or reloading, you must have a chronograph. Without it you have no way of knowing what velocity your loads are producing. Guessing from felt recoil or muzzle blast will produce just that, guesses. Only the chrono knows for sure.

As I have mentioned before, most of the ammunition I shot for the testing came from Black Hills Ammunition. The rimfire ammo came from Hornady, the .500 came from Cor-bon, and the 9mm and .45 I used for some testing came from Zero Bullets. I have found them all to be exemplary sources of ammunition.

.17 Hornady Magnum Rimfire

The 17 HMR is one hot little number, and a new one. Unveiled in 2003, it was joined in 2004 by the 17 Mach 2. The HMR is made on a Magnum Rimfire case, where the Mach 2 is on a Long Rifle case. You will not be reloading either of them, as it is not feasible to reload rimfire cases.

.22 Long Rifle

The target standard for over a century, the long rifle is the most commonly produced cartridge in the United States and probably the world. The production of .22LR is in excess of four billion rounds per year. Which is a lot of plinking, what the long rifle is most commonly used for. As a practice round, or a cartridge to instruct a new shooter to the methods of marksmanship and safety, the LR is the best. You can't reload any centerfire cartridge at the same low cost as buying .22LR, and the recoil is so small it doesn't discourage new shooters. It is also not reloadable.

.32 Magnum

Actually the .32 H&R Magnum, the .32 was introduced in 1984 as a new and improved .32-20. The .32 bore had a large following in the first half of the 20th century, but faded rapidly in the face of the increasing popularity of the .38 Special. The .32 Magnum was intended to run at a higher pressure than the old low-pressure .32-20 loads, but not as high as the rifle-only loads the .32-20 can sometimes be found in. Shooting the rifle-only rounds in a handgun was too much for many, and hard even on those that could take it for a while. SAAMI specifications call for a maximum pressure of 21,000 copper units of pressure, which is just a bit higher than that of a .38 Special+P load. If the .32 Magnum was chambered in solid guns, why not a higher ceiling? Look at the name. ".32 Harrington & Richardson Magnum." The revolvers made by H&R were entirely serviceable, but not as sturdy as those of S&W. Why would they design a cartridge more powerful than their own guns could hold? And that was its downfall. Despite being offered in the most-excellent Model 16, a K frame, in the late 1980s, the Model 16 and the .32 never caught on. It didn't offer enough performance to warrant the hassle. If you could get a .32 or a .38 in the same frame, why not get the .38?

Reloading offers the .32 an option. In the K frame Model 16 you can push it past .38 Special+P pressures and get more performance. The SAAMI specs call for a .312" bullet, usually an 85-grain jacketed hollow point, at 1120 fps. Loading data often tops out at the 1000 fps level with an 85-grain jhp, but Hodgdon shows data over 1200 fps, and under the 21,000 cups ceiling.

For extra-soft practice, any .32 Magnum revolver will also chamber and fire .32 short and .32 Long cartridges.

For soft reloads for indoor shooting, load the Berry's .32 wadcutters.

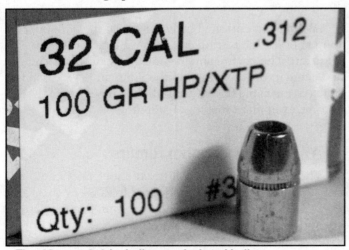

The .32 uses .312-inch diameter jacketed bullets.

The .32 Magnum came from the .32 S&W, through the .32 S&W Long.

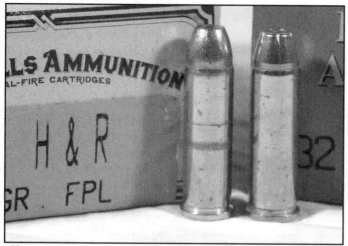
You can have soft-shooting lead loads (as in these Black Hills Cowboy) or hotter jacketed ones in .32.

When reloading, you want to use jacketed bullets of .312" for your high-velocity loads and cast bullets of .313" to .314' for softer loads. Target loads will call for soft cast or swaged lead bullets at .314", while higher-velocity loads would require harder cast bullets at .313" or .314" The belling stem of your sizing die should measure .305", and you should taper crimp to .330" If you use .308" bullets as a substitute (they are a common rifle diameter) then you should have a separate belling stem for the .308" bullet (the CCI "Plinker is a common choice here), one polished down to .302" or .303" in size. Otherwise you will not have sufficient neck tension, and powder ignition may be erratic. Maximum overall loaded length of the .32 is 1.350" as compared to the .32-20 at 1.590". There is the difference for the single-shot silhouette shooters.

9mm Parabellum

The 9 comes to us from Germany, courtesy the German Army of 1904. They liked the Luger, but weren't too hot on the .30 Luger round. Georg Luger opened the case as much as he could (the .30 Luger is bottlenecked) and still be able to fit it in the pistol. Thus the 9mm Luger or 9mm Parabellum was born. The 9mm had a bad reputation for many years as an inaccurate round. The problem was twofold; the guns were often made loose in fit and chamber for reliable feeding. And the ammunition was often surplus, and made for wartime use. As long as it went bang, cycled the weapon, and put a hole downrange, the makers were happy. Accuracy began to improve when the WonderNine Wars began. No police department is going to settle for "acceptable" accuracy when they can get more. No officer wants his scores to suffer, and no department wants the potential liability of using inaccurate ammo.

The 9mm is now a tack-driving target round when you need it to be. The bullets should be .354" for jacketed, and .355" for lead. You do not want soft lead. You do not need it for accuracy, and it will only lead to leading. The belling stem should be .351" or .352" in diameter, and crimping only to .372." I have found that crimping the 9mm too much can be bad for accuracy. Other calibers are more forgiving, but some 9mm pistols are not. And, some 9mm pistols can be touchy about the powder they will like. I have found that some will not shoot well with lead bullets and the fastest powders. In particular Bull's-eye. If your S&W pistol won't shoot well with lead reloads, start checking those variables: Bull's-eye and crimp. The pressure ceiling for the 9mm is 35,000

The 9mm Parabellum came from the .30 Luger. However, except for a few prototypes, there haven't been any S&W pistols done in .30 Luger.

The 9mm is threatening to knock the .38 Special off the top of the hill as the most popular centerfire handgun cartridge.

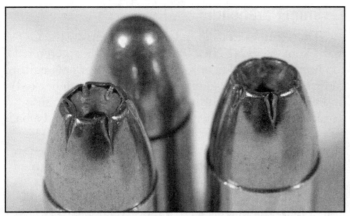
The 9mm can be had in lead, jacketed, hollowpoint and even softpoint loads.

psi, and there is little reason to exceed it. You can get more velocity with more pressure, but only at the cost of working the brass and gun harder. The maximum overall loaded length of the 9mm is 1.170".

When made accurate, a 9mm S&W pistol can easily win matches. They are all over the PPC courses in Any Pistol or Service Pistol categories, and many Action or Steel shooters have found that the combination of accuracy, ubiquitous brass and economy of loading is a hard one to beat.

The 9X19 and the .38 Special are tied for lowest-cost reloads that perform well. For the price of a standard primer, found/range pickup brass, a common lead bullet and 4 grains of powder, you can load and shoot either. At 4 grains per shot, a 7,000-grain pound of powder will load 1,750 rounds.

.38 S&W

Not to be confused with the .38 Special, the "S&W" is a shorter, fatter cartridge using a slightly larger diameter bullet. Despite the superior performance and accuracy of the .38 Special as soon as it came out, the .38 S&W hung on for many decades. And you may encounter WWII production S&W revolvers made for the British Commonwealth forces chambered in .38 S&W.

SAAMI specs call for a 146-grain lead round-nosed bullet at a stately 680 fps, with a pressure ceiling of 14,500 psi. The bullets are supposed to be a maximum diameter of .361", but good luck finding anything to match. You aren't going to be hot-rodding the .38 S&W,

The .38 S&W (right) is not a shorter version of the Special. They are not interchangeable.

Look at the barrel, and you can see the difference between the S&W and the Special.

so use soft .358" bullets meant for use in the .38 Special. The belling stem if you are using original-size bullets of .361" should be .354" to .355." If you are using .38 Special bullets, then use the belling stem for those, at .352" diameter. Crimp to .378". The loading process should be an attempt to duplicate the original power, as almost every revolver you'll ever see in .38 S&W will be a fixed-sight one. So you want your 158-grain bullets going about 725 pfs so they'll hit to the sights. If you want to shoot your old M&P from WWII in a match, you'll have to get a 158-grain bullet up to about 790 fps to make Minor in most competitions. The gun can take it, but you'll find the bullets hit high, and you will have to adjust. The book length for the .38 S&W is only 1.240", but as most of the S&W revolvers you'll find in the caliber are built on the K frame, that is, .38 Special-sized revolvers, you can stretch that if your particular bullet needs the room. I've loaded 200-grain rifle bullets in the .38 S&W, with the loaded length out to 1.400".

.38 Special

The most common revolver round to be found. If there is a place on the face of the earth where you couldn't scare up even a few rounds of .38 Special ammunition, you can be sure you're in some awful gun-banning locale like Bangladesh or New York City. Brass, components, loading data and dies are common. If someone makes anything to do with reloading, they make .38 Special.

The bullets should be .357" for jacketed and .358" for lead. In the +P loadings you can get quite respectable

performance out of a sturdy .38 Special revolver. You may even find in the AirLite models that the limiting factor is not pressure or the revolvers ability to handle it, but your hands. Recoil can be sharp in the very light guns.

The belling stem should be .351" or .352" Your crimp diameter should be .375" the maximum overall loaded length of the .38 Special is 1.550".

With a toolhead all ready, you can be loading .38 Specials (or any other caliber) in a Dillon 550 in a matter of minutes.

The newer cartridge is clearly marked; you just have to look for it on older guns.

.38 Super

The Super was introduced in 1929, in the Colt 1911A1. Meant for police, in an attempt to deal with armed gangs of bank robbers who ere using automobiles as getaway vehicles, the .38 Super penetrated well with its 130-grain jacketed bullet going 1,300 fps. Its short time in the sun was ended when the .357 Magnum came out. Then police could have penetration and their revolvers. The Super is now a competition cartridge, where it does well in USPSA/IPSC competition. For S&W users, it is the round for use in ICORE and IDPA. There, the original .38 Auto performance (what the Super came from) is plenty good enough.

Loaded to "Auto" specs, the .38 Super requires a 9mm bullet, belling diameter and crimp. You want to be using a .354" jacketed or .355" lead bullet. Bell to .352" diameter, and crimp to .372" for light loads. For heavy, IPSC-Major loads, bell smaller, .351" and crimp harder, to .370"

Loading data is now common, due to the enormous volume of .38 Super loading and shooting for IPSC, Steel and action shooting.

Be aware that there are nearly a dozen ".38 Super-like" cases, with the .38 Super, .38 SuperComp, 9mm SuperComp, .38 TJ, 9x23 and 9mm Largo just some of them. Sort your brass and use only the ones marked ".38 Super" or ".38 Auto." They all have a maximum overall loaded length of 1.280", which was dictated by the internal space available in a 1911 magazine.

.357 Magnum

Introduced in 1935, the .357 Magnum was at first seen as more gun than many shooters could handle. The original specs were for a 158-grain bullet at close to 1,500 fps, which is stout even today. Shooters of the day quickly found out that the load was optimistic, and leaded badly. With hard-cast bullets accuracy stayed, leading decreased dramatically, and penetration increased as well. Today the ballistics are not so optimistic, with a 158-grain bullet rarely being clocked over 1,300 fps. But it is still plenty strong. The Magnum is a lengthened .38 Special, designed to run at higher pressures, greatly higher. Where the standard .38 has a pressure ceiling of 17,000 psi, and +P 20,000, the .357 Magnum has a maximum of 35,000 psi. If you expect to load at or near those pressure you should ensure your belling stem is no more than .351" in diameter, and your crimp at .372" The maximum overall loaded length of the .357 is 1.590", not a lot longer than the .38 Special. While there is .135" difference in case lengths, there is only .040" difference in loaded lengths.

There is almost as much loading data for the .357 as there is for the .38 Special, and not all of it at the full-power level. After all, you don't need a 158 at 1,300 fps for anything except hunting and bowling pins. There, the power is welcomed. The 205 power factor will broom pins easily, and with the right bullet will exit the far side of any whitetail that walks the earth.

Many defensive loads feature lighter bullets. For expansion, a 125-grain jacketed hollowpoint works better in the .357 Magnum than a 158 does. The stopping power gold standard for a long time has been the .357 Magnum with a 125-grain jacketed hollowpoint at or above 1,400 fps in a 6-inch barrel. Various experts in the field of stopping power have assigned it "one-shot stop" percentages at or above 96 percent. A hard value to beat.

For defense, the 125-grain JHP in .357 Magnum is usually ranked as #1.

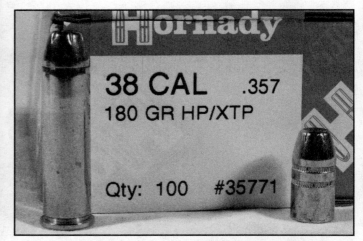

For bowling pins, you want the 180-grain instead of the 125-grain bullet. Mass is king on the pin tables.

10mm

The Ten came along with the Bren Ten, and S&W made a bunch of 10mm pistols back when the FBI thought that was what they wanted. But the current vehicle for 10mm bullet launching is the 610. The bullets for the 10mm are .400" jacketed and .401" lead. The belling stem should be .394" for the maximum loads and as open as .396" for softer, IDPA loads. Your crimp should be .415" I favor a harder crimp on the 10mm in relation to other calibers for uniformity of burn rate, and because all the revolvers and pistols I've tried my reloads in have

The 10mm really benefits from reloading. You can make it just about anything you want, and you have so many more options than factory ammo offers.

shot well with it. I have not yet found a 10mm that was as touchy about crimp as some 9mm pistols I've tried.

The maximum pressure for the 10mm is the greater than the other hot rounds, with a top end of 37,500 psi. Only the 9mm+P exceeds it. At that level you can get .41/.44 Magnum "Lite" performance out of a 10mm, if you can take the recoil. A 200-grain bullet at 1150 fps is not beyond reason. The loaded overall length of the 10mm is 1.260".

40 S&W

The 40 came about when the FBI realized that their agents were not going to post qualifying scores with a full-house 10mm load. The original 200-grain at 1200 fps was beyond reason. The next step, 180 grains at 1100 fps was too much, so how about 180/950? At that low level there is a lot of empty case. (relatively speaking) Why not shorten the case, move the bullet down to the powder, and put it in a 9mm-sized pistol instead of a .45-sized one? Thus Winchester and S&W created the .40 S&W.

The .40 case, chamber bullet and all other dimensions except the primer and case length are the same. The .40 is a short 10mm, but except for the 610 you cannot use .40 S&W in a 10mm. Pistols will not stand for such an arrangement. The excess headspace can create pierced primers and blown cases. The .40 uses a small pistol primer while the 10mm uses a large pistol primer.

The belling stem and crimp dimensions are the same as the 10mm. The .40 S&W is able, just barely, to make Major in competitive shooting. It is not stout enough to load hot enough for bowling pins. Asking the .40 to produce a 195 power factor (say, a 180-grain bullet at 1,085 fps) is asking too much.

The 10mm came out before the .40 S&W, and uses large pistol primers to the .40s small. You cannot use .40 S&W ammo in a 10mm pistol, but you can in a revolver with moon clips.

Lighter loads for practice and IDPA and Steel competition are easy. Just back off of a fast-burning powder until you have a 180-grain bullet going 750 fps over your chronograph, and you're done. The standard overall

The .40 S&W is a "10mm Short" but is not a low-pressure round, like the .38 is to the .357 Magnum.

If you need soft IDPA ammo, load Berry's 135s at 1,000 fps and you're good to go.

The .41 Magnum standard weight is 210 grains. You can load them soft or hot, your choice.

loaded length of the .40 S&W is often quoted as "the same as the 9mm" but it isn't. The .40 S&W comes out at a maximum of 1.135", compared to the 1.170" of the 9mm. The difference is the shape of the bullet tip. If you made the .40 S&W 1.170" it couldn't pivot up out of most 9mm magazine tubes. However, when loaded in 1911-type pistols for IPSC competition, many handloaders load it out to 1.165" to 1.180" in length. They get more useable case capacity, and better feeding in their 1911 pistols. That option is not available to S&W shooters shooting the .40, except for 610 users.

.41 Magnum

The .41 Magnum was to be the best police cartridge, the one all the police experts had been asking for. The problem was, it couldn't be everything they wanted. And it came after the others, the .357 Magnum and .44 Magnum. Introduced in 1964, the .41 Magnum was to be a hard-hitting but controllable police load, and a hunting load. The police load was to be a lead bullet of 210 grains going 950 fps. (Sound familiar?) The hunting load was a 210-grain jacketed soft point at 1,250. The problems it had were many. First, the .41 would only fit the N frame. The N frame was too large for anyone with average or smaller hands. So why pack a great big N frame instead of a "better" K frame, and trade from .357 to .41? The hunting load was not as powerful as the .44 Magnum, so why pack a less-powerful round into the same-size gun? And many police chiefs then didn't want "Magnums" on the street. It could have been different.

If S&W and Remington had introduced the .44 and the .41 at the same time, the .41 might not have suffered in comparison. If they had made it in 1964, but made the hunting load the .41 Magnum and the police load the .41 Special, they might have avoided confusion. Might have. One thing that kept the .41 going, curiously enough, was the Magnum craze from the movie "Dirty Harry." Inspector Callahan made the .44 Mag the hottest thing going. But many shooters were not keen on the waiting lists and premium prices (sometimes outright bribes) needed to get your hands on a real Model 29. They "settled" for an Model 57 instead. The police had the choice of a fixed-sight Model 58, the largest Military & Police style gun S&W made.

The .41 Magnum uses .410" jacketed bullets and .411" lead. The pressure ceiling is 36,000 psi. Belling stem diameter should run .406", .404" if you plan to shoot the heaviest loads, and crimp to .424" The maximum loaded overall length is 1.590"

The .41 is a great hunting cartridge, but doesn't have much utility in competition. It's just a great cartridge that never had a chance.

.44 Special

Introduced with the .44 Hand Ejector in 1908, the .44 Special was for a long time considered quite a powerful cartridge. It was the test bed that Elmer Keith used to develop what later became the .44 Magnum. Now, there is no need to try to load it to anything close to .44 Magnum ballistics. It uses a .430" jacketed, or .431" lead bullet. The belling stem should be .424" and crimp to .446" When loading the .44 Special you have to consider the use, and the gun. For most uses, standard .44 Special ballistics (at least those printed) are good enough. The SAAMI specs call for a 246-grain lead bullet at 800 fps, with a pressure ceiling of 14,000 psi. You'll find most ammo doesn't come close, barely breaking the 700 fps mark. There is a lot of loading data available, and you can match or exceed the SAAMI specs for velocity without exceeding the pressure ceiling. But how far do you want to go? If you get too much, you might as well have had a .44 Magnum to start with. The loaded overall length of the .44 Special is 1.615"

If you are looking to practice with loads equaling a defensive load, then you want a 200-grain jacketed hollowpoint going 900 fps. There is plenty of data that will tell you how to do just that. If you want to replicate the experiments of Elmer Keith and boot a 240-grain to 1,250 fps, you won't find any data. In that case just go right to a .44 Magnum gun, and .44 Magnum loading data.

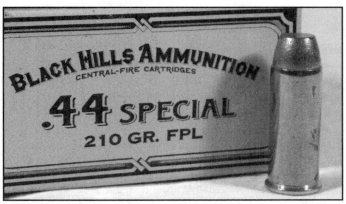

The .44 Special is gaining ground, mostly from Cowboy Action Shooters. It has a place in many other shooting sports, too, and we all benefit from the interest created by the cowboys.

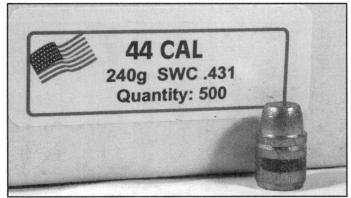

The .44 Special and the .44 Magnum share a bullet weight and design: the 240-grain Keith-style lead bullet.

The .44 Special can be used in .44 Magnum revolvers. And for many shooters, doing so is a wise course of action. You can get a lot of practice with a revolver without risking learning a flinch by using Special instead of Magnum ammo.

.44 Magnum

The magnum is a lengthened .44 Special, operating at a higher pressure. Where the Special tops out at 14,000 psi, the magnum is rated to 36,000 psi. It can be a handful in any gun, and downright painful in compact or lightweight guns. The bullet diameters, belling and crimping and primer sizes are all the same as the Special, only the case length and operating pressures differ.

The .44 Magnum is a "one gun does all" cartridge. It may not be the best in all, but you can do respectably in many. You could load your .44 Magnum down to light .44 Special levels and do well in an IDPA match with a 4-inch Model 29, 629 or the 329. With loads making Major (a simple matter of a 240-grain bullet moving at 700 fps) you could shoot Revolver Division in an IPSC

match. Your reloading times might suffer a bit in comparison to someone with a revolver cut for moon clips, but not much if you practice. And for bowling pins, the power you'd need is still well under the limits of the cartridge. There, you'd need a 240-grain bullet going a mere 825 fps to cleanly broom pins off the tables. For hunting, a hard-cast 240-grain or heavier bullet can be counted on to put holes clean through any deer, and quite often exit even tougher game like wild boar and elk.

The loading data is extensive for the .44 Magnum.

The .44 Magnum was made longer than the .44 Special so you couldn't inadvertently load the big new bruiser in an old Triple Lock.

If you want the heaviest of loads, you can get 300-grain ammo, or load your own with Oregon Trail True Shot hard-cast heavyweights.

The .44 Magnum is the biggest cartridge that can be had in a convenient-carry belt gun. There are bigger and/or more powerful cartridges, but they come in guns you pack, not wear.

.45 ACP

Loaded first for the 1911 pistol, the round came to the Model 1917 revolver a few years later. Bullets are .451" jacketed and .452" lead, with a belling stem of .449" and a crimp of .468". If any cartridge has more loading data available for it than the .38 Special, it is the .45 ACP. You can load from 152-grain lightweights to 265-grain jacketed soft points. It has plenty of accuracy, and power enough for anything up to whitetail deer. With the right load I might even be tempted to try to whack a wild boar with the .45 ACP in a 625-2. The maximum overall loaded length of the .45 ACP is 1.275"

The moon clips make it a viable (even obligatory) choice for action competition, and for defensive carry it is hard to beat if you can pack the weight. In a lightweight gun like the 4513, the .45 ACP packs easily but doesn't beat you up in recoil.

The .45 Auto Rim is simply an ACP case with a thick rim to fit revolvers made to take moon clips.

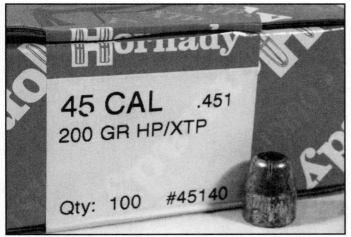

For an accurate, powerful, well-performing load in a .45 ACP, you'd be hard-pressed to do better than Hornady 200-grain XTP bullets.

The .45 ACP is available in lead, full metal jacket, and hollow or soft points.

.45 Colt

Called the "Long Colt" by many, the cartridge was the result of military testing and requirements back in the 1870s. While it is not a longer .45 ACP (as the .38/.357 and .44S/.44M are) you treat it as such when reloading it for S&W revolvers. Unlike Colt SAA revolvers, which sometimes have wide variations between chamber, throat and bore dimensions, the S&W revolvers in .45 Colt are quite stable. You will rarely have to adjust bullet diameter or hardness to accommodate some odd throat size. Bullets should be .451" jacketed and .452" lead. You'll run into many .454" diameter bullets for the .45 Colt, and they will work. It may require some testing to find out if your revolver is more accurate with .452" or .454", and if you have significant differences in leading between them. The belling stem should be .449", but the crimp should be a bit tighter, down to .466" to take into account the sometimes thinner case walls of the .45 Colt as compared to the .45 ACP. The maximum loaded length is 1.600"

Do not try to "magnumize" the .45 Colt. If you want a .44 Magnum, get one. It is a popular pastime among some Ruger owners to load their .45 Colt ammo to much higher pressures, pressures approaching that of the .44 Magnum, to gain more power. In deference to the many older revolvers, specifically the legions of Colt SAA and clones, the SAAMI pressure ceiling of the .45 Colt is kept down to 14,000 psi. Lest you think that presents a problem to getting power, consult the loading data from Vihtavuori. They show several 180-grain bullet loads generating over 1,200 fps, and two with 250-grain bullets at or above 1,000 fps. All under the 14K ceiling.

If you need deep penetration, in any large caliber, you can get it with Cast Performance bullets. The wide flat nose aids, not hinders, penetration.

.500 S&W

If a .44 Magnum isn't manly enough for you, then you're in luck. The .500 makes the .44 Magnum seem tame. The specs are still very new, but we're talking a .500" bullet which would call for a .490" belling stem and a crimp around .510"

The "lightest" loads are the 275-grain jacketed hollowpoints at 1,500 to 1,600 fps, with the heaviest the 440-grain hard-cast bullets at nearly the same velocity.

More power than you need for anything except dangerous game.

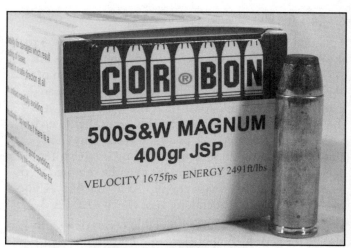

The .500 comes in light, medium and heavy loads. The 400-grain JSP is the "medium" load, stouter than anything else except its own big sibling, the 440 cast.

CHAPTER 25

The 3913LS:
It really did start as a military sidearm

When the Department of Defense expressed an interest in a new sidearm in the early 1950s. S&W was there. The DoD wanted all the newest things: 9mm, double-action, lightweight, hammer-dropping safety. S&W had been working on just such a thing starting right after the war. S&W delivered with the Model 39. The Army wanted single-action, so S&W made six steel-framed prototypes. The DoD hemmed and hawed, and S&W released the Model 39 for commercial and law enforcement sales beginning in 1955. S&W struggled with the Model 39 for some time, as the law enforcement community and military users weren't sure

The Lady Smith is a compact 9mm sidearm for concealed carry. One need not be a lady to pack it.

just what they wanted. Steel frame or alloy, double-action or single, 9mm or even .38 Special or .38 AMU?

But the 39 did have advocates. The Indiana State Police adopted it. Detroit PD approved it. S&W kept improving it. In the expansion of the 1980s it was improved to the 39 series, with the all-steel 3906 as the heaviest,

flattest, softest-shooting 9mm you could get. It was also offered in blue, alloy framed, with fixed sights and adjustable, and in compact versions.

The 3913LS is the result of the evolution. The "Ladysmith" series is S&W resurrection and reclaiming of the slang tern for a certain set of guns from an earlier era.

The underside of the trigger guard is undercut for a higher grip.

The slide is marked "Lady Smith" on the right side.

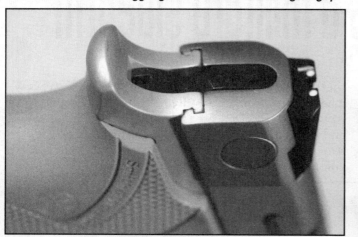
The hammer is bobbed, and the safety is not an ambi, for ease of carry.

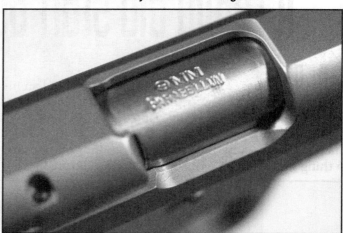
The Lady Smith does not have a loaded chamber indicator port in the barrel hood.

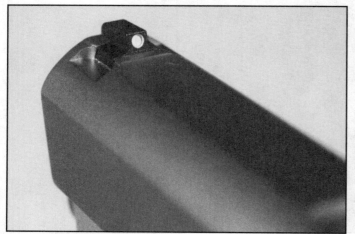
The front portion of the three-dot sights...

...and in the rear, a Novak.

Cocked, safety off, ready to fire.

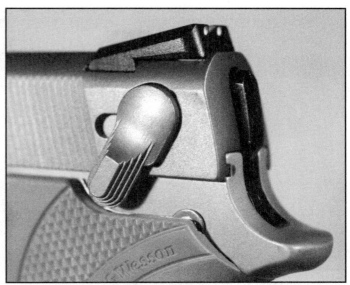

With safety down and hammer de-cocked, it won't fire.

The compact .32 revolvers had a couple of generations ago earned a somewhat shady nickname: "Lady Smiths." As in a defense gun for ladies of the evening. A "Lady Smith" to someone in the Flapper Era was something a prostitute carried. Sort of a predecessor to the "Saturday Night Special" term that has been hung on many compact guns since the 1960s. The new Ladysmith was a series of handguns offered by S&W that had been specially engineered to be more conducive to women, with their smaller hands and generally weaker hand strength.

The 3913LS is a compact lightweight 39-series 9mm pistol. The frame has been altered to make it easier to carry, the grips slimmed to make them easier for smaller hands to hold, and the trigger mechanism worked over to make it lighter in function without compromising reliability. Despite all the attempts to make it a better defensive firearm for women, they do not make it less so for men. Small-statured man will find the changes of great help. And even those of us who are larger than average appreciate the changes.

The slide has Wayne Novak-designed sights. The front is in a dovetail, the rear in a larger dovetail, and the sights have the three-dot combat sights that became so popular in the 1980s. You could easily have them swapped for night sights if you wished, as the S&W/Novak dimensions are so well known that all sight makers

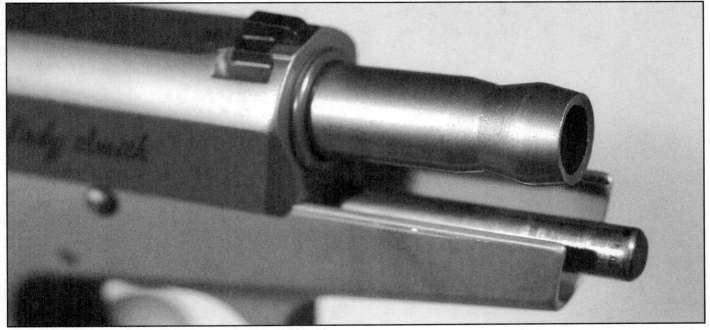

The barrel is shaped to preclude the need for a barrel bushing.

Safety off, ready for double-action shooting.

is pivoted and powered by a coil spring in the rear. I've never seen it broken. The safety is a slightly slimmer than the standard dimension hammer-dropping safety. It is not ambidextrous, and has a paddle only on the left side of the slide. When depressed it locks the firing pin and then drops the hammer. While the safety is down the 3913LS cannot be fired. It must be pushed back up to put the mechanism into the "Fire" mode. Whether you leave it down, or decock and then press it up to be ready is a personal decision, and one you must train with. The most common method depends on your carry mode. If you carry an S&W pistol on duty in uniform it is customary to carry it with the safety down. On the draw you push the safety off before firing. If someone grabs, or attempts to grab your sidearm, the safety being down may slow or foil their attempts at firing your sidearm. In concealed carry it is much less likely that someone will try to grab your (concealed) handgun. Having the safety off is a conscious decision for many, trading a small bit of anti-grab safety for a small bit of ease in getting the sights on the bad guy.

make sights for them. The slide has as flat rib machined on the top between the sights. The extractor is the new S&W Model 39 extractor, changed from the old in the early 1970s. The old was a flat spring steel piece set into the slide, and it occasionally broke. The new design (also incorporated from the beginning in the Model 59)

The 3913LS barrel is the standard S&W barrel design, although shorter than many other 39 series models. It disassembles in the standard S&W pistol fashion.

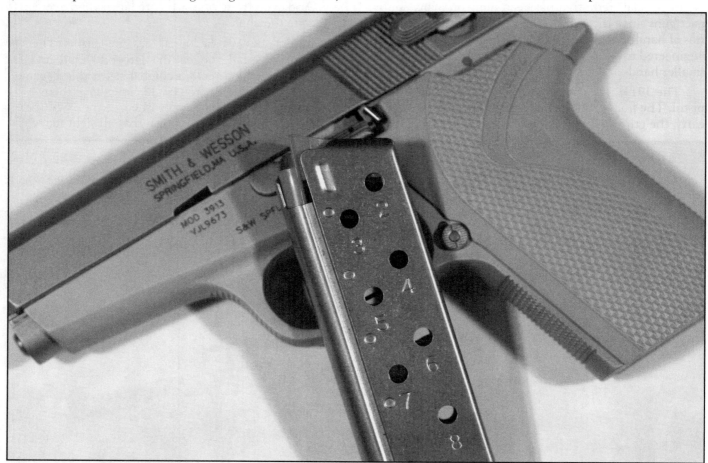

Eight plus one means you're ready.

The checkered front strap, for a non-slip grip.

The hammer of the 3913LS is bobbed. You do not thumb-cock a defensive pistol, so there is no need for a hammer spur. It also makes concealed carry easier. Hammer spurs can catch on clothing on the draw, slowing you down or even snatching the pistol out of your hand. The spur can also abrade your clothing, leading to expensive tailoring repairs. I have worn holes in a number of jackets and coats through the years from guns rubbing the lining and wearing or tearing them. The 3913LS solves that problem.

The frame is contoured in the dust cover area for ease of carry and for looks. The dust cover tapers up towards the slide, unlike the dustcover on other 39 and 59 series models. (Compare the 3913LS dustcover with

The 3913LS goes unnoticed under a windbreaker.

Push your coat open...

that of the 5906TSW elsewhere.) The slide stop and magazine catch are just where you'd expect them on an American gun, and the trigger guard has been scalloped behind so your hand can rise a bit higher in the grip. The rear of the frame has an abbreviated tang. Since the hammer is bobbed so it can't bite, and the spur comes up high enough to block your hand from the slide, why make it larger? Were it a target gun you'd probably want a larger tang so you could improve your scores. But as a concealment gun the tang works just fine.

The grip is one piece and made of a grayish-white polymer. It is held on by the mainspring retainer pin, as all current S&W pistols of the 39 and 59 series are.

The magazine is a single-stack and holds eight rounds. The 3913LS magazines are interchangeable only with other compact 39 series pistols. Their short length precludes using them in larger 39 guns. However, you can use the longer magazines in your 3913LS, where their nine-round capacity gets you an extra shot. The common use is to carry the 3913LS loaded with the compact magazines, and have the larger ones as spares on your belt.

As with all S&W pistols, the 3913LS will lock open when empty. When the magazine is out, the magazine disconnector will prevent the trigger mechanism from working, and the pistol will not fire. As a safety method used when struggling with some bad guy for control of the pistol, it can work great. My friend Mas Ayoob has documented many instances of police officers and civil-

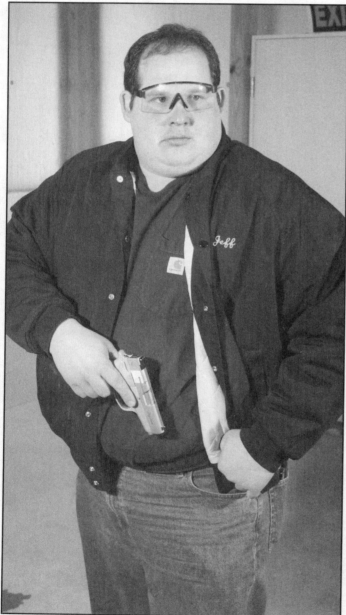

...clear nylon...

...and get on target.

Hard to fault this kind of accuracy, with Black Hills JHP ammo.

ians who, when they felt the pistol being pulled from their grasp managed to press the magazine button and eject or partially eject the magazine. When the miscreant does get control, they usually then waste some time trying to get it to fire, time you can use to flee, get another weapon, or whatever solution works for you.

Firing the 3913LS

The earliest Model 39 pistols were designed to shoot 9mm ball ammo. In the 1950s you would have been called crazy if you had declared that you were going to make a soft-point or hollowpoint that actually expanded reliably.

CHAPTER 26

The CS9:
Compact, light and perfect for packing

The Chief Special 9 is an odd duck. It is the same size as the 3913 LadySmith, but holds one less round in its magazines. The magazine tubes are the same, and you can use the 3913LS magazines in the CS9. So why make a duplicate gun? I don't know, perhaps to offer a 9mm compact pistol to those who want to carry, but not be seen with a LadySmith? I'm not kidding. To some, the name matters.

The CS9 is a single-stack 9mm compact carry pistol.

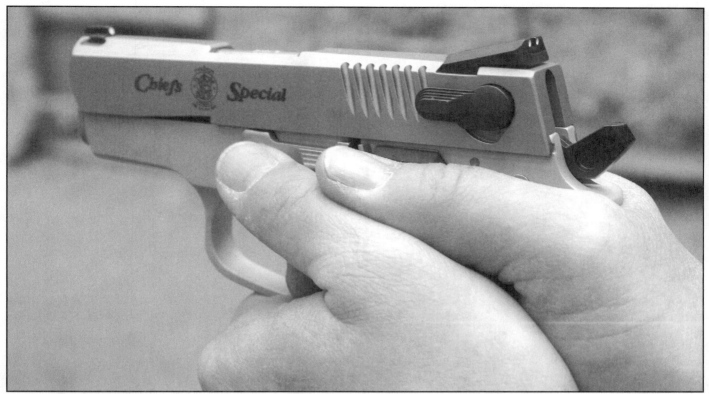
If your hands are too large, you might even have trouble handling it. My assistant with average-sized hands has no problems.

The flat, compact CS9 makes the Cirillo Index a breeze, as the flats provide a good reference.

If you prefer to use the sights, the three-dot CS9 sights are large and easy to see.

What we have here is a compact, lightweight 9mm pistol with a traditional double-action trigger. The hammer-dropping safety is ambidextrous and drops the spur-less hammer when engaged. The sights are three-dot, and pure Wayne Novak, complete with patent number in the sight slot of the rear sight. The slide is slab-sided, with the grasping grooves angled so they are only partially machined in the slide. They taper out two-thirds of the way down, leaving the bottom of the slide sides smooth. The top flat of the slide from the rear sight to the front is also angled, so the flat narrows as it goes

forward. While it begins as wide as the rear sight, it ends as small as the front sight base. The slide is marked on the left with "Chiefs Special" and the S&W logo. Below it on the frame is the Smith & Wesson one-line address, the model number and the serial number. On the right of the slide is the two-line address. The 9mm barrel is marked over the chamber, but does not have the observation port for the loaded chamber indicator.

The grips are two-piece rubber, with the S&W logo on them, and look like they were made for S&W by Hogue. They are held to the frame with a cross screw.

The CS9 is accurate, although if you switch to a hot load like the Cor-bon 9mm 115 grain +P+ your groups will suffer (only from the harder recoil).

The tang comes back far enough to keep your hand out of the path of the slide, without being so large that it makes concealed carry more difficult. The seven-shot magazines fall free when empty, and there were no feeding failures nor failures of any kind.

Carry and shooting

The lightweight CS9 packed flat and carried easily. I would prefer the standard one-piece Xenoy grips for a compact 39 series pistol if they would fit, but that is personal preference. I learned to carry and shoot before rubber grips came on the scene, and old habits die hard. The soft rubber grips made the already mild-recoiling 9mm even softer to shoot. If I hadn't restricted the 9mm ammo, the test fire crew would have shot it all. (Leaving me nothing to test the other 9mm pistols with.) The soft rubber

The right side, with extractor, ejection port and address.

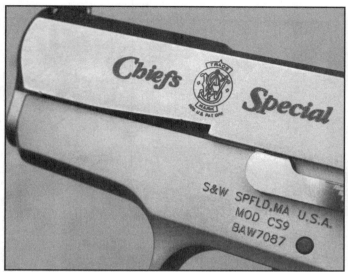

The slab-sided CS9 on the left.

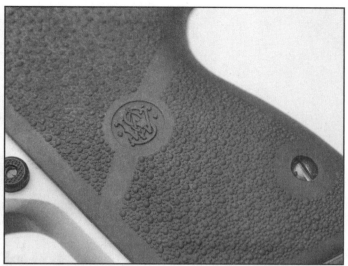

Hogue soft rubber grips.

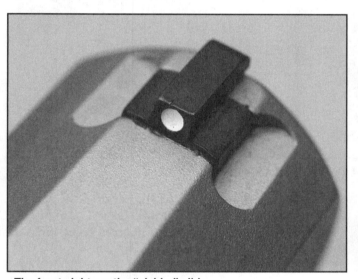

The front sight, on the "slabby" slide.

The Novak-style rear sight: slide and sight are designed to reduce the number of machining operations needed to make both.

The ejection port and barrel, lacking a loaded-chamber indicator.

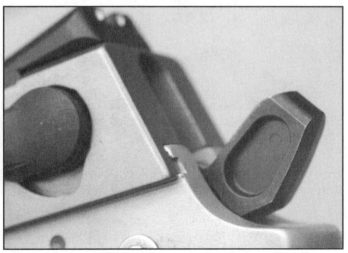

The bobbed and MIM hammer, cocked in single-action shooting mode.

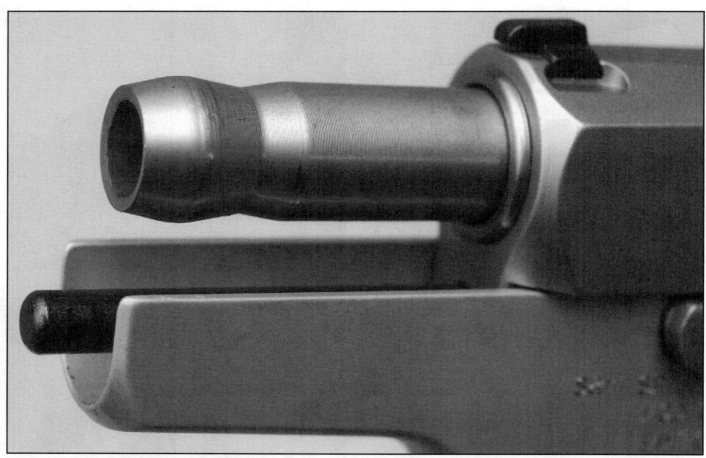

The CS9 with the S&W complex end that locks up with the front of the slide for accuracy.

The safety down, with the hammer dropped and locked out of the mechanism.

grips not only dampened the recoil, but kept the gun from shifting in your grasp, so follow-up shots were quicker.

The CS9 magazines are shorter than the 3913 LadySmith, and hold one less round (seven vs. eight) but the 3913 magazines fit and function in the CS9. I'm not sure the extra compactness of the CS9 grip is worth the loss of one round, but then I am large enough that they are all small guns to me. A short person might find that the CS9 is just enough more compact and hide-able that the loss of one round is not a big deal. After all, you can carry the LadySmith or full-size Model 39 magazines for your reloads, so you're only losing the one round in the magazine in the gun.

Bill Drills were simple, even when starting the first shot with the hammer down and firing it double-action. Cirillo Index drills also were easy, and the flat profile of the CS9 made any mis-alignment obvious. With the spare magazine it was possible to do El Presidente drills, and with the soft recoil and good accuracy of the CS9 I had no problems shooting better than Par. Even with hot +P and +P+ 9mm the CS9 was soft in recoil.

CHAPTER 27

The SW9G:
The practical, tactical polymer pistol

I first saw the Sigma at an S&W Dealers' Seminar in 1989 or 1990. The event was simple: Dealers and their employees gathered at a range in northern Ohio, for the S&W sales pitch and new product re-view. We got coffee and donuts in the morning under the big tent, along with all the news of S&W. The afternoon was spent walking from range to range where S&W had tables piled with ammo, and S&W pistols to shoot.

The SW9 has no magazine disconnector, so the warning is set right into the polymer frame.

Left side view of the SW9.

Right side view.

Among the many new products was the Sigma. S&W had two or three guns, with a pair of magazines each, and five cases of ammo. At first we took turns loading and shooting, but somehow it rapidly turned into a feeding frenzy. Each person would load a magazine and wait until the gun they were in line for was empty, load it and blast at the hill (the targets were quickly shredded) until the gun was empty, hand it off and step back to reload the magazine. In short order the pistols became so hot you could not even touch the slide release without burning your fingertip. We loaded by inserting a magazine and them pressed the front edge of the slide against the shooting bench to release the slide stop, chambering a round. It took less than an hour for the three guns to consume 5,000 rounds of ammo. All the while, the S&W reps stood by, beaming. The Sigmas we were so merrily abusing never failed. Not once did they fail to feed, fire, eject, lock open when empty or otherwise hiccup.

The SW9G in question is the latest, an enhanced Sigma with an improved extractor, a fence around the slide stop, tactical light or equipment rail on the dust cover, and a lower ejection port than earlier Sigma models had. Oh yes, and the frame is O.D. green. The latest tactical "must have" in the 1911 world is a two-tone synthetic finish: black slide and green frame. On the Sigma, S&W simply replaces the black dye with green in the polymer mix. They could probably make it hot pink if they wanted to, but who would buy it?

The 9G Sigma comes in a green plastic box, instead of the S&W blue of the other models. Inside, the foam is brown. The usual owner's manual, cable lock, a pair of magazines and the obligatory fired case in its sealed envelope, and the "Club 1852" card round out the gear.

The sights are three-dot, with a night-sight front dot and plain white rear dots. The Trijicon front dot shows up nicely in darkness. The slide has a shallow rib ma-

The external extractor works very well.

The newest models have a molded fence around the slide-stop lever.

The disconnector bars. Takedown is identical to that of the Glock.

The tactical light rails are molded right into the polymer frame.

The serial number and bar code plate are under the light rail.

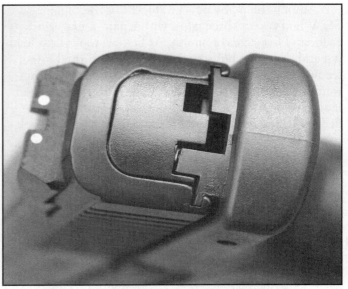

The slide disassembly plate is on the rear of the slide.

The SW9 was meant to have a hi-cap magazine. It can again, in many States.

The magazine follower is marked with the caliber for which it is meant.

The old, "during-ban" magazines cannot be made whole again. If you try to remove the "pinch," the magazine will fall apart. Just buy new ones.

Insert the loaded magazine and rack the slide, and you're ready to go.

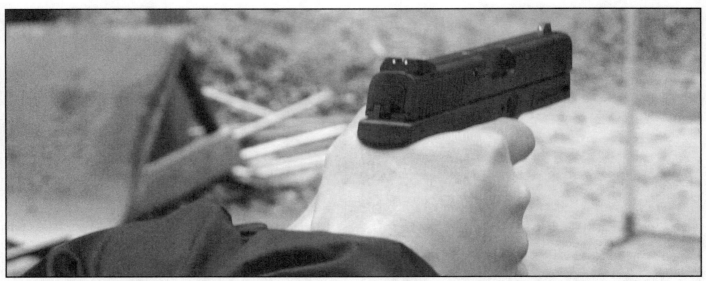
The SW9 is easy to shoot.

chined its length, with the front sight bolted internally through the slide and the rear in a transverse dovetail. The barrel is marked "9MM" and had a small, tapered hole bored in the rear of the hood and the top of the slide at the breechface. It exists solely to provide the regulatory requirement of a "loaded chamber indicator" required by some states. The front of the slide is plain, as the Sigma has no need of a barrel bushing. The rear is the disassembly plate. The Sigma has the light rail up front on the frame dustcover. On the slide it is marked "Smith & Wesson, Springfield MA USA" followed by "SW9G." There are cocking serrations only at the rear. On the frame you can see the disassembly lever just above the trigger, and behind it the barrel-locking block retaining pin. The slide stop has a raised fence protecting it. The magazine catch is behind the trigger, which is pivoted as an additional safety. Underneath the dust cover is the serial number plate, which also incorporates the bar code. The right side of the slide is bare, and the frame has only the warning telling you that the pistol can be fired when the magazine has been removed. The grip is checkered, cast into the polymer, with the S&W logo as part of the design. On the bottom is the magazine well. The magazine has a large detachable baseplate. The magazine shipped with this gun is one of the odious, government-mandated 10-shot versions. Were it not, the standard magazines hold 16 rounds.

In use the Sigma is simplicity: basically it is a box magazine-fed revolver. You pull the slide back and if there is not an empty magazine to hold it open, press the slide stop lever up. Once the slide is open, insert a loaded magazine and press the slide stop lever down. The slide will move forward, chambering a round. (Or, you can simply insert a loaded magazine, pull back the slide and release it.) There are no external safeties to manipulate.

While the recoil looks busy, with lots of movement, it isn't hard, and the sights come right back to the target.

When you need/desire to fire, line up the sights and press the trigger. The next eight steps of the firing sequence will occur in the ensuing .06 seconds. To fire again, release the trigger and press it again.

The action is neither cocked nor rested when ready. When you press the trigger, you pivot the lower leg and cause the safety shoulder on it to swing clear of the frame. Continued pressure cocks the striker until it passes the release point, where the trigger bar cams off and the striker spring launches the striker into the primer. When the slide cycles on firing, the disconnector unlinks the trigger bar from the striker, and the slide on closing brings the striker tail to rest against the sear. When you release the trigger, it moves forward and then springs up to make contact with the striker tail, ready to repeat the firing process. When the system is at ready rest, the striker cannot move forward or back, and the trigger bar cannot move out of the way, releasing it to the primer.

Shooting and carry impressions

In firing, the SW9G is what you'd expect from a middleweight 9mm pistol: the recoil is noticeable but not objectionable. After shooting the AirLite 4040 and the 4513 in the same session, the 9mm Sigma was quite restful in felt recoil. Accuracy-wise it was perfectly serviceable, with respectable performances on the 100-yard gong and good groups in bench testing. Firing over sandbags and using 9mm match ammo I was able to shoot at least one 2-inch group at 25 yards. However, the long and somewhat spongy trigger pull of the Sigma is not at all what match-practiced competition shooters are expecting, so neither I nor my test-fire crew posted the smallest groups with the Sigma. The trigger pull was

not an impediment to shooting well in USPSA/IPSC Production Division, just that if I were doing the "Nickel Drill" on the 100-yard gong, the Sigma wouldn't be my first choice. ("Nickel Drill": Each shooter drops a nickel into the coffee can, and takes one shot offhand with their handgun at the 100-yard gong. When all have shot, each one left drops another nickel and takes another shot. When you miss you drop out. The last shooter to get a hit takes the money.) The Sigma trigger mechanism is similar to the Glock, so any good gunsmith who can lighten and "crisp-up" the trigger on a Glock could probably do the same for your Sigma.

The Sigma trigger made me work for it on Bill Drills. El Presidente was easy, and the tapered-top double-stack magazines reloaded quickly. And the square outline of the Sigma slide was perfect for the Cirillo Index.

The Sigma fits any holster designed for Glocks of the same size. The Sigma is available only in 9mm and .40 S&W, with a small production run in 1998 of Sigmas in .357 Sig. There are no Sigmas in larger calibers, 10mm and .45.

While the SW9 is accurate enough, it isn't up to the 910 we also tested.

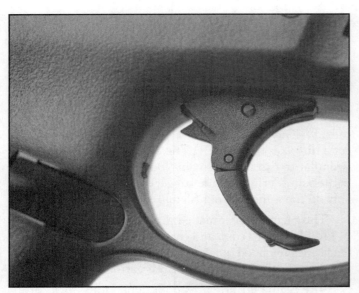

One of the safeties is the pivoting trigger. If your finger does not pivot it when pressing, the trigger can't move back to release the striker.

The loaded-chamber indicator port is on the barrel hood.

The Sigma grip differs slightly from the Glock in that the Sigma is slightly rounded where the Glock is squarish. Whether you like it or not depends on how you come to the Sigma. If you've spent your time with flat pistols like the 1911 (that's me, 25+ years now) the squarish Glock seems better in the hand than the rounder Sigma. If you have spent a lot of time with re-volvers and their rounded grips (again me, over 35 years now) then the Sigma will be comfortable. Some decry the rounder grip of the Sigma as somehow being inferior. I guess I've spent too much time with both, for my scores do not differ significantly when using one or the other.

Loaded with the hottest 9mm ammo you can lay hands on, the SW9G would be a great full-sized carry or duty gun. I'd probably want to be packing Cor-bon 9mm+P+ 115- or 125-grain hollowpoints. The Sigma would have no problem with them.

If your department or agency allows the use of the Sigma, or if you find personal preference has you lean-ing that way, then go for it. You'll find the Sigma to be utterly reliable, light in weight, plenty accurate, and for those for whom it matters, made in the USA.

Glock Vs. S&W

When the Sigma came out, there was an immediate uproar. "Why, they've just made a Glock clone." Cries and hand-wringing about how American ingenuity had failed us, and we were reduced to simply copying an imported pistol ran across the land and were splashed in the gun magazines. There were even rumors of parts interchangeability; why, you could put a Sigma slide and barrel on a Glock, or strip a Glock and rebuild it with all Sigma parts, S&W had cloned it so closely. Which was all nonsense. No one complains that Italian manufactur-ers were copying Colt SAA revolvers, or that Taurus was making S&W-inspired revolvers. Nor grumble at the hordes of 1911 makers. And did anyone pay attention to the fact that when S&W unveiled the Sigma, they also applied for a dozen patent applications on their pistol? So, as such things do, it ended up in court. And ended up fading away.

The various Glock models seem to get a dispropor-tionate amount of press, while the Sigmas keep plug-ging along.

CHAPTER 28

910:
Nothing fancy. Just performance

In the century-plus of Hand Ejector revolver making, S&W has made somewhere in excess of 6 million K frame revolvers. Many of those fit the description, by name or features, of "Military & Police." The name was affixed to S&W K frame .38 Special revolvers early in production, and stuck with them a long time. Even after the name was dropped in favor of numerical designations, I heard shooters refer to a fixed-sight .38 Special K frame as a "Military and Police" model. And it was a durable, accurate, dependable model, then and now.

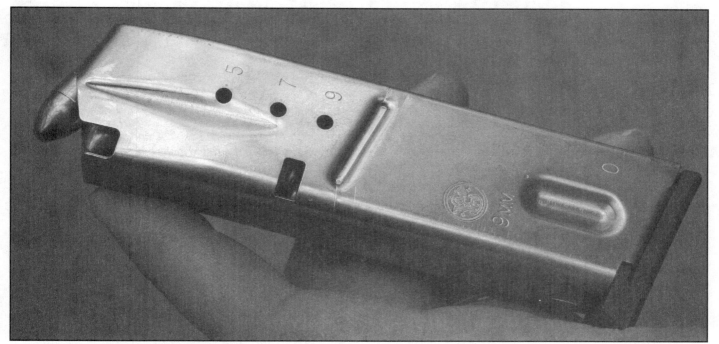

The 910 shipped with two, 10-shot magazines. Now, most of you can get the proper, 15-shot ones.

The slabby-slide 910 points like all other S&W pistols. The 910 is quite comfortable to hold, and you need not have a large hand to get a good grasp on it for firing.

The flat sides make the Cirillo Index easy. Note the lack of an ambi safety lever.

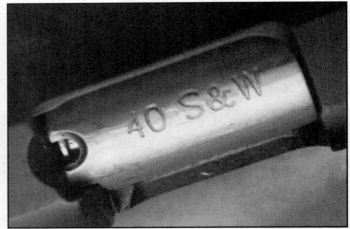

Other models have a loaded-chamber indicator port on the hood to see if there is a round in the chamber.

When Smith & Wesson went with pistols, they determined that while many wanted feature-laden pistols, many shooters wanted basic dependable, durable, 9mm and 40 pistols. They came out with the "economy" or "no-frills" models the 910 and 410. I thought then, and so did my friend John Simon, when we were working at Northwest Gun Shop outside Detroit, that S&W should have tried to use the "M&P" name in the model somehow. The "9mm Military & Police" or the "40 Military & Police" would have kept the tradition going. But they did not, so you will have to look for it as the 910.

Looking at the 910

At first glance the 910 is somewhat blocky. In order to keep the cost down as much as possible, I'm sure the engineers looked to minimize the number of cutter paths and tools in manufacture. When any part is made in a CNC mill or lathe, an engineer has to program (sometimes the engineer suggests to a programmer) the "cutter paths." That is, the route, depth, feed rate, tool rpm and start and end points of a particular cutting tool. A good programmer can make or break a production schedule and cost target. A bad one will break cutters, waste mate-

The 910 was the most accurate S&W handgun I tested for this book. If I did my part, this was the kind of group it produced with boring regularity.

This is a 10-shot group of under an inch, center to center, at 20 yards from a rest.

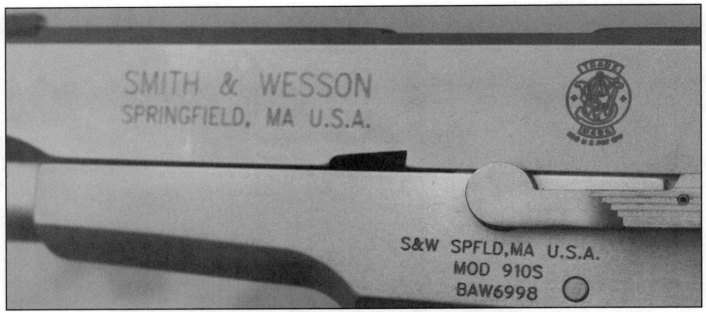

The 910 has the usual S&W markings on a slide that appears to be designed for ease of machining.

The front sight uses a flat spring to produce friction to keep it in place. Judging from the groups it shot, it must work.

The sights are three-dot, the safety a TDA hammer-dropping one, and the hammer has a spur.

rial, scrap parts and eventually get fired. The 910 slide is not so sculpted as the regular S&W pistol slide. The top is a not radius cut, but rather a flat on top and a bevel on each side. Rather than machine a radius, the flats simply contour the slide enough to fit holsters. The dustcover nose is relieved just enough to clear holsters designed for the regular 9mm S&W pistols. The frame gets the same treatment, with slab sides and no grooves or checkering on the frontstrap. Do not be fooled by this apparent (and real) economy. The cost savings have not been carried over into the interior.

On top of the slide the sights differ in design. While they are the standard three-dot Novak-inspired pyramids, they have been designed to be cheaper to make.

The front sight has a much larger dovetail, and inside the sight is a spring steel plate that tensions it, keeping it in place. (Kind of like the steel plate in the Glock rear sight.) The rear is dovetailed, but proportioned so as to minimize the machining needed on the slide and on the sight itself. Unlike regular slides that need the dovetail cut for the base, and another machined flat to nestle the sight body, the 910 sight fits the dovetail and rides on the top flat of the slide. The slide is marked on the left with "Smith & Wesson" and the Springfield, MA rollmark, and the S&W logo. The right side is bare of all markings. The extractor is standard S&W, the barrel is marked "9mm Parabellum" but does not have the loaded chamber indicator hole.

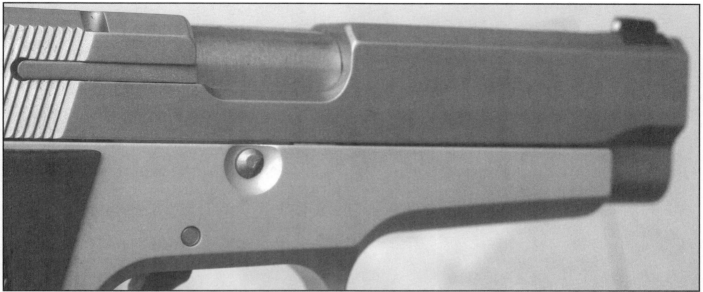
On the right side is the bare slide and external extractor.

The chamber, clearly marked "9mm" and lacking a loaded-chamber indicator.

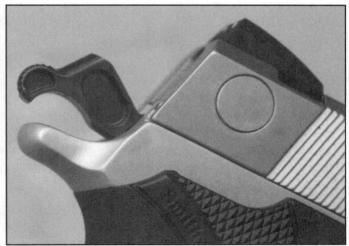
Note the lack of a rightside safety lever. The tang is large for recoil control (like a 9mm needs it), but it also provides a comfortable place for the web of your hand.

The frame is marked on the left side with the model number and serial number, and the required manufacturer's designation. The right side is bare. The grips are the standard one-piece Xenoy plastic grips. The 910 is a traditional double-action, hammer dropping safety with a safety lever only on the left side. The lack of an ambi safety is another economy measure, one that all but left handed shooters will not notice. The hammer has lightening locations in it, easily done with the MIM process.

The trigger is as good as any other S&W TDA pistol that has not come out of the Performance Center, that is, the double-action is smooth and moderate, while the single action is pretty darned close to what you'd expect from a revolver.

The magazines supplied with the 910 are the post-ban neutered magazines, with 10-shot capacity. However, the 910 will work with all standard-length hi-cap S&W magazines ever made. I have a few in my stash, and I tried it with all on hand. One is old enough to date from the first-generation Model 59 production, and the 910 worked just fine with it. While some pistols have a reputation for magazines that can be flaky in function, I've always had good luck with S&W. The third-generation magazines are sturdier than the first or second, and given a choice I'd take the third generation magazines every time. Now that the AWB/94 has sunset (except for a few States) we can get back to hi-cap shooting. The 10-shot magazines were reliable, but the whole point of making a full-size 9mm pistol is kind of lost when you feed it with 10-shot mags. Buy S&W, or a reliable replacement like Mec-Gar, and you can't go wrong.

Show up with a 910 and a bag of 10-shot magazines for USPSA/IPSC Production, or IDPA Stock Service Pistol, and you've got all the gun you'll need. Save the hi-caps for carry. No point in putting undue wear and tear on them.

The one-piece Xenoy grips are tougher than boot leather and comfortable to grab.

Carry and function

In carry, the 910 is not what you'd call a concealed carry gun. It is large and blocky (but light) for a 9mm. If you are going to carry a 10-shot 9mm, you'd be better off with a 3903 or another light, flat 9mm by S&W. If it was all I had I wouldn't worry too much about the size, and just get a comfortable holster. For competition, its size doesn't matter, as you aren't going to be hiding it. The grips, for a pistol its size, are comfortable and manageable to handle. Those with small hands might find it a bit of a reach, but anyone average or larger will have no problem. And the large size helps to spread the recoil of 9mm out to the point where it is not any problem to shoot. Anyone with hands large enough to reach the trigger will not be put off by the recoil of the 9mm, even in the hottest loads.

In shooting, the 910 was stellar. In testing I fire several groups to get a feel for the accuracy, and shoot a photo of the best one. There was no problem shooting the best group from the 910, as they were all spectacular. One-hole groups standing at 15 yards were the norm. All of my testers found it superbly accurate. Hitting the

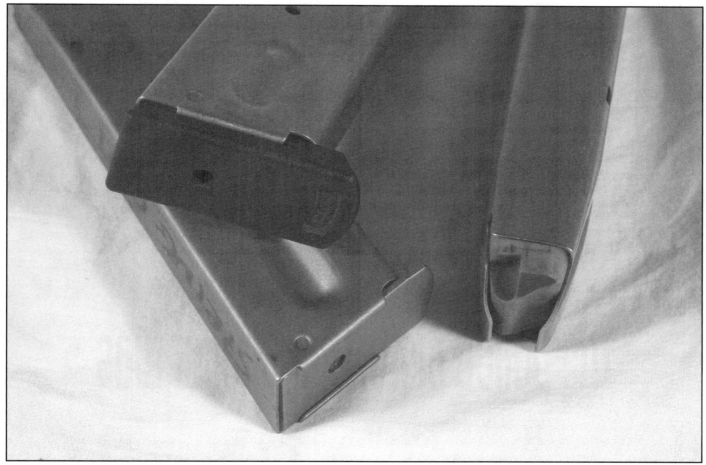

The 910 uses all generations of 59 magazines, from the first through the second and third, and even the emasculated 10-shot magazines.

gong at 100 yards was child's play. Just hold the top of the front sight at the top edge of the gong, and get a hit. It didn't matter what ammo I fed it, it shot it all and shot it well. Better than well. More than one tester handled the 910 and asked "does it make it in Production?" or "Can I shoot this in IDPA?" the accuracy is so good that you could use it as a ringer in PPC matches. Entered in a Service Match, the 910 shoots as well as many tuned PPC pistols you'd find in Open. With a little practice to get back in the groove, I'm sure I could shoot the 910 for a 600 score on an indoor PPC league.

The 910 shoots so well that I'm tempted to ask S&W what they want for it. As a Production gun in USPSA/IPSC competition, or as a Stock Service Pistol (you can't get much more "stock" than a 910) in IDPA, the accuracy this one produces would make it a real sleeper.

CHAPTER 29

5906:
The police pistol that almost was

The 5906 is the all-stainless high-capacity 9mm that S&W almost took the police market with. The original pistol, the 59, came out in 1974 and almost put Colt into the corporate grave. Colt was hanging on with 1911A1 pistols, Single Action Army revolvers, and one variation or another of their double-action revolver. S&W had most of the police market, but Colt was hanging on. Then in 1974 the Model 59 came

The 5906PC wielded by John Flentz works very well indeed in USPSA Production Division. Don't be fooled by the advocates of the "polymer wonder," the S&W can hold its own.

The 5906TSW is not a light gun, but it can be a gun with a light.

The rail allows you to mount a light and use both hands to fire.

Not all S&W pistols have ambidextrous safety levers, but they do all have external extractors.

At the start of the DA stroke, the trigger is fully forward.

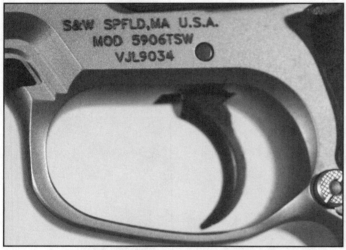

When the hammer is cocked, the trigger rests in the middle of the triggerguard.

The barrel hood has a chamber-loaded indicator port. If you can see in there, you can tell if it is loaded.

The safety pointed towards the muzzle means the mechanism is ready to fire.

Pushing the safety lever down drops the hammer, but blocks the firing pin, and the pistol will not fire.

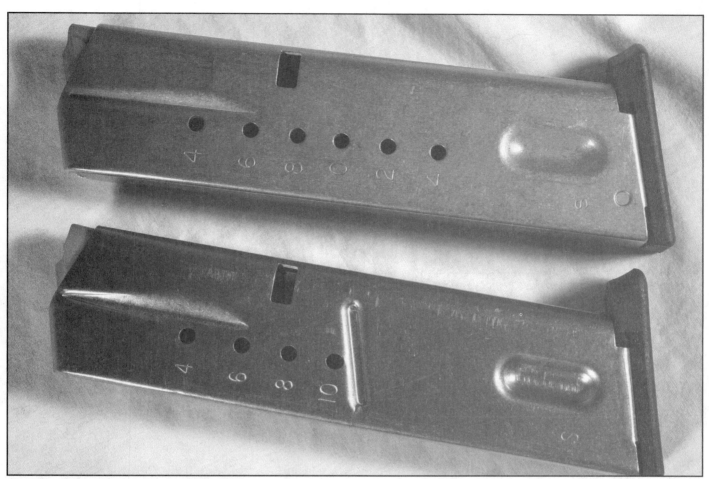

New or old, 10-shot or hi-cap, S&W magazines of the third generation are ultra-reliable.

For practice, or IDPA or USPSA production competition, the 10-shot magazines work just fine. And now, they can be had dirt-cheap.

The front sight has a dot and rides in a dovetail on the slide.

The rear sight completes the three-dot set.

out. Suddenly the 9mm pistol seemed a viable choice for law enforcement. After all, for the holster and belt space a revolver and eighteen rounds took up, you could have an S&W Model 59 and 42 rounds! Within a couple of years Ruger came out with their double-action revolvers, and Colt was in trouble. They had no 9mm pistol, and Ruger was beating them on price on double-action .38/.357 police-type revolvers.

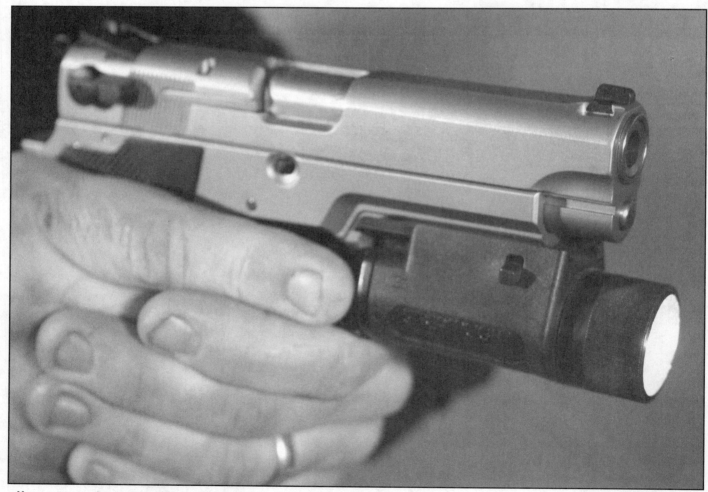
You use your trigger finger to move the light lever on the Streamlight tactical light.

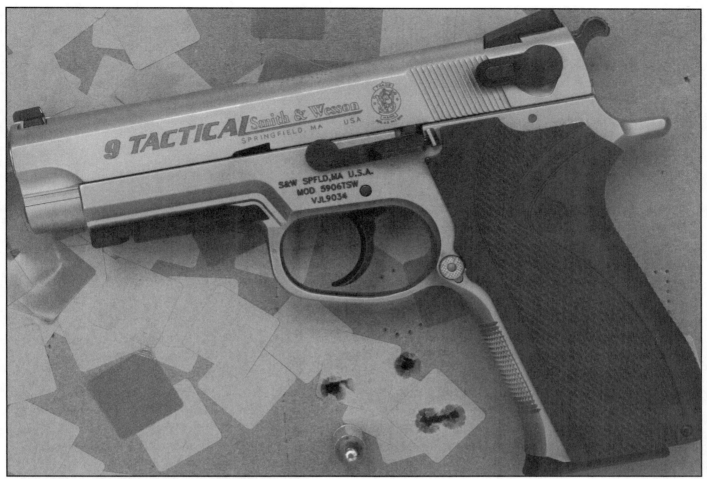

The worst group fired, and still a pretty good one.

But the story of Colt is a different, and sad one we won't get into here.

The Model 59 was upgraded in the second generation, and transformed in the third. The third-generation pistols are refined and tuned. The traditional double-action is smooth and relatively light (when you consider that you're cocking the hammer, it's light) and the single-action pull is nearly that of a 1911 pistol, the exemplar to which all pistols are compared.

The 5906TSW adds a tactical rail on the dustcover, for attaching a light or laser. In 9mm, the standard hi-cap magazines hold 15 rounds, despite the "late" Assault Weapon Ban of 1994 having restricted them to 10. However, pre-ban magazines will fit the 5906, so you can load up if you desire. With the ban over, post-ban mags will again be 15 rounds, reliable and available. The longest magazines in the 59 series, the 5906 magazines will fit shorter guns, but the shorter ones won't fit into the 5906 magazine well. They're too short, and the baseplate stops them before they can lock in place.

The sights are fixed, three-dot Novak sights, the safety is ambidextrous, and drops the hammer and locks it out of the mechanism when down. With the safety down you can work the trigger all you want, the pistol isn't going to fire. The 5906 also has a magazine disconnect safety, so when the magazine is out the pistol will not fire. However, do not assume every 5906 or any S&W pistol you encounter has a magazine safety. They can be removed, and if absent the gun will still fire when the magazine has been removed. You never know when the one you pick up has been worked-on by someone.

In carry the 5906 is a bit heavy. However, the weight can be comforting when you've got the 5906 stoked with 9mm+P or 9mm+P+ ammo. As a duty gun it might be a bit heavy to wear all day, but when you need it the weight will keep it on target. With the weight, it was no problem running Bill Drills with the 5906. The Cirillo Index was also easy, with the long flats of the slide to keep the gun on line. El Presidentes were easy, as the tapered magazine reloads quickly and the gentle recoil of the 9mm in an all-steel gun keeps the sights on target.

The 5906 is potentially the best S&W pistol for the USPSA/IPSC Production Division. The accuracy is great, the recoil soft, the trigger quite manageable. My

One of the good groups the 5906 fired.

friend John Flentz has used his PC5906 to good effect in National and World Shoot matches.

If you get a chance to pick up and try a 5906, you should. You might find that while the attention goes to the polymer wonders of the world, the 5906 is getting the job done without fuss or undue attention.

CHAPTER 30

The 4040:
Tough as nails, light as a feather

The 4040 is a single-stack .40-caliber pistol built on a Scandium alloy frame. Actually, this one is the "4040 AirLite PD" one of the Personal Defense versions that S&W offers. The PD guns are done in matte black finishes, with attention paid to things that make them easier to carry, like de-horning and safety levers only on the left side.

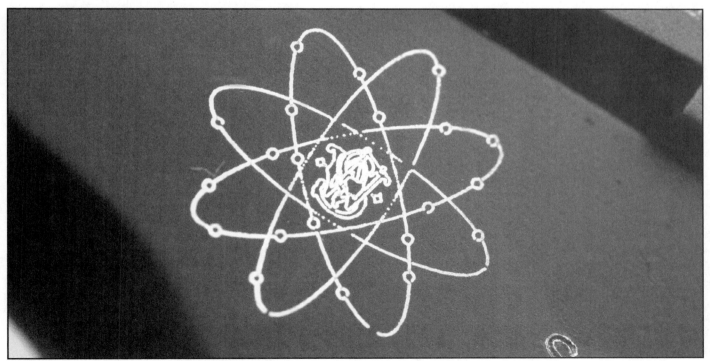

The S&W atomic logo, a sign of Scandium ahead.

The left side of the 4040.

The 4040 safety, down and on safe.

The non-ambi 4040 safety, ready to fire.

The right side of the 4040.

The 4040 follower, with its ball bearing to ensure reliable lift and slide lockback.

The Hogue soft rubber grips go a long way to soaking up recoil from hot .40 loads in a lightweight gun.

A compact, single-stack, .40-caliber carry gun for someone who wants a powerful sidearm.

The standard S&W pistol design does not use a barrel bushing.

As discussed in the "Frames" chapter, Scandium creates a super-tough Aluminum alloy, one with nearly the tensile strength of steel. The .40-caliber pistols specifically benefit from Scandium. One of the problems early in the introduction of the .40 S&W cartridge was slide velocity and early unlocking. It proved to require more than just a heavier recoil spring and a .40-caliber barrel to convert 9mm models to .40 S&W. But with the Scandium alloy S&W could make compact .40-caliber guns that would not fall apart after some hard practice. With the hot .40 S&W loads out there, a non-Scandium gun could be in trouble.

A walk around

The 4040 has a 3-1/2-inch barrel. The barrel/slide junction at the hood has the now obligatory "loaded chamber view port." The slide is flat on top, with Novak three-dot sights fore and aft. The hammer is bobbed, and the safety has a lever only on the left side, for right-handed shooters. The slide is marked "AirLite PD" on the left, and bare on the right.

The dustcover slopes gently up towards the muzzle, similarly to the LadySmith pistols. The right side of

The three-dot sights include the front in a dovetail.

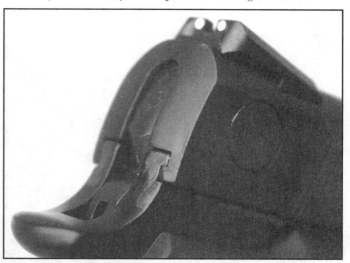
The hammer is bobbed, the sight is Novak, and the result is easy to carry and shoot.

The 4040 shoots very well indeed for a carry gun.

the frame is marked with the S&W logo inside of the "Nuclear" ring, indicating its Scandium alloy. The slide stop, safety lever, magazine button and trigger are all standard S&W, set up for traditional double-action. The grips are Hogue bolt-ons. Unlike the one-piece grips made of Xenoy, the Hogues with their softer consistency have to be made as pairs and held with a screw.

The magazine is blued, single-stack, and holds eight rounds. The follower has a ball bearing set into the right side of it, to keep the follower tracking smoothly and to keep the slide stop tab of the follower on the left side of the tube, where it can lock the slide when empty. The bottom has a curved finger tab on one magazine, while the other has a straight tab.

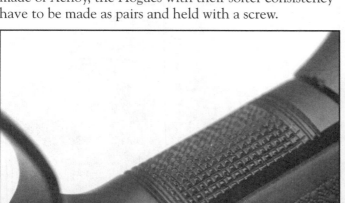

Machine-cut checkering to provide a non-slip grip.

The loaded-chamber indication port.

The 4040 is comfortable in the grip and soft in recoil.

At full recoil, the muzzle hardly comes up.

The grips and magazines called for a lot of comment by my test-fire crew. Some liked the rubber grips, while I preferred that the 4040 have the standard S&W Xenoy grips. Some of the crew loved the curved magazine and disliked the flat. Me, I didn't notice either way. They all commented on the snappy recoil, with hot loads and such a light pistol. The consensus about the grips was that whether you liked them or not they did a lot to take the snap out of the recoil. As shooting grips they are great.

Firing and carry

As I mentioned, the recoil could be noticeable. In its hottest loads the .40 S&W can be quite warm (the heavy bullet Cor-bon loads can post power factors closing in on 190) and the weight of the 4040 does nothing to dampen the recoil. Those who felt the recoil tended to like the Hogue grips. Me, I've spent a lot of time running bowling pin loads through .45-caliber handguns with power factors from 195 to 210, so the recoil wasn't that bad. As for carry, the light weight and compact size are good things. But I'd definitely want to test the Hogue grips on jackets, coats and sweaters to make sure those didn't get "grabbed" by the rubber of the grips and end up printing when it should be concealed. I love Hogue products and the Hogue brothers, but were I carrying this regularly the first thing I'd change would be to go to Xenoy one-piece grips.

(I'd probably also swap the sights for night sights, but then I'd do that with almost all of the guns tested.)

In accuracy the 4040 shot well. With standard-recoil .40 S&W loads it was quite pleasant to handle, the 100-yard gong was easy to hit. Using the Cirillo Index, the 4040 suffered a bit. The short slide/barrel made it a bit harder to keep the gun indexed, as there was less out front to indicate when I'd gotten a bit off the mark. But I could still keep my hits at high speed in the A/C zone. Bill Drills were a snap with the regular loads, but a bit more work with the hottest ones. With only the two magazines I was not able to take the 4040 through any IPSC matches, something I'd have liked to try.

In the course of testing the S&Ws I happened to take a carton of them along with me to a law enforcement class I was teaching. (AR-15, not handgun.) As a duty or off-duty gun, two guns got the most notice: the 4040 and the 4513. Those officers who were enamored of the .45 ACP all looked longingly at the 4513, while those who do not worship at the altar of .45 gravitated towards the 4040. If they had not been loaners from S&W I could have sold both (and several others of the same models) in that class.

If the 9mm is too small, and the .45 ACP too big, then the .40 should be "just right." And if you want your just-right cartridge in a compact, lightweight package, then get a 4040PD.

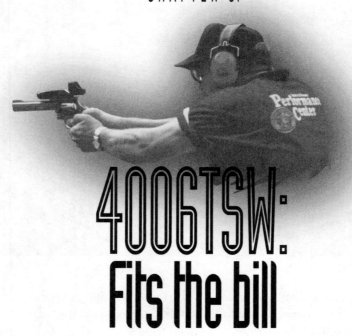

CHAPTER 31

4006TSW: Fits the bill

For some, the 9mm cartridge is too little. It offers high capacity, low recoil, but not enough performance. For others, the .45 was everything they wanted. But it too, has its detractors, who point to heavy recoil, large size and limited capacity as shortcomings. The argument raged for eighty years. The 10mm did not solve the argument, for the simple reason that it wanted to be both and more. Its designers wanted capacity and power, and produced the Bren Ten.

The .40 Tactical S&W in all-stainless for those who want the weight.

The FBI got involved, found the 10mm was too much (too much recoil, too much weight, too much penetration) and wanted less. And what we fund was that sometimes less was more. The 10mm FBI load quickly got turned into the 40 S&W. Derided by some as "Forty Short and Weak" the 40 S&W became the hottest thing since sliced bread. Police departments that had just spent years agonizing over trading in their .38 revolvers for 9mm pistols couldn't dump the 9's fast enough. The .40 as first loaded had some problems. And still does. The

The 4006 is a TDA, with a hammer-dropping safety.

The compact adjustable sight that comes on the 4006TSW is just fine.

A Novak-style dotted front sight makes aiming very easy and accurate.

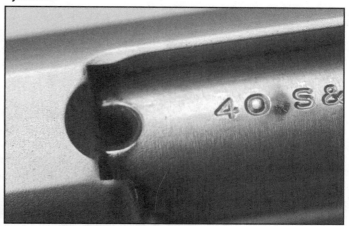
Mandated in some states, the loaded-chamber indicator is just a port on the barrel.

The light rail allows you to mount a light if you so wish.

The one-piece Xenoy grips are comfortable and non-skid.

original load of a truncated-cone jacketed 180-grain bullet at 850 fps is one that penetrates excessively. Where we have come to find that 12 to 18 inches of penetration in ballistic gelatin is sufficient for almost all defensive uses, the 180 fmj load will penetrate more than 36 inches. In testing I have found I need to drape a Kevlar panel over the back of a set of ballistic gelatin blocks in order to retain the bullet. Otherwise it will exit the 3 feet of gelatin and keep on going

The solution was to back off in weight and bump up velocity a bit. The hot setup for the .40 is now a hi-tech expanding hollowpoint of 165 grains, at about 1100 fps.

(From a full-size gun.) The combination is relatively easy to shoot, expands well, doesn't over penetrate, and is plenty accurate. And when fired in something like the 4006, really easy to handle.

The tire-kicking

The 4006TSW is built on an all-stainless steel frame and slide combo. The extra weight the stainless frame adds helps dampen the felt recoil of the sometimes-hot .40 loads. The slide is the regular .40 slide, with the top of the slide milled with a radiused cutter, for a smooth

The slide stop on S&W pistols contains its own spring-loaded plunger to unlock when you load.

With its steel frame, the 4006 handles recoil well.

The 4006 is easy-handling, all-steel and nicely accurate.

arc across the top except for the flat that leads up to the front sight. The front sight base, dovetail and slide flat are complex (easy once programmed) arcs and flats that are attractive but expensive. (Hence the 910 and 410 economy models.) The sights are easy to see. The sights are three-dot, with the front in a dovetail and the rear adjustable. The adjustable sight is proportioned to fit the standard Novak dovetail for rear sights on many S&W pistols. The safety is an ambidextrous one, as the 4006TSW is a traditional double-action.

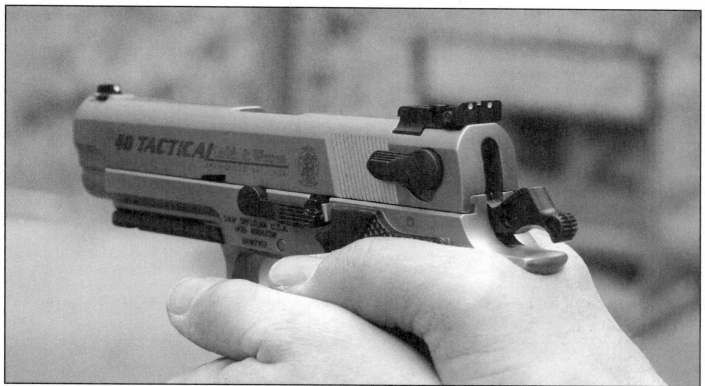

The 4006 at the shot.

The 4006 at the top of its recoil.

The frame is checkered on the front strap, with one-piece Xenoy grips, and an accessory rail on the dustcover. The 4006TSW is meant as a tactical pistol, for a SWAT team or similar use, where a light or laser designator can be a useful thing. One thing you can count on, the 4006 frame is not going to flex under recoil. Some Glock 40 models with light rails have demonstrated malfunctions with a light installed. The solution for Glock was to increase the magazine spring strength, which in some magazines can reduce magazine capacity. No need to worry here, as any load that will flex stainless steel is one you will not survive.

The slide is marked "40 Tactical" and the serial number and model markings are all in the usual locations.

Introduced in 1997, the 4006TSW has a magazine capacity of 10 rounds as dictated by the high-capacity magazine ban enacted in 1994. The ban expired in September of 2004, but as of this writing, S&W has not announced plans to increase the magazine capacity of the 4006TSW. Even so, 10 rounds of .40 S&W is as many as anyone is likely to need, and the 4006TSW's extremely fast reloading capability makes a high-capacity version somewhat superfluous. The firepower of the 4006TSW is limited only by the number of extra magazines the shooter can carry.

Carry and shooting

As a carry gun the recoil-dampening weight of the 4006 works against it. While it is great to shoot, the full-up weight makes it a drag to carry concealed. But that is what the models such as the 4040 are for, light in carry and not a lot of shooting. As a tactical gun carried on duty, the 4006TSW has a lot going for it. The weight makes shooting it a real breeze. Even the hottest loads have their recoil soaked up by the weight. The accuracy was plenty good, with El Prez drills and Bill Drills a snap. I tried the 4006TSW on a few Cirillo drills, and while it worked well there, the sights just kept attracting my attention. I taped them over and still did well.

The accuracy was plenty good (although it did suffer in comparison to the 910 along at the same session, but then all the other firearms suffered, too) and the gong was no problem. A 15-yard group off the bench that is under 2 inches is not something to sneer at, and the 4006TSW could do that pretty regularly.

In use, the 4006TSW would make a great sidearm for on duty. Were you limited to a traditional double-action, and could get what you wanted in the way of high-performance .40 S&W ammo, the 4006TSW would serve you without fail.

An accurate shooter, the 4006 will not let you down.

For mild IDPA loads, or hot defense-equivalent, 135-grain bullets will serve you well.

In competition, the 4006TSW is something that is neither fish nor fowl. As a traditional double-action pistol it fits the definition of both USPSA/IPSC Production guns, and IDPA Stock Service Pistol. But the scoring works against it. In both IPSC and IDPA it would run against 9mms, and the recoil would hurt your scores. You couldn't use it in any other category of IDPA, for it is not a revolver and not a single-action pistol. You could run it in Limited 10 in USPSA/IPSC matches. There, your .40 could be scored Major along with .45s, and the 10-shot magazines would not be a hindrance. But you'd have to start the first shot double-action, against a bunch of cocked and locked 1911's. A good shooter would not have a problem at the club level.

As a defensive gun it is a bit heavy for concealed carry. But as a carry gun in a business or home, it would work very well. And as a stationary defensive gun, the light rail might come in handy. With a light on it, you can investigate noises in the night with a light on your firearm.

CHAPTER 32

CS45:
Power in a small package

The CS45 is the most compact traditional double action .45 pistol you can get your hands on. The 4513 was a smaller duty gun, compact enough to be carried concealed, but large enough to be useful as a duty gun. The CS45 does not try to be a duty gun, except if your duty requires concealed carry. The layout and features of the CS45 are identical to the CS9, so if you don't see them in context you'd be hard-pressed to

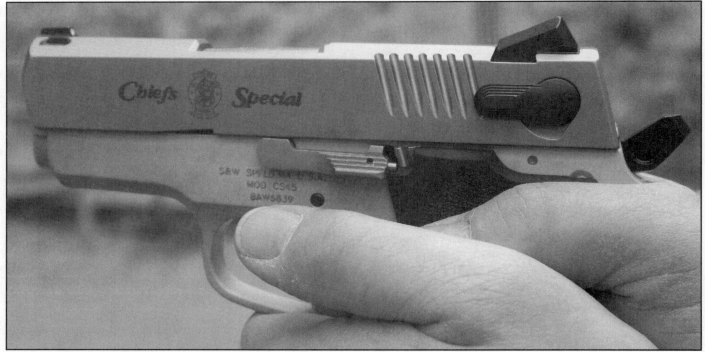

Even with average hands, my test-shooter has no problems getting a good grip on the CS45.

tell which one you were looking at. As soon as you pick one up you'll now, for the most compact .45 pistol is still a large handgun.

The slide is stainless, the frame aluminum alloy hard anodized clear so the aluminum color shows. The grips are the two-piece Hogue rubber grips with S&W logo

that served so well on the CS9, but they are scaled up. They fill the hand without making the pistol bulky. It has the same style three-dot Novak sights, and MIM lightened hammer that the CS9 has, just scaled up.

For its compact size, the CS45 is remarkably soft to shoot. I don't know if it is the rubber Hogue grips, the

The CS45 just before the shot.

Remarkably soft in recoil, this is all the CS45 rises with Black Hills 230-grain hardball.

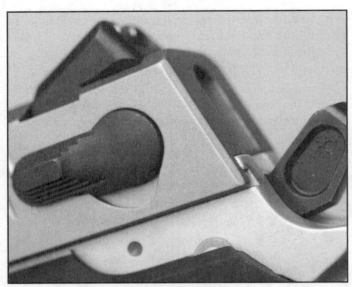

The TDA safety lever and bobbed MIM hammer.

The front sight. Notice that the CS45 is a much "slabbier" gun than most S&W pistols. The slide is mostly a series of flats with no curves.

For a compact gun, the CS45 is very accurate. If you can't hit something with this, don't blame the gun.

loss of velocity you get from such a short barrel (not much, really, the .45 mostly works by weight and diameter) or what, but shooting the CS45 was such a pleasure that on one outing not only was all the test-fire ammo consumed by my crew, some of them went back to their vehicles to get more of their own. You can't get a better endorsement than that.

The CS45 uses shorter than usual .45 caliber third generation magazines. They hold only six rounds each, making the CS45 a seven-shooter. However the pistol will work with the longer magazines for the 4513, with seven rounds, and the full-sized pistols which hold eight. So, if you plan to pack the CS45, you would be doing well to invest in some full-size magazines that hold eight for your reloads, and holster the CS45 with the standard magazine for compactness.

Required by law to put their name on it someplace, S&W can barely fit what they need on the front of the slide.

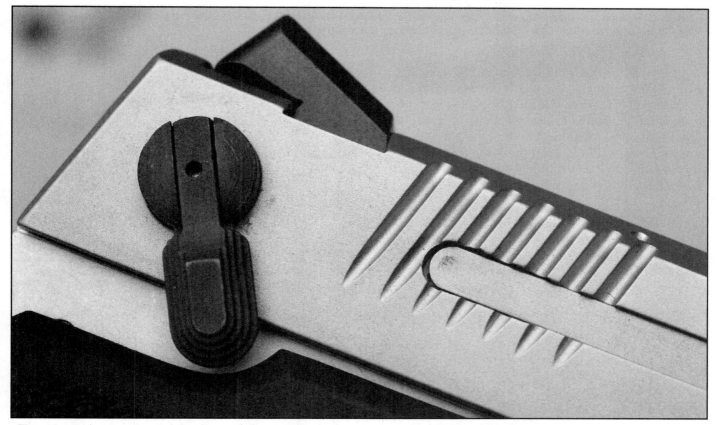

The safety is ambi, and notice that the grasping grooves don't come down the full side of the slide.

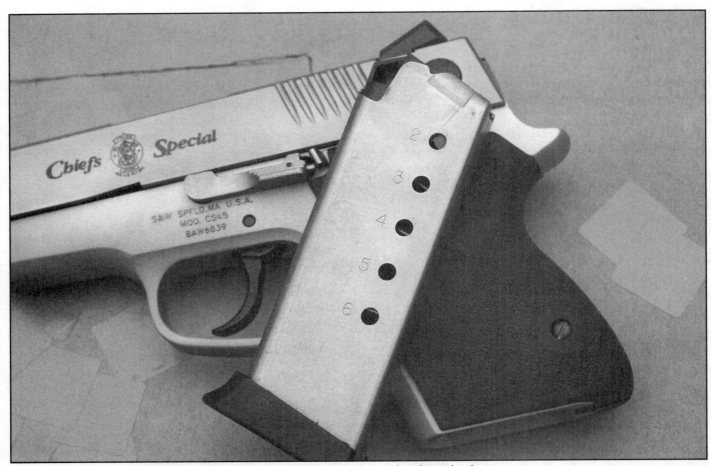

With six and one, the seven-shot CS45 offers plenty of ammo, and more in a fast reload.

On the range the CS45 was quite accurate. You don't usually associate small groups with small guns, especially not those with big bores, but the CS45 delivered the goods. Bill Drills were some work, but manageable, the Cirillo Index was a snap, and El Presidente Par times were easy to beat. Plinking on the 100-yard gong produced a satisfying number of hits, more so than the crew expected from the short sight radius.

The CS45 isn't the smallest gun around, nor the lightest. But it is the smallest and lightest you can get a .45 ACP in traditional double-action. For those who want the .45 ACP, or whose departments allow its carry, the CS45 would make a great concealed carry or off-duty gun.

Hogue, soft rubber grips help make the CS45 a soft shooter.

CHAPTER 33

The 4513TSW:
A tactical .45 with flair

When the first 645 pistols arrived in the mid-1980s we were amazed: It was all-stainless, it was .45, it was double-action. And it was big and clunky. For those who were tired of their 9mm pistols, it was the only choice. But, it suffered in comparison to the custom 1911s we were starting to see and build. The choice would have been to make it in an alloy frame to lighten it somewhat, but S&W was in

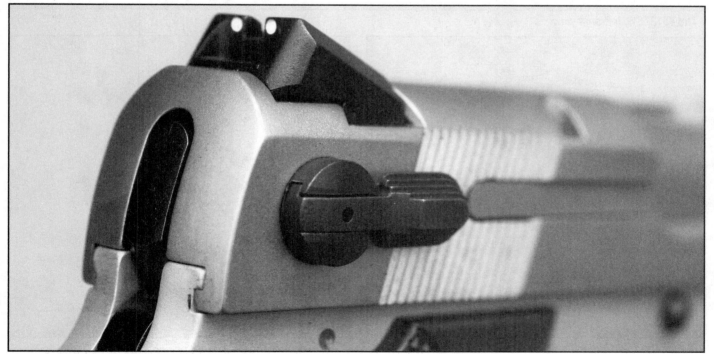

The ambi safety ready to fire.

The 4513TSW, left-side view.

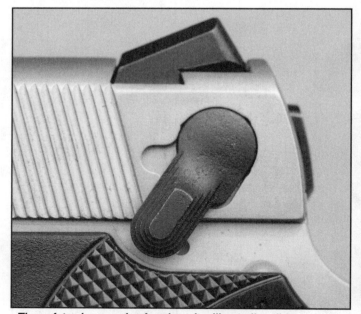

The safety, down and safe, where it will not allow firing.

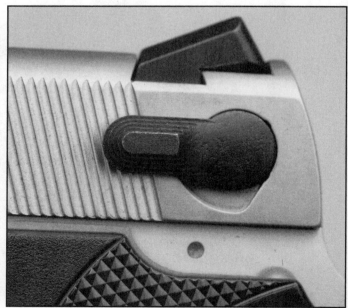

The hammer is bobbed, and the sights are Novak. While a bit big, the 4513 is still compact for a .45.

a bit of a bind there. You see, soon after the 645 came out, the FBI decided that what they really wanted was a 10mm sidearm. (The 1986 Miami shootout was the impetus, and it has been covered quite a bit. Simply put, the FBI put a lot of blame on the 9mm cartridge when training, tactics and procedures were more to blame.) The FBI also insisted at first on full-power 10mm ammo. S&W was not going to put the hot 10mm ammo into an alloy-frame gun. (They could now, with the new Scandium alloy, but the 10mm is long past saving for general

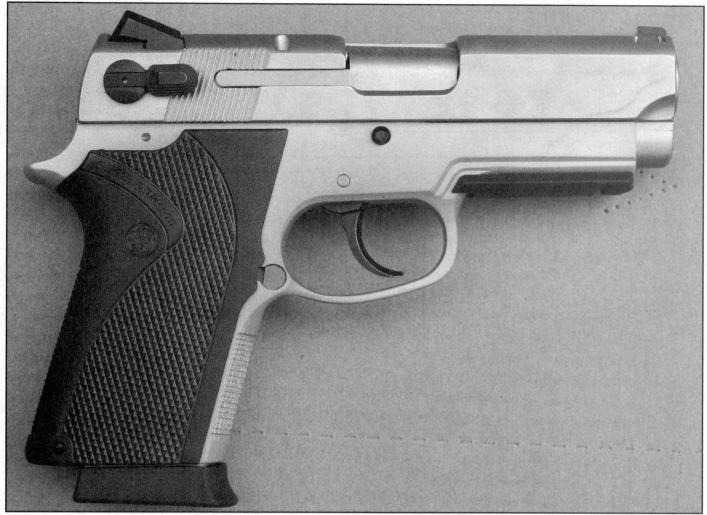

Right side.

The slide stop, with its integral plunger and spring.

The laser-etched Tactical logo is distinctive.

No bushing, but a big muzzle.

The front sight, of the three-dot sights, rests in a dovetail.

Seven rounds in the magazine and one in the chamber give you plenty of ammo — with more on the reload.

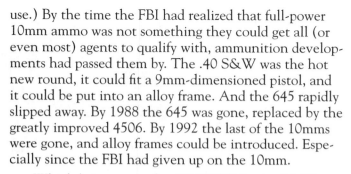

The chamber and loaded-chamber indicator port.

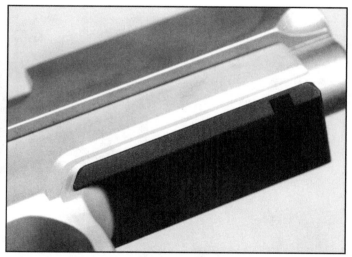

The tactical light rail is all the rage these days.

use.) By the time the FBI had realized that full-power 10mm ammo was not something they could get all (or even most) agents to qualify with, ammunition developments had passed them by. The .40 S&W was the hot new round, it could fit a 9mm-dimensioned pistol, and it could be put into an alloy frame. And the 645 rapidly slipped away. By 1988 the 645 was gone, replaced by the greatly improved 4506. By 1992 the last of the 10mms were gone, and alloy frames could be introduced. Especially since the FBI had given up on the 10mm.

Which brings us to the 4513TSW. In the S&W numbering parlance, it is a .45 ACP pistol in a single-stack lightweight frame with a tactical light rail. For those paying attention to equipment, it is one of the nicest .45 launching systems available.

The 4513TSW comes in a standard S&W Blue plastic box with the nail-breaking gray latches. Inside are a pair of magazines, the standard owner's manual, fired case in sealed envelope and card to join "Club 1852."

The pistol is done in stainless slide and natural hard-coat aluminum frame. On the top the sights are Novak three-dot, in transverse dovetails. The slide has a machined flat on the top. On the left side the slide is laser-etched ".45 Tactical Smith & Wesson" and has the S&W logo. On the right, the slide is bare of markings. The serrations are only at the rear, just ahead of the ambidextrous hammer-dropping safety. The frame is marked on the left with "S&W SPLFD,MA USA" above the model number and serial number, all laser etched. The equipment rail on the dustcover is black, contrasting the frame. The black slide stop has its own internal plunger to power it, bearing on an angled shoulder on the arm of the hammer pivot pin. The frame has red dots on both sides under the safety levers. If you see red, it is ready to fire. The one-piece Xenoy grips have a flat backstrap, and

are quite comfortable. The magazine release is behind the trigger on the left side of the frame. The magazine is a single-stack, stainless, and holds seven rounds. The bottom lips hold a removable baseplate for cleaning. Should you find an enterprising machinist, he (or she) would machine you hollow, extended baseplates to increase capacity. Bumping the magazine capacity from seven to nine or 10 rounds would be very useful indeed.

The trigger is the Traditional Double Action, where the safety decocks but does not fire it, and blocks the trigger while it is down. The DA is a re-strike double-action. The magazine disconnector makes the pistol incapable of firing while the magazine is out. The magazines are generation-specific. If you have any old Model 645 magazines, they aren't going to work in the new third-generation pistols. But the longer magazines, the eight-shot ones made for the 945, will.

Shooting and carry impressions

The 4513TSW is lighter than the all-steel S&W pistols, but it isn't as light as say, a lightweight Commander 1911 is. It can't be, as there are simply more parts that have to be fitted, and extra steel means extra weight. But it is light enough that daily carry is not a problem. And compact enough that you are much less likely to suffer from "grip in the kidneys" pain than you would with larger guns. The recoil is manageable, and the grips help a lot. They are large enough to fill your grasp, but not so large that you feel like you're trying to hang onto a hard-kicking 2x4.

The barrel is only 3-3/4 inches long, but long enough to get good velocity from a .45 round, and long enough to do accurate shooting. In single-action the trigger is heavy enough to keep you out of trouble, but light enough to shoot accurately.

The magazine has "out" bottom lips, so in the future you could extend it for more capacity.

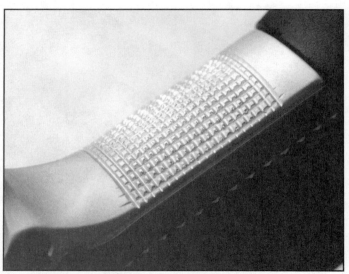

The checkered front strap aids in a non-slip grip.

Loaded magazine in, slide forward, and you're ready to go.

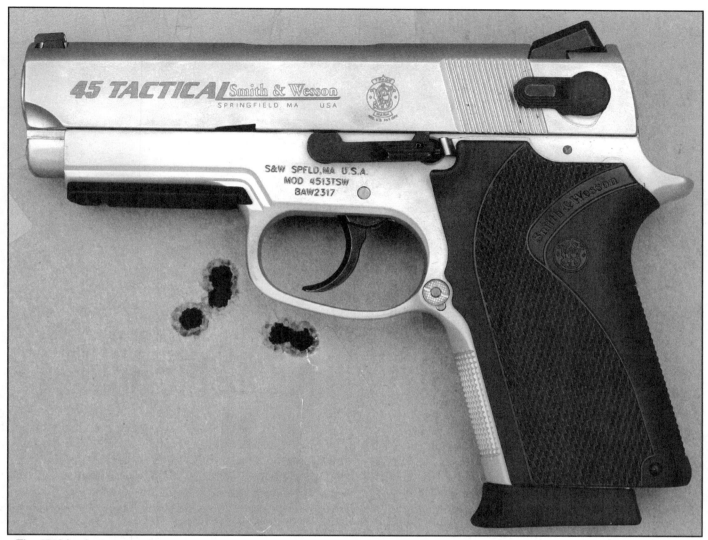

The 4513 is plenty accurate.

Holsters might be a problem. The equipment rail, even when you don't have equipment in it, adds enough size that you might not be able to get it to fit some holsters. With a tactical light on it you'll definitely need a holster designed to hold a sidearm with a light.

On the standard drills and on the gong, the 4513TSW handled nicely. I was able to post passing times at will on the El Presidente even using the trigger-cocking feature on the first shot. And the equipment rail rested nicely on a carpeted shooting block, letting me shoot some amazingly tight groups. The El Presidente was a breeze, and the Cirillo Index produced all A-zone hits. Were I packing for a tactical team and allowed a .45, the 4513TSW would definitely be high

on my list of sidearms. For regular concealed carry, I think I'd opt for the regular 4513, lacking the tactical rail. It would just be a lot easier to find holsters to fit that I could conceal.

The handling of the 4513, and its ability to handle recoil without causing you to regret your choice of .45, was impressive enough that I wish I had talked S&W into sending a fistful of magazines along with it. I would have loved to try it on an IPSC course. It would have been only eligible for Limited 10 Division, but I'm sure I could have done well with it. However, a pair of seven-shot magazines only gives you 15 rounds (one in the chamber to start) and with many stages set at 20 rounds or more, there just was no point to it.

CHAPTER 34

P99:
Where the Old World meets the New

The P99 is a collaboration between S&W and Walther. Starting with the 9mm, the arrangement was that the frames would be made in Germany, but that the assembled firearms would be made here in the United States, with U.S.-made parts and labor.

The P99 was quickly offered in .40 S&W, and then re-engineered to take the .45 ACP. The test gun is one of the .45 ACP P99 pistols. The layout is similar, but not identical to many other self-loading pistols. The magazine is "mid-capacity" designed to be only 10 rounds from

The S&W P99, in .45 ACP, is a really good choice for a sidearm.

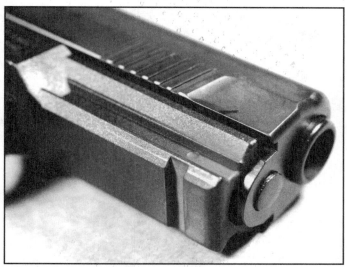

The polymer frame has an integral light rail.

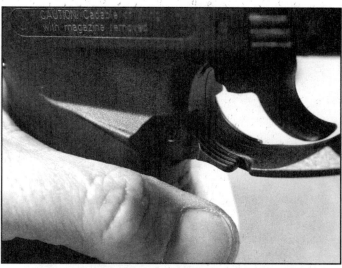

The magazine release is located behind the trigger, at the bottom of the trigger guard.

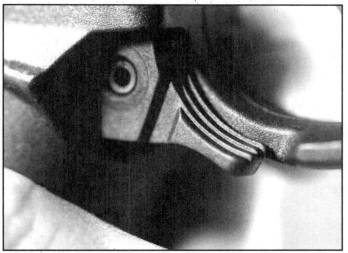

You can lever the magazine release on either side, with trigger finger or thumb.

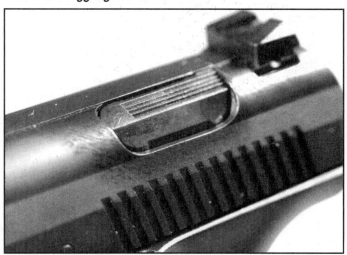

The decocking "lever" is a button in the top of the slide.

The frame is clearly marked, "Made in Germany," but the pistol is assembled in the United States.

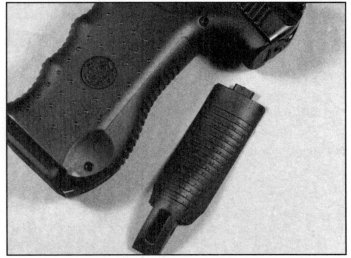

The P99 comes with two backstraps, one arched, one flat. Install the one that feels the best or produces the best scores for you.

The mid-cap magazine holds 10 rounds, but is not a modified larger-capacity one. It was designed to be 10 shots.

You can see the difference at the base between the P99 magazine and a 1911 magazine.

the beginning. The taper starts sooner than many other hi-cap magazines, and that and a slightly narrower tube width makes the P99 a relatively slender gun for being a 10-shot .45 ACP. The frame is polymer with metal reinforcements that also allow the engineers to add a refinement to the grip; replaceable grip straps. The rear of the frame is a panel that can be replaced. The P99 comes with two, an arched and a flat panel. If the arched is too large, drift out the retaining pin and replace it with the flat one. Or vice verse.

Moving up the frame, the magazine catch is a dual paddle on either side of the rear of the trigger guard. To release the magazine, press the paddle down on either side. The magazine will drop free of its own weight when unlatched. Right above the trigger, behind the "Walther" logo are the disassembly panels. To take the P99 apart, unload it. Then dry fire it. Pull the slide back a fraction of an inch, and pull both panels down. While holding them down, run the slide forward off the frame. Once off, pull the recoil spring guide rod slightly forward to release it from its seat in the barrel, and then lift out. Pivot the barrel out of the slide and pull it away from the muzzle end of the slide.

The front of the frame has a tactical rail cast into the polymer frame for a light or laser.

The trigger of the P99 is a decocking double-action. When at rest, you stroke through the trigger to finish cocking the hammer and fire the pistol. If you do not wish to fire, press the button set in the top of the slide to relax the striker.

The P99 carries like any mid-weight large bore pistol. You'll need a holster, for it won't fit any pocket, and the relatively short barrel/slide length calls for a secure holster. Otherwise the weight and bulk of the grip might lever the slide out of some holsters.

In firing it is surprisingly mild. It is lighter, due to its polymer frame, than a steel-framed pistol, yet the lighter weight doesn't seem to translate into a harsher recoil. I found quick precision drills were harder to do than with a cocked and locked pistol like a 1911 or an already cocked TDA like the 4513TSW. However, that didn't prevent me from managing Bill Drills, and the Cirillo Index was no problem. The tapered magazines of the P99 made quick reloads a snap, so my first three attempts on El Presidente were all faster than Par times and scores.

Where does the P99 fit in? Well, the grip is smaller than that of the Glock 21, especially with the flat mainspring cover in place. If you wanted a .45, and were locked into a DAO-type or Safe action pistol, that was American made, you'd have a P99 in your holster.

CHAPTER 35

The SW1911:
A solid soldier in the clone war

It was an open secret for a few years that S&W provided many of the 1911 manufacturers, other than Colt, with the basics to make their products. To understand why, we have to delve a bit into manufacturing and the costs associated with it. Working from the end of the line back we have the assemblers. They take the finished parts and assemble them into a working firearm. Depending on the manufacturing tolerances they may have to do anywhere from a little to a lot of hand-fitting to make things work. The parts come to them from the machinists. In the old days, the machinists were just that, row upon row of machinists who stood at a

Since the 1911 has no magazine disconnector, the SW1911 carries the standard factory warning.

single machine each, which performed a single operation (or two or three at most) on a single part. With a dozen machinists making the same part, the minute differences between them would call for hand-fitting.

Now, we use computer-controlled machining stations. The precision and repeatability of the machines reduces the need for hand-fitting. Instead of 100 mills costing $1,000 each, and requiring 100 operators, a modern

The S&W 1911 is a modern iteration of the classic.

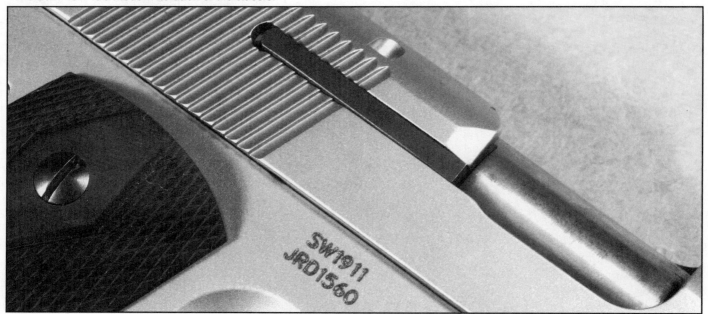

The extractor is external and thus not prone to the tension problems sometimes found in the original design.

manufacturer pays (or leases) a $100,000 dollar mill and pays two or three operators. A top-notch CNC machining station can cost a lot more than a "mere" $100,000. But the cost can be borne.

Getting the material to mill, that's the rub. You see, for many applications forgings are best. You don't go out and buy a forge for a few hundred thousand dollars. You need a forge (and the bigger, the better) you need a furnace (again, bigger is better) you need forging dies and the die sinkers to machine and maintain them. You need pyrometers to read the heat of the steel. And you need skilled operators at every turn. Investing in a forging setup to produce your parts can be a breath-taking financial undertaking. Which is why many parts, firearms included, are promoted as being "milled from bar stock." A CNC mill can do that. What it can't do is forge.

So, Smith & Wesson, having big forges, lots of experience, and a well-trained staff, forged parts for other people. Not just guns, although the forges made for firearms-sized parts can't forge really big stuff. One of their clients was Kimber. Kimber slides and frames were forged at S&W, and then shipped to the Kimber plant to be fed into their CNC mills and lathes. In case you haven't been paying attention over the past few years, Kimber makes 1911 pistols, and very good ones. What with the seemingly bottomless demand for 1911 pistols, it was only a matter of time before S&W began feeding those forgings into their own CNC machines.

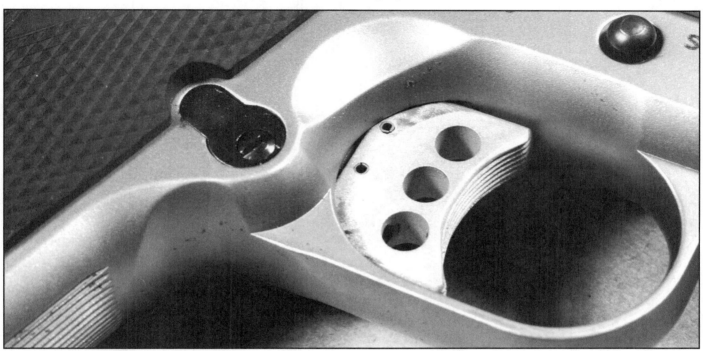
The trigger is long, aluminum and lightweight.

The extractor is held in place by a pin coming down from the top of the slide.

The sights are classic three-dot Novaks.

SW1911

If you have been around 1911 pistols, the S&W will seem familiar. Very familiar. If your experience has been with DA revolvers and TDA pistols, then it is time for the walk-through. The SW1911 is a Government-size pistol chambered in .45 ACP. (There is a Scandium-frame Commander with a shorter slide and barrel coming out any day now as I type this.) The sights are Novak, as you'd expect, with three dots. The top of the slide is the standard arc, no flats or ribs. On the left side the slide is marked "SW1911" with the S&W logo laser etched. On the right side, the slide is bare of markings, but the ex-

tractor is clearly visible. Unlike the internal, spring-stock extractor of the original 1911 pistols, the SW1911 has an external extractor. It pivots on a pin driven in vertically, and is powered by a coil spring opposite the chamber end. One problem with the old-style extractor is that the extractor itself provides the tension for it to work. If the old extractor is abused it my lose its tension and fail to reliably extract or eject. The external extractor is much less prone to that sort of problem. The ejection port is lowered from the old 1911, but not as low as some custom gunsmiths provide. Ejection is more positive and less likely to "ding" the case mouths, something not favored by reloaders.

The thumb safety is not ambidextrous.

The grip safety works the firing pin block lever.

The one-piece recoil spring guide rod keeps the spring under control. Some like guide rods, some don't. If you don't, it is easy enough to change it.

The plunger in the slide is the bottom of the firing pin block.

With a standard bushing, the SW1911 would be accepted in IDPA and at the Single Stack Classic.

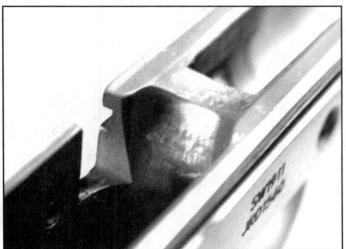

The feed ramp is the classic style, with ramp on both frame and barrel.

The frame is standard government model, lacking (at this time) a tactical light rail. It is marked on the left side with "Caution: Capable offering with magazine removed" as a warning to those who might be very familiar with S&W pistols but not the 1911. As the magazine disconnector in the other S&W pistols precludes them from firing with the magazine removed, S&W didn't want someone to look at it and thinks "Oh, it's an S&W. I can take the mag out and it won't fire." Thus the warning. On the right side the frame has the serial number and required manufacturer's mark.

The initial SW1911 production uses stainless slide, frame and barrel, with the sights and operating controls carbon steel with a durable black finish. So the slide stop, thumb safety, the plunger tube that holds their spring and plungers, magazine catch and grip safety are blued steel. The mainspring housing is black plastic. The grips are molded rubber with an internal stiffener, with checkering molded into the surface for a non-skid grip.

The trigger is a long one, with three lightening holes in the aluminum (left bright) front. The thumb safety is small enough to be out of the way but large enough to be useful. The grip safety is the modern high-ride style, with a "speed bump" on the bottom to ensure a solid grip and grip safety deactivation on the draw. Internally the SW1911 is a mix of old and new. The feed ramp is standard, not an integral barrel ramp. Thus should you wear out or become tired of the excellent accuracy the S&W barrel provides, fitting a new one will not be expensive. (As compared to the cost of acquiring and fitting a ramped barrel.) However, the firing pin of the SW1911 has an additional safety. The firing pin safety plunger blocks the firing pin from moving forward until the plunger has been levered out of the way. The lever is in the frame. Unlike the Colt Series 80 safety, the lever is not moved by the trigger. In the SW1911 it is moved by the grip safety. If you grasp the SW1911 your grip moves the grip safety and the lever unlocks the firing pin safety plunger as it should so you can fire when needed. If you drop the SW1911, as soon as your hand leaves the grip safety the lever pivots down, and the spring-loaded firing pin safety plunger again blocks the firing pin. The firing pin is blocked without potential problems with a proper trigger pull, as can happen in the Series 80.

The SW1911 comes in the usual S&W Blue plastic box with all the usual accouterments (manual, fired case, cable lock, etc), and includes a pair of Wilson 47D magazines. The Wilson magazines have justly earned a reputation as one of the best. The sturdy stainless tubes are extremely durable, the plastic followers last a long time and provide reliable feeding, and the plastic base plates are removable and thus encourage regular cleaning and maintenance, adding to reliability.

Shooting and carry impressions

My first chance to shoot the SW1911 came at a law enforcement class I was teaching. The SW1911 arrived just before I left, so I packed it along with some ammo in the hopes that I'd get a chance to shoot it after class or during breaks. As it turned out, I'd get a bunch of shooting. The law enforcement officers who go to classes, and those who teach, tend to be gear-oriented. And many have a fondness for the 1911. When word got out that I'd brought the new and as-yet unseen SW1911, well, ammo just started showing up. After a few boxes had gone downrange, I had a DEA agent walk up with a carton of ammo and ask "Can I try it?" In the course of a short afternoon, we put about 700 rounds of ammo through it. Except for a box of factory ammo that had been sitting on the floor when a police storage room flooded (and thus would not reliably fire) everything fed, fired, ejected and worked exactly as you'd expect. And shot accurately. So accurately that I was accused of bringing a "special writer's gun" to show off. Shooting from the 7-yard line I was able to place two full magazines of hot Winchester Ranger LE-Only 230-grain hollowpoint into a single ragged hole. And no, it wasn't a "special writers gun." I'm not sure such guns exist, and most manufacturers don't have a sufficient inventory that they can keep a storeroom full of slick, tuned, accurized guns just so they'll have what a writer wants.

After that I brought it home and let my test-fire crew have a go with it. As they are all experienced 1911 shooters, I hadn't expected any surprises, nor were there any. They didn't find any sharp corners or edges that would bite. The gun hit right to the sights for all of them, and worked reliably with any ammo we fed it. I ran a couple of matches with it, since I had a ready supply of 1911 magazines with which to feed it. It never failed me. The only thing I'd change for competition shooting would be to put some kind of a magazine funnel on it. In many high round-count stages you can lose a lot of time with a bunch of slow reloads. A magazine funnel speeds up reloads and improves your score. For carry they can be helpful, but only so long as they are small enough to be unobtrusive.

As a full size all-steel 1911, it would be a bit much for a daily carry gun, concealed. I did just that in the old days, and found the size and weight were a lot by the end of the day, week and month. With a good holster and dressing properly you could do it without a problem, but for everyday use I'm looking forward to the Scandium commander.

As a duty gun for departments that allow the 1911, the SW1911 would be an excellent choice. As it takes all standard 1911 accessories, you could easily put a magazine funnel on it. It will use all standard 1911 magazines, so you could carry it with the eight-shot Wilson 47D and use 10-shot Wilson or McCormick magazines for your reloads. It will stand up to all the ammo you can feed it, and keep doing so for years.

In all, the SW1911 is a worthy adversary in the "1911 Clone Wars" that we seem to be in the midst of.

The SW1911 uses standard 1911 magazines, seven-, eight- and 10-shot versions.

CHAPTER 36

The 945:
More than just a quarter to 10

In the decades of developing, manufacturing, marketing and improving their pistol design, S&W kept bumping into one inescapable fact: a large segment of the American shooting populace desires a .45. Indeed, there are segments who view anything smaller as something unmanly, something less than desirable, even embarrassing. They do not like the 9mm, and avoid it if at all possible.

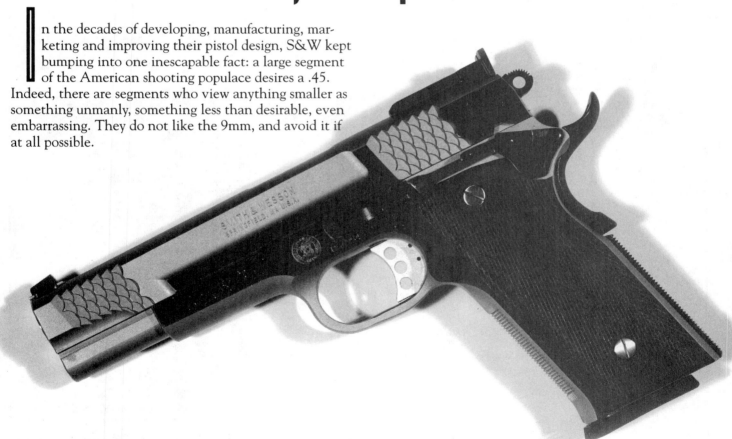

The S&W 945 is a great gun you might never see.

When S&W first came out with the Model 39 in the 1950s, they did so because the Army had been expressing a desire for something "better" than the 1911. They wanted 9mm for its low recoil, greater penetration and ease of shooting from lesser recoil. They wanted less weight. They also wanted a double-action trigger for greater safety. Never mind that they finally got all that in 1985 with the Beretta Model 92, and also never mind that all the attributes they sought were phantoms and not worth seeking. In the 1950s they knew what they wanted, and S&W provided it. But as much as they

The external extractor solves some problems.

wanted it, the Department of Defense would not buy it. After all, while the 1911 was "old and heavy, kicked too much and was unsafe" (all untrue) there were lots of them in warehouses. So S&W turned to the police market. They had some success, as the Model 39 has real advantages over a double-action revolver. The Indiana State Police went with it, and acted as the test bed for other departments that later switched wholesale to pistols fromm revolvers.

In 1974 S&W unveiled the latest improvement of the Model 39, the M-59. It had 14 shots in a magazine instead of the nine of the Model 39. In the early 1970s, the 9mm was still hot, and police departments who may have been thinking of switching could be lured to pistols from revolvers via capacity. While nine shots was greater than six shots it wasn't enough for some. But 14 shots? Departments started switching. The design iterations accelerated in the 1980s, when S&W unveiled the plethora of trigger and safety options, and in the mid 1980s the 10mm guns. For those who wanted something bigger, like Detroit and Chicago, S&W scaled up the pistol frame and unveiled the 645: a .45 ACP SA/DA pistol in stainless steel. Now we're talking. Except by that time the .45 position had begun to harden: it wasn't enough to have a .45 pistol, it had to be a 1911 pistol. Hammer-dropping

If you have a chance to lay hands on a 945, you should do so. You will not be disappointed.

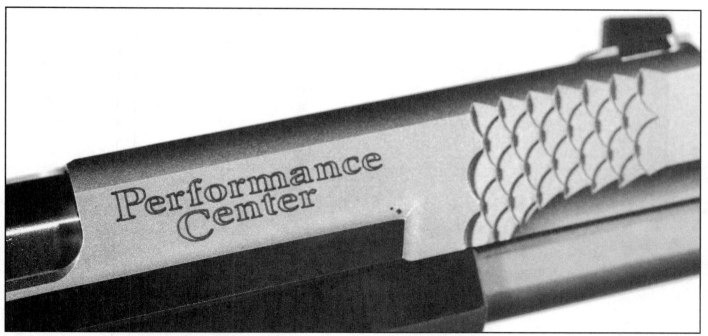

Note the fish scales used for a better gripping surface.

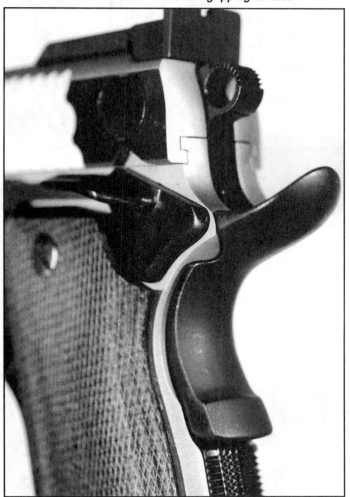

The S&W pistol frame is machined to take a 1911-style grip and thumb safety.

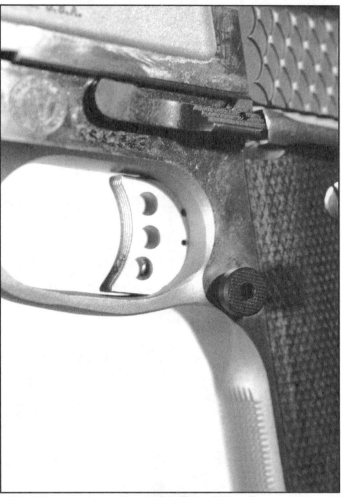

The trigger looks on the outside like a 1911 unit.

safeties were OK for street cops, but SWAT cops and competition shooters had to have a thumb safety that didn't drop the hammer.

Luckily, S&W had another ace up their sleeve. The 945.

Unlike the rest of the S&W pistols at the time, the 945 has a frame-mounted thumb safety that does not drop the hammer. It also has a grip safety. It is the closest design you can come up with to the 1911, starting with an S&W pistol mechanism. And a very good one.

Overview

The 945 is a full-size pistol, laid out as you would expect a pistol designed for the American market. The magazine catch is on the left side behind the trigger, the slide stop is on the left side just below the slide. The outline is very 1911-ish. But you can still see the S&W pistol lines. The slide is machined with fish-scale or snake-scale cocking "serrations." The process involves tilting the slide on a milling machine and then bringing

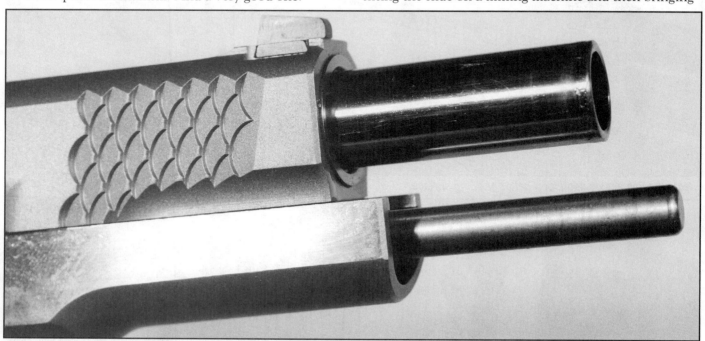

The full-length recoil spring guide rod, expected on an S&W.

The slide stop is pure S&W. Note the extra machining on the slide to sculpt it.

an end mill into contact with the slide in repeated steps. The effect is striking, and provides an excellent grasping surface. The front of the slide has an interior bushing, very much like the Briley spherical bushing. The actual bushing surface is a (what appears to be) Titanium nitride-plated ring inset in the slide front. The ring can be removed or inserted by turning it sideways and pushing

The S&W 945 uses a Briley bushing, not a 1911-type bushing.

The front sight, a Novak-style in a dovetail.

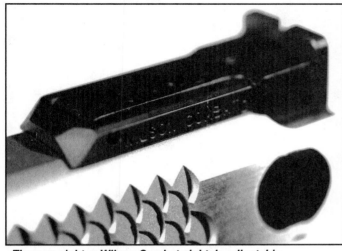

The rear sight, a Wilson Combat sight, is adjustable.

it through the clearance slots. Once in place and turned to receive the barrel it will not exit the slide, but will tilt to allow the barrel to tilt to unlock and lock as the slide cycles. In all a very precise bit of machining but one that allows for a tight fit of barrel to bushing and bushing to slide, and provides the freedom for the barrel to move in the desired direction. The front of the slide is machined under the flats in pure S&W style, with the remnants of the slide rail slots continued forward to the muzzle.

The barrel is pure S&W. It has the side cams and integral feed ramp that you'd expect from an S&W pistol. On top the front sight is pressed into a transverse dovetail. The rear sight is a Wilson Combat. We see a lot more cross-parts/manufacturers use of things like sights. After all, why should S&W dedicate machine tools and production time for a sight when they can simply buy the most-excellent sight from Bill Wilson? In between the front and rear the slide is machined with a flat, but the flat is not grooved or ribbed. Even on a semi-custom gun there are limits to what you can get without writing a check for extras. On the right side the ejection port is

With Black Hills Red 185 JHP ammo, the 945 was a tack-driver. Here is a cluster under an inch, center-to-center.

nicely lowered to clear the empty brass (and occasional live or dud round you might eject) and behind it the extractor. Pinned through the middle, with a spring at the rear to pivot it, the extractor never failed in the test-firing sessions. You could probably even use it with steel-cased ammunition, although I am not a fan of such rounds. It would not suffer as traditional 1911 extractors do to such abuse. The rear of the slide is smooth and matte in texture. If you want serrations or checkering you'll again have to pullout the checkbook.

The frame is hand-filling but not overly large. If you've spent any time with a 1911 you'll warm right up to the 945. (I hate to keep making comparisons to the 1911, but as the 945 was meant to go head-to-head with it, and designed to have its virtues, I simply must keep comparing the two.) The dustcover is similar to the 1911, and if you feel the need you could easily mount a tactical light rail there. The wall thickness is greater than that of the 1911, so it will provide a secure mounting point. The trigger guard, trigger and curve under the trigger guard of the frontstrap are so much like the 1911 that you'll have to look to see what you're holding. The magazine catch falls easily under the thumb. The thumb safety is right where you'd expect it to be, and is fitted with a secure but easily managed detent tension. In between the slide stop and thumb safety is the spring and plunger housing. Well, the spring and plunger housing for the thumb safety. The slide stop has its own internal spring and plunger as a captured assembly, so the "plunger housing" simply has a ramped surface for the slide stop to bear against. When the magazine tension is off the slide stop, and you retract the slide, the angled surface cams the slide stop down and out of the way. There is no room in a thumb safety to do that, so the spring and plunger for the thumb safety is in the housing, and not in the safety.

The thumb safety is ambidextrous, with paddles on both sides. There are a whole host of ambi safeties I do not find comfortable. My grip is such that many of them have the right side paddle located so it binds against the knuckle of my trigger finger. I either have to shift my grip to clear the safety, or it doesn't work. On my competition guns with ambi safeties I simply machine the paddle down until it clears my hand. It isn't as useful as a safety then, but it does work.

At the rear is the grip safety, something you've not seen before on an S&W pistol. The grip safety has the lines of a Caspian safety, and has a "speed bump" on the bottom to ensure that your firing hand fully presses the grip safety so you can fire. The controls are blued steel in contrast to the stainless of the slide and frame.

The 945 shot nicely with Zero reloads (just over 2 inches).

The grips are thin and sculpted to match the frame edge contours. Unlike the rectangular 1911 grips the S&W 945 grips curve under the thumb safety and follow the rear of the frame curve. They are held on with a pair of screws each, tightened into bushings secured to the frame. The grips cover the mainspring housing pin, and you'll have to drift it out to remove the mainspring housing, spring and cup.

The 945 magazines are stout and dependable. Derived from the earlier 645 model, they are not inter-changeable with the older magazines. Each holds eight rounds, with a removable baseplate for cleaning.

You get the 945, two magazines, and the obligatory cable lock and fired case for your local law enforcement officials, in a lockable case from the Performance Center.

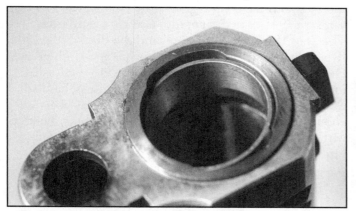

The Briley ring bushing keeps the barrel aligned without potential binding.

The plunger tube only has a spring and plunger for the safety. The slide stop has its own spring and plunger.

And with 230-grain hardball, the 945 was plenty accurate for anything but the Bianchi Cup.

The 945 in use

At the range my testers and I put a goodly amount of Black Hills and Zero ammunition through the 945. As they are almost all regular 1911 shooters they found the 945 pleasant indeed to shoot. At the rifle range the 100-yard gong was in serious jeopardy with almost any ammo, but the Black Hills Red, with a 185-grain JHP was particularly effective. A hold on the top edge of the plate and a clean trigger break almost assured the shooter of a hit on the 10-inch gong. All the empties were ejected to the right and slightly behind. None failed to fire. The magazines dropped free of their own weight when empty. A small note for those who might be accustomed to the more traditional S&W pistols: the 945 will fire when the magazine has been removed. I repeat, there is no magazine safety, and pulling the trigger when the magazine is out will cause the hammer to fall. If there is a round in the chamber that round will fire.

The trigger pull was simply beautiful. It broke crisp and clean, and on the scale it held almost 4 pounds despite feeling a lot closer to 3 in weight. As a competition gun it is great. Were it a carry gun I'd have a gunsmith get in there and boost the trigger pull by another half a pound or so. (I'd really rather carry something with five pounds than three, but four and a half will do nicely.) As clean and crisp as the break was, you would not likely notice it if the pull was increased.

Groups fired at a later session showed me just why the 185s were such a threat. Off the sandbags at 15 yards, the 945 drilled them into a single ragged hole. The Zero 185-grain JHP ammo and the Black Hills 230 JRN did not do as well, but that you'd expect. The Black Hills Blue is loaded in used brass. The Zero is reloaded in mixed cases. And no one ever said that 230 hardball was the most accurate ammo available. Plenty accurate enough in both cases, but if I was going to shoot a match with one of the three loads, in this 945, it would definitely be the Black Hills 185 JHP red box.

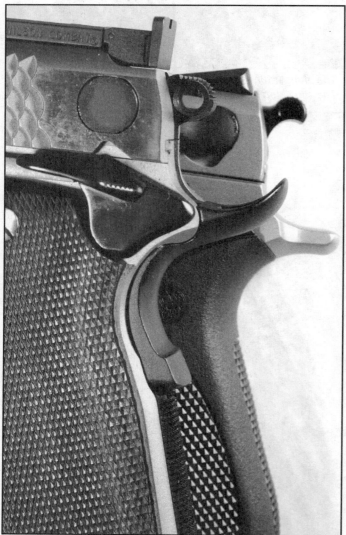

Note the upsweep of the 945 grip safety, allowing your hand a higher ride on the frame.

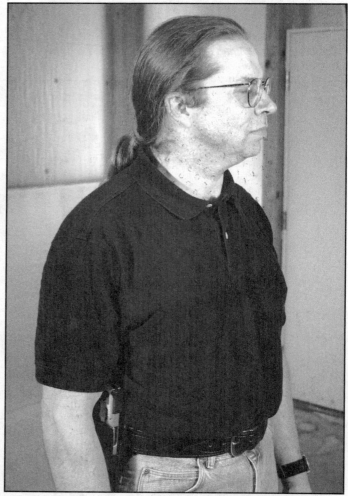

The 945 fits perfectly in an Uncle Mike's kydex belt holster, which is perfect for IPSC or IDPA (check the IDPA list to make sure it is approved, first).

The Draw: grasp the pistol...

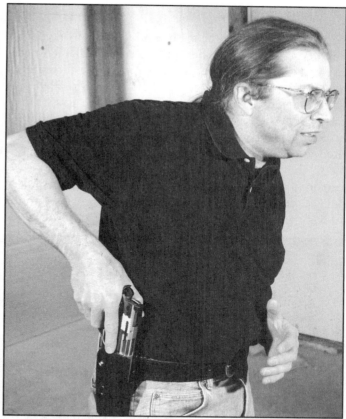

...snatch it upwards...

...clear "leather" and shove it forward...

...get the weak hand on the gun, underneath and without sweeping your fingers, and you're almost there.

Uses of the 945

And we finally come to the end. Having worked for four decades to perfect their pistol design, make it a near-clone of the 1911 and get it to fire (and quite accurately, too) the .45 ACP cartridge, what is it good for? Well, there is defense. While heavy, it would make a superb carry gun. And locked in a tactical holster, it would be a brilliant backup gun for a SWAT officer who was authorized to carry cocked and locked. There are some departments that allow officers trained on the 1911 to carry one on duty. For them the S&W 945 would be a wonderfully accurate and dependable sidearm. Again, for duty I'd want the trigger pull to be at least 4-1/2 pounds.

In competition, we have a different problem. Many matches won't allow it, and others will greet it with little enthusiasm. Don't bother showing up at a GSSF match. The Glock shooters may appreciate its qualities, but you can't use it in the match. Ditto the Single Stack Classic. Only real 1911s need show up. In a Steel Challenge match the trigger and accuracy will serve you well, but you'll be shooting a .45 against a bunch of soft-recoiling 9mm or .38 Super guns, and your times will suffer. At the American Handgunner Shootoffs it would be great, even if the eight-round magazines limited you some. For that, and for USPSA Limited 10 competition, I'd find or make magazine extensions. By removing the plastic baseplates and replacing them with brass or aluminum ones ma-

Disassembly is easy; line the slide-stop notch up with the pivot of the slide-stop lever, and push the lever out.

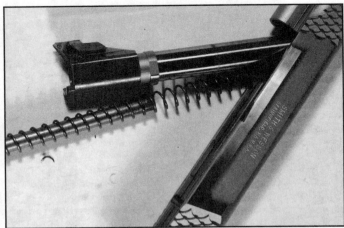

The barrel comes out from underneath and behind, like all S&W pistols.

The 945 may look like a 1911, but inside, it is still an S&W.

chined to be hollow, you could increase the magazine capacity to 10 rounds. You might have to ask Wolff for longer springs to fill the slack, but the whole project would be do-able. Once done you could shoot in USPSA Limited 10 without giving up anything to the crowds of 1911 shooters. The same gun and magazines would work great in the Shootoff. The only thing you'd need then would be a magazine funnel, and those are easy to make if you can't find one that fits.

The 945 is a beautifully-crafted .45 that shows the skill of the Performance Center and the abilities of the design engineers at S&W. If you ever get a chance to shoot one do not turn it down. If someone offers you one at a price you can swing at the moment, don't hesitate. You won't be disappointed.

Endnote

As I wrapped this manuscript up, I got word from the factory that the 945 was being dropped. Darn. The cost is too great, and what with the success of the SW1911 the 945 was getting beaten up in the marketplace by its own stablemate. So the Performance Center dropped the 945. Which is too bad, as they were great guns. I probably should have told the factory that I wanted to keep the one they'd sent me, and sent them a check. Now the opportunity has passed, which is a shame. It bears repeating, that if you are offered a 945PC at a price you can swing, you should give in to opportunity. You will not be disappointed.

The 945 does not use 1911 magazines but rather current S&W 4506 magazines.

The 945 case comes from the Performance Center.

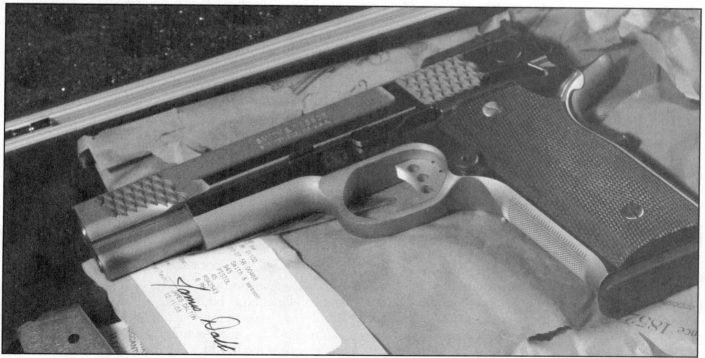
Inside the 945 case, you'll find the magazines, fired cartridge case, cable lock, etc.

CHAPTER 37

Triggers, Controls And Extras

S&W has made revolvers for a century and a half, and pistols for over a half century. They have not stuck with just one way of doing things. If you pick up a Colt SAA you know exactly how it works, for Colt has not changed its operation since 1873. Ditto the 1911, which has not changed since then. However, S&W revolvers can be had or found several ways, and pistols are all over the map.

Revolvers

We're accustomed to the S&W single-action and double-action revolvers. You can thumb-cock the hammer and fire by pressing the trigger. Or you can trigger-cock the hammer, which falls when you finish the stroke. However, there are some single-action-only S&W revolvers around. If you find one, and it is factory-made (a quick look at the lockwork will tell you) it is a rarity. S&W made some for target shooters back when Bull's-eye shooting was still done with revolvers. To shoot most accurately, Bull's-eye shooters would thumb-cock their revolvers. Since there was no need for the DA sear, S&W made some where the hammer had no DA sear nor any provision for one. A single-action-only revolver made as a DA but with the DA sear gone is just a revolver missing some parts.

Double-action is different. From the factory, there are several approaches. There are models made (usually for a police department) where the single-action sear is missing, never having been machined into the hammer. Then there are guns where it has been removed, again usually for police departments. For a while it was something of a fad in police circles to make revolvers double-action-only (DAO) to avoid inadvertent discharges. The usual route for the problem was an officer or officers who made a point of expressing their desire for peace, or to threaten a suspect, by drawing their revolver and showily cocking it. Or, officers who were so uncertain of their double-action shooting skills that they'd cock their handgun on drawing it. Inevitably they'd have to un-cock their revolver, and done enough times you have a certainty of an inadvertent discharge. The correct solution is proper training and supervision. The easy solution is to make the guns DAO.

There are also models that can only be DAO, like the Centennials. With a completely hidden hammer there is no way to shoot it except DA.

Some revolvers will have the hammer spur cut off, but still function as both single-action and double-action revolvers. However, without a spur, getting the hammer safety cocked in single-action is a problem. And there are revolvers modified for DA use that are almost DA to SA by design: PPC guns. It is not uncommon to modify

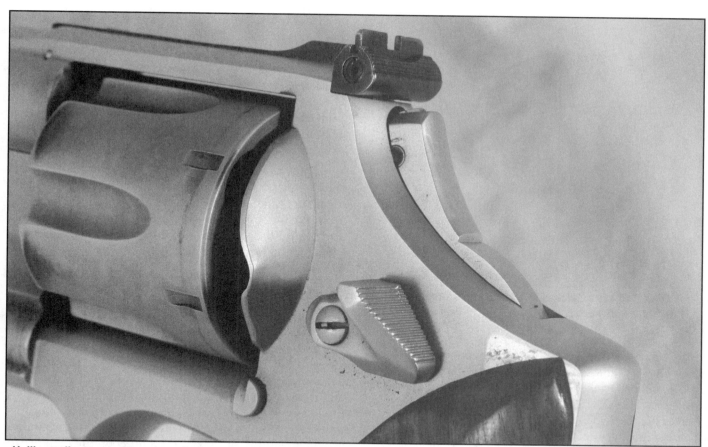

Unlike earlier competitions, we all shoot double-action today. Thus many shooters have the hammer spur removed. (It also aids concealment, too.)

S&W pistols (except for the SW9 & SW40) have a safety assembly of some kind on the slide. Even this double-action-only 4046 has safety parts in the slide.

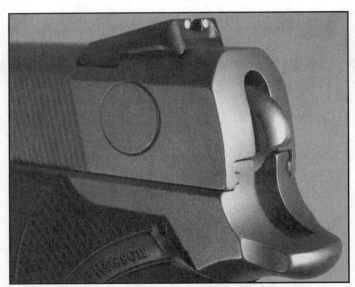

This DAO 4046 has a "slick side" safety, which simply holds the firing pin and plunger in place.

a PPC gun with a rubber-backed trigger stop or special grips. On trigger-cocking, the hammer comes to full cock but stops, requiring a small additional press to fire it. The rubber-backed trigger stop pauses the hammer at full cock. Then the shooter presses enough to compress the rubber, clearing the hammer and firing the revolver. The alternative method is to have a small shelf built into the grips on the left side, where the shooter's trigger finger contacts at full cock. The method of shooting is to quickly trigger cock, and then refine the aim as the last pressure is being applied. Properly done, a good PPC shooter can place all his shots on or touching a business card at the maximum indoor range of 50 feet. This method is not seen in other competitions. In IPSC, bowling pins, Steel Challenge or the American Handgunner Shootoff there is no time to be pausing and refining one's aim. You keep the front sight buried in the middle of the target while you smoothly stroke through the trigger. In PPC the center of the target is 2 by 3 inches. In IPSC and steel the center ring is 8 to 10 inches. In pins or the Shootoff, the target is 6 inches or more.

One new addition to S&W lockwork is the action lock. The small keyhole on the left side of the frame, above the cylinder release latch, is the lock. In use, you insert the special key and rotate the lock counter clockwise to lock the action. When you do so, a small flag pops up next to the hammer, marked "locked." The action cannot be cycled when locked. Why is this here? Because there are those who do not understand the quote from Jeff Cooper, founder of IPSC; "Safety is not something that resides between your hands, but something that resides between your ears." Well-meaning firearms non-experts feel that when a firearm is stored, it isn't enough to lock it away. It should be disassembled

or locked to prevent function. Thus, the action lock for those jurisdictions. While the lock is unobtrusive, and actually a rather elegant solution to a non-existent problem, the danger lies in "if some is good, more is better" attitude. If not met with reason and training, who knows where it might lead? To a pristine Triple Lock or Registered Magnum being turned over to a government-certified gunsmith, to either be machined to fit a new action lock, or destroyed? I hope not.

In any case, if you live in one of the jurisdictions that require a handgun be locked when stored, use the lock. If you don't, or you have need of a handgun ready for defensive use, use your best judgment. Just be aware that the lock is not intended to be used when you are carrying a holstered, loaded handgun.

Pistols

The initial M-39 trigger and controls are the baseline from which all other S&W pistols are derived. The initial trigger press (with the safety off) cocks the hammer and then fires the pistol. The cycling slide cocks the hammer for subsequent shots. If you use the safety, pressing it down decocks the hammer without firing the pistol. Leaving it down means the pistol won't fire. Pressing the safety up unlocks it, and allows you to once again fire it double-action. Or, you can thumb-cock the hammer to start the firing sequence. However, thumb-cocking won't work when the safety is down, as the hammer won't stay cocked nor will the pistol fire if you thumb the hammer back and let it drop. This is the DA/SA also known as the TDA, or Traditional Double-Action. DA/SA or TDA pistols have what is known as "re-strike" capability. That is, if you stroke through the trigger double-action and nothing happens, you can release and press again and the hammer will rise, fall and strike again. If the primer is willing to cooperate, you'll get a "bang." If not, or if there is no round in the chamber, you won't. Some DA/SA pistols are not re-strike capable, and the Safe Action of the Glock is not either.

A feature found on the early IPSC guns was SA/No Drop. The pistol fired only from the single-action, not double-action. The safety did not drop the hammer when engaged, it simply blocked the mechanism. In operation you'd simply use it like a 1911, push the safety off and start shooting.

When competing manufacturers offered designs that had desirable (to some) features not on S&W pistols, the engineers found a way to design those features in. As a result you'll sometimes see trigger and safety controls that might not be what you'd expect for an S&W. One is the decocking lever guns. Instead of the slide-mounted safety, the decocking lever is a spring-loaded lever above

The S&W DAO, from ready...

...through the trigger stroke...

the magazine button and below the slide stop. Pressing the lever down decocks the guns, but does not put it on safe. When you release the lever it springs back up in place, leaving the pistol ready to fire with a DA stroke. The Decock guns came about when the FBI wanted 10mm guns, but wanted them with SIG-style decocking levers. S&W made the changes, but the FBI wasn't satisfied. The word was that the FBI also had required internal changes, changes that didn't work as well as the Bureau had expected. (Hey, they're accountants and lawyers, not mechanical engineers.) The option was available for a while, but foundered from the simple fact that those who wanted a SIG-style safety usually wanted it in a SIG pistol.

Then there are the DAO guns. The popularity of the Glock, and the desire in New York City in particular for a double-action-only pistol led to the DAO guns. The safety lever is gone, and there is no decocking lever. Instead there is simply a trigger and a rebounding hammer. Stroking the trigger cocks the hammer and fires the pistol. The hammer follows the slide down but does not fire it again. You must release the trigger and press it again to fire. The DAO pistol is not a re-strike action. If the primer is a dud you must work the slide to reset the action so you can press the trigger to cycle the hammer again. Since you have to work the slide a small amount

anyway, the reaction that all competent firearms instructors teach to a "click instead of a bang" is to work the slide fully, ejecting the dud round, resetting the action, and trying again.

The last mechanism found is the "1911" style. The safety is a lever on the frame, and only blocks the trigger parts. It does not decock the hammer.

Know what you're handling, or check the function, before you go to shoot an S&W. Considering the versions, models and variants made through the years, plus the amount of gunsmithing you can run into, you can eventually see everything.

Extras

Current-production S&W revolvers have an internal lock built in. The lock requires a key, and is meant for storage, not carry. The lock came about thanks to legislation in some jurisdictions requiring some sort of "safe storage" and to prevent unauthorized use. Being lawyers and legislators, the elected representatives often pass legislation mandating some nebulous goal, leaving it to regulators to define the steps required to accomplish that goal. So, you get two locks in the box with your brand-new revolver: the internal keyed lock and the external cable lock.

...to hammer fall. If the primer is a dud, you'll have to manually cycle the slide to prep the action (and also extract and eject the dud round).

Pistols do not have the internal lock, and get the cable lock. However, S&W pistols from the beginning of the modern era (not the .35 and .32 pocket pistols) come with a magazine disconnector. (An M-D.) But not all. The magazine disconnector is an internal lock that interrupts the trigger mechanism if the magazine is not locked in place in the frame. Remove the magazine and the pistol won't fire. However, not all police agencies greet magazine disconnectors with the same level of enthusiasm, and some models lack the disconnector. Those made that way from the factory will be marked on the frame: "Warning! Firearm can be discharged when magazines has been removed" or similar warnings. An enterprising gunsmith could remove and work around the magazine disconnector on a model built with one. There have been a number of accidental deaths and injuries due to users who are familiar with S&W pistols picking up other brands, assuming that "all pistols have magazine disconnectors" and shooting themselves while "showing off." Every time it happens some politician gets up on a soapbox and announces that all pistols should have an M-D built in. Political grandstanding aside, not all mechanisms can have an M-D retrofitted, and any could be removed. To quote Jeff Cooper again; "Safety is not something that resides between your hands, but something that resides between your ears."

The box will also contain a small envelope (known in the printing and paper trade as a "coin envelope") sealed and labeled, containing a fired case. Another intrusion of the technically uneducated legislators intended "for our safety." The idea is that fired cases can be traced back to the firearm in which they were fired. Crime scene investigators have been doing do for decades. The idea is that instead of waiting until the crime

occurs, and then testing likely firearms, the government should test all of them beforehand and have a database of cases to compare after a crime. The problem is, it hasn't worked yet, and isn't likely to. Those interested can do a web search for the study done by the State of California. The short form is this: the State had the Highway Patrol test-fire several hundred .40 caliber pistols that were new in inventory. The fired cases were then entered into a database. Then another set of cases fired from the same pistols was sent for comparison. The results were appalling, with matches between the two sets not much better than you'd get tossing a coin. But each and every box will still have a fired case, and likely will for decades after the whole idea has been abandoned.

In the box you'll also find a small screwdriver if your firearm has adjustable sights. The screwdriver is meant for the sight, not the sideplate of your revolver. You'll also find the owner's manual, registration card and other advertising inducements. (It would be prudent to fill out any NRA applications you might find, too.) And last, for revolvers that use moon clips, and pistols, you'll find ammo holders. The moon clips will hold a load of ammo to fill the cylinder. The magazines will hold up to 10 rounds. In the event the Assault Weapon Ban of 1994 ever gets repealed.

In the old days boxes were cardboard. Now they're plastic, with latches and handles. You can further lock the case by using a padlock on the handles. Once closed, a tight lock on the handles keeps it from being opened. The Performance Center handguns will come in a lockable case with a combination lock at each latch.

If you're buying a new S&W, check the box to make sure you're getting the full compliment of "goodies."

CHAPTER 38

Buying used handguns

So, having read about all the neat Smith & Wesson revolvers and pistols, you decided you want one? But the budget won't permit buying new? No problem. With a little prudent shopping you can get a good deal on a used S&W, and not feel buyer's remorse. But in order to do so you have to do a little homework. And ask yourself a few questions.

You may pay more at a gun shop, but one that stands behind its sales is worth the extra money.

What are you going to be using it for?

Setting out to buy a concealed carry gun, and ending up picking up a 625-2 Model of 1988 because "It was a good deal and you always read the .45 was a great stopper" will lead to remorse. Remorse at the backaches of packing such a big gun concealed; remorse at the torn clothes from the hammer spur; and at the expense of good leather to keep it from falling out of the cheap holster. Again. At being asked "Why such a big gun?" Every time your concealed carry buddies see it. Do you want a light, comfortable carry gun? A competition gun? A practice gun? A plinker to start new shooters with? Be clear what you want and why. If you're shopping and have a need (or a "need") for something in several categories, then get what fits the task and is in your budget. But don't jump to something else because the price is good without realizing that you have done so. And still need what you were originally looking for.

What models fit your needs?

If you are shooting USPSA/IPSC competition or bowling pins, you'll want a .45 ACP revolver and a fistful of moon clips. You may stumble across a great deal on a pinned and recessed Model 29, but as good as the deal may be it won't help your scores. If you're intent on shooting IDPA Stock Service Pistol, a fabulous price on a Performance Center 945 isn't much use. The IDPA rules won't allow it in SSP, so your bargain isn't one. At least not for that use.

Will you need accessories?

If you carry, you'll need a comfortable and concealable holster. For competition, you'll either need something fast or something that conforms to the rules of the game you're playing. (Or both.) You'll need a means of carrying extra ammo. No right-minded person who is carrying a handgun for defense goes out the door without extra ammo. Many competitions will require strings of fire that take more ammo than your gun holds. For pistols that means spare magazines. For revolvers that means speedloaders or moon clips. If you don't already have the right ones, you'll need more. Magazines, moon clips and speedloaders are caliber and model specific. One size does not fit all, and you'll need some for each handgun you have.

Can you get ammunition suited to your needs?

The Performance Center 356 guns are great. But .356TSW ammunition is not easy to come by. If you insist on using or carrying one of them, you'll end up in short order having to reload your own ammo to keep in practice. (Save the factory ammo for carry. You do not want to be using your own reloads in the event of a shootout.) As much as I like the little .32 Magnum guns, I'd be leery of using one as a carry gun. But only due to factory ammunition supply. If the supply of factory ammunition stops, you are faced with a pair of unenviable choices: use reloads for carry ammo, or carefully hoarding a few boxes of suitable factory carry ammo (as much as you can squirrel away) for years while using reloads for practice.

A high-volume competition gun might see more in a year's shooting than most owners would put through it in a lifetime. If possible, find out how much a gun has been shot before buying it.

A Shorty Forty is a great carry gun. But is will not be easy to make Major in one for USPSA/IPSC competition. And impossible to load it hot enough to take bowling pins off cleanly.

Last we come to the questions that most think of when contemplating buying used: Is it in good condition? Is it a good price? Price depends. If you're looking for the same model everyone else is, the price is not going to be soft. If you find something that fits your needs but no one wants, then let the bargaining begin. You can use *The Standard Catalog of Firearms* as a guide, but remember there are still regional differences.

Is there a warranty?

A good gunshop will stand behind their sale. The best shop to buy from is one with an experienced gunsmith on premises, one who is likely to have looked over the used gun when it came in, and will diagnose and fix (or return to S&W) it in the event something goes wrong. Get the shop policy in writing, and test your new/used gun right away so you can report back if there is a problem. Buying something and then testing it months later is sure to cause hard feelings. How are they to know it sat in your safe for all those months? If you've been using it all that time, they shouldn't be responsible for a sudden (and out of warranty) problem, should they?

The best place possible to buy used is a gun shop with an indoor range and an on-site gunsmith. You can buy the gun, rent some range time, and shoot it right there.

If you cannot get a warranty, or are buying at a gun show or form a private seller, look it over carefully. Any problems you find later will be your problems alone.

Checking condition

We'll start with revolvers, as there is more that can go wrong, more to look for, and a lot more revolvers in circulation (over 6 million K frame guns alone) than pistols. And always check to make sure it isn't loaded before beginning an inspection.

Finish

Is the finish even? That is, in a blued gun is the finish the same color across the frame, sideplate and barrel? In the century-plus that Hand Ejectors were made, it is entirely possible for a gun to be completely rebuilt. A decent armorer could easily take a box of parts and build a gun. A replacement frame could have been rebuilt from parts stripped off of confiscated guns. I've seen some. For a long time it was common for police departments to strip parts off of confiscated guns for departmental use.

Is this gun ugly? You bet. But it is tight, accurate and reliable. And it has won me a bunch of loot in various matches through the years.

The Michigan State Police is the agency tasked with feeding confiscated guns into the various smelters in the State, and they got tired of melting "partials." So they told departments that they'd accept complete firearms only. (What they do when the confiscated guns are partials to begin with, I don't know.) However, in the decades before this decision many "parts guns" showed up. I've seen some of the ugliest guns you could imagine, and they were obviously mis-matches. Look at the fit of the sideplate; is the line a hairline all the way around? Does the curve in the trigger guard match, frame to sideplate? If not, it has been replaced. And not at the factory, where great pride is taken in getting it right.

If it has been re-blued, the blue sometimes doesn't always "take" evenly on the various parts. Or, the barrel or cylinder may have been replaced, and the slightly different alloy of the new part doesn't blue the same as the rest.

Continue your inspection, looking at corners, screw heads and screw holes. Are the screw heads crowned? Polished and reblued gun often have flattened screwheads. Check the screw hole edges. Again, an indifferent polisher will "pull" the hole, rounding the crisp edge letting the polishing wheel get down in the hole. Are the letters clear? Repolishing often pulls or distorts the lettering. A new finish is not a crime in and of itself, but being handed an obvious re-blue with the assertion that it is "new in the box" should send up warning flags in your head.

If the wear is honest, the edges of the muzzle might show wear through the blue. In heavy use the frame edges

Check the bore and muzzle. Look for wear, nicks, dents or abuse. Seeing none, move on.

might be worn bright, and the overall color of the blueing might be dulled. As long as the wear is even, and something you can live with from the look standpoint, wear isn't a problem. If, however you find signs of dropping, like dents on a muzzle, scrapes and rock marks, be cautious. A dropped revolver with a bent frame is an expensive fix. Crushed sights on an adjustable sight gun are a sign of either being dropped, or hitting a doorframe while holstered. Regardless of cause you should get assurances.

Don't mistake an uneven rollmark with a polish job. This rollmark is lighter at one corner, but has never been refinished.

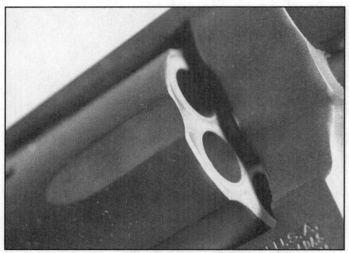

Dropped guns often show nicks and dents on the cylinder. Check the edges, and eyeball the cylinder gap while you're at it.

The forcing cone can tell you a lot. Is it worn, eroded and does it have rounded edges? It has seen a lot of ammo. Is it caked with lead and powder? It needs cleaning, and might be hiding something.

Look at the standing breech for wear, pitting, and evidence of blown primers.

Open the cylinder and look at the standing face. The breech will have a circular shield in it if it is an older revolver, with the firing pin attached to the hammer. Inspect the shield. It should be smooth, and in a well-fired revolver, worn to bright metal. It should not be pitted, and if it looks markedly different than the rest of the breechface, it may have been replaced. Now look at the forcing cone. Is it clean? If not, see about cleaning it. If it is heavily crusted in powder residue and leading, it may be hiding a crack or chip. A cracked or chipped forcing cone means a new barrel is called for. Use your thumbnail to reflect light down the bore and peer in through the muzzle. Is the bore clean and shiny? There should not be pits or dark rings. A pitted or ringed barrel will lead faster than a correct one. You can get away with shooting a tired bore, but accuracy will suffer and should be replaced.

Look at the barrel shoulder. Is the very end of it, against the frame, peened? A replacement barrel, or an older one that works loose, was sometimes in the past tightened by peening the end of the shoulder enough to create a crush fit against the frame. Properly done it is no strike against an otherwise suitable revolver, but you should pay attention to it and point it out to the seller. If it turns out the person who did the work struck the barrel too hard and ovaled it inside, accuracy will always be bad. If you didn't point it out during the sale, the seller has no way of knowing that you didn't do it, voiding the warranty.

With the cylinder open you can't cock the action. So close it and cock the hammer. Look at the tip of the firing pin. Is it clean, round and smooth? If it shows any pitting, is chipped or bent, pass unless you can get it tended to. Now gently lower the hammer and hold the trigger back. Look through the rear opening between the cylinder and breech. Do you see the firing pin? If not, something is wrong. If you do, continue.

Next, you want to check the action. With the owner's permission (some people are not cool with dry-firing a firearm) slowly cock the action. Then keep your thumb on the hammer while you pull the trigger, and ease the hammer down. Does the cocking action have hard spots? Does it seem to bind partway back? A binding or "knuckling" may be as simple a problem as a mainspring not properly tightened. And it could mean someone tried to re-time it and didn't finish the job. Unless you can get the on-site gunsmith to look at it, pass. Then cock it and leave it cocked. Gently press the hammer forward. Don't use more than a couple of pounds of pressure. The hammer should not fall. Here in Michigan we have a

"State Safety Inspection" which is little more than a de-facto registration system. I once had a desk officer in the inspection office of Detroit PD who kept rejecting otherwise fine revolvers. They all "pushed off." What I came to find was that he was pushing them off using both thumbs, pushing as hard as he could. I finally had to make a copy of the S&W armorer's manual showing the proper method and amount ("not more than three pounds") for him to stop doing it. A hammer that pushes off might be a too-light rebound spring, and it might be a stoned SA sear (and thus a trashed hammer) that is expensive to fix.

Now press the trigger, and ease the hammer down. Holding the trigger back, see if the cylinder moves when you try to turn it with your other hand. It should not. Now release the trigger and try turning the cylinder again. It should wobble but not turn. If it turns, the cylinder stop is worn, chipped or the spring is weak, or the stop slots in the cylinder are worn. The stop or spring is not too bad a fix. The cylinder slots are expensive: a new cylinder.

Open and close the cylinder. Does it open smoothly, or does the cylinder stick when opening? When you close it, do you have to press a little harder once closed to get

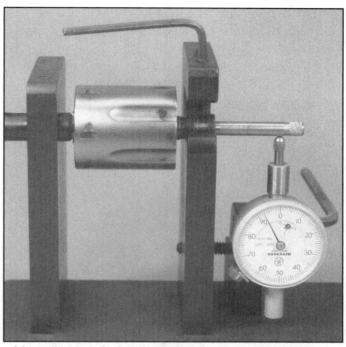

A bent ejector rod takes the correct fixture to straighten properly. If you spin the cylinder and the ejector tip wobbles, you'll need this, or someone who has it.

Use your thumb to drag the cylinder as you cycle the action. If it fails to carry up, it needs work.

the centerpin to snap into the pivot hole? If you feel binding, catching or you have to press hard, the centerpin or crane might be bent.

Now close the action, and while using a thumb to drag on the cylinder, cock the action. Does it carry all

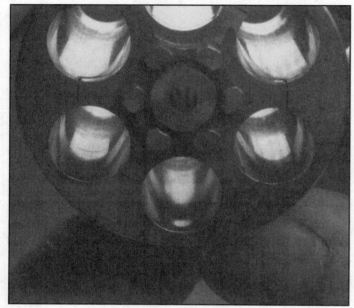

Someone loaded this gun too hot, and the charge hole on the bottom is bulged at the cylinder top slot. It cannot be repaired, and requires a new cylinder, an expensive fix.

the way up to lock in a slot? If it does, great. If not, the timing needs work. Then check the carry-up while dry-firing in double-action. The drag on the cylinder by your thumb precludes inertia finishing the cylinder's rotation. If you simply cock the hammer, the cylinder will keep rotating until it locks up, hiding a lack of carry-up.

The last things to check you can only do if you have the tools along with you that you'll need: a range rod and feeler gauges. The range rod checks barrel-to-cylinder alignment. You cock each chamber inline with the barrel and then attempt to slide the range rod from the bore to the chamber. If it passes, withdraw the rod, cock and try again. If it fails, the cylinder is so out of alignment on that chamber that the rod can't get from bore to cylinder. Which is the same problem the bullet has. In a mis-aligned revolver, the bullet must carom off the forcing cone to make it to the bore. As you can imagine, accuracy suffers. The feeler gauges are for the gap check. A properly-fitted barrel-to-cylinder gap should not be over .006" However, there were a few years when the factory would ship any revolver with a gap less than .013". I had an acrimonious conversation on just that subject concerning a customer's Model 686. The factory refused to re-fit a barrel with an out of the box gap of .012". While that was 15 years ago, revolvers of that era are still out there. (I ended up setting the shoulder back and re-gapping it to .006".)

A bent crane is easy to feel, but hard to measure and fix. You need more tools to set it right.

Pistol checks

Pistols are a lot easier to check, partly because there is less to go wrong, and partly due to less parts and functions being user-serviceable items.

Again, give it a thorough visual check, looking to see if you spot things like signs of dropping, mis-matched finish, etc.

Remove the magazine, make sure the safety is up, and try the trigger. It should spring back and forth, but not activate the hammer. If it does, someone has been messing with the mechanism. Of course check the frame to see if it has the "Caution" warning. It may be a police trade-in, and never have had a magazine disconnector. Put the magazine back. Pull the slide back. Does the slide lock open? If it doesn't the likely cause is a bad magazine. Drop the magazine part-way out and pull the slide back. It should release from the slide stop. If it does not, there is something going on, most likely with the recoil spring. (Someone may have installed a shock buffer. They can reduce slide travel enough to prevent you from using slide overtravel to unlock the slide stop.)

With the slide closed, press the magazine back into lock, and try the trigger. A traditional double-action should allow you to repeatedly work the hammer double-action. Then cock it and try the single-action. DAO and Decock-only guns also must be tested. Now take the pencil you've brought along and point the muzzle up. Cock the hammer. Drop the pencil (eraser end first) into the bore. Use the safety to decock. If the pencil stays put except for some vibration caused by the hammer fall, the safety is working. If the pencil moves at all, the safety is not working as it is supposed to. The fix is to get it to a factory-authorized armorer, or the factory. Many gunsmiths are competent to solve and fix the problem, but when it comes to a safety I prefer the authorized "fixers."

Buying New

New, you have the manufacturer's warranty. You want to check things over just to be sure that what you are getting is what you think you are getting. You may have an assembly mistake, where you've got something improperly assembled. Highly unlikely, but possible. Just check to make sure there is rifling in the bore, the controls work, and the serial number on the box matches that of the gun.

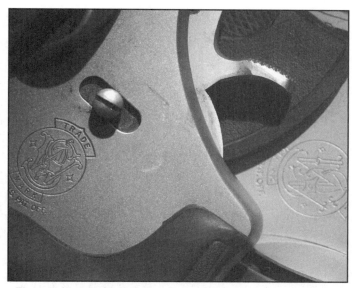

The revolver on the right has been polished too heavily. The rollmark is "washed out," as you can easily see compared to the one on the left.

Buying Collectibles

This is a very different scene. First, you may find that some collectibles are "sealed." The owner does not want everyone who handles them (and not everyone will be allowed to handle them) to turn the cylinder and "ring" it. That is, leave marks around it from the cylinder stop bolt. So there will be a cable tie sealing it. Once you've bought it you can do what you want, but the seller is protecting his investment. Don't be offended if after you've handled it he wipes it down with a silicone cloth. Some people have corrosive perspiration, and he is again protecting his investment.

If you are buying a collectible, get a detailed description and invoice with the sale. If the seller sells it to you at a premium because a famous person or organization owned it, get the paperwork to prove it. Make sure the invoice or letter with the gun states something like "seller offers such-and-such firearm as having been owned by XYZ and will refund in full if not true." It may not help much if you have to get to court, but it will slow down some of the big-talking sellers who will promise you anything if you just buy it.

And buy because you want it, not because you think in X years it will be worth so much more. Collect to collect, not to invest.

CHAPTER 39

Competitions:
A great way to increase skill

Actually, we should be talking about "competitions and training." Competition shooting can greatly increase your skill in handling a handgun; your aim in shooting, your ability to deal with stress. But if you are going to be carrying a handgun for defensive use, you need more than pleasant afternoons on the range punching paper and tipping over steel. You need training. For defensive carry I can recommend three places: Lethal Force Institute, Defensive Tactics Inc. and Gunsite.

Massad Ayood teaches the least "gun gear" and most legal-based class of the three at Lethal Force Institute. You'll do a bunch of shooting at an LFI class, but you'll also spend classroom time learning the legalities of defensive use. It doesn't do any good to prevail in "Problem 1" (the bad guy) only to fail in "Problem 2" (the court system) and end up in prison next to friends of the offender you shot.

John Farnam is in the middle, with emphasis on both legal and practical problems. Like Mas, John travels the country (and into some foreign countries) teaching defensive tactics, so if you want to know what the current problems are in NYC or Johannesburg, he can tell you. You'll do a bunch of shooting and learn the problems of dealing with the legal system.

Gunsite is not a person but a place. Founded by Jeff

In the old days, Jeff Cooper taught the classes personally. Age has caught up with him, but the able staff carries on under his principles.

Yes, IPSC can be less than practical. But it can be as practical as you make it. And you are always better for being more skilled at handling firearms.

Cooper, the task at Gunsite is to teach you the skills to prevail in an armed encounter. Since the students come from all walks of life and all corners of the U.S. and the globe, Gunsite cannot be so detail-oriented on legal matters. The school teaches you how to deal with the tactical problem with which you are faced, in a moral framework, and it is your job to determine exactly what the law requires of you where you live, work or happen to find yourself in harm's way.

It is fashionable in some places and social settings to be squeamish about the use of firearms in general, and handguns in particular, on people. Let us be clear about what some of us face: There are bad people in the world. Some of them are so bad that only the threat of violence, or actual violence, directed at them, will keep them from doing bad things. Those of us who are not so inclined do not always have an option about interacting with the bad people of the world. Sometimes they seek us out. And sometimes it is our job to go find them. Some people feel that violence is not the answer. That is their choice. Those people do not have the power to make that the choice for all of us. The law recognizes that there are situations where a good citizen is authorized to use violence up to and including lethal force, to save his or her life or the lives of others from the consequences of violence by bad people. In order to do so effectively you need good firearms and good training. To do so legally you need to know the basics of the law as it affects you and a lethal-force encounter. When it comes down to

considering equipment, ammunition, holsters, training and practice, do not be squeamish about your own safety. But there is also no need to be pugnacious about it, either. Consider your options and make your choices, but don't become the obnoxious gun club member who has iron-clad opinions and won't shut up about them. We all make our own decisions, and while some conversation can be interesting, the obnoxious get shunned.

If you need training for competition, you can go to any one of a host of top-notch competition shooters who will do their best to impart to you the skills needed to succeed in practical shooting competition. Jerry Barnhart, Todd Jarrett, Jerry Miculek and Ron Avery all teach those who wish to shoot better. It is fashionable to decry many competitions as being "untactical" or that some build skills that "will get you killed on the street." Nonsense. Shooting builds skills. Whether they are skills that are relevant to your particular defensive predicament is something you will have to consider and decide. Some of the best street gunners I know had the sum total of: police academy training, annual qualification, and no competitive shooting or tactical training of any kind, and prevailed in all the shootouts in which they were involved. I know school-trained shooters who were careful to get the best tactical training they could, who hit exactly nothing in real shootouts. Anecdotes prove nothing except the individuality of shooters. If you want to shoot competitively for fun, then have fun, stay safe, and do your best. If you want to improve your skills for defense, then whatever competition you shoot, approach it with the thought "How will this stage/technique/equipment improve my chances of surviving an encounter?" You can shoot IPSC (the supposed "competition that will get you killed") in the most practical manner possible and greatly improve your chances. Or you can shoot IDPA (the supposed "practical street-savvy match") in the most unpractical manner, and learn nothing. It is up to you, not the match organizers, to improve your defensive skills. All they are doing is presenting a competitive shooting challenge you can enter.

The competitions

There are a number of organizations in which you can shoot your S&W. One we can strike off the list immediately is the GSSF. The Glock Sport Shooting Federation is by Glock, for Glocks. Nothing personal, they just hold matches for Glocks. In all the rest of the competitions, you have to make sure you read the rules and be sure you're shooting the correct S&W in the correct division. Those groups are the USPSA, IDPA, ICORE and NRA/PPC. The big matches are the Steel Challenge, American Handgunner Shootoff, and the Bianchi Cup. Bowling pin shoots are specialty matches you will find scattered across the Midwest and through Pennsylvania.

USPSA

The United States Practical Shooting Association is the U.S. organization associated with International Practical Shooting Confederation. The common reference to "IPSC shooting" here in the United States refers to the USPSA. In IPSC shooting you will not be presented with the typical Bull's-eye course of fire. Every stage will be different, requiring a different number of rounds at different distances. You'll draw to shoot, you have to reload when you need to (no one will tell you when to reload, only to load to start the stage) and if you have any malfunctions you must deal with them. There are no "alibis" in IPSC. If your gun breaks you get a zero on the stage and don't get to do it over. If you have a malfunction you have to clear it and get on with the stage. In many stages, if you miss you can fire again to make it up. Mistakes of shooting can be corrected by shooting again, although the clock is ticking while you do so. You'll encounter doors, windows, walls, barricades and all manner of everyday objects or their representatives. You must maneuver among them to engage the targets, and keep your muzzle safely downrange while doing so. Many feel it is more fun than many other sports. The USPSA has five Divisions; Open, Limited, Limited 10, Production, and Revolver.

Open is just about no-holds barred. You have to shoot a 9mm Parabellum or larger, you can't have a magazine longer than 170mm, and that's about it. There is no catalog firearm from S&W that is suited to Open. However, you could build an Open gun with a 5906 by adding a comp and red-dot sight, and building hi-cap magazines to 170mm (they'd hold 25 rounds or so) and be ready to go. Back when S&W had a Team, they (Brian Enos, J. Michael Plaxco and crew) shot 5906s with comps on them, chambered for .356TSW. The "TSW" was longer than a 9mm in the case, but the same in overall length. Run hot (as in well past the 34,000 psi the 9mm is limited to) they made Major and the guns worked fine. Should you want to step back into the storied past, you could do the same.

The Limited category restricts you to magazines of up to 140mm in length, you cannot have a comp or muzzle brake, and you can't have optics. And you must use a caliber of .40 or larger to shoot Major. If you are really slick with a traditional double-action, then a 4006 with

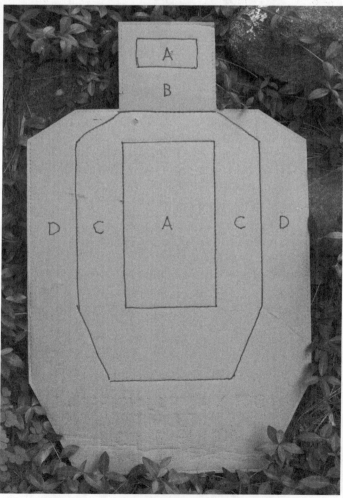

The USPSA target. Normally the rings are not visible (they are highlighted here so you can see them). As your hits move out from the center, they are scored with fewer points.

In the years before Revolver Division, Jerry would often show up at the USPSA Nationals with an Open Revolver, to shoot in the Open class. Using an eight-shot wheelgun against 28-shot pistols, he still did quite respectably.

extended magazines would work well. If not, then you'd want a 4006 rebuilt to an original 745 trigger system: safety down does not drop the hammer, so you'd have a cocked and locked .40.

In both Open and Limited you'll have to locate a source for high-capacity magazines. And they will have to be extended for you to be competitive. But the guns are up to it.

Limited 10 offers the same restrictions as Limited, with the added limit of not more than 10 rounds in a magazine. The obvious choice would be the new SW1911. A 945PC would be a great choice the moment you could get the magazines up from eight rounds to 10 rounds each. You can also use one of the high-capacity revolvers, too. While an eight-shot wheelgun will have a hard time keeping up with ten-shot pistol it isn't as bad a time as a six-shot would have. And you can shoot the .357 Magnum at Major in that category.

Production is where S&W can really shine. The limits on Production are severe: first, it has to be a production gun. No prototypes. Then, it can't have more than 10 rounds. No compensators, no optics, and everything is scored Minor. That's right, it doesn't matter what you shoot, it will all be scored the same as if you were shooting 9mm ammo. The idea for Production was to offer the "9mm carry gun" guys a place to play in the IPSC sandbox. As if all the other hindrances they faced

John Flentz getting ready to smoke a course with his 5906PC, shooting in Production.

weren't enough (DA/SA or DAO guns, 10-shot mags, no factory comps or optics) the Major/Minor scoring hurt 9mm shooters. In production there are two camps: the TDA guns and the Glock shooters. Some, like my friend John Flentz, who shoots a 5906PC, feel the first shot DA is a small problem, and on a tuned gun the small advantage is offset by the crisp SA trigger and weight of the steel frame of a traditional double-action gun. The Glock shooters tune their triggers to be as "1911-like" as possible and don't worry about the lighter weight. You can go either way with S&W, shooting any 39, 59 or even 40 series pistol (just load the .40s lighter to get them closer in feel to the 9mm) and run. Or stoke an SW9 and shoot like it was a Glock. With the scoring disadvantage of the 9mm out of the way, you can shoot whatever surplus or big-box discount store 9mm ammo you want and never have to reload to shoot. Many Open shooters, having paid $2,000 to $3,000 for an Open gun (and $150 each for tuned hi-cap magazines) then have to reload specialty ammo that ends up costing them $100 per 1,000 rounds or more. And load their ammo on expensive machines weekly to keep up with their practice and match consumption. The Production shooters can buy surplus for not much more than that and never reload.

Revolver shooters were early into IPSC, but fell behind when technology really ramped things up. When the typical IPSC gun was a slightly-tuned but essentially box-stock 1911, a wheelgunner with a slicked-up Model 25-2 or Model 27 could keep up. But when gunsmiths

started applying their skills to the 1911 (and not so much to the revolvers) wheelguns fell by the wayside. And when hi-cap guns, with comps and optics showed up, it was all over. To give the revolver shooters a place, USPSA added Revolver. The rules are simple: six shots, .38 and over, no comps, optics or extra weights added. You can shoot your hi-cap revolver, but if you shoot more than six shots before a reload you will get bumped to Open. And find your scores compared to 28-shot, comped, red-dot Raceguns. What it means is that everyone shoots one of a few guns: old Model 25-2s, newer 625-2s, and 610s. While you might do well at a club match with a non-moon gun and a bag full of speedloaders, if you want to move up you pretty much have to have moon clips. The good news is that the USPSA doesn't care if you take your K or L frame gun off to someone like Mark Hartshorne and have him apply his skills to make it accept full moon clips. The basic working principle for revolver modifications is "If the factory did it, you can too." You don't have to hunt down one of a limited run of L frame guns cut for full moon clips. If the factory did it, you can duplicate it. Ditto barrel lengths. If you

USPSA/IPSC courses will have lots of movement. And you are expected to manage your ammo supply without the Range Officer reminding you.

Reloading is stressed in practical shooting, but in USPSA/IPSC shooting, the revolver shooters are also stressed.

Often in IDPA matches you will have to draw from concealment.

stumble onto a bargain 25-2, and want to change the barrel to some other factory configuration, go for it. For that, give Scott Mulkerin a call at SDM Fabricating. He can replace barrels, or carve you one out of a barrel blank. Just don't get more than a few ounces over what a factory gun of the same barrel length would be, or you might find yourself in Open. Consult the current rules closely before jumping into that level of custom work.

Fair warning: if you wish to run with the big dogs in USPSA competition, be prepared. You will sooner or later get your clock cleaned by Jerry Miculek. To give you an idea of just how bad it can be, at the 2003 USPSA Factory Gun Nationals I placed third. The second, third and fourth place shooters were very close (16 points between second and third, 50 between third and fourth) Jerry won the Division, and he lead us by nearly 400 points with a score in the mid 1,500s. He was High Revolver shooter on 15 of the 17 stages. (I beat him on one, Rudy Waldinger beat him on the other.) The thing is, Jerry is such a nice guy, and he shoots so well, that is isn't like he's crushing you, its more like you're part of a revolver-shooting seminar. Watch. Learn. Practice. You'll get better.

IDPA

The origins of IDPA are eerily familiar: shooters who felt the current shooting method was not practical enough, and had strayed too far from its roots, set up a new organization. However, instead of it being IPSC shooters leaving Bull's-eye and PPC, it was IDPA leaving IPSC. IDPA has much stricter rules on just about everything. Equipment is just one example. In IPSC there are things you can't do. As long as you don't do them, you're cool. In IDPA there is a list of things allowed. Anything else is not allowed. The same with holsters. IPSC doesn't care (with a few exceptions) while IDPA has an approved list. Not on the list? Can't use it in a match. In IDPA you will also be moving among walls, doors, etc. However, you'll be doing less shooting. One of the restrictions in IDPA is that no course can be more then 18 rounds. In IPSC, stage designers sometimes go overboard, with stages running 30, 40 or even 50 rounds. (Many shooters do not complain about it, they actually like it.) The IDPA originators did not want competitors festooned with magazines. They wanted a competition more closely based on what the average shooter with a concealed carry permit might actually be stepping out of the house wearing.

The scoring is also changed: where IPSC primarily uses Comstock, IDPA uses elapsed time plus penalties. In IPSC, your score fired has penalties applied, then is divided by the time it took you to shoot the stage. So the classic El Presidente is (for the old Par time) 12 five-point hits divided by 10 seconds, or a "factor" of 6.0 In

IDPA it is simply the time it took to shoot, with an extra second tacked on for each shot outside the "A" ring. In IPSC you can shoot fast enough (at least until the Grand Master level) to outrun penalties for lesser hits. Not so in IDPA, where each non-A hit costs you a second. As with IPSC, you can generally make up misses with extra shots.

Also, IDPA has penalties for not using cover well, and a curious penalty called "Failure to Do Right." In IPSC, the course is set up and you find any means to score well while staying safe. In IDPA, the stage designer wants you to do it a particular way. If you get too "game-y" he'll give you an FTDR. The discussions between IPSC and IDPA can get quite acrimonious at times. Consider it a peculiar religious argument, like how many angels can dance on the head of a pin, and you'll be fine. Both are games, both are fun, and both can require some interesting gear. Oh, and you may at times need a "concealment garment" for IDPA. A photographers' or fishing vest seem to be the "gear du jour" for IDPA.

IDPA has no Major or Minor scoring, just threshold for each Division. For Custom Defensive Pistol is it 165, for the others it is 125. Exceed the threshold and you can play. If not, you shoot for fun as your score doesn't count. You cannot load the lesser categories to 165 and gain more score.

The Divisions in IDPA are four, and there is an S&W for each of them: Custom Defensive Pistol, Enhanced Service Pistol, Stock Service Pistol and Stock Service Revolver.

CDP is set up to be the "1911 in .45 ACP" Division. Use a box-stock SW1911 and you'll be set. You cannot use your 10-shot magazines as you would in IPSC Limited 10, so leave them behind. Bring the eight-shot ones that came with it, plus an extra or two. You'll only have two spares and the one in the gun on you at any time, so leave the speed mag pouches behind.

ESP is for all the guns that aren't .45, but aren't traditional double-action or some variant thereof. Were I shooting an S&W in ESP, I'd be torn. The 59 series reload quickly, and the weight and fat grip handle the minimal recoil well. But the 39 series are flat and index well for me. The fact that I'd be shooting against 1911 pistols in 9mm or light-load .38 Super wouldn't be a problem, as the times are generous and the A zone big in IDPA.

SSP is usually the Glock playground. You could go with a 39 or 59, or use an SW9. There is no advantage in using a .40 in either ESP or SSP, as you don't get more score. You do have a wider bullet, so you might nick a scoring ring you'd otherwise miss. But weighing against that is the need to either reload your own .40 ammunition to bring it down to 9mm recoil, or accept the extra recoil of factory 40 vs. 9mm recoil.

SSR is the place for wheelguns. One big difference between IPSC and IDPA is in barrel length. In IDPA it must be 4 inches, max. If you want to shoot something shorter you can. Even if you can hide something longer, you can't shoot it. There was a big fuss a couple of years ago when the word came down that the five-inch 625s were no longer going to be allowed. We'd all have to either get new guns or get new barrels on our guns. Now that the dust has settled, everyone gets along with four-inch barreled guns. The choice here is between the 625-2 and the 610. The 625-2 reloads slightly more quickly, and the larger bullets will give you the occasional higher-value hit from nicking a line. The 610 can use 40 S&W ammo, for theoretically faster reloads, and certainly less recoil than 10mm ammo. In either you have to reload to get your ammo down close to the threshold of 125 power factor.

ICORE

The International Confederation of Revolver Enthusiasts was formed before IPSC had made a place for revolver shooters again. One way to describe ICORE is "IPSC with Bianchi guns and targets." Like IPSC you'll be dealing with freestyle stages, not set-in-stone strings of fire. You'll have to reload on your own, when and if necessary. You'll draw to fire, move, reload, and scramble over, under and around obstacles. And it will all be against the clock. Like Bianchi, you'll be shooting on a target requiring accuracy and not blistering speed. The scoring is, as in IDPA, simple: elapsed time plus time penalties. Lowest time wins the match. The target is different from IPSC or IDPA. Where they both use a vaguely person-shaped silhouette, the Bianchi Cup and ICORE use the "Tombstone" target. The target is a sheet of cardboard with scoring circles on it, and the top cut on a radius. The rings are the penalties. The X and A ring are zero penalty. The B ring is one second, and the rest of the target is two seconds. A miss is a five-second penalty. Some stage designers like to use the X ring as a "negative time" ring, where an X hit will remove a second from your stage time. The shooting pace in ICORE (except for Jerry Miculek) is more like that of IDPA than it is of IPSC. I occasionally shoot my first ICORE stage in a match at IPSC speed, and my score suffers. As an example, one year at Handgunners' Revenge, (The Midwest ICORE Championship) I shot the first stage with an 18-second time and 18 seconds in time penalties. I then slowed down and didn't add eighteen seconds of time penalties in the whole rest of the match.

With the penalty for a non-center hit being a full second, it is easy to shoot to fast and end up with a big time. You can make up misses or bad shots with an extra shot or two, but you will have to do so while the clock is ticking.

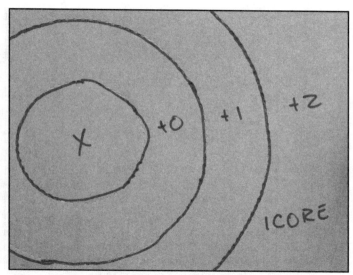
The scoring system of ICORE: Added time to your run.

Every stage is designed for a six-shot revolver (and no pistols need apply at an ICORE match, thank you) but that doesn't mean seven- and eight-shot guns are not allowed. They are, and can give an advantage to your shooting in some stages. The scoring requires that you have (sometimes the stage designers will vary it) two hits per target. You can shoot more, and the best two hits will be your score. So, if you have a seven- or eight-shot gun, you can shoot three times on a relatively distant target, counting on two of them being good enough to keep you from being penalized for shooting them so quickly.

There is no Major/Minor scoring in ICORE, only a threshold of 120 power factor. And ICORE also allows the use of .32 Magnum revolvers, where the others do not. While you might not want to be shooting ICORE with a Model 332, you could. Enterprising shooters often go the other way. Vic Pickett has built a .32 Magnum revolver that holds nine rounds. (Of course it uses moon clips!) With nine in the gun Vic has a lot of leeway to run close to the edge. Should he shoot so fast he throws a "+2" or even a Miss, he can make it up. After all, he has plenty of shots on hand.

The equipment rules are pretty simple. You have to use a revolver. If it has ports or a compensator, or optics, or both, it is an Open gun. If it doesn't, then it is a Limited or Stock gun. Many ICORE shooters are Bianchi Cup shooters or PPC shooters looking for something more challenging and more active. A PPC revolver will be a Stock gun, and your "typical" Bianchi Open gun will be an ICORE Open gun.

What wins an ICORE match? Usually the Open shooter, but that depends on what the best shooter is using. At the International Revolver Championships, the ICORE world cup, Jerry Miculek has been the winner. At local or regional matches, you'll find that the winning gun is what the best shooter is using. There are equipment advantages, but someone who has practiced will beat you even if you have the best gear and you didn't practice.

The basic starter gun would be a .38 or .357 K frame. A Model 15 or 19 will be plenty accurate, have a nice trigger to start with (all shooting will be double-action, just because you can't thumb-cock a revolver fast enough to win this game) and can easily be tuned to be better. You can use speedloaders, or get it machined for full moon clips. Moving up, the various Performance Center guns using moon clips would be great guns. The Model 627-5, a six- or seven-shot L frame, anything in .38 special, .38 Super or .357 Magnum will work excellently. Larger would be the Model 610 and the 25-2 and 625-2 and all the variants. Since reloading is such an important part, anything with a moon clip will probably (but not always) beat something without moon clips. The hard part with the larger guns is loading them down close to the threshold but still having an accurate and clean load. Many powders do not like it when you throttle back from 176 PF to 130PF, and the results are often a dirty-burning load. The gunk can eventually bind the gun, and leave you with a miserable score.

NRA/PPC

The PPC course is pretty much the same one the FBI developed in the 1930s. And therein lies the rub. While it is so familiar it can be set up on almost any range, it can become so routine that boredom sets in. I shot mostly the indoor course, to stay in practice during the cold Midwest winters, and there were times when even I was practically hallucinating while shooting, the pace was so slow. The basics are pretty much the same, and while you might find some regional variances what you'll face will be pretty much the same. You need 60 rounds and three speedloaders or four pistol magazines to shoot the indoor course. The indoor course goes only to 50 feet, while the outdoor course goes back to 50 yards, and requires 150 rounds if all stages are fired. There are also some differences in the strings, times and positions, but there isn't a lot of variation. While I shot indoors with the local sheriff's department league for four years, I shot outdoors only twice. Hence I describe indoor shooting in detail. If you've shot indoors, or know the strings, the outdoors course will differ only in distance.

PPC has been described as "Position, double-action Bull's-eye" shooting. You shoot everything double-action. (Pistol shooters shoot what the gun does. TDA, DAO, single-action, however it works is what you do.) You do all shooting two-handed, and may use the barricade for support when you are required to use it for "cover."

Seven yards, string one

Facing the targets, when the targets turn (Unlike the shooting events already mentioned you are not on the line by yourself. Everyone's targets turn to face all of you, and turn away when time it up) you have 20 seconds to draw and fire six rounds, reload and fire six rounds. All the rest of your shooting will be done at 50 feet.

Fifty feet, string two

On the start, draw and shoot six shots kneeling, reload, six shots right-hand barricade, reload, and six shots left-hand barricade. The shots on the left side of the barricade must be shot with your left hand, but you can use both hands and the barricade for support. You can use your right eye to aim, if you are right-eye-dominant.

The target now has thirty holes in it, so you change for a fresh target.

Fifty feet, string three

On the start, draw and fire six shots in 12 seconds. This is perhaps the only difficult string in the course. All the others are either close or supported, and shooting a bunch of "10" with many "X's" is relatively easy. But the 10-ring is only the size of a playing card, and at fifty feet getting all six shots into it in 12 seconds isn't easy.

Fifty feet, string four

On the start, shoot six shots sitting, six shots prone, six shots right hand barricade and six shot left hand barricade. Reload in between each set of six. Total time allowed, 2 minutes and 45 seconds. Yes, you read that correctly, 165 seconds for 24 shots. It was common when I was shooting with the local sheriff's department deputies in the winter league for the targets to turn on string four and no one would shoot for 15 seconds while they drew, got into a comfortable sitting position, aligned the sights and began their initial trigger press. Even when I learned to slow down, I'd be done before the rest of the line had finished their third of four positions.

The grand total is 60 rounds, with a potential of 10 points each. The best shooters will score 600, with a high X count of 30, 40 or 50 Xs. You may not take extra shots to make up for misses or bad shots. Every shot you fire will be scored, good or bad.

There is no power factor in PPC. As long as your bullets pass completely through the target and its holder, you have enough power. The lower limit is on caliber, where you must use a .38 special or 9mm cartridge. The typical load for indoor shooting was a 148-grain lead wadcutter going at or less than 700 feet per second for a 103 power factor. Some PPC shooters look at ICORE shooters as wild men, shooting those "powerful" 120 power factor loads.

There are no optics nor any porting, compensators or muzzle brakes allowed in PPC.

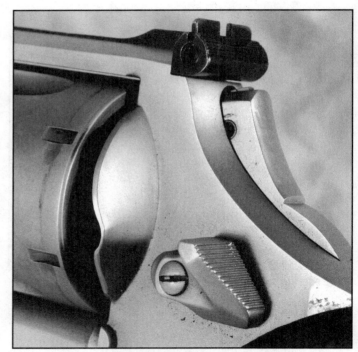

PPC guns started the trend to bobbed hammers.

Divisions in PPC vary, again depending on local preferences. Generally, you'll have Open Revolver, which is almost always a slicked-up K frame with a bull barrel and a rib sight with position-adjustable front or rear. There is no catalog equivalent from S&W to a PPC Open revolver. I'm not sure anyone makes one. What would work well would also work in the Service category. A Service revolver is limited to 6 inches (some places deem only 4-inch barrels as "Service") and has to be factory stock except for the grips. If you've made changes inside no one will know, but before you go down that path there isn't a whole lot you can do to gain advantage that hasn't already been done by everyone else on the line. Service Pistol requires something that is accepted for Duty, usually a traditional double-action pistol. Some leagues allow a cocked and locked pistol like the 1911, others don't. Find out before you show up.

To shoot a Service Revolver match, I'd use a 6-inch (if it were allowed, four if not) Model 686 with a post front sight and plain black rear. No dots, no red ramp, no white outline. For Service Pistol, a Model 5906 with plain black sights. Factory Match ammo is available for both, and good-quality reloads will deliver all the accuracy you'll need or can use. As much as a SW1911 would tempt me for the Service Pistol category, I'd turn it down until I can get one in 9mm or .38 Super. I shot a .45 in the league matches, and found that I simply could not reload my ammo soft enough to keep from shooting a cannon compared to the loads the rest were shooting. I carried a 596 average with a .45. When I built a .38 super 1911 to shoot PPC (In 1984, that was a wild gun to show up with!) I immediately went up to a 598 average, and closed the league with a string of 600s.

Getting to a match. Finding matches was not always easy. Before the Internet it was a matter of keeping glued to the grapevine and hearing word of this league or that league. Now, you can just do an Internet search for "PPC+shooting" and find plenty. What you have to be aware of is a particular NRA rule. The NRA is the organizing body for PPC shooting. In some ways, not only has PPC not left the 1930s, but neither has the NRA. They still view it as "police training" and if you are not a police officer you can't shoot a match. Well, you can't shoot a match above a certain level. The various clubs and leagues that shoot PPC allow anyone who wants to, to shoot. The clubs and the NRA don't look too closely at who shows up, to avoid having to exchange words. But when you get to a big match, the rule is enforced. So, if you want to shoot PPC, search for a club or league. Then ask them if you will have to be a police officer to shoot. Don't bother complaining to the NRA, I've already been there.

Bianchi Cup

The other shooting sport administered by the NRA, the Bianchi Cup was the brainchild of John Bianchi, the holster maker. He wanted in the early 1980s to find a bridge between the various factions of handgun competition; IPSC, PPC, Bull's-eye. The idea was to find a course in which each found something of their own, but did not favor any one more than the others. For the state of the art in the early 1980s, he did well. As they all evolved, the Bianchi Cup became less a bridge and more another specialized match. It has Open and Stock division. One thing that stopped the Bianchi Cup becoming more popular was that an Open gun evolved in such a peculiar way that it wasn't useable in any other shooting sport. While that doesn't seem to bother the shotgun shoot-

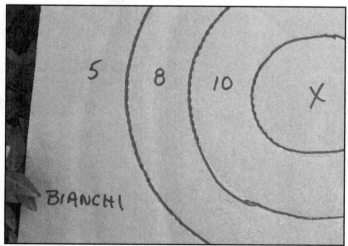

The Bianchi Cup scores points. The top shooters shoot perfect scores with lots of X hits.

ers who shoot Trap, it does bother handgun shooters. A Bianchi Open gun is similar to a PPC gun, but it also has "wings" to lock against the barricade, and the rear sight is adjustable to deal with the moving target. The Stock category is something you can shoot with almost any factory-stock gun, and many S&W products would do well.

The match is four courses, the Barricade, Practical, Plates and Mover. Each is composed of six-shot strings, and each comprises 48 rounds. You cannot make up bad shots, or fire again to correct for a miss.

The barricade match involves a pair of targets, and you engage them in increasing distances and set times on both sides of the barricade. Bianchi barricades are unlike other shooting discipline's barricades, and part of the specialized gear is due to the barricades. They are made of angle iron and plywood. You can grasp the barricade (at least in Open, not in Stock) and thus Open guns have special "wings" on the barrel to fit the gun to the barricade. Shooters will draw, slap the gun against the barricade, clamp the winged barrel against the barricade with their free hand, and then shoot their string with the other hand. The times and distances are: 10 yards in five seconds, 15 yards in six seconds, 25 yards in seven seconds and 35 yards in eight seconds.

The Practical is more complicated. Instead of six-shot strings on a single target per run there are a pair of targets. You must fire on each of the two, with a single, two or three rounds per run. The closest distance, 10 yards, requires weak-hand-only shooting on the run where you fire three rounds on each target. The firing distances are 10, 15, 25 and 50 yards.

The mover is a target (unlike the other stages, you fire it by yourself) that moves back and forth. You fire one, two or three rounds per pass (depending on distance). The mover takes six seconds to cover the open space, and the number of rounds decreases as you move back.

The plates are a rack of falling plates that you must engage at various distances and times. At 10 yards you have six seconds to down six plates, at 15 you get seven seconds, at 20 it is eight, and at 25 yards you get an interminable nine seconds. The scoring is simple; ten points for an X or center hit, eight for the next ring and five for the rest. It seemed impossible in the 1980s for anyone to shoot a perfect score. Now, the winner is decided by the number or X hits, as the top shooters all shoot perfect scores. And the big two stages are the mover and the plates. You win the match at the plates and lose it at the mover. The mover is where most of the "almost perfect" shooters drop their two, five or 10 points of the 1920 points possible. The plate rack used to be simple: once someone would shoot the rack "clean" then the match organizers would simply have them shoot the hardest string, six plates at 25 yards in nine seconds, again and again until they missed. Well, that went by the wayside when my friend Brian Enos shot clean on the rack. And then just kept hitting from the 25-yard line. He kept shooting and shooting, and not missing. His friends had to scramble to find ammo for him to use. Finally, with darkness coming on, other shooters ready to shoot, and the whole thing becoming a bit silly, Brian decided to miss. And found that he had to work to do so, he was so grooved into hitting. The record of 505 plates was never even approached, let alone surpassed. And the organizers changed the tie-breaking procedure. But the plates are the place to rack up your X count to win the match.

As mentioned in the ICORE part, many Bianchi Cup shooters also dabble in ICORE as a way to get some practice in, and find another venue to use their special-purpose Open guns. Their Open guns are perfect ICORE Open guns, and anything Stock for Bianchi is certainly Stock for ICORE.

Steel Challenge

The Steel Challenge got started in 1981 when IPSC shooting was still in its early growth stage. The pace of shooting had greatly increased from the earliest days, and Mike Dalton and Mike Fichman decided to see if they could increase the speed even more. The basics of the Steel Challenge are simple: five plates arranged in a simple pattern, with one of them designated the "Stop" plate. (The stages have changed through the years, and sometimes there were not always five on a stage.) On the start signal you draw and hit the plates, ending with the stop plate. There is no power factor, the plates do not fall, and the plate array is re-painted between each shooter. The stop plate was needed in the beginning because we used stopwatches for the earliest IPSC and practical competitions. Without a stop plate, the job of stopping the watch at the correct moment is too difficult. Without knowing which was the last plate the shooter was going to shoot, the timer had no way of determin-

Jerry Miculek at the Steel Challenge, with a scoped revolver.

ing that the shooter was, indeed, done. With electronic timing it doesn't matter, but tradition holds, and the use of the stop plate continues. Despite the lack of a power factor, you still have to use something that is chambered in 9mm or .38 Special or larger. I always loved to watch the Japanese Squad shooting. They would save their vacation time all year so they could go to Southern California for two or three weeks. They'd arrive a week or two early, pick up their revolvers they'd stored since the last Steel Challenge (they can't take them home, no one owns a real handgun in Japan) and practice. If they were lucky they could have an Airsoft revolver at home, and practice with little plastic pellets. To minimize recoil they'd load the lightest possible load. Commonly they'd be using short wadcutter bullets, 100-grain or so, at the softest load that was accurate. After all, all they have to do is scuff the paint on the plate. Sometimes you have to see someone who has to work a whole lot harder at something in order to realize just how much fun you're having. Stop grumbling about having to fly or drive from Texas or Illinois. These guys have it a lot worse.

The traditional scoring method has been to run each stage five times and total up your fastest four runs. Lowest time total on a stage wins the stage, and lowest time total for the match wins the match. Some stages have not been "best four of five" but "best three of four" due to their extra time required for shooting. That is, (and only as an example) you have a super-fast stage that takes two seconds a run to shoot. The total of four runs is eight seconds. A badly messed-up stage would have you doubling that time. Then compare it to a long-range stage that takes 10 seconds to shoot. Four runs would be 40 seconds! If someone only shot marginally faster (say a second a run) they'd chop four seconds off their time, half the fastest total of the faster stage. So, the stages are adjusted to even the scoring. The match is the total time it takes you to shoot through seven stages.

With speed the overriding variable and your score simply the time it takes you to hit the plates, the draw is critical. At the current structure, with Outer Limits (one of the stages) only scoring three runs, your seven-stage total (best four of five on six stages, plus best three of Outer Limits) 27 stages, with 27 draws. An IPSC match that has as many rounds fired might have a total of only seven to 10 draws. And the time totals magnify the disparity even more. That IPSC match with 189 rounds fired (the Steel Challenge minimum) with its field courses might take a running time total of almost 200 seconds. The winning times in the Steel Challenge are commonly in the 70- to 80-second region. As a result, the Steel Challenge has a multiplicity of shooting Divisions, because the holster is so important. Someone using an IPSC speed holster will have the advantage over someone shooting IDPA, with those concealable holster requirements. So, when deciding to shoot the Steel Challenge (and you should go at least once, if for no other reason than to watch the best shooters shooting at incredible speeds) you have to decide what holster rules you want to follow. Once you've selected a holster, then you can proceed to select a firearm with which to shoot.

Then it is simply a matter of backing up a few paragraphs and reading the selections for that category. For instance, if you are going to be shooting IDPA CDP at the Steel Challenge, then your holster selection must come from the IDPA approved list. And then you have to be shooting a cocked and locked pistol in .45 ACP. That narrows it down pretty much to the SW1911. And similarly with the other categories. With the strings of fire only needing five shots, you can do it well with a revolver. Jerry Miculek has done well many times through the years. A seven- or eight-shot revolver is a distinct advantage, however. If you plan to get heavy into steel wheelgunning, you definitely want to consider a Model 686+ or a 627-5.

Once the bug hits, converts will go back to their gun clubs spreading the gospel of steel. And the courses only require plates and stands, a timer and a shooting box. If your club doesn't allow holster work you can even start with the pistol in hand, muzzle touching a tabletop.

American Handgunner Shootoff

Paul Miller was an early IPSC shooter, and a good one. He found that the best, and most fun part of the match was the shootoff. In the shootoff, the top eight or 16 shooters would be paired off. They'd shoot a set of falling plates shoulder to shoulder. The one who knocked down his plates fastest was the winner. Then the survivors would pair off, and the whole process continued until there was one shooter left. At a club match you could select the top eight or 16 at every match. When 20 guys shot, the best eight slugged it out and everyone had fun. But at a larger match, with 100, 200 or more shooters, the top 16 was an exclusive club that most never entered. Paul was determined to design a match that was "nothing but shootoffs." He succeeded.

The design is simple, it just takes a whole lot of ranges. Each of the 15 stages at the Shootoff has a matched set of falling plates. In the middle (sometimes right in between the two falling plate racks) is a pair of pepper poppers designed to overlap when they fall. The shooting is simple: you stand next to your competitor. On the start signal you shoot down all the falling plates on your side, then knock over the pepper popper. The popper on the bottom wins. If you miss a plate (that is, leave it standing) then you've faulted the run, and despite your popper being on the bottom you lose. Shoot until the bout is over, for you never know if the other guy will fault on his run.

The categories are divided by class and gear. For instance, you could shoot in the "B Stock Pistol" category or the "GM and Master Revolver" category. You will find that all the other shooters at the match who are in that category are in your squad. As a result, some squads will fill up right away. The squads can only have 32 shooters, maximum, in them. So the "C Class Stock Pistol" squad fills right away, while the "GM and Master Open Pistol" squad might have eight or 10 shooters in it. Yes, the perk of being an average shooter is that the average shooters do more shooting. At each stage you'll find a loose-leaf book with your squad's page in it. Each page has a "ladder," the pairings and descending pairings, printed on it. The computer randomly assigns you a starting slot on each stage. The shooters than pair off and shoot the plate rack. Each win gets you a point. At first you shoot for best two out of three bouts. When you lose you sit down. The winners continue until there is one man left standing. Your "score" for that stage is the total number of bouts you won. You'll draw and shoot an incredible amount of ammo, and begin competing directly against shooters with similar skill and equipment. At the end of the match, your match score is your bout win total. And you can be up and down from stage to stage. In one stage you could win a bout but lose the pairing, getting one point. On the next stage you could "click" and win the stage, racking up 10 or more points.

After all the categories have been sorted out, Paul matches category winners against each other in the Finals, until there is one shooter who has beaten everyone else to stand alone.

I can tell you from practice that while a .357 Magnum will hammer pins, it isn't easy from a snubbie.

If all you did was show up, shoot your gun dry on each stage and lose both bouts, and sit down, you would shoot a minimum of 180 rounds of revolver ammo or 300 rounds of pistol ammo. With any skill at all, and some wins, you could easily double those totals. If you are in a big squad, and on a roll, you could easily exceed 1,000 rounds of ammo before you get to the finals.

To make Paul's life easier, he simply follows the class and equipment divisions of IPSC, IDPA and the Single Action Shooting Society. So your decisions concerning gear there determine your squad and class ranking at the Shootoff.

Bowling Pins

Begun in the mid 1970s by Richard Davis of Second Chance, the Second Chance Combat Shoot had a 24-year run and ended up as the testing and development arena for many guns, gunsmiths, and shooters. The requirements are simple: You place a stated number of bowling pins on a table (preferably steel for longevity) at 25 feet, and then shoot them off the table. The fastest shooter in that array is the winner. The categories that ended up as the finished products were many, but can be summed up in three: 5-Pin, 8-Pin and 9-Pin.

In all categories, the clock starts on the start signal, and ends when the last pin of the table being fired hits the ground. As long as there are pins on the table, the clock continues. Pins tipped over but not pushed off the table (known as "deadwood") must be dealt with by the shooter. Many matches have a 15-second time limit, just to keep the match moving. If you have pins left at the fifteen second mark, time is called and your score is entered as "15.0"

5-Pin

In the early days, five pins on a table with a 4-foot by 8-foot steel top. The pins were 25 feet from the shooting rail, and three feet from the back edge of the table. On the start signal, lift the gun off the rail and shoot the pins off as fast as you can. The final table design was the SuperTable, a two-tiered structure of three 5-foot-wide boxes. Each box was a "table." Each had five pins, three on the bottom and two on the top shelf. Scoring remained the same, time ran until the last pin struck the ground. It took a hot load to reliably move a pin 3 feet back and off the table. Luckily, many handgun rounds were/are hot enough. A full-weight bullet in a .357 Magnum would do it. Anything larger with the exception of the .40 S&W would do it. The measurement of Major/Minor has little meaning in pin shooting. The pins determine what works. What we have found is that

Mas Ayoob, with a revolver and a New York Reload, shooting Mixed Doubles at Second Chance.

you want to be generating about a 195 power factor to reliably clean pins, which is a bit out of reach for a .40 S&W. But anything else; .357 Magnum, 10mm, .41 Mag, .44 Special (some loads) .44 Magnum, .45 Colt and .45 ACP all had enough power.

And as it is five pins, a revolver is not at too much of a disadvantage. However, Richard felt the wheelguns needed a bit of a boost, so he adopted the "New York Reload" for 5-Pin. If you're shooting a revolver you can use a spare loaded revolver. If you run the first one dry, drop it (you had to bring your own box and padding) grab the spare and keep shooting.

Not all local clubs hold with the "NYR" on wheelguns. But many do.

The 5-Pin is also called the Main Event. You shoot six tables of five pins each. Your best five runs are your score, and your sixth is the tiebreaker. Traditional timing is with stopwatches, taking the average of three watches, rounded to the nearest tenth of a second. Some clubs run shooters one at a time, using an electronic timer. In the Main Event you can have two or three categories. A Stock gun is pretty much that. You can have a factory barrel on a revolver and port it. You can use a pistol, ported through the slide and barrel. You can't add a compensator or muzzle brake, and you can't have optic

sights. Pin guns can have a bull barrel in a revolver, and both revolvers and autos can have a compensator added. A Space gun is allowed optics. In all of them you are limited to eight shots in the guns at any time. In the adventurous tradition Richard blazed, you can always "Shoot Up" in equipment. That is, if you want to enter Pin Gun while using a Stock-category gun, knock yourself out. You won't be given any bonus, and your scores will be directly compared to the Pin guns being used. And there is no distinction between revolvers and autos.

That said, some local clubs added a separate 5-Pin Revolver category. Local rules, and local variations of events can vary.

What to use in 5-Pin? I've seen everything. You could use an SW1911, or a 945PC. You could use any N-frame in .357 Magnum or larger. It all depends on how quickly you can hit five pins and drive them off. You do not want to be using full-power .41 or .44 Magnum ammo. The extra recoil will slow you down. You do not want to be using light bullets in .357 Magnum, or standard .44 Special loads. They will not have enough momentum to push the pins off. And do not try going to extreme weights unless you keep your velocity above 750 fps. The hard wood and tough plastic skin of bowling pins makes penetration important. If you do not penetrate to the pin interior, you can be setting up a bounce-back situation. A bullet flush with the surface of a pin, or barely lodged into the pin, can bounce another bullet back, or be squeezed out and launched. In 14 years of shooting at Second Chance I had a number of minor bouncebacks hit me, and two heavy ones. None drew blood. My friend Mas Ayoob is a bullet magnet, getting hit every year he shot the match. Sometimes more than once. He took to shooting the match wearing a bulletproof vest. Some made fun of him, but had I been hit that many times I'd have worn one, too.

8-Pin

The 8-pin event is restricted to revolvers only. And you must reload in it, you cannot use a New York Reload. The old tables were eight pins straight across the 4x8 table. Again 3 feet from the back. You needed the same hot load, and you absolutely must have a 25-2 or a 625-2 to win. You can use a 610, but the reloads will not be quite as fast and reloads in the 8-Pin are everything. The new tables had eight pins, four on each shelf, in each 5-foot wide box of a SuperTable. The 8-pin is an optional event. That is, if you go to a pin shoot and enter, the only event you must shoot is some or all of the 5-pin. You can opt to shoot 8-pin, 9-pin and the others. As an optional, scoring is different. Your single best run in an optional is your score, with your second-best run your tiebreaker. There may be limits as to how many times you can enter the optionals, and the limits may be the thickness of your wallet.

8-Pin traditionally is run as two divisions, pin and stock. A Stock gun is a 4-inch (some clubs allow 6-inch barrels) gun but it can only have porting if the porting is done through a factory or factory-profile barrel. A Pin gun is allowed ports, a compensator, but no optics. And regardless of category, when you fire your six (you cannot use a higher-capacity revolver unless you start with only six rounds in it) you must reload to continue.

9-Pin

Not everyone wanted to spend all their time at Second Chance (each match lasted nine days, with plenty of time to shoot on one or all of the 18 Optionals) shooting .45's and Magnums. The hi-capacity guns needed something to play at, too. The 9mm cartridge could not be loaded hot enough to move a pin back 3 feet, so the pins were moved. The pins were at first spaced along the back of the 8-foot table, one foot from the rear edge. When the tables were made into 5-foot boxes, the pins got crowded in a 5- foot span. The effect was to make it seem impossible to miss. It was not impossible. In fact it was quite likely that you'd miss if you weren't paying attention. The 9-pin guns were allowed comps and porting but no optics. There is no capacity restriction, but if you need more than 10 or 11 shots to clear the table you are just having fun. You won't be winning.

A full-size 39 series guns, with eight in the mag and one in the chamber, has just enough. Better to use a 59 series, a 40 series or the SW9 or SW40. There, you've got a minimum of 10 shots in the magazine (post-ban) plus one in the chamber. Eleven hits wins the event, as those who win hit the last pin twice or three times in order to speed its exit. With the pins a foot from the back you don't need more power than a 9mm delivers, but you do need that much power. Loading down will result in disappointing times as the pins fail to fall off the table, and the resulting deadwood is impossible to broom off with a mere 9mm.

As in all optionals, your single best time counts for score, with the second best as your tiebreaker. Tiebreakers can matter. I once failed to back up a blazing time of 2.7 seconds in the Shotgun Optional. ("Hey, who's going to match that?") and left my "tiebreaker" of 12.7 seconds as my second time. My friend Terry O-Hara matched me, and his tiebreaker was better. As a result, he went to the prize table before I did, and got listed as the record-holder for that event.